D1190540

304.809 Sch2

IMMIGRANT NATIONS

Nyack College - Bailey Library
One South Blvd.
Nyack, NY 10960

IMMIGRANT NATIONS

Paul Scheffer

Translated by Liz Waters

polity

First published in Dutch as *Het land van aankomst* © Paul Scheffer 2007

This publication has been made possible with the financial support of
The Dutch Foundation for Literature

This English edition © Polity Press, 2011
Reprinted 2011

Polity Press
65 Bridge Street
Cambridge CB2 1UR, UK

Polity Press
350 Main Street
Malden, MA 02148, USA

All rights reserved. Except for the quotation of short passages for the purpose
of criticism and review, no part of this publication may be reproduced, stored
in a retrieval system, or transmitted, in any form or by any means, electronic,
mechanical, photocopying, recording or otherwise, without the prior permission
of the publisher.

ISBN-13: 978-0-7456-4961-0
ISBN-13: 978-0-7456-4962-7(pb)

A catalogue record for this book is available from the British Library.

Typeset in 10 on 12 pt Adobe Sabon
by Servis Filmsetting Ltd, Stockport, Cheshire
Printed and bound in Great Britain by the MPG Books Group

The publisher has used its best endeavours to ensure that the URLs for external
websites referred to in this book are correct and active at the time of going to
press. However, the publisher has no responsibility for the websites and can
make no guarantee that a site will remain live or that the content is or will
remain appropriate.

Every effort has been made to trace all copyright holders, but if any have been
inadvertently overlooked the publisher will be pleased to include any necessary
credits in any subsequent reprint or edition.

For further information on Polity, visit our website: www.politybooks.com

GG89 4669 1

So from an early age I developed the habit of looking, detaching myself from a familiar scene and trying to consider it as from a distance. It was from this habit of looking that the idea came to me that as a community we had fallen behind. And that was the beginning of my insecurity.

V. S. Naipaul, *A Bend in the River*

Contents

⁊

1 **A Suitcase in the Hall**
Tolerance Under Strain   1
The Conservatism of Migrants   7
The In-Between Generation   14
Native Unease   20
Integration Requires Self-Examination   27
So What's New?   33

2 **The World in the City**
The Proximity of Strangers   42
Segregation and Inequality   47
Ghetto Culture   53
Black and White Schools   57
Dispersing Without Mixing   62
Back to the Garden City   67

3 **The Great Migration**
The Globe Is Fragile   72
All the Colours plus Grey   79
Classic Countries of Immigration   86
Migration and Development   91
A Morality of Mobility   97
The Citizens' Revolt   103

4 **The Netherlands: A Culture of Avoidance**
As Others See Us   109
Migration and Nation-Building   113
Tolerance is not Laisser-Faire   118

Organizing Islam   124
Postcolonial Lessons   130
Identity and Openness   135

5 **European Contrasts**
From Emigration to Immigration   141
Early Opposition   147
Republican Answers   152
Foreigners After Genocide   160
Taking Leave of Empire   168
At the External Borders   177

6 **The Cosmopolitan Code**
The Colonial Trap   182
'Enlightened' Racism   188
The Value of Cultures   193
Beyond Multiculturalism   197
Prejudice Weighed   203
World Citizens in the Making   209

7 **The Rediscovery of America**
The Colonists' Creed   216
In the Melting Pot   221
Opposition to Immigrants   227
The Golden Door Shuts   232
The Lingering Shadow of Slavery   237
Affirmative Action   244

8 **The Divided House of Islam**
Islam and Imperialism   252
In a Secular Environment   258
Conservatism and Radicalization   265
Reformist Voices   272
Believers in an Open Society   278
A World Without an Emergency Exit   285

9 **Land of Arrival**
Rituals of Citizenship   292
Everything of Value Must Defend Itself   298
A Triptych of Integration   303
Dilemmas of Equal Treatment   308
Tomorrow's Immigrants   314
Accepting What We Have Become   319

Epilogue: After the Multicultural Drama   325

Acknowledgements   334
Notes   336
References   355
Name Index   377
Subject Index   382

I

A Suitcase in the Hall

Tolerance Under Strain

'Welcome', someone calls out unexpectedly from across the street. 'You like it here?' Absolutely I do; there's a lot to like about this place. The Moroccan port city of Tangiers is an inviting chaos in the summer months. Young and old, wrapped and unwrapped, parade along the promenade. The city is packed with returned migrants, their children often fashionably dressed, and behind the wheel of their roomy cars they're the embodiment of success to those who stayed behind.

I'd often heard that kind of welcome over the previous few weeks, as Morocco has a tradition of hospitality, but this time the greeting came from a young Moroccan who addressed me in my own native tongue, with an Amsterdam accent no less. He spoke with the pride of a host: 'This is my country. So what do you think?' We exchanged a few comments about here and there, then he got into a car with his friends and disappeared into the traffic.

I was left slightly perplexed. The man who'd welcomed me was a compatriot of mine. As soon as he opened his mouth the market traders of Tangiers would realize he was a foreigner by birth, if they hadn't already concluded as much from his bearing. Prices were higher for him than for the locals; he too was primarily a wallet on legs. He was a tourist in a country he knew only superficially, really only from the stories his parents had told him.

In his 'welcome' I detected not just ritual hospitality but bittersweet vengeance. At last he could show off about something that truly belonged to him. At last the roles were reversed. The guests he welcomed were people who often gave him the cold shoulder back home. That 'welcome' was almost a challenge, drawing the attention of Dutch visitors to short-comings in their own dealings with outsiders. At least, that was how it felt.

Compatriots in a strange country, yet strangers in our own. That's the state of uncertainty this book explores, a confusion that has its milder side, but an agonizing side as well. Behind that verbal welcome in a foreign country lay a no-man's-land, a feeling of not really being at home anywhere. That young man wanted to be proud of a place he mainly knew about second hand because he couldn't be proud of the place where he grew up.

If we retrace the routes taken by migrants back to their countries of origin, we discover an insecurity that has become our own. Immigrants from all over the world have changed the face of our cities. The original intentions, whatever they were, theirs and ours, ceased to matter a long time ago. The world has settled into our neighbourhoods, and it's a confusing and shocking experience. Our markets, places of worship, schools, sports clubs – everything and everyone has been affected by the great migration that's under way and whose end is nowhere in sight.

We're in the midst of profound changes and it's unwise to pretend they're inconsequential or simply to close our minds to them. How often do we hear the unanswerable 'immigration has always been with us', the notion that people are always on the move and our own time is no exception? The Amsterdam municipality writes, matter-of-factly: 'Almost half of all Amsterdammers were born outside the Netherlands. This is nothing new. For centuries Amsterdam, as a city of immigrants, has been open to people of different origins and faiths. Think of the Portuguese Jews, French Huguenots and seasonal workers from Germany.'

Even if we accept that from a historical perspective there's nothing new under the sun, no one can doubt we are witnessing a profound change to the composition of Western populations. People certainly moved around a great deal in the seventeenth century, but that surely does nothing to mitigate the upheaval that cities are going through now. The guest workers from Morocco and Turkey who are changing Dutch neighbourhoods aren't simply counterparts to the seasonal workers from Germany who spent time in the Low Countries in centuries past. The fact that Jews from Portugal fled to the Netherlands to escape the Catholic Church's Inquisition doesn't make it a matter of course that refugees from Islamist despotism in Iran and Afghanistan should come to live here.

In any case, how much is it possible to know about the newcomers who made Amsterdam into a city of immigrants in earlier times? A recent study by historian Erika Kuijpers speaks of 'the innumerable' and 'the invisible' and demonstrates that our knowledge about them is limited, aside from a social elite that left a heritage of public works and charming houses on the city's main canals.[1] It's hard to find out anything about the lives most migrants lived; even the numbers are a rough approximation. The lack of information alone makes that stalwart 'there's nothing new under the sun' little short of exasperating.

How long can you downplay the significance of what's happening to you by talking about those who shared the same fate in the past? How long can a deeply felt experience be declared off limits? There's a growing feeling that today's migrants and the reactions provoked by them have not as yet done much to move Western societies forward. This feeling refuses to be placated. Here in the Netherlands and in neighbouring countries, tolerance and freedom are under strain.

In a time when progress is all that counts, when the sense that something is being lost is dismissed as nostalgia, we've become adept at transforming reality, blithely describing impoverishment as enrichment, allowing semi-lingualism to pass for bilingualism and treating narrow-mindedness with sympathy. But compliant language doesn't make reality any more amenable. Turning a blind eye to the clashes caused by the arrival of immigrants is no longer an option.

Today's migration cannot simply be described as making receiving societies more open, since as a result of the traditional beliefs many migrants bring with them, old questions about the position of women have suddenly resurfaced and freedom of expression has become controversial. People have started to talk about blasphemy again, even apostasy. It may all seem familiar from recent history, but having to repeat the emancipation struggles of 50 years ago can hardly be described as progress.

There's a need to go beyond the simple assumption that the migration of past decades amounts to an enrichment of the societies in which newcomers have arrived. In fact, the continual use of the word 'enrichment' is rather unfortunate, considering the difficult circumstances in which many immigrants and their children live. Schools are suddenly faced with a multiplicity of special needs, and this alone causes significant problems. Set against the benefits, the costs of migration have so far turned out to be high, in some periods perhaps even higher than the returns, although such calculations are always complicated.

This has nothing to do with the question of guilt that comes up in so many contemporary discussions of immigration. Receiving societies are hesitant in their dealings with newcomers; established populations are becoming noticeably more rigid and tending to turn away from the outside world. It has even proved possible to find majority support for measures to limit immigrants' civil rights. Nevertheless, many migrants could have done more to create a place for themselves in their new countries. They ought to have rid themselves sooner of the 'myth of return', the belief that their stay was only temporary. As someone remarked in a debate: 'The price of staying is that you take the trouble to learn. Learning and spurning are two quite different things.'

It's not difficult to point to shortcomings on all sides, but there's a good deal more to be said. This book examines how the conflicts surrounding migration can bring about a renewal of society as a whole, taking us closer to our aim of creating an open society. There's a need for a more candid approach to the frictions and clashes that always result from the arrival of sizeable migrant groups. Earlier generations of historians and sociologists have left us a remarkable body of work to draw upon. Oscar Handlin, the best-known historian of immigration in America, is one source of inspiration. In *The Uprooted* (1952) he describes the causes and effects of migration from Europe to America. They can be summed up in one sentence: '[T]he history of immigration is a history of alienation and its consequences.'[2] Alienation and loss are key features of any description of the arrival of migrants in a strange environment.

Handlin is thinking primarily of those who came, 'for the effect of the transfer was harsher upon the people than upon the society they entered'.[3] He tells the story of the millions who were set adrift by industrialization and by the astonishing population growth of the second half of the nineteenth century. The dislocation and poverty that resulted, especially in rural areas, led to mass emigration from countries including Ireland, Germany, Italy, Sweden, Norway and Poland. Huge economic and social forces were at work, and people were torn loose from environments they had occupied for centuries. Hardly anyone welcomed this liberation, Handlin says, since above all it meant separation. He describes with great empathy the often atrocious journey they made across the Atlantic and their arrival in a new land where they had to make their way as immigrants, often utterly destitute and with no idea what the future might bring.

In unfamiliar surroundings many sought refuge in the certainties of their religion. 'In that sense all immigrants were conservatives. . . . All would seek to set their ideas within a fortification of religious and cultural institutions that would keep them sound against the strange New World.'[4] This hankering after old structures and customs served as an aid to survival in an urban environment. It's easy to see why many migrants tried to perpetuate village life in foreign cities, which makes it all the harder to understand why immigrants are so often described as great innovators.

In their new country, so confusing and full of dangers, people felt a need for the support of their religion, but maintaining religious faith was a challenge: 'The same environment, in its very strangeness and looseness and freedom, made it difficult to preserve what could be taken for granted at home.'[5] The end result was all too often a sense of not belonging anywhere any longer. 'They had thus completed their alienation from the culture to which they had come, as from that which they had left.'[6] This is an experience shared by many contemporary migrants as they try to connect with a new society.

It was not only the migrants themselves who were afflicted by insecurity. Those already living in the new country, which after all was not a blank canvas but had customs and traditions of its own, were thrown off balance. Handlin acknowledges their side of the story: 'Everything in the neighbourhood was so nice, they would later say, until the others came. The others brought outlandish ways and unintelligible speech, foreign dress and curious foods, were poor, worked hard, and paid higher rents for inferior quarters.'[7]

In an earlier study Handlin had examined the reaction of nineteenth-century Bostonians to the arrival of Irish immigrants, who came in huge numbers. After the two groups clashed it took at least half a century for the city to regain its balance. 'Group conflict left a permanent scar that disfigured the complexion of Boston social life.'[8] Yet Handlin's approach was subtle and he avoided laying the blame on one side or the other. He used cautious terms like 'latent distrusts' and 'social uneasiness' to describe the attitudes of longstanding residents.[9]

It's not hard to understand reactions like these. People saw their world changed by immigrants and instinctively harked back to a shared notion of the community as it had been before. It serves little purpose to impress upon people who no longer feel at home in their neighbourhoods that we all have to move with the times. In the often hostile expression 'stranger in your own country' lies a recognition that migration has brought people from all over the world to settle in today's major cities. We need to face up to the feeling among established populations that a tried and tested society is being lost, just as we need to acknowledge the feeling of uprootedness among many newcomers.

For far too long, those who didn't live in the neighbourhoods where migrants settled were the warmest advocates of the multicultural society, while those who did live in them steadily moved out. Their opinions were ignored, or they were belittled for suddenly giving voice to their own latent xenophobia. Now that the middle classes can no longer escape the changes migration brings – in part because they can no longer fail to notice migrants' children in the classroom – the argument has broken out in earnest and there is a need to think seriously about both the life stories of immigrants and the experiences of indigenous residents. It is indeed true to say that the history of immigration is a history of alienation and its consequences.

Yet that alienation does not last for ever; quite the reverse, in fact.

Back in the 1920s American sociologist Robert E Park described what was then generally referred to as the race relations cycle as beginning with isolation and avoidance and moving on via contact, competition and conflict to accommodation and assimilation.[10] There is an underlying logic here: on arrival, migrants tend to keep themselves to themselves, partly as a result of the attitude of avoidance they detect in the society around them. In the years that follow, migrants and their children struggle to claim a place for themselves in the new country, and this leads to rivalry and strife. The question of how everyone can live together becomes unavoidable. If a satisfactory answer is found, the descendants of the original migrants will be absorbed more or less smoothly into society. This is a hopeful view and it suggests the familiar model of three generations.

Of course, the process can't really be divided into phases or generations as neatly as this, but the important point is that every story of migration involves conflict. That was and is the case in America, and the pattern is being repeated in contemporary Europe. It's difficult to say how long or how severe the period of conflict will be, but the phase of avoidance is gradually coming to an end. We should see today's frictions as part of a search for ways for newcomers and the established population to live together. Conflict has a socializing effect.

Immigration is the most visible aspect of globalization, which gives many people a sense that their familiar world is vanishing. This is not yet felt to be an improvement. In European countries many people are convinced that a period of stagnation or even decline lies ahead. Few still believe their children will have a better future, whereas the post-war generation enjoyed the prospect that their offspring would live more freely and have more prosperous lives. It doesn't really help to say that future generations will see these as the good old days. Right now, all that counts is that a sense of loss has taken hold and people are looking for ways of reaching beyond that experience.

Literary critic Svetlana Boym discerns a pattern: 'Nostalgia inevitably appears as a defense mechanism in a time of accelerated rhythms of life and historical upheavals.'[11] Newcomers and natives react in similar ways – and no wonder, since the cause of their unrest is the same. Migrants personify a world set adrift, and those they come to live amongst are swept along by changes to their everyday environments, but shared experience does not bring the two sides together, Boym concludes. 'The moment we try to repair longing with belonging, the apprehension of loss with a rediscovery of identity, we often part ways and put an end to mutual understanding.'[12] That is exactly what's happening now: the desire for a firm footing in a turbulent world is driving old and new citizens apart.

In the history of immigration the pendulum swings back and forth between openness and withdrawal. Later we'll examine the American experience at some length, but we should note at this point that after 40 years of mass immigration, between 1880 and 1920, new legislation was introduced that kept the numbers to a minimum until 1965. The similarity with present-day Europe is striking; here too, after decades of mass immigration, there's a widespread desire for tighter controls.

In other words, the call for the influx to be curbed is not an exclusively European phenomenon, nor does it represent an inability to get along with migrants, a failing that could perhaps be ascribed to Europe's relatively short history of immigration. A more restrictive policy as a means of restoring the social balance is an option that ought to be taken seriously. History shows that spontaneous rapprochement between indigenous populations and newcomers is rare. The risk that each side will keep raising the stakes with opposing declarations of loyalty – both in effect openly saying 'my own people first' – means we must take the trouble to explore what lies behind this hostility. Let's first take a closer look at the experiences of the migrants we encountered on the promenade in Tangiers.

The Conservatism of Migrants

People rarely leave hearth and home simply to seek their fortunes in the wider world. They are usually trying to escape deplorable living conditions in their native countries. Guest workers were motivated by economic misery, migrants from former colonies were set adrift by worries about the repercussions of independence, refugees are by definition fleeing political or religious persecution, and migration arising from the formation or reuniting of families is often the result of emotional attachments or of problematic circumstances at home.

So although people's motives for leaving differ appreciably, migration almost always arises out of need, and not everyone has the talent to make a virtue of necessity. Nowadays we're often presented with a romantic image of the migrant as the personification of an increasingly mobile world. He is described as a forerunner, part of a reluctant advance guard. We should be aware that it requires an immense effort to make the best of what is often a traumatic experience. Some writers, entrepreneurs, sporting heroes and politicians have acquired prominent positions for themselves in their new countries, an admirable achievement, not to mention the innumerable teachers, shopkeepers, police officers and nurses who have made a success of migration.

The early work of Anil Ramdas, a Dutch writer from Surinam, shows that migration need not be a sombre story of loss and homesickness. The migrant's journey will often entail a broadening of horizons: 'This means a gulf opens up, a breach in the memory, a void in recollection, as wide as the ocean he has crossed. And I want to insist that this emptiness, this blank space, this vagueness of the past, far from being tragic can be a fortunate thing, that it can be interpreted as a liberation.'[13]

Generally speaking, Ramdas's view of his old fatherland is affectionate and steeped in a tone that allows the reader to share it. Yet we can sometimes taste a bitterness in his verdict on what he has left behind. He does not baulk at writing: 'Surinamese literature has failed. And the most obvious explanation for this is that Surinam has failed. Surinam as a community does not exist and has never existed.'[14] Even for Ramdas, who clearly sees the benefits of migration, the relationship with his native land has its painful side.

It's been called a 'brutal bargain': to gain entry to another culture you have to relinquish many things you hold dear.[15] Securing a place for yourself often involves disloyalty to family traditions. Learning a new language distances many migrants little by little from the parental home. It takes a great deal of effort to balance on a slack rope slung between the country of origin and the country of arrival, and there's a great temptation either to have done with the past completely or to cling to old memories and react with hostility to the new environment.

Later we'll look in more detail at how far relocation is an experience of uprooting, even though we know that people don't have roots, they have legs. There are significant differences between migrant groups and between migrants as individuals, but some of the general characteristics of the experience of migration are worth examining. Let's start by looking at the first generation, before moving on to see how their children have fared. Imagine the journey through time from a small village community in the Rif Mountains or Anatolia, for example, to big city life in Amsterdam or Birmingham, Lyon or Frankfurt. There's a Moroccan saying about guest workers: 'By donkey to the airport.'[16] It refers to the fact that many had not laid eyes on the modern world before, never having visited their country's own major cities. In that journey several stages were missed, and no one should be surprised at the culture shock that resulted.

Weighing against the desire to get ahead was a familiarity with the landscape of home. Take one characteristic passage from the life story of a migrant: 'I didn't really want to leave. I didn't talk to anyone about it, but I couldn't make up my mind. It was such a huge step. I was a country boy. I loved life there intensely. It was simple, fathomable, you knew everyone, you knew what they meant to you. But every day was the same. You never made any progress. Still, did I dare to head off into the wider world?'[17]

Earlier generations of migrants, leaving Europe for America, often faced a similar challenge in the transition from village to town. A greater familiarity with the classic accounts of the past might have helped in anticipating some of the problems of the present day. Back in the 1920s, Park described the migrant communities of Chicago, especially the spectacular growth of ghettos. Tellingly, Chicago's Little Italy, with 15,000 illiterate peasants from Sicily crammed together in appalling conditions, was also known as Little Hell.

The immigrants' lives were affected not only by poverty but by the challenge of cultural adjustment. As far as possible, they held the new, unfamiliar world at arm's length. Migrants were drawn to each other in specific districts: 'Our great cities turn out . . . to be a mosaic of segregated peoples . . . each seeking to preserve its peculiar cultural forms.'[18] Park sums up the different legacies as a conflict between individuality and communality. 'Energies that were formerly controlled by custom and tradition are released. The individual is free for new adventures, but he is more or less without direction and control.'[19] He goes on to conclude that 'the result is a cultural hybrid, . . . a man on the margin of two cultures and two societies, which are never completely interpenetrated and fused.'[20] Park describes this type of person as a 'marginal man'.

The parallels with today's migrant communities are obvious. No wonder there are frictions in societies where so many villagers find themselves living in cities. In fact, the same difficulties can arise in their countries of origin; migrants from the Moroccan and Turkish countryside have to make complicated adjustments to life in Casablanca or Istanbul. Even some years ago, the more enlightened residents of Istanbul could be heard complaining to anyone who would listen about the 'hordes of barbarians' from Anatolia who had seized control of the capital. They talked endlessly about their many compatriots who were being carried away by traditional beliefs, and how this was destroying the open atmosphere of their city. When the devout mayor of Istanbul suddenly announced proposals to segregate men and women on public transport, the liberal elite felt its most dire predictions were becoming a reality.

Immigration as a threat to tolerance – that's at the very least an interesting concept, certainly as a response to those who claim without giving the matter much thought that immigration enriches society and makes it more open. And this was domestic migration from rural communities to Istanbul. Inevitably, the sense of disorientation is even more extreme when on top of a transition from village life to the anonymous city comes the transition to another language and a secular society. The change could hardly be more abrupt and profound.

It may seem as if migrants have voted with their feet – by leaving home they have declared a preference for life elsewhere – but many had prosperity in mind rather than anything else. People who wanted to improve their lot economically have now come to see the norms of liberal societies as tarnishing all that is dear to them. Far from avidly embracing the freedoms on offer, they experience them as a threat. Anyone who takes the trouble to imagine what most newcomers go through will realize that arrival in a totally unfamiliar world has a dizzying effect. French historian Gérard Noiriel describes the feeling of displacement: 'On top of the shock of transplantation and the discovery of a new universe characterized by the speed of the assembly line and the complex topography of metro tunnels comes incomprehension in the face of the new dominant norms.'[21]

The tensions that arise from the difficulty of settling down in a new country are felt mainly within migrant families themselves. It's there that the gulf between newcomers and their adoptive societies is most keenly felt. Farah Karimi, a native of Iran and a former member of the Dutch parliament, makes this point: 'There certainly is a multicultural drama going on. It plays itself out primarily in the living rooms of immigrant families.'[22] A fundamental conflict emerges as traditional beliefs come up against modern attitudes towards men and women, parents and children, believers and non-believers. Those involved are deeply affected.

It's not easy to find a compromise between a fate-based culture and one that puts individual freedom first. In traditional societies everything is pretty much set in stone. The class, caste and religion you're born into mould your life from cradle to grave and escape is difficult, if not impossible. In the Western world, to an increasing degree since the Second World War, life is seen as an invitation to self-fulfilment. The notion that a person must take his fate into his own hands is incompatible with a culture that lays all the emphasis on the community, in which the individual has little or no room for manoeuvre.

Much of the insecurity we're witnessing now has its origins in this collision between authoritarian cultures and the relatively liberal societies of the West. The social divide in Morocco or India is far greater than in Europe, where class differences manifest themselves rather informally, although they certainly do exist. It surely can't be easy for newcomers to navigate countries with so many implicit codes.

Kader Abdolah, who arrived in the Netherlands as a refugee from Iran, describes the confusion beautifully: 'We had suddenly fallen out of a culture in which everything happened behind curtains into a semi-naked society. I thought I'd better keep my mouth shut for the time being and watch carefully, listen carefully to the world around me.'[23] His family falls prey to the same culture shock; his wife wants less and less to do with him: 'I really had nothing attractive to offer her any longer. In my own country I was a man with a future. My position was clear. But who was I now? An applicant for temporary jobs.'[24]

It's a story we hear all too often: families come under huge strain because of the father's loss of status. In many migrant families this results in an inverted form of intergenerational conflict. Instead of children being dependent on their parents, the parents are in many ways dependent on their children. There is something humiliating about the sight of an elderly-looking man in a caftan standing at the pharmacist's counter holding his small son's hand, needing the help of his child because he hasn't mastered the language of the country in which he now lives. It's especially painful when he comes from an unambiguously authoritarian culture.

This loss of status among immigrants is another classic theme in the history of migration. Under the heading 'the demoralization of the migrant', Park describes the way it affects families. How can children believe in paternal authority if it's personified by someone struggling to hold his ground at the margins of society? The breakdown of communication in many migrant families is largely attributable to the weak social position of immigrants, who have often received only minimal education.

Moroccan-Dutch author Hafid Bouazza presents a compelling portrait of the first generation of guest workers and their isolation: 'He enjoyed all this, but he didn't feel part of it. It existed outside him and would continue to exist without him, and that made him sad. It was a sadness he shared with other visitors to the tea house, and which in other men sometimes turned into anger and disgust.'[25] Indeed, the paths of melancholy don't always lead people in the same direction, but usually they will cling stubbornly to the ways of life they have brought from home, sticking closely to their companions in adversity, people they can always turn to when problems arise. Anyone who steps into the hall of a mosque will feel this atmosphere all too powerfully: Turkey or Pakistan are everywhere, while the Netherlands or Britain seem a distant illusion.

Many immigrants don't fully command the language of their adoptive countries, and this adds to their isolation. Postcolonial migrants, who generally did speak the language of their former motherlands and knew a fair amount about their future homes, had an easier time than people who arrived in Germany or Denmark as guest workers, poorly educated and not expected to have much knowledge of a place that was offering them a temporary stay and, most importantly for all concerned, dirty, physically demanding work.

The language, with all its emotional nuances, stands for more than just straightforward meanings. A German immigrant to America in the early twentieth century wrote in an autobiographical account: 'Whenever we must decide quickly we judge subconsciously. The subconscious life was destroyed and badly disorganized. I never knew if my reactions would be in line with the new code of conduct and had to think and reflect. . . . To act instinctively in an American fashion and manner was impossible, and I appeared slow and clumsy.'[26]

Many of the everyday misunderstandings and conflicts in cities with a high proportion of immigrants arise from this poor command of the country's mother tongue. The hesitancy of newcomers is obvious, especially when it comes to expressions with an ironic slant or a double meaning. The room for anything more than superficial communication shrinks; if people want to understand each other, they must limit themselves.

Parents' unfamiliarity with the language of the new homeland affects the future of their children, large numbers of whom grow up in environments where nobody speaks the native tongue of the country in which they live. They arrive at school with considerable language deficits compared to children from indigenous families. Aside from the impact this has on their performance in school – and it turns out they hardly ever catch up completely – it's hard for them to establish contacts outside their own communities. German-Turkish sociologist Necla Kelek has criticized childrearing in Germany's Turkish community. 'Their parents were unable or unwilling to teach them German, since either they hadn't mastered it themselves or they didn't feel it was necessary for their sons to speak the language of the country they lived in.'[27] She acknowledges the aloof attitude of the receiving society, but concludes that 'for their part the Turks – a few exceptions aside – made no effort to accept their second home'.[28]

A reticence towards their countries of settlement can be found in all stories about first-generation migrants, but this self-isolation is particularly prevalent in Europe, where many did not initially see themselves as immigrants. All too often a temporary stay bogged down to become a permanent presence. Whether Algerians in France, Jamaicans in Britain, Turks in Germany or Moroccans in the Netherlands, in each case the notion 'one day we'll go back' gave their lives in the new country a transient character. They lived with a suitcase in the hall; their real lives had been put on hold in the expectation of a glorious return. In most cases nothing came of that dream, usually because they wanted to remain close to their children, who had never lived anywhere else. So a child says of his mother: 'She doesn't want to go back until her grandchildren have grown up too. And found their feet. In other words: never.'[29]

The way back is also closed off to most migrants because, for all their conservatism, their lengthy stay outside their own countries has changed them. This becomes evident for the first time when they go back on holiday, staying with relatives. In their home villages it may not be at all natural for women to go out on the street by themselves to shop, for instance, let alone simply to take a walk. People would soon start to gossip. They cannot go back. They could never get used to corrupt officials again, or to police intimidation, or the way society controls them. Too much of what they once took for granted has gradually become alien, even repellent.

Moving changes people, even though they often fail to realize it. Noiriel poses a question that at first seems cryptic: 'Isn't the paradox of the immigrant that the more he is one the less he is one?'[30] He means that the true immigrant, who has settled in a new country permanently and therefore left behind the 'myth of return', is really less and less of an immigrant, since he's making every effort to put down roots in his adoptive land.

To put it another way, the conservatism of many immigrants is not a permanent condition. The work of Oscar Handlin, which has been quoted here with approval, is sometimes criticized for the importance it attributes to alienation in the history of migration. Later historians, such as Kristian Hvidt, with his study into the backgrounds of Danish immigrants in America, have shown that Handlin placed undue emphasis on the transition from the countryside to the city. Although in many cases emigration did mean exchanging rural life for an urban existence – almost half of Danish Americans were originally agricultural labourers – a fair number of newcomers had lived in towns or cities back home.[31] Another historian, John Bodnar, has argued that Handlin saw migration too much as a one-way street, from tradition to modernity, producing an inevitable culture shock.[32]

Important though that transition may be, this book argues more generally that the conservatism of immigrant communities should be understood as a reaction to the loss of social and cultural certainties that migration brings with it. Bodnar writes that migrants 'had to devise explanations of their status in terms intelligible to themselves by drawing on folk thought, religion, ancestry, and similar devices close at hand'. Harking back to cultural traditions was a means of survival in a time of economic struggle. 'They had to devote nearly all their attention to that portion of their world in which they actually could exert some power and influence: the family household, the workplace, and the local neighborhood or community.'[33]

Alienation should be seen as a phase in the biographies of migrant families. Gaining control in unfamiliar surroundings marked the start of a process of integration. Mastering a new language, dealing with unfamiliar working conditions, deciphering the prevailing rules of etiquette and practising the old faith in a new environment – all these things changed their lives, and even more so the lives of their children. The more time they spent in the new environment, the more treacherous the route back to a remembered youth. In Zorgvlied cemetery in Amsterdam a little plot of Islamic gravestones is shyly emerging, a literal and figurative 'we're never going to leave', but that decision – 'I want to be buried here' – is a difficult and deeply emotional one. The isolation of many older migrants, tied by their children to the place where they've settled but in their minds still living in their native countries, should not be underestimated. And who will look after them when they need it? 'I do secretly hope that my children will care for me.'

The In-Between Generation

A skewed relationship with the children is one of the most painful consequences of migration. This is particularly clear in the case of migrants from Pakistan, Morocco and Mexico, for example, whose rather conservative lifestyle is now meeting with growing resistance from their sons and daughters, but in many other cases too the generation gap is wide, and traditional communities in many countries of origin fail to acknowledge intergenerational conflict. Parents have few means of preparing their children for a society whose language and customs remain in many ways strange to them. Their resignation is all too obvious, as is the sense that everything they once had has been taken away.

In his novel *Judith and Jamal*, Fouad Laroui, born in Morocco, describes a father–son relationship. 'Abal-Khail loved his son, but he didn't know how to tell him. He worried about him, there in that country where he understood so little. It was his fault that Jamal was growing up in a land of infidels. He had wanted to protect him against every danger, against the temptations, the traps.'[34] If anything, the boy's mother has an even more tenuous connection to the world around them. Can you stay somewhere and yet not be there? Laroui asks himself, looking at Jamal's exhausted mother asleep on the couch. 'The answer is a sorrowful yes. In the mornings she hurries through the streets of Paris, wrapped in an exotic djellaba, but what is she actually making of her life? In all things she's an outsider, irrevocably an outsider.'[35]

The powerlessness of such parents is obvious. As one of their children has said: 'It's not that they didn't want to offer us any support, it was simply that they couldn't. You can't give something you don't have to begin with.'[36] Many are so detached from society that they have no idea what their offspring get up to when they leave the house. The children move between separate worlds: home, school and the street. The norms that prevail in the family sphere have little to do with the rules that apply outside it and the resulting conflict seems almost inevitable. The distances that have to be bridged every day are simply too great for many parents, and for their children.

One difference between the first and second generations is that for adults the shock of the new country comes after they've already been shaped to a great degree by the cultures of their countries of origin, whereas the problems of adaptation for their children come at a point when they're in the midst of their personal development. This explains why children are even more susceptible to the confusion that migration inevitably brings with it. They can't stand aloof. Their resilience and flexibility are tested, and often their parents can do little to help them.

Journalist Margalith Kleijwegt has recorded their stories: 'At home Mehmet never says anything about school, about what happens there, who his friends are. He claims he does his homework, but does he? Mrs Demircan has no way of checking. School is an abstract concept to her. She has no idea where the building is or what her eldest son does there.'[37] So the gulf between migrants and society inevitably creates a gulf between parents and children. Kleijwegt sums up her impressions: 'For most of the parents, childrearing seems more like staving off catastrophe than something beautiful or fun that they can enjoy. They lack confidence in themselves, in the world and in their children. Parents feel pushed into a corner. They react defensively to everything.'[38] People outside the family are kept at a safe distance as a matter of principle.

Follow the trail in the other direction. Anyone who travels back with a migrant family to the place where its older members were born will soon become aware of the gulf between here and there. People accustomed to living as part of an extensive family network are suddenly transformed into a nuclear family in a rear apartment on the third floor. Husband and wife living on top of one another – surely that's unnatural. The emotional balance is upset; family conventions have to be rethought. In the new country, relationships are strange: men and women, boys and girls treat each other differently.

It is of course quite natural for parents to defend their own notions of propriety. This tendency expresses itself most clearly in traditional beliefs about marriage as a bond that arises not so much out of love as from a sense of social duty. In her novel *Brick Lane* Monica Ali describes the married lives of two migrants from Bangladesh. Nazneen was given away to Chanu by her father when she was young: 'Her husband had a proverb for everything. Any wife is better than no wife. Something is better than nothing. What had she imagined? That he was in love with her? That he was grateful because she, young and graceful, had accepted him? That in sacrificing herself to him, she was owed something? Yes. Yes. She realized in a stinging rush she had imagined all these things. Such a foolish girl. Such high notions. What self-regard.'[39] All that's left to her is rebelliousness. There's no way out. 'If I had known what this marriage would be, what this man would be . . . ! What? What then? I would have run away?'[40]

Arranged marriages also reveal clear notions about the role of women, and these increasingly conflict with liberal ideas after 50 years of female emancipation. Fatiha, another second-generation migrant, says: 'Mother thinks, like father, that I should just give up my studies and get married soon. Studying isn't terribly important in our family. As a woman you've little to gain by it. You're going to marry anyway and be a housewife, so working for a diploma is a waste of time.'[41] Many girls from migrant families see school as a chance to escape their parents' plans for them. But how many women take their lives into their own hands when they leave full-time education and use the knowledge they've amassed to pursue a career?

This collision over marriage is a constant theme in the history of migration. Handlin wrote of European migrants in America that 'here was the ultimate barrier between the generations: they would never understand each other's conception of marriage'.[42] Getting a daughter to marry young was a way for parents to prevent her from being lost to a liberal outside world that was felt to be a perpetual threat to her chastity. Fatiha says: 'Because of all these things I haven't spoken to my father for a long time, nor he to me. I find my parents' constant distrust of me the worst thing of all.'[43] Yet even today most of these girls, however modern they may appear at first glance, fall back into a more-or-less traditional marriage.

One of the causes of troubled relationships in many migrant families is that the father usually left first. Ten years or so passed before he arranged for his family to follow him. The children grew up without their father, who visited only at holiday time, laden with gifts. Indeed, the pressure to have his family join him usually arose from the fact that mothers were being forced to bring up their children alone. Often these holiday dads agreed to reunite the family only with some understandable reluctance, since they'd learned to value the freedom of their new country in their own way and had entered into all kinds of relationships. With their wives and daughters came religion and a more conservative outlook.

These clashes within families, complicated enough in themselves, are compounded by a legacy of educational disadvantage. The expectation that children from migrant families would quickly make their way up the social ladder has met with disappointment in many cases. The statistics on training and work speak for themselves. The second generation is clearly over-represented on the lowest rungs. Exclusion and discrimination are exacerbated by language deficits, a limited range of personal networks, inadequate knowledge of the social environment and, of course, a low level of education among parents.

A new social question has arisen. On average, the children of migrants lag behind their peers significantly in cognitive development and linguistic ability, which puts the better jobs out of their reach. Researchers have concluded that there is a 'considerable reserve of talent', yet, at the same time, that 'the majority of children from non-native families reach a level of education little different from that of their low-skilled parents. Clearly the weak social position of the first generation is being passed on to the second.'[44] Not only does their advancement seem less spectacular than expected, progress in relation to the parents is not what ultimately matters, however valuable it may be in terms of family history. Children don't compete within their own communities but within society as a whole. What counts in the end is whether they have a real chance in the jobs market.

Amid all this attention to falling behind, we shouldn't neglect the existence of a growing middle class of migrants and their children. Migrant communities differ, and social distinctions within them are bound to increase in the future. Disadvantage tends to be concentrated in non-Western communities, although many migrants from Asia are doing extremely well. The impatience of this new middle class is unmistakable and its achievements are crucial in determining the degree to which immigrants feel their new country is truly their own. A society that affords little space to talented newcomers will pay a high price.

Good jobs aren't everything, however. Those who succeed often feel remarkably uncomfortable. In societies that haven't yet adjusted appropriately to the permanent presence of migrants and their children, they soon find a role thrust upon them, as George Alagiah, a well-known BBC journalist who came to England from Sri Lanka as a boy, reflects in his autobiography. 'I had never asked to be an example to anyone. I never wanted to be the best black journalist. I simply wanted to be the best reporter that I could be. Later, I came to understand that I performed a function regardless of whether I wanted to or not.'[45]

That feeling of continually being judged by where you come from, or are presumed to have come from, is pernicious, but the reaction of those it affects is ambiguous: 'Don't judge me by my background but never forget where I come from.' The hedgehog response comes naturally to people struggling to gain a foothold in a society that in many respects remains closed to them, and it can lead to willed victimhood among those not endowed with any outstanding talent: 'I'll never fit in.'

The psychology of this middle class of migrants and their children may be complicated, but it's become impossible to imagine Western countries without them. Anyone casting an eye across university lecture halls knows that in 10 or 20 years at most, people with a background in post-war migration will be in positions of responsibility of all kinds. Their presence will seem increasingly natural, and the question 'Where do you come from?' will gradually be replaced by 'What kind of work do you do?'

The lives of children from migrant families can no longer be evaluated using the common denominator of social disadvantage. This in itself is reason for hope. But a large group remains that is failing in the education system as it stands, a group with little chance of finding decent jobs. What will happen to them? How will they vent their frustration in an environment of seemingly limitless opportunity? The trouble they cause won't be cancelled out by the success stories that run in parallel to theirs, and which must also be told.

Most worrying of all is the level of criminality. Even today it's spoken of with great trepidation. While we're all willing to accept that social class is an important factor, statistics showing high crime rates for certain ethnic groups, among them Moroccans in the Netherlands, Pakistanis in Britain, Somalis in Sweden and Algerians in France, cannot be ignored. Spokesmen for these communities are heard to excuse them by saying: 'We have a crime problem precisely because we're excluded.'[46] The perpetrators become the victims.

It's unwise to ignore resentment simply because confronting it is unpleasant. In a fascinating interview, psychiatrist Zohra Acherrat-Stitou described the situation that people of her generation find themselves in: 'They're angry with a society that exploited their parents, and angry with their parents for failing to put up any resistance. Many young Moroccans, I notice, see themselves as victims. A victim feels mistreated, misunderstood, insecure. They'll have to shake off that victimhood if they're to find an identity.'[47] This is something we often hear discussed by immigrants who are troubled by the resentment and hostility towards society they detect in their own communities, especially since many such 'victims' quickly build careers for themselves as criminals, thereby jeopardizing the opportunities available to fellow migrants.

A high juvenile crime rate among the second generation is nothing new. Research by Park and his colleagues recorded no fewer than 1,300 youth gangs in Chicago, mostly made up of the children of migrants. His study detected overwhelming uncertainty among parents about how to handle their children. What were they allowed to do and what not? A Polish woman wrote to her sister about her unruly son, 'You say, "Beat". In America you are not allowed to beat; they can put you into a prison. Give them to eat, and don't beat – such is the law in America. Nothing can be done, and you advise to beat! Nothing can be done; if he is not good of himself, he is lost. . . . I regret that I took the children from our country so soon.'[48]

With a view to prevention, it's important to talk about the background to juvenile criminality. Crime isn't imported by migrants, but current crime rates are a product of the confusion that arises from the contrast between different ways of exercising authority. Young people accustomed to a fairly authoritarian upbringing in immigrant families laugh at police officers who prefer to negotiate with them than to arrest them, and they're not afraid of judges who, with a clear conscience, impose one community service order after another. The appeal for self-control isn't working and the unwillingness of migrant communities to take stock of their own responsibilities doesn't help matters. Parents who bury their heads in the sand are no doubt prompted to do so by shame, or impotence, or apathy, but meanwhile their sons are wrecking the image of the entire community and thereby disadvantaging everyone.

There's no doubt that some neighbourhoods have developed a subculture in which both serious and petty criminality flourish, most famously the *banlieues* in cities like Lyon and Paris, although comparable stories emerge from other urban districts, such as Berlin's Rollberg-Viertel.[49] Lucienne Bui Trong, who for 10 years headed the urban violence section of the French police intelligence service, writes that although the children of migrants are involved in crime to a disproportionate extent, 'the attachment to a territory seems to be stronger than comradeship based on ethnic origin; a coloured youth from a different part of town is not regarded as a brother.'[50] Clearly crime shouldn't be perceived as a product of a young man's country of origin but, rather, as an outcome of the violent street culture that turns some deprived neighbourhoods into no-go areas.

We'd do better to call the second generation an in-between generation. Its members are themselves often unsure where they belong. Although many young people in Europe describe themselves as Turkish, Bangladeshi or Moroccan, once on holiday in their parents' countries they quickly discover they don't belong. In his novel, Laroui takes a humorous look at this confusion. When Jamal and his friend pay a brief visit to relatives in Morocco they're upset by the arbitrary behaviour of the police and much else that seems outlandish to them. Back in Paris we're privy to the following dialogue: '"Didn't we invent couscous?" "Who do you mean by 'we'? What are you then, actually?" "Well, I'm an Arab aren't I?" "Crap. What on earth do you know about the history of the Arabs? You don't even speak Arabic. There's no way you're an Arab. That's what I think and no one's going to tell me any different." "You sure do take the prize for making simple things complicated. Suddenly I don't know who I am any more. But I'm a Muslim anyhow, aren't I?"

"Don't make me laugh. You? You wouldn't last 15 minutes in Teheran. The only thing that connects you to Islam and the Arabs is your name. And even that's nothing but hot air." "So where *are* my roots then, dammit?"[51]

And so on. The misunderstanding is endless. Many children of migrant families have considerable reservations about the countries in which they were born and raised. Some are proud of an identity borrowed from their parents' native land, a place they can't really fathom. All this follows a familiar pattern and at the same time it's a pity, because clinging to the culture of the country their parents left behind will not help them to thrive in new circumstances. There are two sides to their reticence, however. It signifies the gulf that exists, but it also represents the beginning of critical engagement. Indeed, there is a growing number who rise above the idea that they're not fully at home anywhere. If asked whether they'd like to go back to their 'native country' they answer with a simple 'I'm already there.'[52]

Native Unease

Migrants aren't alone in feeling that a familiar world is being lost. People who in some cases have lived in the same district for generations have seen their surroundings changed out of all recognition by the arrival of people from other parts of the globe. Anyone who chooses to listen can hear countless stories of people who no longer feel at home in their neighbourhoods. So-called white flight is one result, a phenomenon associated with all major waves of immigration in Western countries. The steady departure of the original inhabitants contributes to the creation of districts in which the majority has become a minority and minorities are now the majority. We shall return with some regularity to the relationship between the two, but now let's look for a moment at the unease felt by native populations.

The history of immigration is a history of alienation, Handlin wrote, and this applies not just to the immigrants themselves but to a fair few of the longstanding inhabitants as well. The documentary film *All White in Barking* focuses on what was once a traditional working-class district of London. Dave, one of the central characters, walks through his old neighbourhood and comments: 'This was the best part of Barking and Dagenham. Everyone wanted to live in this area; now no one wants to live here. Well, none of the indigenous population wants to live here now anyway.' He worries about those left behind: 'Clive and Chris, what's going to happen to them? They can't move. They've got to suffer it all.'

The filmmaker asks him about the town he's chosen as his new home. 'It's a nice place, only your own people there. I just want to move out of this bloody borough and be safe again, like I used to be.'[53]

Sometimes discontent may arise from rather more symbolic changes to the built environment. In the Berlin district of Pankow residents rebelled against plans for a mosque, which was finally built despite years of opposition. It's a relatively modest building, hidden behind a Kentucky Fried Chicken, but the people involved in the protest – whom the mayor of the borough describes as predominantly moderates – are convinced the new house of prayer won't be of any benefit to their neighbourhood. One reason may be that its imam is fairly orthodox and tries to convince believers that their German neighbours will one day understand why they cannot shake hands with women.

Of course it's perfectly possible to dismiss such experiences as the trivial complaints of citizens who've never had it so good – the mosque really is here to stay and there are more important things in life – but it would be better to listen first. During a debate in Antwerp several people commented that a third of the city consisted of declared and undeclared xenophobes, since they'd voted for the populist Vlaams Belang, while others asked why so many voters were refusing to take part in a rational conversation about a changing world. Perhaps it shouldn't surprise us that people will not be favourably disposed towards dialogue if their concerns are dismissed as knee-jerk reactions. Besides, does a term like 'racism' really increase our insight into the fears of the native population? No one would deny that xenophobia exists, but British urban sociologist Ruth Glass opted for a more cautious approach in her early study of Londoners' responses to the arrival of immigrants from the Caribbean in the late 1950s: 'The keynote in the situation of the coloured minority in Britain is not inflexible prejudice, harsh segregation and discrimination; it is muddle, confusion and insecurity.'[54] She concluded that 'the majority have an attitude which can be called "benevolent prejudice" – a combination of passive prejudice and passive tolerance'.[55]

Glass was writing about the 1950s and '60s, but this undoubtedly applies to present circumstances too. Avoidance of such monolithic terms as 'racism' allows a more accurate picture to emerge. In a speech about race relations in America, Barack Obama attempted not only to find words for the anger and frustration of the black community but to say something meaningful about the sense of resentment among his country's white residents. 'Most working- and middle-class white Americans don't feel that they have been particularly privileged by their race. . . . They are anxious about their futures, and feel their dreams slipping away. . . . When they hear that an African American is getting an advantage in landing a good job or a spot in a good college because of an injustice that they themselves never committed; when they're told that their fears about crime in urban neighborhoods are somehow prejudiced, resentment builds over time.' He told his audience that 'to wish away the resentments of white Americans, to label them as misguided or even racist, without recognizing they are grounded in legitimate concerns – this too widens the racial divide, and blocks the path to understanding'.[56]

The anxiety Obama talks about has everything to do with a loss of social and cultural certainties. Established populations are reacting in ways that are reminiscent of earlier periods of mass immigration, in America and elsewhere. We have already looked at the cycle of ethnic relations, in which three stages can be discerned: avoidance, conflict and accommodation. In this context, avoidance involves a refusal to accept a new reality; people deny that anything essential has changed. As long as they never actually meet any migrants, because of segregation in the cities where they live, it may seem as if the arrival of newcomers hasn't really affected anything.

Avoidance is often the first phase in a long process of settlement. Research in cities like Detroit and Chicago – where the one-time majority now finds itself a minority of the urban population – reveals the unease of white residents. Maria Kefalas describes an overwhelmingly 'white' district of Chicago called Beltway, populated by the lower middle class and located not far from one of the city's black ghettos. Her aim is to chart the aversion felt by its residents, since she is convinced that 'tolerance only comes after every voice of dissent is heard'.[57] In her judgement, the defensiveness of residents goes 'beyond the old notions of racial antagonisms and fears'.[58]

They are the children and grandchildren of working-class people who struggled to survive at the margins of society, so home ownership is extremely important to them. They feel themselves partial owners of their neighbourhood, which is well maintained. Graffiti is regarded as a serious assault on the orderly social environment. 'Consumption, ritualistic displays of house pride, and a fanatical concern for order serve as talismans to keep socio-economic insecurities at bay.'[59] For many residents, Beltway represents a last stand. If bad neighbours arrive they have nowhere else to go. Their lives are far more bound to a specific place than those of the better off.

Their insecurity has to do with both class and colour. Anthropologist John Hartigan is firm in his views about white districts of Detroit that feel similarly threatened. In one case he writes of 'the interplay of class anxieties and racial confusions at work in the transformations of this neighbourhood'.[60] The importance of social class is clear from reactions to white migrants who arrived from the South from the 1950s onwards, the so-called 'hillbillies', who were far from welcome despite their skin colour; in fact they were often labelled 'white trash'. 'The overall focus of negative feeling was on recent arrivals, both white and black, native-born and foreign.'[61]

Clashes such as these, Kefalas says, can be seen as arising from resistance of a kind that excludes any 'ambiguity about what distinguishes the garden from the ghetto'.[62] Ambivalence is a privilege reserved for those who have already secured a place on the social ladder. 'Safety, a sense of belonging, security, and undisrupted routines – these are the things neighbors want to preserve and these are the things they would mourn if the last garden ceased to exist.'[63] Hostility towards newcomers – who, as in Detroit, include white immigrants – is one result. 'Even though many Beltway residents are the children and grandchildren of European immigrants, second- or third-generation Americans demonstrate little empathy for the latest wave of arrivals from Eastern Europe to settle in Chicago.'[64]

Classic competition for resources lurks behind much of the resistance to further immigration and no one would deny that it's especially intense at the bottom of the labour market, where people are forced out of their jobs by a low-paid and non-organized work force, or subjected to downward pressure on wages. Perhaps those with most to lose are the insecure lower middle classes. American economists Timothy Hatton and Jeffry Williamson conclude soberly that hostility today, as in the past, arises from the admission of large numbers of migrants with little education or training, leading to 'rising inequality' and a growth in the number of 'crowded-out native unskilled workers'. This opposition is made all the harder to ignore by 'the greater voting power of those hurt most – the working poor'.[65]

The stories relayed by writers like Hartigan and Kefalas should not be allowed to obscure the fact that however durable a phenomenon avoidance may be, it represents an early stage in an ongoing process. A time always arrives when segregation becomes untenable. Today, in cities like Marseille, Birmingham, Stuttgart and Malmö where 40 per cent or more of residents are migrants or the children of migrants, newcomers and established residents can no longer avoid one another. Nor can they disregard the question: How much must we have in common in order to live together in a diverse but peaceful society? The end of avoidance provokes a good deal of conflict, which is not to say that integration has failed.

Once the permanence of the changes unleashed by immigration can no longer be denied, loss becomes tangible on both sides and tensions emerge. To take the enrichment of a society that immigration brings about as a starting point and ignore the disappearance of a familiar world is to demonstrate an inadequate understanding of the history of immigration. Recognition of the resulting sense of loss opens up the possibility of a rational explanation for many of the accompanying experiences people go through. Clashes are an integral part of immigration history and they often seem to help people accept their new social environment.

The malaise in native populations arises from a sense of insecurity, which has social and cultural causes. It's not always easy to distinguish between the two, but whether it's a matter of the freedom to publish cartoons that ridicule all that is sacred, the wearing of headscarves by prosecutors and judges, dual nationality, sex education, or the kind of history taught in schools, each dilemma arrives with cultural or symbolic baggage. Of course people's living conditions must be improved and access to education extended, but an important part of the unease felt on all sides is at precisely this symbolic level: 'We're losing our culture.'

Since 9/11, if not before, opposition to immigration in today's Europe has been bound up with the sense of insecurity arising from the emergence of Islam as a major European religion. In many neighbourhoods, hostility towards newcomers is generated by the precarious circumstances of residents' lives, but the debate about the place of Islam in a liberal society has little to do with class divides or traditional distinctions between left and right. There's a widespread belief that the achievements of liberalism are at stake, from freedom of speech to sexual equality.

Sometimes it's simply a question of etiquette. A resident of a mixed neighbourhood in Rotterdam describes an incident in her own street: 'Those young Turkish women don't say good-day to me. They look away arrogantly if a man comes towards them. I can't stand that. Last week I stood talking in my doorway with a Turkish woman. That was quite something. Later that day I saw her on the street with her mother. She didn't say a word. The next day I said to her, "Listen, if you don't even want to say hello to me in public, then I don't need to talk to you indoors any more either." She just shrugged.'[66] It's interesting to note that the failure to greet a neighbour was interpreted as arrogance, whereas it might equally well have been a sign of embarrassment or shyness.

Everyday friction of this kind is common. It may revolve around the withdrawal of a child from mixed swimming lessons, the introduction of halal food in a staff canteen, concern about whether state schools should celebrate Christmas, a firm's decision to stop giving piggy-banks as promotional gifts, the provision of separate citizenship courses for men and women, the granting of planning permission for a mosque, or the refusal of a policeman to shake a woman's hand because it's against his religion. Sometimes a compromise could easily be reached, but when norms are radically different they will collide.

In the case of Muslim communities, attitudes to homosexuality and unequal treatment of men and women are particular sources of discomfort among their non-Muslim neighbours. Before finding fame in the Netherlands and beyond as a populist politician, Pim Fortuyn wrote a polemical book about what he called with characteristic hyperbole 'the Islamization of our culture'. Precisely because he was aware of parallels with the emancipatory struggles of women and homosexuals – of which in the latter case he had direct experience – he believed the gains made needed to be defended against 'a culture of reticence and silence'. He wrote: 'Emancipation is a basic right of all those who live here and we have a duty to do all we can to promote it, in the case of Muslim men and women as well as everyone else.'[67]

Another bone of contention is the visibility of Islam in public places, as demonstrated by recent heated debates in Switzerland over a proposed ban on the building of minarets. The building of a new mosque of any size tends to cause conflict, but this ban goes far further than the usual objections to the granting of planning permission. In the autumn of 2009 the proposal won 57 per cent of votes in a referendum. A majority of those eligible to do so had voted. Its supporters, many of whom thought of themselves as moderates, spoke of the way Islam mixes politics and religion. Like the wearing of the burka, which has been outlawed in France, the minaret was seen as a political statement, a symbol of dominance. This was a reversal of the argument that such a ban would erode religious freedom; neutrality is clearly far easier before Islam became so noticeable, and its new visibility is now provoking profound hostility. The abolition of the constitutional right of a minority by majority vote violates a taboo and should serve as a warning.

Alongside the temptation to curb religious freedom in the case of Islam, fierce arguments have arisen about freedom of expression, although the temptation in this case is to limit what critics of Islam are allowed to say. Some governments have tried to introduce new clauses to blasphemy laws, aimed mainly at protecting Muslim communities and preventing their radicalization, and this too has provoked a good deal of opposition. In Britain new legislation was proposed that would have tightened the law governing 'the intent to stir up religious hatred'. Actor and comic Rowan Atkinson gave a speech in the House of Lords in which he expressed his opposition to the Racial and Religious Hatred Bill, saying: 'The freedom to criticise ideas – any ideas even if they are sincerely held beliefs – is one of the fundamental freedoms of society. And the law which attempts to say you can criticise or ridicule ideas as long as they are not religious ideas is a very peculiar law indeed. It all points to the promotion of the idea that there should be a right not to be offended. But in my view the right to offend is far more important than any right not to be offended.'[68] The row over Danish cartoons that ridiculed the prophet Mohammed (which British newspapers unanimously decided not to publish) and the murder of filmmaker Theo van Gogh were further occasions for what could be described as secular discomfort.

Just as racism is a catch-all term and therefore inadequate to describe current hostilities, the overused word Islamophobia can lead people to mistake legitimate criticism of religious intolerance for a rejection of the principle of religious freedom for Muslims. Especially when equated with anti-Semitism, thereby evoking a whole range of unjustified historical associations, it blocks the route to any understanding of the controversies surrounding Islam. The unease created by the emergence of European Islam requires more detailed examination than this, if only because the threat of terrorism casts a shadow over attempts to see Muslim communities as part of the 'imagined community'.

The social and cultural dimensions of integration both deserve attention. Currently, the experiences of migrants are often interpreted as primarily socio-economic and those of native populations as cultural in origin. Neither interpretation reflects the full picture. It's also important to stress that problems surrounding migration are embedded in general social issues, that they never arise in isolation but are part of far broader changes to society. The unease felt by established residents results from the general impression that there are more and more gaps in the social fabric, that neighbourhoods are losing their cohesion.

The fundamental dilemma of our times is the growing divide between social elites, able to move around at will in a world that has fewer and fewer borders, and an increasing proportion of the population that feels threatened by globalization and is turning its back on the outside world. A vague and unrealistic concept of world citizenship has encouraged a return to parochialism. While some sing the praises of a borderless world, others are resorting to cut and dried notions of their own identity. Conservatism can never be the complete answer and there's a need to look beyond the self-affirmation of slogans like 'my own people first', but self-abnegation, the dream of a world without borders where nationality will no longer matter, isn't a long-term answer either.

Societies cannot progress from avoidance to acceptance without evolving a new sense of themselves. What is citizenship and who are our fellow citizens? Avoidance, conflict and accommodation occur simultaneously, since immigrants continue to arrive, but societies aren't fated endlessly to repeat the same clashes. History teaches us that new groups are continually being absorbed into the imagined community, thereby enlarging it. There was a time when the Catholic Irish were unwelcome in Protestant America, whereas nowadays we can't imagine that country without them. Their history is similar to that of other migrant communities of past centuries, such as the Italians in France or the Poles in Germany.

During a debate in Amsterdam with representatives of the Surinamese community, someone said in a slightly injured tone: 'No one talks about us any longer.' The current focus is on problems involving young Moroccans and Turks. Contrary to the speaker's intentions, that complaint was actually an encouraging reflection of immigrant history: those once seen as outsiders have become, little by little, established residents. The Surinamese immigrants of 40 years ago have slowly come to be part of the imagined Netherlands (although there is still some way to go), and in the process they have changed the country's image. The search for a sense of who we are today is never-ending, since new groups of outsiders are arriving all the time.

Genuine acceptance of the changes brought about by migrants does not imply resignation, a sense that things are the way they are and there's nothing anyone can do. In every discussion of immigration controls, people in the West are told that they live in a borderless world and people will come whether they like it or not, indeed that what they're experiencing now is only the start of a vast wave of immigration. Statements of this kind certainly haven't helped to encourage tolerance. Too much has been obscured by a factual observation: 'People are increasingly mobile.'

Immigration and integration should be part of a civilized ideal that functions both as an aspiration and as a subject for public debate. If discussion is stymied by a belief that globalization means people can no longer shape their own societies, then we shouldn't be surprised to see freedoms brought into disrepute. How can anyone value a democracy that declares itself impotent in the face of the most far-reaching issues affecting citizens' daily lives?

Integration Requires Self-Examination

The movement of peoples over the past few decades has had a considerable impact. Natives and newcomers often seem far apart, and beneath a veneer of harmony countless stories can be heard – by those willing to listen – about daily cultural clashes. A conflict successfully avoided for years has erupted all the more fiercely. Where silence reigned for so long, too much is now being said and too stridently. Multicultural diplomacy alone will not be enough to build mutual trust, but for a long time few awkward questions were asked, both because no one was particularly interested in the answers and because it was felt too much would be stirred up if they were. Noiriel remarks that crises surrounding migration 'are moments in which the social rules for the whole of the receiving society are ruptured and redefined'.[69]

This process is now well under way. In migrant communities, one generation after another puzzles over the nature of its relationship not just with the society it finds itself in, but with its countries of origin. In an autobiographical account Ziauddin Sardar writes: 'As we, the Asian community, became more British, more rooted in time and place, here and now in Britain, we also needed to build more barricades against losing touch with where our parents came from. We needed barricades to protect us from the increasing sense of being rejected by British society.'[70]

Ambiguity is rife in countries of immigration and it can easily lead to distrust on all sides. When relations between people are coloured by suspicion, anything anyone does can be interpreted as malicious: on closer examination an offer of help is mere meddling, a question can easily sound like an order, apparent uncertainty is taken as some kind of subterfuge and, before you know it, all attempts at sincerity have run into the sand. The conclusion drawn by German writer Hans Magnus Enzensberger seems justified: 'Today the preparedness and ability to integrate cannot be taken for granted in any country or on any side. The multicultural society remains an empty slogan as long as the difficulties the concept raises are declared taboo but not resolved.'[71]

There has been too much avoidance on the part of receiving societies, and it goes some way to explain the current impasse. The twentieth century was marked by attempts to reduce social inequality and bridge cultural divides; no issue has disturbed European public life so much as the effort to elevate a whole range of population groups so that full citizenship would be available to everyone. This determination to achieve equality of opportunity arose out of a fear of social unrest, but it was also inspired by moral convictions.

Generally speaking, past efforts to integrate all social groups could be described as successful. Rank and class lost their edge; people became less and less bound by their origins. This makes the resigned response to the rise of a new, perhaps more pernicious divide seem all the more troubling. Newcomers and their families often lag behind, and at the same time institutions are not sufficiently open to new talent. The absence of urgency was the product of a consensus that prevailed for decades, the idea that integration is purely a matter of time, a natural outcome of socio-economic progress. What's lacking now is a clear notion of citizenship that goes beyond a plea for improvements to the position of migrants in the jobs market and in education.

Timidity on the subject points to a more general failing. The call for integration prompts the response: 'Integration, fine, but into what?' A society that has little or nothing to say for itself will quickly be exposed as flawed. This has not escaped the attention of migrants, who respond with a combination of 'What do you actually want from us?' and 'For heaven's sake leave us alone'. As one student remarked: 'You never know where you stand here. What is integration, in fact? What are Dutch or French or British norms and values? I have a feeling politicians are deliberately vague about them, so that they can always say: no, that's not what we meant.'

Such reactions are all too often expressed in aggrieved tones, but anyone aiming to close the chasm nevertheless needs to come up with a convincing response. 'Diversity' is a commonly deployed concept, but it does little to clarify matters. It ought to go without saying that an open society is characterized by divergent outlooks, lifestyles and beliefs, but even in a liberal democracy there are limits: not everything that's different is valuable. Embracing diversity indiscriminately is tantamount to protecting traditional habits and customs from critical scrutiny. There's a tendency to address migrant families as members of the groups to which they're presumed to belong. This applies not only to the first generation, which is to some extent preserving the traditions of its countries of origin, but to the children and grandchildren of migrants as well. They are regarded as perpetuating a particular culture, whereas it may well be that many 'Turkish' children prefer listening to American rapper 50 Cent than to Turkish pop star Sezen Aksu – quite apart from the fact that many different influences can be found in Aksu's work.

There's another reason why the prevailing view of diversity doesn't necessarily represent progress. If minorities continue to see themselves primarily as ethnic groups, there's a real danger that majority populations too will increasingly conceive of themselves in ethnic terms, especially when in many cities they find themselves outnumbered. American sociologist Charles Gallagher has observed: 'Like it or not, middle-class and lower middle-class whites see themselves as a minority and have adopted a posture of being the victims.'[72] This is the risk we run by emphasizing ethnicity. Why should one group be allowed to appeal to its own ethnic identity if another group is not?

It's important always to keep in mind the aim of creating a society in which people are asked how they see their futures, not one in which they're judged according to their pasts. Getting there will be a process of trial and error, and all citizens will need to look beyond ethnic dividing lines.

It's often argued that integration should engage both newcomers and natives, but what does this actually mean? Instead of emphasizing the differences between minorities and the majority, we should concentrate on shared citizenship as an ideal to which everyone can aspire. Migrants can be invited and challenged by a society only if it has a strong culture of citizenship. Problems surrounding migrants and their children are general social issues writ large. They concern not only important institutions such as education but constitutional rights like freedom of expression. This is the reason migration cuts so deep: it goes to the heart of institutions and liberties.

The basic principle is simple: native populations cannot ask of newcomers any more than they are themselves prepared to contribute. Those who encourage others to see themselves as fellow citizens must have at least some notion of what it means to be a citizen and, as far as possible, turn that notion into practical reality. Hence the embarrassment that typifies debates about integration. An established population that asks newcomers to integrate will sooner or later find itself facing similar demands. This is all part of an ongoing quest, a process of social renewal.

Take linguistic skills. There can be no doubt that the command of a country's official language is a prerequisite for all those trying to hold their own as citizens. The Dutch have therefore talked a great deal over the past few years about language deficits in migrant families, a problem currently referred to as 'low literacy'. It was only a matter of time before people started asking: How good are the reading and writing skills of the indigenous Dutch population? It quickly became clear that hundreds of thousands are struggling, and initiatives are now being implemented that are aimed at raising levels of literacy across the board.

This is just one example of how debates about integration can make hidden social problems visible, introducing issues that go far beyond the emancipation of migrants. The growing divide between low-skilled and educated people demands attention; Flemish writer David van Reybrouck regards this as the most important cause of current dissatisfaction with democracy. Many people with little more than a basic education no longer feel represented: 'As in the Netherlands, a parallel society has grown up in Belgium. The low-skilled are in the majority, but they genuinely feel themselves to be a minority that is subjected to discrimination.'[73]

Integration conceived as a reciprocal process confronts society with profound questions about what it means to be a citizen. What skills are essential? What kind of knowledge is required? Those who think migrants should know more about the development of their adoptive country's constitution, for example, cannot avoid the question: What exactly do you know about it yourself? This has revealed another weakness of Western societies. Doubts about the historical awareness of the average citizen matter, because citizenship involves a realization that something came before us and something will come after us. It's hard for any sense of responsibility to develop unless people see themselves as part of a continuing history.

This prompts a number of questions. What image of the past is presented to newcomers? Might there not be a need to discuss this image with everyone, irrespective of background and origin? The issue of integration has forced many countries to take a fresh look at school curricula. Are schoolchildren taught in any meaningful sense about colonial history? Is any attention paid in schools to migration into and within Europe over the centuries? It would change the way history is treated. Gestures are of little use. It's essential to hand down as truthful and self-critical an account of the past as possible.

Self-examination is going on outside schools as well. New museums are being established, such as the French museum for the history of immigration and the Dutch National History museum, while those already in existence are reassessing the stories they tell. The aim is not so much to win people over as to use migration as the starting point for a re-examination of commonly held assumptions.

There's an even more fundamental sense in which the principle of reciprocity prompts societies to question themselves. It concerns the rights and duties attached to citizenship. Citizens are now well aware of their rights but far less likely to have been given a clear understanding of their duties. This is a crucial problem, since freedoms unaccompanied by a sense of responsibility will start to erode. The issue of religious freedom illustrates the point. Muslims invoke the right to practise their religion and that right is non-negotiable, as long as it's exercised within the bounds of the constitution, but it also confers upon them a responsibility to defend the rights of people of other faiths or none.

There's a need for shared norms to which both the majority and minorities feel bound, and they include the right to freedom of conscience. The question that needs to be addressed is: What do the difficulties surrounding integration tell us about the strengths and weaknesses of society as a whole? The search for ways to live together demands self-examination on all sides. That's the deeper significance of the reciprocity we seek: those who ask migrants to take a critical look at their traditions must be prepared to hold their own cherished assumptions up to the light.

Citizens, whether newcomers or otherwise, should not be required to absorb themselves into society as it is now but rather to identify with society as it has the potential to be. Everyone should feel invited to help society move closer to its ideal of equal treatment. Reciprocity as a basic principle of citizenship means that anyone trying to combat discrimination against migrants and their children must be prepared to oppose forms of discrimination within migrant families, against unbelievers, for example, or homosexuals. We can't pick and choose when it comes to equality.

This became clear on a visit to a school in Antwerp where a large majority of pupils are from Muslim families. One commented, as a joke: 'I've counted the Belgians at our school. There are 23.' The school has a long tradition and many of the children do well, but the teachers say it's become difficult to talk about evolution in biology lessons, about the Holocaust during history lessons and about 'perverts' like Oscar Wilde in literature lessons. A choice has to be made. Should teachers give in to the religious prejudices many children bring from home, or oppose them, with all the patience and dedication that requires?

The reverse is also true, of course. A society that cherishes the principle of equality must be willing to listen to those who claim they've been discriminated against at work or in pubs and clubs. Sometimes legal action is necessary, but in many situations the key to success is persuasion, not compulsion. Campaigns and rules may help to combat discrimination, but we all need to confront prejudices publicly, challenging them as a step towards developing mutual trust.

Not everyone favours such reciprocity, as is clear from comments like: 'They came to us, we didn't go to their country.' This amounts to saying that the majority has the right to force minorities to adapt. Such an imbalance of power can never produce a truly integrated society, if only because the protection of the rights of minorities is a defining element of democracy. The opposite view is equally unproductive. It often takes the form of claims that there can be no reciprocity while the imbalance between the established and newcomers is as great as it is now. In other words: 'You can't ask the same of those at the bottom as you do of those at the top.' This attitude leads nowhere, except to the paternalistic notion that people in migrant communities are not responsible for their fate. Shared citizenship means, by definition, that we are all invited to enter the public arena as equals.

We started by identifying a sense of alienation and loss among both immigrant and indigenous populations. If the shock of the new can inspire self-criticism and change, real progress will have been made. Efforts to ensure that people from all regions of the world can be part of today's urban society should prompt a reassessment of prevailing notions. This is not a matter of being disloyal to everything Europe and America have contributed to the ideal of an open society, but of becoming more faithful to that ideal.

In other words, the arrival of migrants is not only irreversible, it offers a unique opportunity for introspection. American sociologist Henry Pratt Fairchild was aware of this almost a century ago. Much of what he wrote is now outdated, but surely he was right in saying that the degree to which migrants were able to feel part of a new country was not down to them alone: 'Before laying tardy assimilation too readily at the door of the immigrant we should thoughtfully consider whether our own house does not need to be set in order.'[74] In short it makes sense to talk about integration only if it's seen as part of an effort to improve society as a whole. As Fairchild puts it: 'If the immigrant is to love America he must first have the opportunity to experience America, and having experienced it he must find it lovable. No amount of lecturing, legislating, and threatening can make the alien love America if he does not find it lovable, and no amount of original strangeness and unfamiliarity can keep him from loving it if in the final event he finds it worthy of his love.'[75]

The subject of immigration and integration – and therefore of citizenship – creates uncertainty because it affects so many areas of life: education systems, welfare provision, constitutional rights such as freedom of expression. The public debate now under way sparks conflict time and again. This book is an attempt to reach beyond existing divides. That will be possible only once we've explored the causes of discontent and developed a realistic view of society as it is now, irrevocably altered by migration.

Perhaps integration has in fact been successful in recent years and newcomers are now just as disengaged as the established population. A society without clear ideas about citizenship will be unable to inspire migrants to see themselves as citizens. It's time for some thorough renovation. An open society cannot survive without self-criticism. We must aspire to become what we say we are.

So What's New?

Immigration is all about crossing borders and its study requires not only specialists but generalists who are willing to step beyond the boundaries of disciplines and genres. In making clear how deeply migration affects society as a whole, I have drawn freely on a wide range of sources, including the insights provided by urban sociology, history, cultural anthropology and studies of international relations. This approach is reflected in the book's essayistic style. The essay is a genre that combines academic study with journalism and literature, and although a great deal of academic research is included here, I've also been inspired by reportage, novels and the public debates of the past 10 years.

I've sought to clarify the experience of migration, placing less emphasis than is usual on the differences between countries and migrant groups, thereby revealing patterns that fail to emerge from studies of those groups in isolation. Turkish and Pakistani migrants obviously differ in many respects, just as Turkish migrants in Germany are different from those in the Netherlands. Indeed, close examination reveals a contrast even between Turkish immigrants in Berlin and Cologne. All this is relevant – and later we'll focus specifically on these diverse groups of newcomers

– but the aim here is to develop some well-founded generalizations about migrant experiences and the reactions their arrival provokes.

I'm interested above all in the social dynamics that result from migration, especially of post-war migrants from what used to be called the third world – more so in fact than in policy or in models of integration, although these will certainly come up. An undue emphasis on differences between models, such as French republicanism and British multiculturalism, tends to obscure the many similarities between living conditions in the major conurbations of Europe. This book focuses on comparable developments in cities such as Lyon, Rotterdam, Bradford and Malmö.

Views that touch upon policy will frequently be discussed, but this is not a political book, ending with a list of recommendations on how to proceed. A great deal of the existing research on the subject of human migration focuses on policy, since its funding is provided by governments. Nevertheless, we will look at opinions about which kinds of immigration may or may not be desirable, as well as at adjustments to the welfare state in societies of immigration, how to deal with segregation in neighbourhoods and schools, ways in which Islam can find a place in an open society and much more along those lines.

What are the consequences of this approach? First, experiences in America and Europe have more in common than we tend to assume. Here lies one hallmark of this study: a comparison between the two continents crops up time and again. Of course, the differences are discussed as well – especially the impact of Islam in Europe and the consequences of the continent's comprehensive welfare state – but it soon becomes clear that behind the proud self-image of America as a 'nation of immigrants' more uncertainty and conflict lurk than is generally recognized. Further examination reveals that European and American experiences are broadly comparable as far as the extent of immigration, public opinion, the degree of segregation and the patterns of integration are concerned.

I therefore disagree with American writers such as Christopher Caldwell and Walter Laqueur, who are extremely gloomy about the future of Europe in this respect and at the same time see America as a fairly unambiguous model. Caldwell writes: 'Immigration is not enhancing or validating European culture; it is supplanting it. Europe is not welcoming its newest residents but making way for them.'[76] He is quick to contrast this with the situation in the United States: 'Mass Hispanic immigration can disrupt a few local habits . . . but it requires no fundamental reform of American cultural practices or institutions. On balance, it may strengthen them.'[77]

While accepting that a contrast exists, it's important to realize the extent of the similarity. The history of America teaches us that practically every sizeable new group encounters opposition, and this has been the pattern in Europe too across the centuries. It will suffice to cite the conclusion of French researcher Denis Lacorne, a view shared by most historians: 'A land that receives immigrants of every provenance and every social class, the United States is also, paradoxically, a country that rejects immigrants.'[78]

A recent comparative study shows that 55 per cent of Britons and 50 per cent of Spaniards believe there are too many immigrants in their countries, while 48 per cent of Americans are of the same opinion, although less resistance is expressed in Germany, France and the Netherlands, with figures of 28, 29 and 32 per cent respectively.[79] Furthermore, 61 per cent of Americans are worried about illegal immigration, compared to an average of 67 per cent in the European Union, while 58 per cent of Americans think illegal immigrants cause crime and an average of 61 per cent of citizens of the EU agree with them.[80] The proportion of those questioned who favour the granting of legal residence status to illegal immigrants is practically identical: a minority of 44 per cent in America compared to 43 per cent in the European Union.[81] In short, attitudes to legal and illegal immigration coincide.

Europe and America are converging in another sense too, namely in the extent of immigration over recent decades, measured as a share of the population. Until the First World War, America received far more migrants; indeed in the nineteenth century millions of Europeans crossed the Atlantic. By 1900, roughly 15 per cent of the US population was foreign-born. The figure is slightly lower today, but it's now in line with the percentages in member states of the European Union: in the United States 13.6 per cent of residents are immigrants, compared with 12.9 per cent in Germany, 10.2 per cent in Britain, 10.7 per cent in the Netherlands, 13.4 per cent in Spain, 8.5 per cent in France, 11.4 per cent in Austria and 6.5 per cent in Italy. The average for Western Europe is around 11 per cent.[82]

The degree to which populations live apart is another example. If we leave aside America's history of slavery and the forced segregation of its black population – a past still at work in maintaining the profound divides seen in cities such as New York, Detroit and Chicago – and look at how migrant communities in Europe cluster together in their own neighbourhoods, then we may well share the conclusion of Amsterdam social geographer Sako Musterd: 'The differences are much smaller than perhaps expected and in some European cities they are even comparable with US metropolitan area averages.'[83] Generally speaking, although the level of segregation is higher in America, it does not differ dramatically from that of migrants from Bangladesh and Pakistan in cities like Birmingham, Bradford and London. The spatial concentration of Moroccans in Brussels, Turks in The Hague and Iranians in Stockholm is considerable as well.

Finally, and this will come as no great surprise in light of the foregoing, integration has taken a roughly comparable course on the two continents. The cycle of avoidance, conflict and accommodation described by American sociologists in the early twentieth century contributes to an understanding of contemporary Europe, and indeed of contemporary America, which is now facing mass migration from Mexico. Of course reality is rather messier than this model suggests, if only because new groups are continually arriving and in large cities all three stages of the cycle occur simultaneously.

Out of this situation arises another hallmark of my approach: the dynamism of societies of immigration is generated by the loss of familiar worlds and the need to come to terms with new environments. The attitudes of both the established and newcomers are coloured by that experience, and both points of view must be taken into account by anyone studying immigration and integration. This would seem to go without saying, but much current research concentrates primarily on the fortunes of migrants and their children. If the native population is discussed at all, it is mostly seen as a hindrance, its members regarded as the personification of prejudice and all too rarely as citizens helping to shape a new kind of society.

The cycle of avoidance, conflict and accommodation can be understood as resulting from ways of dealing with this loss of certainty. Some commentators, such as author Geert Mak, have drawn a parallel with the grieving process.[84] It's an enlightening analogy. What after all are the phases of grief, in which we cope with loss? Surely they include at the very least denial, anger and acceptance. At first people refuse to acknowledge what has happened, next they rebel against it – why me? – before finally coming to terms with circumstances they cannot change and making the best of things. This reflects the cycle some historians of immigration have described.

The stress on a shared experience of loss throws fresh light on the role of prejudice. The conflict that accompanies all major migratory movements means that prejudices on both sides will be challenged sooner or later. Much of today's research, however, is rather one-sided in its approach. In their informative survey of population movements, Stephen Castles and Mark Miller write of anxieties about Islamic fundamentalism but insist that 'such fears are based on racist ideologies rather than social realities'.[85] They go a step further by assuming that a fearful response by the majority fuels Muslim fundamentalism and therefore amounts to a self-fulfilling prophesy. This is to ignore 9/11 and the influence of worldwide radicalization on Muslim communities in Europe and America.

We come upon an identical tendency in the work of German immigration historian Klaus Bade, who ends his wide-ranging historical account by saying that European reluctance to admit refugees is 'an historical scandal by which future generations will judge Europe's understanding of humanity in the late twentieth and early twenty-first centuries'.[86] He clearly has no sympathy for 'fortress Europe', but should we not try to comprehend the desire to reduce the influx of refugees in the 1990s before describing it as a scandal? Should we not also, in passing judgement, take into account the large groups of refugees that have already been given access?

Surely neither avoidance nor the conflict that arises in countries dealing with large-scale immigration can be laid entirely at the door of majority populations. The causes of prejudice described in a classic study by American social psychologist Gordon Allport – including a precarious position in society, strict religious beliefs and an authoritarian upbringing – are to be found in migrant communities as well.[87] This too affects relationships between the established and newcomers. Hostility is no less deeply felt in migrant circles, nor is it merely a response to rejection by the majority. The imbalance in power between majorities and minorities is obvious to all, but in many major cities in Europe and America the majority is gradually becoming a minority, and migrants and their descendants now have considerable influence.

Which brings us to another hallmark of my approach, namely the argument that integration requires both natives and newcomers to engage in self-examination. Migration brings about changes on both sides, such that the phrase 'integration with the retention of identity', which has been used to define multiculturalism, becomes an unhelpful concept. Many changes may pass unnoticed, becoming obvious only when migrants return to their countries of origin after many years and suddenly realize the extent to which they have been moulded by their new homelands. Aside from this tacit form of integration, one of the potential benefits of migration can be derived from a conscious reassessment of routines and traditions long taken for granted. Once again this applies both to newcomers and to members of receiving societies.

As long as reciprocity is its guiding principle, this kind of re-evaluation will not be directionless. The open society is founded upon equality before the law. Consistent application of this principle encourages a sense of responsibility, especially in societies of immigration, as regular visitors to a Turkish mosque in Amsterdam found out when, to their astonishment, they won a court case against the local authority. The experience of victory in a legal battle against a powerful city council certainly made an impression. The constitutional state became *their* constitutional state. Outcomes like this build trust of the kind that oils the wheels of social interaction between people of widely differing backgrounds.

But beyond equality, reciprocity means 'do unto others as you would have them do unto you'. Those who hate being treated with condescension on the grounds of their convictions or disposition would do well to avoid treating others with condescension for similar reasons. Those who require of others that they question their own habits and customs must be prepared to do the same. Those who ask questions must be not only open to the answers, but willing to think about the questions others are asking. In an open society, reciprocity is not something people can be forced into; it needs to be accepted freely. Philosopher of law Dorien Pessers writes that it means 'people do more than they are legally obliged to do, and more is expected of them than the law demands'.[88]

What if people refuse to acknowledge others as equals, because of their faith or lifestyle or ethnic background? What if they demand freedoms for themselves that they are not willing to grant to fellow citizens? Is freedom of expression, for example, a constitutional right that must be accorded even to those who attempt to use it to restrict the freedom of others? To take a concrete example: Should that particular right be defended in the case of people who want to place limits on the religious freedom of Muslims? Should Muslims be expected to feel obliged to defend such people's rights? If so, and if equality matters, then freedom must be safeguarded for all, even for Muslims who embrace radical beliefs and advocate the introduction of *sharia* in whole or in part – just as long as they are merely voicing their opinions, not inciting others to violence.

To put it another way, the open society must make room for those who adhere to a closed worldview and reject reciprocity. This is the liberal paradox: orthodoxy, whether religious or secular, has a place in a lively democracy. Equality extends that far. But an open society needs a majority of its citizens to believe fundamentally in reciprocity, to try to live according to the notion that the right of one entails the duty of another. Such a majority will not come into being of its own accord. Indeed, this is precisely the reason the open society is vulnerable. There can never be any guarantees.

One final hallmark of my approach is therefore that it takes history seriously, although without drawing the unambiguous conclusion that all migratory shifts will ultimately end in accommodation. There are clear indications to that effect, and historian Leo Lucassen is right to remark that current developments point more 'in the direction of ongoing integration than toward the dawn of a multicultural society where descendants of immigrants remain visible and culturally distinct groups'.[89] Yet however familiar this trend may seem from history, it's impossible to derive from the past any assurance that integration will be successful in the future.

Indeed there are a number of features of post-war immigration that make its long-term outcomes uncertain. While religion has always been of crucial importance to immigrant communities, Islam is a new phenomenon in the Western world. The fact that around 15 million Muslims are living in the member states of the European Union is a challenge in every sense. For a religion that has always held either a majority or a monopoly position in migrants' countries of origin, existence as a religious minority means practices will have to be reshaped to suit quite different circumstances. Receiving societies, for their part, need to look for ways of dealing with a religion that has not been part of the modern history of Europe, aside from the Balkans. The migration of Muslims is an unprecedented event and we cannot be certain that Islam will find a natural place for itself in the Western world. The attacks of 11 September and since do not make any of this any easier.

In regions such as the Arab world where Islam is dominant, religion, culture and politics are intertwined, whereas in modern societies they have become separate domains. If Islam is to be part of liberal society it will have to free itself from the cultures of its countries of origin, if only to prevent certain customs and traditions from acquiring an aura of sanctity. Canadian Muslim Irshad Manji is unimpressed by the argument that critics of Islam fail to draw a clear distinction between religion and culture. 'Why would Islam be so hard to extricate from local customs – tribal customs – if there wasn't something profoundly tribal about the religion to begin with?'[90] No one should be forced to abandon Islam as a spiritual tradition, but Muslims must find ways to live as a religious minority in a democracy.

For the receiving society too, the arrival of a new religion ought to be an incentive to ponder afresh the issue of religious freedom. Many countries have regulations that are at odds with the principle of the separation of church and state – think of the church taxes Germans and Danes have to pay, the constitutional status of the Anglican Church in Britain, faith schools in the Netherlands or the crucifixes in Italian courts and classrooms. Only if there is a willingness to re-evaluate the relationship between church and state will it be possible to formulate a proper response to the arrival of Islam.

Past and present migration differ in another sense too. That migrants are often poor is nothing new, but the extent of unemployment in migrant communities, in Western Europe especially, certainly is. One of the causes of low participation in paid work is a generous social benefits system. The combination of mass immigration and the welfare state is unique, lacking any historical precedent. The consequences are plain to see: large groups of migrants find themselves in a situation of dependence. What ought to be an innovative segment of society – immigrants are the pre-eminent survivors – has become the most passive segment of all.

Indeed, the subsidized isolation of all those migrant families has turned out to be an obstacle to them, to their children and to society as a whole. The entrepreneurial instincts of those who left their home countries to earn money abroad is stifled by a society that attempts to protect people against every conceivable risk. In Amsterdam, for example, more than half of all Moroccans and Turks are unemployed or classified as unfit for work. A comparative study leads American researcher John Mollenkopf to conclude that Amsterdam is doing less well than New York, where over 90 per cent of the first generation is in work. He shows that labour inactivity among migrants in Amsterdam has led to 'a polarisation between productive, employed natives and unproductive, unemployed immigrant minorities'.[91] If arguments in favour of large-scale migration are based on the contribution newcomers make to society, then the high rates of long-term unemployment among them make it harder to justify.

There is one other difference between old and new migration. The fact that the first generation of migrants is still steeped in its countries of origin should come as no surprise. It's a feature of all immigration. Irish-Americans have always been profoundly engaged with their mother country's struggle for independence. Similarly, Germans in America remained concerned about the changing fortunes of the old country, and this had a direct impact on them during the First World War. After 1918 they paid a high price for their neutrality during the conflict. It was no longer desirable to be identified as of German extraction and many changed their names.

Relations with the country of origin are a recurring theme in the history of migration, but because of modern communications technology and the growth in opportunities for cheap travel, ties with the old country are now easier to maintain than they were. Nowadays migrants are occasionally described as transnational citizens, meaning they have a presence in more than one society. Many commute, if only in a psychological sense. Will today's migrant groups increasingly function as diaspora, or will they, as in the past, become more oriented towards their new countries with each generation that passes?

The fact that governments in their countries of origin are keen to keep a grip on migrant communities often escapes attention. Dual nationality is important in this respect. Many countries, including Germany and Japan, resist the concept, while others go even further. The Moroccan government believes it can control its subjects and their descendants as it sees fit; it's impossible to relinquish Moroccan nationality. This autocratic stance is bound up with economic interests, since around 13 per cent of Morocco's national income is derived from its emigrants. The refusal of governments to leave emigrant communities free to choose their own path also stems from a fear that liberal ways of thinking will be brought back from the countries where migrants have settled.

All these novel circumstances – the presence of large Muslim communities, the rise of the welfare state and the increasing importance of transnational ties – may mean that integration will no longer follow the old pattern of three generations at most. 'It is questionable whether the cycle that would see the third and subsequent generations of all population groups living in the Netherlands thoroughly absorbed into society will run its course if the second generation has achieved so little progress.'[92] In the decade since that conclusion was drawn, the picture has grown more mixed. There are indications that generational change is developing according to familiar patterns, but the most recent generation to emerge, composed of the grandchildren of immigrants who arrived from the early 1960s onwards, is still relatively few in number, and the effects of new circumstances are hard to predict. For this reason alone, patience is a bad councillor. Living together requires commitment on both sides. Integration really is more than a question of time.

2

The World in the City

The Proximity of Strangers

Over the past few decades, street scenes in the major cities of Europe have changed radically. The arrival of migrants from every part of the world has produced neighbourhoods with a colour all their own. They range from more or less successfully multiethnic areas to poverty-scarred sink estates. Sometimes a district may change beyond recognition. Take London's Notting Hill. In the late 1950s it was the scene of race riots; now, with its famous carnival, the neighbourhood is decidedly in vogue. There are plenty of examples of historic districts revitalized by the arrival of immigrants.

Unfortunately there are also many urban areas where changes to the make-up of the population have placed a severe strain on the quality of life. Which is certainly not to say that the responsibility for their decline can simply be placed at the door of the newcomers. The concentration of overwhelmingly poor migrants in these areas results from a combination of free choice and necessity, since public housing in Europe and America is almost always built in clusters in certain parts of town, and it's hard to blame migrants for the departure of the original residents.

None of this alters the fact that sizeable waves of migration tend to create neighbourhoods characterized by greater than average poverty, illiteracy and violence. Most migrants who succeed in working their way up the social ladder therefore move out of these problem areas to settle – along with the indigenous middle class – in more prosperous districts. This process is now in full swing. Amsterdam's middle-class Surinamers, for example, are leaving the city for satellite towns, where houses rather than flats are still available and affordable. In other European countries the picture is no different.

Those who remain find themselves living, along with the newcomers, in deplorable conditions. The situation was incomparably worse in the 1960s, when Champigny in France was the biggest slum in Europe, although in the suburbs of Lisbon, for instance, the hovels that were once so common can still be found. Provision of public housing has driven out the worst abuses, but even so, living conditions in these areas could not be described as pleasant or even acceptable, if only because of the latent and blatant violence experienced there. It's clear to everyone that the local authorities are finding it extremely hard to improve matters.

Walk through parts of Lyon or Rome or Malmö, and you'll be confronted with almost identical images. It's striking how districts built in the 1960s seem as badly eroded as the grand ideals of that time; everywhere the stairways are covered in graffiti and the first signs of concrete rot are showing through. Public spaces created as an invitation to social intercourse are poorly maintained. Broken bottles and food waste lie everywhere – rubbish that would have been cleared away long ago anywhere else in the city. 'Indefensible spaces' is how one city planner has described the open areas in many modern neighbourhoods, places that no longer belong to anyone, where social control has fallen away and criminality can become entrenched. All major cities feature neighbourhoods where aggression hangs in the air, where the police and other emergency services are inclined to retreat. Eventually they become districts most people tend to avoid. French cities are home to perhaps the most famous and infamous examples, but similarly dilapidated areas can be found in many other countries, even if outbursts of repressed aggression are rather less frequent there, and less spectacular.

Living in environments like these doesn't encourage residents to get involved with the local community. The monotonous high-rise blocks are speckled with satellite dishes tuned to a different reality. 'Dish city' symbolizes a world that's growing smaller in both senses, in which technological innovation helps to perpetuate a parochial way of life. A global village, indeed, but did the people who thought up that slogan ever consider the ways in which global communications can foster a village mentality?

Migrants often find themselves in the cheapest parts of town, which are also the worst maintained. That's the way it's always been. Most have few means of support and must start at the bottom. An Indian migrant in London, writing in the 1960s, describes a fairly typical impression: 'There were many people, I thought maybe waiting for me to come, but when everybody went away there was still fifteen or sixteen people,

Indians, staying at the house. In the front room, two double beds, in the bedrooms upstairs, each bedroom two double beds and in the small room, one three-quarter bed and those beds with like the metal springs and big wooden headboards. No carpets in the house, it was lino in all the rooms. The food was kept under the beds. . . . No hot water system, the toilet was outside.'[1]

A close relationship exists between migrants and the city, between immigrants and urbanization. American historian Lewis Mumford made the connection a long time ago: 'Perhaps the most gigantic fact in the whole urban transition was the displacement of population that took place over the whole planet. For this movement and resettlement was accompanied by another fact of colossal import: the astounding rise in the rate of population increase.'[2] In 1800 London had a population of around 800,000; 60 years later it had grown to three million. The story of New York is similar, although industrialization happened later there: in 1840 it was a city of around 400,000 souls; another 60 years and there were getting on for ten times as many, some 3.5 million. This population explosion and the nineteenth-century shift from the country-side to the cities also produced huge waves of migration from Europe to America.

In the developing nations of Africa, Asia and South America, the historical transition from an agrarian to an industrial society seen in Europe and North America is repeating itself along roughly similar lines. Declining job prospects on the land and the simultaneous rise of modern mass production is causing a great trek to the cities, a transition entailing social displacement on a massive scale. We are witnessing a historical reversal. For the first time in history, a majority of the world's population lives in cities. This process of urbanization has been extremely rapid. Whereas in 1980 only 39 per cent of people were city-dwellers, by 2000 they amounted to 47 per cent and by 2020 they will account for an estimated 57 per cent. This growth is not evenly spread. In the developed world the urban population will stabilize at around 80 per cent, while in Africa, Asia and especially South America the growth in urbanization is galloping on apace. Predictions for these continents suggest that respectively 49 per cent, 50 per cent and 85 per cent of the population will reside in cities by 2020. By that time there will be 27 mega-cities worldwide with more than ten million inhabitants each, and more than 500 with populations of a million or more.[3]

The expanding cities of the industrial age, where millions of migrants were left to fend for themselves in heavily polluted environments, were machines that devoured human beings. Child mortality gives us some idea. In New York the rate doubled in the course of the nineteenth century: in 1810 there were between 120 and 145 childhood deaths for every thousand births; by 1870 the figure had risen to 240.[4] This goes a long way to explain why, at the end of the nineteenth century, when the effects of an unrestrained market economy were plain for all to see, the first social legislation was put in place to tackle unacceptable working conditions and housing.

In his novel *The Jungle* (1906), Upton Sinclair paints an unforgettable picture of the Lithuanian migrants in Chicago who worked in the city's abattoirs. It was nothing short of a descent into hell in broad daylight: 'They were trying to save their souls – and who but a fool could fail to see that all that was the matter with their souls was that they had not been able to get a decent existence for their bodies?'[5] Working conditions may have improved, partly as a result of Sinclair's novel, but today's Mexican illegals, who have followed those Eastern European migrants into Chicago's meat-processing industry, still in many respects teeter on the edge of existence.

The nineteenth-century city was often seen as the triumph of a mechanical worldview destined to obliterate human relationships, and no one would deny that outside their much older centres they were often repositories of filth and misery. Mumford concluded that social development had not kept pace with mechanical achievement and scientific knowledge; instead it had been left to chance, 'as if the scientific habit of mind had exhausted itself upon machines, and was not capable of advancing further'.[6] He contrasted this with an alternative image of the city as 'a place in which the social heritage is concentrated, and in which the possibilities of continuous social intercourse and interaction raise to a higher potential the activities of men'.[7]

For better or worse, cities are laboratories of change. Their transformation can be ascribed in large part to waves of migration, which is reason enough to take a closer look at them and in doing so to examine segregation in particular. Why do we see migrant groups everywhere clustering together in specific districts, sometimes so much so that whole villages can be found sharing the same street, transplanted there straight from their home countries? What are the consequences of this spatial concentration of migrants, for them and for those already in residence when they arrive?

The close link between migration and urbanization makes cities into training grounds for interaction with strangers. In an essay on the city as a way of life, American sociologist Louis Wirth describes the city as 'a relatively large, dense, and permanent settlement of socially heterogeneous individuals'.[8] The gathering together of large populations reveals a new human quality: the ability of people of vastly different origins to live together on small patches of ground.

Many in fact see this as a deficiency. Big cities, with their high levels of anonymity and superficial contact, are to them the opposite of the traditional community with its strict social control. The freedom on offer in cities is therefore often seen to epitomize licentious and irresponsible behaviour. Wirth sounds rather ambivalent about the social consequences: 'The reserve, the indifference, and the blasé outlook which urbanites manifest in their relationships may thus be regarded as devices for immunizing themselves against the personal claims and expectations of others.'⁹ They need to do exactly that, since the increasing scale of cities creates opportunities for a division of labour that makes an individual likely to have relatively impersonal relationships with a large number of people.

The city continually forces us into contact with strangers. Of course newcomers turn up in villages as well, but in rural settings they immediately attract attention, whereas in cities they are a commonplace. The modern city is the product of unprecedented mobility. The lumping together of so many people with utterly different lifestyles creates a need for special forms of etiquette and for defence mechanisms. Urban sociologist Lyn Lofland recognizes the benefits: 'The cosmopolitan did not lose the capacity for the deep, long-lasting, multifaceted relationship. But he gained the capacity for the surface, fleeting, restricted relationship.'¹⁰ Despite this optimistic view, her study on the subject of the proximity of strangers is above all else the story of increasing spatial separation between population groups in the modern city. In an environment full of strangers, anonymity reigns and people seek ways to reduce the unpredictability that results. We can cope in the city only by learning to read people's backgrounds quickly.

Lofland compares interaction between strangers in pre-industrial cities with forms of interaction in industrial cities. In earlier times appearances were more important, precisely because in public spaces people and their activities were far more mixed. Children were taught in the squares and streets, executions were held in public and trade was carried on everywhere. This degree of spatial integration meant that everyone needed to be able to distinguish clearly between people by the way they looked. 'Socially defined differences among persons were emphasized in costuming, in body markings, and in language.'¹¹

In modern cities the opposite applies. We can tell less about people nowadays from their appearance. Despite the individualism of today's urban societies, the distinctions visible on the streets are now much reduced. At the same time there's far more separation and structuring. The enormous growth of cities makes it possible to divide public and private space, and to segregate groups more and more into their own neighbourhoods or districts. Lofland writes that this means people are increasingly identified by where they live. 'In the preindustrial city, space was chaotic, appearances were ordered. In the modern city, appearances are chaotic, space is ordered.'[12]

The up-and-coming middle class plays a crucial role in the evolution of cities; its desire to steer clear of the underclass or 'dangerous classes' is an important stimulus to segregation. Avoidance is part of modern city living: there's a place for everyone as long as everyone knows his place. Looked at in this way, segregation emerges as a far more deeply ingrained pattern than many of us realize. Acknowledgement of this fact has important policy implications.

Segregation and Inequality

Segregation is the product of a strategy for dealing with strangers in a city. Crudely put, it's a manifestation of the 'birds of a feather' principle: people of comparable backgrounds are drawn to each other. Patterns of settlement show we are separating out into identifiable groups. Analysis of Western cities suggests that the crucial factors are social class and, to a lesser extent, family circumstances and ethnicity. The rapid numerical increase in ethnic minorities in the wealthier suburbs and satellite towns demonstrates that socio-economic circumstances weigh heavily. The abandonment of old city neighbourhoods by the rising middle class of migrants is well under way. By 2000 a quarter of America's ethnic minorities were living in the suburbs, rechristened 'ethnoburbs', and this has sparked a new 'white flight' further out of the city. The willingness to live in a mixed community is still quite rare among established residents.

Let's look first at the causes and extent of segregation, before moving on to examine its social and cultural consequences. Lastly we'll consider whether deliberate attempts to mix population groups offer any solutions. Social geographer Paul Knox outlines the motives for the observable desire of minorities to live together in certain areas: 'The spatial segregation of different "communities" helps to minimize conflict between social groups while facilitating a greater degree of social control and endowing specific social groups with a more cohesive political voice.' Segregation arises 'from the desire of [a community's] members to preserve their own group identity or lifestyle'.[13] In short it's all about 'defence, support, preservation and attack'.[14]

Knox pays little attention to white flight as an explanation. While he sees segregation primarily as a matter of free choice, with migrants electing to live in certain districts and send their children to certain schools, others point primarily to its involuntary nature. Behind that distinction lies a difference in how migrants are perceived: as enterprising individuals who seize opportunities or as people subject to forces beyond their control. Irrespective of which point of view they take, people have always warned of the consequences of too great a concentration of ethnic communities. The first US president, George Washington, was concerned about the migrants of his own time, noting how they retained the 'language, habits and principles (good or bad) which they bring with them'.[15]

A further qualification to place beside Knox's view is that segregation doesn't always solve problems, it can sometimes create them. The separation of different communities may dampen hostilities, since where there's little contact there will be little friction, but when the distances become too great they can in themselves become a source of conflict. Again: avoidance will always end at some point. Social control that limits deviant behaviour within a particular group can also lead to serious tensions within that community if more and more individuals decide to follow rules of their own. There lies the dilemma of all emancipation: the formation of groups may help but it can equally well be a hindrance, as we shall see.

An outlook in which the separation of groups is seen primarily as a form of self-defence that relies upon the creation of a political force and on social control is a useful corrective to the view that segregation is attributable above all to the majority community's fear of contact. Both motives come into play – self-defence on the part of newcomers and avoidance on the part of the established population – and each should be seen in the context of the other. Only then does the impasse surrounding segregation become visible.

How widespread is this phenomenon? The concentration of migrants in specific areas is measured by means of the segregation index, used to determine whether the presence of a certain group in a given district diverges from its average share of the population of the city as a whole. In other words, it's a relative measure. If 30 per cent of a city's population is of Indian, Pakistani or Bangladeshi extraction, then a neighbourhood where 40 per cent of residents are from the subcontinent is not particularly segregated. The index can be criticized on the grounds that it pays little heed to historical change within neighbourhoods. Residential preference – or, more bluntly, the flight of indigenous populations – is based on absolute rather than relative numbers. To see the real extent of change we need to look at majorities, which is to say at neighbourhoods where an indigenous majority has become a minority – areas like Vénissieux in Lyon, Rosengard in Malmö, Lozells in Birmingham and Molenbeek in Brussels, where the transformation has taken place within a period of 25 years. It's a perspective that reveals different patterns altogether.

Nevertheless the index does give us a clear idea of the extent of segregation in certain districts relative to other places and other times. The classic example of segregation is the formation of black ghettos in the northern United States after the emancipation of slaves and the subsequent migration of black people from the south. The segregation level has been measured at 46 for the year 1860, 59 for 1910 and 89 for 1940. In the Midwest and the north-eastern states especially, black people remain highly segregated to this day. For Chicago, for example, the index stands at 80. The 40 largest cities still exhibit a noticeable degree of black segregation, although in the past 20 years the figure has fallen from about 73 to 64. The index records less extreme levels for other ethnic groups, such as Asians, 41, and Hispanics, 46. In New York the segregation of black, Asian and Hispanic populations has been measured at 82, 48 and 66 respectively.[16]

From all this it is clear that the history of the black population in America – beginning with slavery and forced segregation – is unique, and quite different from that of migrant groups. Amsterdam geographer Sako Musterd points this out in comparing the US with Europe. In a general sense the level of segregation in Europe is lower than in America but, he warns, when we leave aside the extreme segregation of America's black population, there is a far smaller difference between levels on the two sides of the Atlantic. Certain cities in Europe, including Brussels, Rotterdam and Bradford, stand out as examples of above average segregation.[17]

General agreement exists about the degree of segregation that commonly emerges and about how persistent it is. Over the past few years, expressions of concern about the phenomenon have been heard from various quarters, relating both to the trend that has been identified – an increase rather than a reduction – and to its presumed impact on integration. The unspoken assumption is that the separation of population groups – the most visible example being 'black' and 'white' schools – is detrimental to the social advancement of migrants and adversely effects the extent to which they feel part of society. The findings of a Dutch parliamentary committee of investigation in 2004 were hesitant: 'The concentration of ethnic minorities reduces their chances of contact with the indigenous population, but that concentration has no clear influence on an individual's level of education or position in the jobs market.' This last phrase was then further refined: 'It is not inconceivable that reduced socio-cultural integration leads on to reduced socio-economic integration.'[18]

Issues surrounding segregation and its consequences demand more thorough treatment than this. Before taking a closer look at its cultural effects, we must turn our attention to a social issue: does life in a neighbourhood where many people are poor increase an individual's chances of becoming stuck, like them, at the bottom of the social heap? In a fairly general sense there is evidence of increasing polarization in major cities; a clear rift has emerged between those who make the leap to join the middle class and those at risk of forming an underclass, with all the troubled family relationships, above average crime, and poverty passed down from generation to generation that characterize such a phenomenon.

The same goes for migrants. Sizeable groups come onto the jobs market insufficiently qualified. There's a clear divide between work for a highly skilled elite and uncomplicated jobs for short-term employees who can easily be laid off. The formation of a social underclass creates an environment in which less than fully integrated migrants can survive, and such an underclass tends to perpetuate itself. British researcher Peter Hall concludes: 'The good news, if any, is that the cities will be where some of the more exciting new economic developments are taking place. The bad news is that these groups may not be playing much role in them. . . . [Planning faces] a nightmarish return of the oldest of urban problems, which more than any other originally brought it into being and gave it its legitimacy: the problem of the urban underclass.'[19]

It's important to ask whether segregation contributes to social inequality. Opinions on this point differ quite markedly. Some researchers dismiss any link as relatively unimportant, while others suggest that a strong connection exists. American sociologists Douglas Massey and Nancy Denton summarize their research into the formation of ghettos in the United States as follows: 'Racial segregation is the institutional nexus that enables the transmission of poverty from person to person and generation to generation, and is therefore a primary structural factor behind the perpetuation of the urban underclass.'[20] A concentration of poverty and inequality has its own independent effect on the opportunities open to individual residents of these neighbourhoods. Irrespective of talent or personality, people who live in areas of enduring poverty are more likely to become mothers at a young age, to cut short their schooling prematurely and to have low incomes.

According to Massey and Denton, a culture develops in such neighbourhoods that defines itself in opposition to middle-class conventions, departing from widely accepted norms in its attitudes to marriage and success at school, for example. They point out that at the level of language a growing divide can be seen between black and white America. The black dialect that has developed in the ghettos has less and less in common with standard English. 'Thus black educational progress is hampered not only because segregation concentrates poverty within ghetto schools but also because segregation confines blacks to an isolated linguistic community.'[21] America's black ghettos are perhaps an extreme example, but they may well illustrate a general problem: segregation has a real impact on social mobility.

America differs in various ways from Europe, where social inequality is tempered by highly developed welfare states. But those welfare states, while guaranteeing a subsistence-level income, have brought with them widespread inactivity. This is particularly noticeable in migrant communities, which have relatively high levels of unemployment. Low labour participation rates in former guest-worker communities in particular have stood in the way of integration, with inevitable consequences for children growing up in them.

Sociologist Eric Maurin concludes that, in France at least, the formation of ghettos in areas of public housing contributes to social inequality. Social and ethnic segregation in French cities has persisted over the past 20 years. Social mixing is a universally accepted ideal, but the actual behaviour of the middle classes and social elites is another matter. Maurin describes this as 'ghettoization from above' and 'ghettoization from below'. He talks of a three-way split in almost all major cities: the elites install themselves in the old city centres – where prices have shot up since the 1980s – while the middle class moves to single-family dwellings in the suburbs and the lowest educated remain stuck in high-rise housing estates.[22]

On the positive side, ethnic neighbourhoods are seedbeds of entrepreneurship. The concentration of migrant communities enables them to organize all kinds of services geared mainly to their own consumers. Shops selling Indian cuisine or halal meat immediately spring to mind, followed by businesses offering cheap international phone calls and bookshops stocking Islamic reading materials. The list is endless, but this ethnic economy thrives by virtue of a certain amount of segregation. Sociologist Jan Rath believes that diversity has economic value and sees it not as a passing trend but as a consequence of the changes to Western cities brought about by globalization. 'The commercial use of ethno-cultural diversity, or more specifically the rise of "coloured neighbourhoods" as places of entertainment and consumption, is not an isolated phenomenon but part of the economic change that cities are currently going though.'[23]

A great deal has been written about the economic significance of ethnic enclaves. Based on examples both from the past (Manhattan's Jewish community and the Japanese on the West Coast) and from our own time (the Koreans in Los Angeles and Cubans in Miami), Alejandro Portes and Robert Manning conclude that such enclaves can present significant economic opportunities. There are a number of preconditions, however, including the presence of a considerable number of migrants with experience as entrepreneurs in their native countries, and the availability of sufficient capital and manpower. Most migrant communities have labour to spare but they often lack capital and entrepreneurial skills.[24]

However prosperous some ethnic enclaves may become, the question remains: How far can emancipation through your own economic networks take you? Do they offer a starting point from which you can conquer the wider world or does the ethnic economy also represent a self-limitation that is ultimately involuntary? The picture is mixed. There are many new enterprises but also many bankruptcies; high ambition is accompanied by the exploitation of workers from the same community, who have nowhere else to turn. Sad stories about the Chinese restaurant business are familiar to us all. The trade in ethnic products and services presents opportunities, but the risk that migrants will become shut into an exotic niche in the name of a celebration of diversity is a real one, however fascinating the Chinatowns of Sydney or London may be. In the end, the main route to emancipation for the majority of migrants and their children surely lies in participation in economic life of a broader kind, where a person's descent is irrelevant.

An extensive comparative study of the second generation in New York lends weight to this suggestion. Dynamism is not created by a 'retention of identity'. As the authors put it: 'This rapid incorporation into American life does not stem from the second generation's maintaining social or cultural ties with the parents' immigrant communities. The group experiencing the most dramatic upward mobility – the Chinese – is actually the *least* likely to retain the parents' language.'[25] They conclude: 'Members of every second generation group who work in predominantly ethnic work sites earn less than those who work in mainstream settings.'[26] This is not to say, in the researchers' view, that such children rebel against their parents' culture. Rather, their social ascent takes place largely outside their own communities.

The upshot of all this is that while the outcome of segregation for social inequality is far from unambiguous, in areas where population groups live apart according to both class and colour, a 'culture of poverty' may develop, adversely affecting people's chances of social advancement. We can deduce as much simply from the avoidance of such districts by those who are doing rather better, whether natives or newcomers. As soon as a good opportunity presents itself, they flee the area. Other motives are at work here besides a desire to escape social disadvantage, motives that have to do with the quality of life in a more general sense. Neighbourhoods of this kind often struggle with above-average crime and aggression. Feelings of isolation and frustration seek an outlet; the trouble caused by many children of migrants must have its origins somewhere.

Ghetto Culture

Along with forms of social exclusion, cultural alienation is often a feature of the neighbourhoods where immigrants end up living. It's expressed in ways that have now claimed everyone's attention. Take the riots in the French *banlieues* in the autumn of 2005. They were prompted by a single incident. On the night of 27 October in Clichy-sous-Bois, two teenagers running from the police hid in an electricity substation and were fatally electrocuted. Their deaths triggered disturbances that spread across France like an ink-blot, especially after the future president, Nicolas Sarkozy, dubbed the rebellious youths *racaille* (variously translated by English-language media as rabble, ruffians or scum).

This outburst of disaffection and violence should have surprised no one; the public housing estates of France had been the setting for ferocious clashes several times over the previous quarter century. Lucienne Bui Trong has listed no fewer than 47 disturbances of varying degrees of severity between 1991 and 2000 alone. But this was different from previous riots. The uprising in Minguettes in 1981, for example, had been seen as a sign of hope – not long afterwards the children of North African migrants held a protest march and were received by President Mitterrand. This time, the disturbances were interpreted as above all an expression of nihilism, not just because of the extent of the violence but because the rebellion was not marked by concrete desires or specific demands. The arsonists had no message and no doctrine. Not only were thousands of cars torched, institutions whose very existence was intended to improve life in the *banlieues* were destroyed too, including schools and libraries. Much was wrecked and little was said.

Once the initial shock had passed, there was a need to contemplate why the aggression had erupted. The silence called for subtitling. While politicians talked at length about a social problem (*'fracture sociale'*), most commentators took a different tack, describing a cultural or ethnic conflict. Sociologist Jacques Donzelot wrote that the ethnic background of the youngsters involved was undoubtedly one reason for their marginalization, while economist Yann Moulier Boutang compared the disturbances with race riots in America: 'The young people of the *banlieues* of Europe are on their way to becoming the blacks of the United States.'[27]

Other commentators too detected a deep malaise in the indiscriminate violence of that autumn and felt that choosing to see it mainly as an outcome of poverty was an insult to the many families on the bottom rungs of the social ladder who, despite difficult circumstances, bring up their children to be respectable citizens. They discerned increasing cultural disengagement, one indication of which, as they saw it, was the language of the *banlieues*. Initially the backslang seems relatively innocent, playfully transforming *français* into *céfran* or *noir* into *renoi*. This could be regarded as an attempt to make a virtue of necessity: you may have absolutely no status in society, but at least you can be lord and master in the universe of your own language. Nevertheless, violent rap lyrics reveal a mental detachment, which does not bode well. Psychiatrist Theodore Dalrymple's interpretation of it is apt: 'Having been enclosed in a physical ghetto, they respond by building a cultural and psychological ghetto for themselves.'[28]

In these areas the family–school–work triangle no longer functions as a social framework. The breakdown of communication in families is the main focus of attention. Rootless youths are growing up in the inner suburbs of Paris and Lyon with insufficient parental support. Their fathers have lost all authority and feel constrained by the many people watching over their shoulders as they bring up their children. Harsh disciplinary measures are no longer permitted and nothing is available to replace them. It all seems very familiar – in some parts of Bradford or Brussels the situation is much the same.

The development of a ghetto culture in America was described as far back as the 1920s. In his study of the Jewish ghetto, Louis Wirth quotes Israel Cohen, who analysed in detail the mechanisms of closing off and shutting out: 'Ignorance of the language of the new country, of its labour conditions, and of its general habits and ways of thought, as well as the natural timidity of a fugitive from a land of persecution, compels the immigrant Jew to settle in the colony of his co-religionists.'[29] Their settlement in the ghetto was usually a transitional phase between the old world and the new, a temporary refuge, even though some might live there for many decades.

According to Wirth, the ghetto isn't just a physical reality, it's a state of mind. The narrower the gateway to the outside world, the easier it becomes for a community to stick to its own norms and to obstruct individuals within that community who try to take their lives into their own hands. The freedom of the community is in many respects inseparable from the lack of freedom of the individual. Nevertheless, Wirth valued the emotional certainty the ghetto could offer its residents: 'Here he could relax from the etiquette and the formalism by which his conduct in the gentile world was regulated.'[30] The price was perhaps high, especially for unbelievers or apostates who were despised and ostracized, but the attractions of that intimate world where people had an unambiguous status were a counterweight to those of the wider world, which seemed from a distance to offer immense freedom. 'What it lacks in breadth of horizon, the ghetto life makes up in depth of emotion, in strength of familial and communal ties, and in attachment to tradition, form, and sentiment.'[31]

Jewish experience is illustrative in a number of respects. 'The history of the Jews and the history of the ghetto are in essence a history of migrations.'[32] In areas of Western cities that are populated by migrants, we see the same national and religious fault-lines. The search for a form of leadership that works in the new circumstances, which is to say for leaders who have their origins in the new country, is familiar too, and once more we come upon the moral constraints of orthodoxy: 'The synagogue and the rabbi . . . leave scarcely a single phase of the life of the congregation free from their control.'[33]

So to some extent the formation of ghettos has to do with a particular mentality. As soon as we take a broader view, rather than looking purely at economic disadvantage in the groups involved, we begin to see how segregation impacts upon the integration of migrants. If in turning our attention to patterns of social integration we ask how great the chances are that natives and newcomers will come into contact, then we arrive at some firm conclusions about the consequences of segregation. Dutch researcher Jaco Dagevos observes: 'Immigrant groups with a strong tendency to keep away from the native population are generally also living at quite some remove from the values bound up with the process of modernization that Western societies have been through.'[34] He believes there's a real danger that 'separate worlds' will develop, affecting opportunities for finding good jobs: 'A strong focus on one's own group hampers socio-economic integration.'[35]

Quite apart from the need to improve prospects for the population groups concerned, the vitality of democracy is at stake. A city can cope with the existence in its midst of small, isolated communities, but not when sizeable immigrant groups shut themselves off from the wider environment. This is a question not just of the advancement of ethnic communities but of society as a whole. It's all about the degree to which a new social fabric can grow. If ethnic minorities lead separate lives, their emancipation may well be limited, but perhaps even more importantly, segregation will eventually undermine a society's capacity for peaceful conflict resolution. Most researchers look only at the material advancement of migrant groups, paying no attention at all to this aspect of the multicultural drama.

Muslim communities in many major European cities have created a space of their own. Flemish journalist Hind Fraihi, born to Moroccan parents, offers a touching portrayal of the Muslim community in the old Brussels district of Molenbeek: 'Ever since childhood I've been coming here with my parents. Like so many Moroccans, they do their shopping in this Muslim village in Brussels where the prices are low, a cheerful chaos prevails, the main language is Arabic and the meat tastes halal. Shopping in Molenbeek is like spending the summer in a sunless Mediterranean.'[36] In the midst of this beguiling jumble, social problems mount and with them an aversion to Belgian society: 'Youth unemployment is astronomical, good for some 40 per cent. In certain districts the figure is as high as 80 per cent. And it shows. Just look at the youngsters loitering in the cheerless streets.'[37]

In environments like this, a ghetto culture develops. Reliance on welfare is the norm and, as usual, dependence leads not to gratitude but to resentment. A coherent community of faith can quickly become a second home, all the more so when the parental home has little to offer. Parents don't have much to set against the street, with its freedom without responsibility, other than responsibility without freedom. No wonder they lose control of their children.

One of those to whom Fraihi spoke, a young man who hangs around at a metro station and lives from street robbery, said: 'See those rails, and the sleepers the rails are bolted to? Well, that was my father's job. He worked his fingers to the bone here, so that the Belgians could be transported about like rats under the ground. The Belgians think we, the children of hardworking fathers, are going to get our hands dirty too. But they're wrong.'[38] He and Muslim youngsters like him pose as victims of colonial exploitation on a small scale, an outlook that neatly coincides with the indictment of full-scale imperialism that turns Muslims into victims in the world at large.

Concerned voices are being raised in Germany too, with talk of 'parallel societies' (Parallelgesellschaften), especially in areas where Turkish migrants are concentrated. Researcher Bassam Tibi, originally from Damascus, writes: 'Within these parallel societies, poverty is in reality bound up with religion and ethnicity, and it therefore stands in the way of integration. This form of migration therefore manifests itself as the ethnicization of the culture of poverty, producing an enormous potential for conflict that forms a significant threat to the security of the host society.'[39] He is not at all confident that the migrant diaspora will eventually connect with the European environment, especially since the isolation of part of the Muslim community is accompanied by an ongoing international confrontation.

In essence this has to do with an age-old dilemma faced by all emancipation movements: the strength of the community is based on the weakness of the individual. Group thinking can function for a time as a bulwark against a hostile environment, but what is often seen as a temporary refuge or a springboard to advancement can easily degenerate into narrow-mindedness. In his novel The Human Stain Philip Roth sums up this form of oppression perfectly as 'the tyranny of the we and the we-talk and everything that the we wants to pile on your head'.[40] What matters to Roth in the end is the liberation of the individual, who is 'free to enact the boundless, self-defining drama of the pronouns we, they, and I'.[41]

These are all aspects of the way migrants are drawn to each other in specific districts of their adoptive cities. It's a form of self-defence that can easily turn into isolation, such that the outside world grows increasingly distant, and where social inequality and cultural unfamiliarity already exist, the growing apart of population groups can further estrange them and make barriers more durable. Segregation should not be seen purely in the context of worsening social inequality; we must also be willing to perceive urban life as a training ground for democracy.

Black and White Schools

In schools segregation has taken a very stark form indeed. Is the emergence of 'black' and 'white' schools problematic? Or should we see ethnic dividing lines in education as temporary phenomena of little real consequence? It's worth looking again at the French *banlieues*. In these areas of social housing, school is the vital institution as far as integration is concerned, if only because schoolchildren from migrant families receive little support from home in finding their way in mainstream society. Many if not most schools in these neighbourhoods are unable to cope with their task. The most important route to social advancement is therefore jeopardized and we should not underestimate the frustration this causes.

A book by Karen Montet-Toutain called *Et pourtant, je les aime* ['All the same, I'm fond of them'] is the account of a committed teacher who was stabbed by a pupil some years ago during a lesson. As a young art teacher she had deliberately chosen to work at a troubled school in a poor district on the outskirts of Paris and she soon encountered a climate of threat. At first it was merely a matter of sexual intimidation during lessons – 'I want to **** you' – but a year later came the attack that almost cost her her life. She describes her work at the vocational secondary school with great affection and clearly states that schools in the *banlieues* are all too willing to see their pupils as problem children, keen to be rid of them at the earliest possible opportunity. Their diplomas are no longer worth very much, a fact not lost on potential employers. She's convinced there's 'buried treasure' in this generation of migrants' children, and that it's now going to waste: 'There is no poor soil, only poorly irrigated soil.'[42]

She describes in detail a general malaise. The building is inadequately heated and poorly maintained. At her introductory meeting she's advised not to wear jewellery, and to hide her mobile phone. In fact her colleagues feel it's altogether a bad idea for a young woman to stand in front of the kind of class she's about to encounter. The scissors used in lessons have rounded tips as a safety precaution. 'Teaching under the perpetual threat of an incident is exhausting,' she remarks.[43] The pupils know there's little future for them and this translates into an atmosphere of aggression, with teachers continually running the gauntlet: 'We have to choose our words carefully to avoid being accused of racism, even though we're bombarded with the worst kind of abuse all day long.'[44]

Keeping order under such circumstances is often more important than actually teaching anything. After the attack, in which she was stabbed seven times with a kitchen knife, Montet-Toutain felt abandoned. Her book is therefore also an indictment of a climate of wilful indifference. She comes to the conclusion that those who report disciplinary problems to school administrators merely raise doubts about their own capacities. Add to this the policy many schools have of hushing up violent incidents for fear of a bad reputation and all the conditions are in place for a culture of silence, a silence she was hoping to break with her book.

Her school in a district of Paris could stand for many in European cities. Everywhere we see ethnic minorities becoming a majority at specific schools. What motivates white families to remove their children? It begins with the assessment that school is the most significant factor in the struggle for social advancement, a place where crucial decisions are made about a person's future. 'White flight' reflects the importance of school: parents fear their children will adjust downwards if they attend a 'black' school, so they move to 'white' enclaves. Maurin talks about 'intimate fears and ambitions' as the motives behind this avoidance.[45] It's interesting to note that the switch from 'white' to 'black' lies somewhere around the point where one third of pupils are the children of migrants. This appears to be a critical threshold; in schools parents are voting with their feet on the issue of mixed classrooms.

Too little thought has been given to the fact that the meritocratic society – in which everyone is judged on his or her merits – has a merciless side to it. As education becomes increasingly important and access to the better schools increasingly competitive, we see the best educated trying to distance themselves as far as possible from the least educated. A meritocratic society means stricter selection, and this is reflected in the growth of 'black' and 'white' schools. Patterns of segregation are far more deeply ingrained than many people realize. Parents make every effort to give their children the best possible start in life, even if it means committing fraud when filling out application forms, or moving house. British research shows that house prices are strongly influenced, to the tune of some 10 per cent, by the quality of the schools into whose catchment areas properties fall.[46]

Dutch researchers have concluded that 'as soon as the proportion of weaker pupils tends towards 50 per cent, the positive effects on socially weaker pupils disappear, while the performance of "white" middle-class children declines significantly'.[47] This means that in cities where the majority of school-aged children come from low-skilled migrant families, the avoidance of 'black' schools by the middle class (irrespective of origin) is an understandable choice in itself. Yet the most profound consequences of ethnic segregation in schools impact upon the children of migrants. Segregation has a negative effect on their opportunities in life.

As well as 'white flight', we need to look at another cause of segregation, namely the rise of religious schools in countries including the Netherlands and Britain. They are still relatively few in number, but they amount to the expression of a desire in some migrant communities for seclusion among their own kind. The constitutional guarantee of freedom of education in the Netherlands gives religious communities the right to found their own schools, but this only reinforces segregation according to class and colour.

Amartya Sen regards the policy of the British government, which plans to give state support to religious schools for Muslims, Sikhs and Hindus, as a great mistake. It means children will continue to be poured into the mould of a religion before they are old enough to judge for themselves. 'The importance of non-sectarian and nonparochial school education that expands, rather than reduces, the reach of reasoning (including critical scrutiny) would be hard to exaggerate.'[48] Nobody whose attitudes are rooted in the principle of freedom can want young children to have a choice thrust upon them. They ought to come into contact with a number of different worldviews. The fundamental debate on this issue has been avoided up to now, but sooner or later it will have to take place.

Looking at schools, we are forced to conclude that, generally speaking, segregation by class and colour is already far advanced. Take the statistics from Amsterdam that give the proportion of primary school pupils with low-skilled parents from non-Western backgrounds (they are registered as such in the Netherlands, since for many years almost twice the usual resources were allocated to them): 127 of the 201 primary schools in Amsterdam have a concentration of such pupils of more than 50 per cent and in 102 (in other words, half of all the city's primary schools) more than 70 per cent of pupils are the children of immigrants of this type. In some districts this applies to all schools.[49]

In discussions about the consequences of the way schools are growing apart, two issues become intertwined: how do pupils perform in these schools and what are the social consequences of groups of pupils growing up separately? Opinions differ widely as to the results in performance terms. One Dutch study calculates that the difference between black and white schools is around 10 per cent.[50] Maurin estimates the effect of school segregation in French cities at around 20 per cent of academic performance.[51] It seems safe to conclude that discrepancies do exist and that attending even a slightly less successful school can have a significant effect on the rest of an individual's life. After all, even a minor reduction in exam results can determine the choice between a track to basic training and the route to a rather more ambitious form of higher education. Exams are therefore decisive for later careers. The early consignment of many children from migrant families to the lower streams of education is undeniably a huge problem in cities where such children form a majority of school-aged youngsters. Societies cannot afford to lose the 'hidden treasure' Montet-Toutain talks about – and that's exactly what's happening now.

Researchers looking at effects like these always apply a corrective for socio-economic background. A statistical bias will of course be produced if, in attempting to judge the significance of ethnic differences, we compare the child of two doctors with the offspring of unskilled workers. But this correction threatens to obscure the real situation in schools. For research purposes we may want to filter out of our analysis differences based on class, but in the day-to-day reality of a school, the over-representation of children from disadvantaged backgrounds clearly has an effect on academic performance and on the atmosphere in general.

Questions about the consequences of ethnic segregation are often avoided because head teachers are apprehensive about the demotivating effects of linking colour with poor performance. But surely the first priority is to understand exactly what's going on. Researchers have concluded that there is a connection between ethnic and social segregation. Migrants' children have measurable language deficits, partly as a result of the fact that many grow up in areas where hardly any indigenous children live. This has led to calls for pre-school reception classes and extra coaching for children from migrant communities.

There is less disagreement about the adverse consequences of school segregation in a socio-cultural sense. Studies in the Netherlands have reached some unambiguous conclusions: 'Mixed schools are a crucial means of passing on middle-class norms and attitudes. In other words, mixing helps children to get on in life.'[52] A school is more than a factory for learning; it's an exercise in living together for children from diverse backgrounds. The ability to interact across social and cultural divides is important for society as a whole, and apart from the neighbourhoods in which people live and grow up, school is the only place where children can relate to each other in a natural way. The results are obvious.

Dagevos sums them up as follows: 'For the Netherlands as a whole it has recently been established that over the past ten years the tendency of people belonging to minorities to have circles of friends composed of members of their own group has steadily increased. The main reason for this seems to be greater segregation.'[53]

Comparable findings have been reported elsewhere. Almost all Western Europe's major cities abound with stories about 'black' schools. One disturbing example is the Rütli school in Berlin, where over 80 per cent of pupils are of Turkish or Arab descent. In some areas of the city, including the northern part of Neukölln, the Arab population has become larger than the traditionally most strongly represented migrant group, people of Turkish extraction. In the spring of 2006 teachers at the Rütli school wrote a desperate letter about the impossible situation in their classrooms: 'We are at our wits' end. In many classes behaviour is characterized by a complete rejection of the material and by inhuman behaviour.' They used three key words to describe the atmosphere at their school: aggression, disrespect and ignorance.

The letter provoked a debate in the Federal Republic about the integration of children from migrant communities. There was criticism of the 'multicultural language police' who had obscured all these problems for years, and the real-life police pointed to the large proportion of migrants' children in crime statistics. It was proposed that an upper limit of 50 per cent should be set to the number of pupils of foreign origin. Questions were also raised about the future of the type of school represented by the Rütli, the *Hauptschule* or vocational secondary school, which has in reality come to function as a social dumping ground. As someone remarked, 'Vocational schools are losers' schools.' It's clear that a concentration of migrants' children from socially disadvantaged backgrounds presents schools with serious problems. The teachers at the Rütli school wrote: 'In most families our pupils are the only ones who get up in the mornings.' What are the staff supposed to tell those children about the importance of going to school?

The Rollberg-Viertel, where the school is located, is a district where 30 different nationalities live, many of them Middle Eastern. A large majority of the pupils who register at its schools have a poor command of German for their age. In these and other areas a counter-culture is developing, breaking free little by little from the majority culture, and within it success at school has become the exception. As in the French *banlieues*, the language – '*Kanak Sprak*' – is a mixture of cheerful provocation and far less cheerful intimidation. Clearly people can always find ways to survive in a niche, but the drawbacks are obvious, as Polish writer Ryszard Kapuściński observed. This kind of separation is 'also a way of creating a climate of self-veneration for yourself, since a niche offers one great advantage: we can fill it entirely with ourselves, which protects us from the plague of confrontation, from comparison, from the judgement of others'.[54]

Again and again we come up against the same reality. The over-representation of migrants in specific districts is a phenomenon seen throughout the history of migration. Often such areas have been jumping-off points for people on their way up, but now there are indications that a good many children remain stuck in them. There's a real danger of creating a permanent underclass of migrants and their descendants. Although many have managed to overcome depressing circumstances and do well at school, for a considerable proportion of the second generation – in some cities, including Amsterdam and Lyon, perhaps even a majority – things are not looking so good.

Dispersing Without Mixing

It's important to reach this diagnosis independently of ideas about ways in which the situation can be changed. Segregation is not easy to influence, if only because immigration over past decades has brought with it an irreversible change in the composition of populations. In quite a few cities a majority of school-aged children come from migrant families. Furthermore, the separation of population groups by social class has become deeply entrenched. The whole world has arrived in our cities and avoidance is one result. It's disturbing to note that wherever you look, people are withdrawing. Many do not feel at home in a globalizing world and want to build walls around themselves, both figuratively and literally.

This is clearly illustrated by the recent history of Rotterdam. The atmosphere of the Afrikaander district emerges in countless interviews with native Dutch residents. One says, 'Why do I want to move? Because it's a lousy neighbourhood these days. It used to be really friendly here, and now it's ruined. What ought to change around here? I want it to be reasonably normal again, reasonably respectable. To have a few Dutch shops around again. There's not a single Dutch shop left. Every time a Dutch shop goes, a foreign one opens in its place. I've got nothing against foreigners, but it's not Rotterdam any longer.'[55]

In recent years greater attention has been paid to this kind of reaction. In 2003, in an attempt to justify a newly restrictive policy towards the arrival of low-skilled migrants, the city council wrote: 'The absorptive capacity of certain districts is being exceeded by a continual influx of underprivileged people and the departure of the better off, who can afford to go and live somewhere else. Along with nuisance, illegality and criminality, this is the essence of the problem we face.'[56] It emphasized that 'colour isn't the problem, but the problem has colour' and concluded that 'the speed of inflow and outflow makes it hard for the residents of Rotterdam to develop a bond with the city and with each other'. In 20 years from now a majority of the city's current residents will in turn have been replaced by newcomers. The most controversial aspect of Rotterdam's plan was a proposal to restrict settlement in certain districts to those with a specified minimum income – 120 per cent of the legal minimum wage – so as to put a brake on the influx of people dependent on welfare.

The agonizing that has gone on in Rotterdam, an international port that would prefer to have city walls, shows how immigration places cities under strain. Rotterdam is far from alone in this. Some years ago the mayor of Malmö appealed for a temporary halt to all immigration. This and other attempts to implement an immigration policy at a municipal level can be seen as indicating that too much is being asked of residents and that they no longer feel protected by their national governments.

All over Western Europe in the past few decades, there have been attempts to promote the mixing of populations by establishing numerical limits to the number of immigrants in given neighbourhoods or schools. In the 1960s, for instance, the British minister of education set a limit of 30 per cent to the number of children from migrant families in any one school. In the 1970s, Rotterdam set the maximum number of migrants in any given neighbourhood at 5 per cent, a proposal blocked by central government on the basis that it conflicted with the principle of non-discrimination. The move had been prompted by riots in the Afrikaander district in the summer of 1972 that targeted Turkish guest workers. In West Germany at around the same time a cap on immigration, the so-called *Zuzugssperre*, was proposed for the five largest cities. It was to come into force as soon as the total proportion of migrants in their populations passed 12 per cent. More recently there have been attempts in France to oblige the better-off suburbs to build social housing until it made up at least 20 per cent of the total, in the hope that this would bring about a dispersal of the migrant population.

It's clear that each of these attempts has failed. Enforced dispersal either proves impossible to implement or is condemned as discriminatory. Everyone feels that dispersal ordered from on high soon comes into conflict with constitutional rights such as freedom of settlement or the freedom to choose a school for your child. Indirect methods of mixing populations seem to work better. By demolishing cheap rental accommodation and building more expensive owner-occupied dwellings, local authorities are attempting to nudge areas towards greater diversity.

This approach is currently being tried in many European countries, and in America. Some say the best idea is to create a greater ethnic mix by explicitly encouraging residents of other neighbourhoods to move into areas where many migrants live. Others have set their sights on social diversity instead and are concentrating on trying to persuade middle-class migrants to stay in their neighbourhoods, providing better housing to dissuade them from moving out. Whichever priority is uppermost, population policy in one form or another lurks behind recent urban reconstruction projects.

The thinking that inspires these initiatives is in itself perfectly defensible. The accumulation of disadvantage is to no small degree the result of well-intentioned city planning, which made social housing so predominant in certain areas that the result was the opposite of the emancipation intended. In large-scale housing projects the clustering together of problem families meant that the districts they lived in quickly deteriorated. There are countless examples, the best known being Pruitt-Igoe, a project in St Louis that won a prize when it was completed in 1955 but within 17 years had turned into an uninhabitable no-go area and in the end was literally wiped off the map. Or take the Amsterdam suburb of Bijlmer. On completion in the mid-1960s, it was praised as a dream neighbourhood. But 20 years later it had descended into a downward spiral of poverty and violence.

Processes like these have been experienced everywhere and they have not escaped the attention of observers such as Peter Hall: 'The evidence was accumulating in the 1990s that the underclass phenomenon, once thought a product of the Anglo-American deregulated economies, was appearing also in very different kinds of society and kinds of city: large public housing projects in Paris and Amsterdam were increasingly populated by the structurally unemployed and their children, and – just as in their New York and London equivalents – violence was simmering just below the surface.'[57]

It's therefore high time to take a close look at the unintended consequences of the disproportionate amount of social housing in major cities. Here lies one of the keys to change. Increased home ownership will strengthen ties with the city and encourage a mixed composition of neighbourhoods. In countries like the Netherlands or Sweden especially, where home ownership in the most important cities is extremely low – in Amsterdam, for example, less than a quarter of dwellings are owner-occupied – such interventions can help to create more balanced neighbourhoods.

Yet this approach too has its limitations. We tend to assume not only that mixing boosts the economic vitality of a neighbourhood, providing it with a thriving middle class, but that it stimulates social interaction as well. Is this actually how it works? Attempts to create mixed communities are often prompted by the simple idea that familiarity breaks down barriers; as people get to know each other, they'll become more tolerant. American urban sociologist Herbert Gans, however, believes that a 'balanced community', one whose composition reflects that of the population as a whole, is in itself problematic. He writes: 'The balanced community would probably experience intense political and cultural conflict.'[58]

Up to a point, imbalance within a population can actually be helpful in everyday life, and indeed there is something to be said for the notion that segregation has damped down conflict over many years. Different groups had barely any contact with each other and when they did the indigenous population voted with its feet. The fact that even the middle classes are now being affected by immigration has undoubtedly contributed to a change over the past few years; the extent of immigration is such that leading separate lives no longer works as a way of avoiding conflict. This is not to say, however, that combining populations by housing rich and poor or black and white next to each other will produce integrated neighbourhoods.

Sociologist Jan Willem Duyvendak points to a real problem with the attempt to create more socially diverse neighbourhoods by means of demolition and reconstruction: 'The weakest groups of residents then run the risk of being forced out of the neighbourhood "for their own good".'[59] If you speak to council leaders in the western suburbs of Amsterdam or in Rotterdam neighbourhoods like Charlois, they continually bring up the subject of public support for reconstruction, since feelings of unrest and discomfort have been created among many residents, who have the impression they're being cleansed out of their own neighbourhoods. You hear comments like: 'Along that way you'll find new privately owned houses. Sorry to be so blunt, but that's an enclave of high-income whites in what's really a ghetto for immigrants. Groups shut themselves off. No one has anything to gain by it.'

These are all useful qualifications to set beside attempts to encourage local residents of different social and ethnic groups to mix, initiatives that run the risk of disrupting more social networks than they create. Large-scale interventions do perk up the appearance of a neighbourhood, but that's not to say social relations will improve very much in the long term, one reason being that a neighbourhood is more important to some of its residents than to others. There are those who want to make intensive use of the area they live in, while for many a home may be not much more than a base of operations. So it's only partly true to say that a neighbourhood is a community; people who live in cities increasingly have relationships that extend far beyond their own part of town. The notion that local communities have gradually fallen apart is based on more than nostalgia alone.

There's another factor to bear in mind. Much of the recent reconstruction of urban areas has been prompted by concerns about public order. This in itself is nothing new, in fact it's an aspect of all urban planning: the established middle class wants to prevent the emergence of an underclass, fearing social tensions and the creation of crime-infested neighbourhoods. But striving for the maintenance of public order is not the same as wanting to live together. People are keen to do away with 'ghettoization at the bottom' while not really wanting to change 'ghettoization at the top'. The better off would in fact like to see dispersal without too much mixing. Of course this is a rather self-contradictory desire, but it demonstrates that a conflict of interest has come into play, in which the boundaries of class and colour soon become hard to tell apart.

The middle classes have an increasing tendency to isolate themselves. Why else do we see more and more 'gated communities', small fenced-off welfare states with their own security arrangements that look much like medieval fortress towns? Anthropologist Setha Low has researched the phenomenon in the country in which it has grown most rapidly, America, where as long ago as the late 1990s more than 16 million people lived in 20,000 of these settlements.

People's motives in opting for this kind of self-imposed isolation have to do primarily with the quest for a safe community. 'It transforms Americans' dilemma of how to protect themselves and their children from danger, crime, and unknown others while still perpetuating open, friendly neighbourhoods.'[60] At the root of this self-seclusion lies a fear of the rapidly increasing social and cultural differences we see in today's cities, but there's also, Low says, a longing to replicate childhood memories imbued with emotional certainties and a sense of protection. Closing off a neighbourhood by building a fence around it, with private security guards at the entrance, reduces individual freedom and opportunities for easy access, but that's a price people are happy to pay for enhanced social control. Of course, one of the effects of this kind of privatization is that it reduces residents' sense of responsibility for security in society at large.

Dislike of ethnic minorities is one factor in the decision to live in a gated community. By shutting themselves off, people are attempting to preserve some degree of homogeneity and to secure control over who can settle in their immediate vicinity. As a result, the ability of others to build a community is undermined, that is to say 'community in the sense of an integration of the suburb and the city, community in terms of access to public open space, and community within the American tradition of racial and ethnic integration and social justice'.[61]

Here we see, in a magnified form, the impasse that segregation has created. The middle classes react with fear to the formation of ghettos housing primarily low-skilled migrants, but they regard the mixing of schools and local populations as a prospect no less threatening. In cities where the majority of school-aged children belong to migrant families, dispersal imposed from above elicits yet more avoidance strategies among members of the 'white' and 'black' middle classes. They can easily leave. By doing so, they undermine attempts to achieve mixed communities. Clearly, along with the rebuilding of neighbourhoods, the positive effects of which relate mainly to economic capacities and the safety of residents, other means must be sought to encourage and enable people to live together.

Back to the Garden City

In a time of globalization, not all cities are places of freedom and experimentation, and those that are will not automatically remain so. Indeed, the cultural differences that characterize all major cities today may make us wonder what can possibly hold urban communities together. Communities are never boundless; they are always demarcated in some way, and it's in the city that the perpetual tension between heritage and openness is most obvious. Historian Piet de Rooy writes: 'It will be possible to recover cohesion in urban society only if we can develop new ideas about citizenship.'[62] That will not be easy in places where more than 100 different nationalities are required to live together.

Countless cities in Europe and America are trying to find solutions. Social interventions have been set in train, but patterns of segregation are stubborn, especially in neighbourhoods where a large majority of the population is composed of migrants. These patterns cannot be swept away completely, or even largely, by the interventions of planners. The renovation of entire districts will end in huge disappointment if the social environment – as manifested above all in schools and the jobs market – doesn't change at the same time. Donzelot is right: What is the point of replacing the stairs and the lift in a high-rise block if it's impossible for residents ever to climb to a higher social level?

This is generally recognized. But there is more. The debate sparked by the riots in the French *banlieues* made clear, if nothing else, that urban societies are divided along cultural as well as social lines. Attempts to give neighbourhoods and schools a more mixed character and to improve social mobility through education will not suffice on their own. The 'cultural pillar' has been neglected, the idea that a handing down of culture in the broadest sense is essential for the preservation and development of an urban society.

The first generation of city planners clearly believed in the connection between urban planning, social integration and cultural advancement. The garden city movement, which marks the beginning of town planning in its modern form, was inextricably bound up with social issues. The background to this movement in Britain was plain to all. The indescribable poverty and chaos in the slums of London, a city of millions, was seen in Victorian England as a moral scandal and at the same time as a threat to social order. One feature of the garden city movement was a culturally motivated distrust of the city, which was blamed for the decline of civilization. By contrast, the healthy countryside was regarded as an environment in which traditional norms and values flourished. The best aspects of city and countryside could be combined in a new project: the garden city. Small, self-sufficient towns were created outside urban areas. In the words of the movement's founder, Ebenezer Howard, these were intended 'not as a temporary haven of refuge but as a permanent seat of life and culture, urban in its advantages, permanently rural in its situation'.[63]

The old social question was addressed not merely through social regulation and house building – those initiatives were embedded in a civilizing offensive that we'd now no doubt be quick to label patronizing. In early twentieth-century Amsterdam, councillor Floor Wibaut said: 'The starting point for an enhancement of civilization among the working classes must lie in the improvement of housing.' At the same time, however, he recognized that it would also be a question of 'stimulating and strengthening the desire for a more elevated life' among members of that working class. Planning was advocated by urban elites that adhered to clearly defined cultural ideals.

This attitude should be revived. Writing about life in modern cities, sociologist Manuel Castells explains why. 'It opposes the cosmopolitanism of the elite, living on a daily connection to the whole world, . . . to the tribalism of local communities, retrenched in their spaces that they try to control as their last stand against the macro forces that shape their lives out of their reach.'[64] We need to let that phrase about 'their last stand' sink in. What we have too easily dismissed as nostalgia is in fact an attempt to get a grip on the huge and therefore anonymous forces that increasingly affect daily life. Opposition to immigration among a significant majority of the population can be seen as an indication of this. Castells is entirely correct in concluding that 'the most important challenge to be met in European cities . . . is the articulation of the globally-oriented economic functions of the city with the locally-rooted society and culture'.[65]

How we can reconcile these two worlds? How can ties to the city be reinvented and social cohesion strengthened? How can the sense of being part of an urban community take root? The desire to achieve all this forms part of a broader reassessment. The mass demolition that once accompanied urban renewal has been replaced by interventions that show more respect for the historical stratification of the city. This way of dealing with a city's history could become a guiding principle, helping city-dwellers to see themselves as residents of an environment that existed before them and will continue to exist after them.

In European cities, history is everywhere. In some we find relics more than 2,000 years old. Architectural historian Leonardo Benevolo stresses the significance of the physical presence of past generations: 'Coexistence with the "ruins" of the ancient world would remain a constant of European civilization and transmitted the physical sense of another, ever-present civilization, both foreign and familiar at the same time. It also inspired a series of general reflections on the fragility of human works and on those great forces – the ravages of time, the fickleness of fortune – which have long accompanied both the individual and collective European sentiment.'[66] History understood in this way is not an invitation to arrogance or hubris but rather – above all, perhaps – to modesty and moderation.

Why are children told so little about the history of their cities? Why do they learn nothing about the stories behind the buildings and the streets, about manners and customs? Why are children not encouraged to develop a historical sensibility by looking at paintings or other works of art? British urban sociologist Ali Madanipour writes: 'The question of social exclusion and integration, it can be argued, largely revolves around access. It is access to decision-making, access to resources, and access to common narratives, which enable social integration.'[67] The emphasis is always placed on the political aspect, access to decision-making, and the economic aspect, access to means, whereas in fact the cultural aspect of integration, access to shared stories, is no less crucial.

There is a need to create a new majority among city-dwellers, made up of those who feel responsible for the future of the city, a majority that straddles the dividing line between indigenous populations and newcomers. In doing so, more attention must be paid to the rising middle class of migrants, in short to those with the greatest potential for citizenship. There is so much to be gained here, although a great deal of suspicion will have to be overcome. A deliberate effort needs to be made to broaden the urban elite; it often fails to care enough, but, at the same time, too little is asked of it. Writers, artists, entrepreneurs – the possibilities are endless. They should all be invited to think for themselves about the way the urban fabric can be strengthened.

Over the past few years much has been said about the creativity of cities, and clearly those urban conurbations that have more technology, talent and tolerance do better than those with less. The tension between creativity, pre-eminently the province of individuals, and cohesion, a matter of communities, is something cities will have to address in a time of globalization. In these new circumstances we must reinvent the city as a place where new ways are constantly being found of combining creativity and continuity. This will be possible only if we understand that freedoms can sometimes fall into disrepute. There's no guarantee that tolerance can be preserved in cities that accommodate vast social and cultural differences.

Some say diversity is valuable in itself and talk of a 'diversity dividend'. We hear little about the cost. American researcher Robert Putnam concludes from one study that diversity certainly comes at a price. Although in the long term today's immigration brings new opportunities with it, in the short term the costs and benefits look rather different. 'In highly diverse Los Angeles or San Francisco, for example, roughly 30 percent of inhabitants say they trust their neighbours "a lot", whereas in the ethnically homogeneous communities of North and South Dakota 70–80 percent of the inhabitants say the same. In more diverse communities, people trust their neighbours less. . . . People living in ethnically diverse settings appear to "hunker down" – that is, to pull in like a turtle.'[68] He therefore advocates 'more opportunities for meaningful interaction across ethnic lines where Americans (new and old) work, learn, recreate, and live'.[69]

Research shows that cities that are ahead in a technological sense do not score highly on measures of social capital. The latter refers to things like the degree to which people join clubs or do voluntary work. Clearly the new elites that populate the creative city are less tied to a specific place, preferring to operate in quasi-anonymous surroundings. This disengagement at the top of the social spectrum is matched by alienation at the bottom. More and more people feel neither at home nor represented. Odes to the creative city notwithstanding, the questions raised by Putnam continue to dog us. How can we ensure that cities remain places where, despite being surrounded by strangers, we can live with a reasonable degree of trust and confidence?

A city of creativity and freedom cannot exist in complete isolation. It requires the context of a society that can answer the questions thrown up by migration in a more or less balanced manner. Particularly in a time of speculation about 'the abolition of distance', there's a need to understand the boundaries within which people move. In the globalizing world of the internet and other means of mass communication, distance seems less and less important, and it's all too easy to assume that the spatial dimension will slowly dissolve into a general mobility of increasingly footloose citizens.

This is to overlook something: the city walls of old were not just a way of protecting a place against intruders from outside; they also enclosed a community, an animated inner space, as the German philosopher Peter Sloterdijk describes it. He points to a need to animate a large number of people within a 'sphere of significance with shared motives and unified spatial concepts'.[70] The walls that shelter us are growing ever thinner in a world where borders are fewer and people have been set adrift. Sloterdijk writes of a 'globalization drama': the social ties that protect people are gradually dissipating without anything new arising to take their place. Modern man is suffering moral panic, finding himself a kind of vagrant in a chaotic world.[71]

The turnover rate of people, goods and ideas is increasing all the time and in response the need for spatial and mental anchorage has grown. The urban environment has a major impact on all this. In a global economy there's nothing natural about open cities. The problem for elites is that they have not yet found ways of relating to the insecurity many citizens feel and their resulting tendency towards self-isolation. It doesn't help to remind people that they've become citizens of the world unless at the same time we look for ways to answer their need for continuity and a sense of community.

3

The Great Migration

The Globe Is Fragile

On the borders of the affluent world, the dramas come thick and fast. People risk literally everything for a share in prosperity and freedom. On the Mexican border illegal migrants lose their way in the desert cauldron and die of thirst. In the Mediterranean, people attempt the crossing in unseaworthy small boats and drown. Sometimes the bodies wash up, spotted from afar by holidaymakers settling down for a day at the beach. A horrified reaction follows every time, then ebbs away until the next disaster grabs our attention.

On 19 June 2000, British customs officers found 58 Chinese illegals in the back of a lorry. They'd died of suffocation. The driver, a Dutch national, was arrested on suspicion of agreeing to hide them for a fee and was eventually sentenced to 14 years in prison. The stowaways had probably put their fate into the hands of professional people smugglers. Estimates suggest that since the mid-1990s some 7,000 deaths occurred in the cat-and-mouse game between border guards and illegal immigrants.

We've stepped into a new world, but by no means everything we're experiencing is new. On 21 October 1927, customs officials in the port city of Fremantle on the west coast of Australia found 54 Chinese stowaways in one of the ballast tanks of the Dutch ship *SS Almkerk*. They'd hidden there intending to come ashore unnoticed. The air in the tank was so stale that eight were dead by the time they were found. The rest had lost consciousness.[1]

People have been crossing borders, legally or illegally, throughout human history. What we now call globalization – its most visible feature being widespread human migration – is the latest manifestation of a long process of interconnection. It was the colonial expansion of Europe, beginning with the discovery of America in 1492, that created today's boundless network of economic and cultural interdependence. Immigration into the Western world has a prior cause: if it hadn't been for the overseas possessions of European colonial powers, the inhabitants of those other worlds would not have been cut adrift so soon.

Globalization as expressed in widespread migration is not a steadily advancing process. It has peaks and troughs. There was mass migration from Europe to America between 1850 and 1914, and in terms of the numbers involved that period was remarkably similar to our own, but the intervening years saw a deep dip. Between 1900 and 1910, 8.5 million people emigrated to America, whereas between 1950 and 1960 only 2.5 million crossed the Atlantic permanently. At the end of the twentieth century, immigration almost equalled the level it had reached just before the First World War, producing 9 million new Americans between 1990 and 2000.

Migration experts Stephen Castles and Mark Miller point to an histor- ical continuity in immigration trends, but at the same time they indicate what's new about our own era. 'While movements of people across borders have shaped states and societies since time immemorial, what is distinctive in recent years is their global scope, their centrality to domes- tic and international politics and their enormous economic and social consequences.'[2] Castles and Miller predict a further 'globalization' and 'politicization' of the issue as more and more countries are affected by global waves of population movement and at the same time the impact of migration becomes so great that it sparks political conflict.

Estimates of the number of migrants in the world today are inherently unreliable. In 2005 several reports stated that more than 190 million people had spent over a year outside their own countries. It has been estimated that in 2010 this figure, which includes illegal migrants, will pass the 200 million mark. Distribution across the continents is roughly as follows: Africa 17 million, North America 45 million, South America a little under 7 million, Asia 25 million, Western and Central Europe 44 million, Eastern Europe and Central Asia 25 million, the Middle East 19 million and Oceania 5 million.[3]

As a proportion of a rapidly expanding world population, the rise in migration in the years 1970–2005 from 2.2 to 2.9 per cent may not have been spectacular, but the average for the richer parts of the world – Europe, North America, Japan, Australia and New Zealand – rose enormously. In 1960–5 it stood at half a million per year, in 2000–5 at 3.3 million. The figure is expected to fall back to 2.5 million a year for 2005–10.[4] In the case of Western Europe it actually increased more than threefold between 1965 and 2005 to around 11 per cent, meaning that in terms of the influx of newcomers, this region now differs little from the United States. Moreover, the proportion of total population growth in the rich world attributable to immigration has increased enormously, from one-eighth to more than two-thirds. In Europe it's as high as three quarters. Were it not for the arrival of migrants, Europe's population would now be falling. Together with a rise in average age and changes in ethnic composition, this lends a considerable emotional charge to the issue of immigration.[5]

The number of people fleeing their own countries grew particularly rapidly in the 1980s and the first half of the 1990s, reaching ten times that of a decade earlier. There was a fresh peak around the turn of the century, then the figure stabilized and measurably decreased before slowly rising again over the past few years. The number of refugees worldwide is estimated at 15 million, with a majority still in their home regions. Almost half of all requests for asylum made in the West in 1983–2007 were received by the three largest European countries: Germany, France and Britain.[6] Given the environmental disasters now predicted, it seems logical to assume that more people will be forced to leave their native countries in the not too distant future.

Globalization has undoubtedly brought about a politicization of migration. There's a need to find democratic ways of influencing world-wide flows of humanity. Of course, a tension exists between calls for more effective controls on human mobility and attempts to create an open economy sustained by cross-border trade and investment. If economic liberalism is to be consistent, it cannot favour the free movement of goods and capital alone, but must aim to dismantle barriers to the free movement of people. Few liberals, though, are willing to live up to the creed they espouse.

It's often said that immigration is out of control. Historians Piet Emmer and Hans Wansink write: 'Little can be done to prevent the arrival of migrants. The fact is, rich countries are the favoured destination for immigrants from poor countries.'[7] If they aren't allowed in legally, they'll come illegally. Yet the conclusion reached in their book is that 'only a fraction of intercontinental migrants can be allowed into Europe as legal migrant labourers, and if we don't succeed in allowing the best to come in, we'll have further problems'.[8] This illustrates a profound feeling of uncertainty. How can it make sense to opt for selective labour migration if all controls are doomed to fail and 'little can be done to prevent the arrival of migrants'?

Emmer and Wansink are not alone in thinking this way. All too often a decision in favour of more relaxed immigration laws is presented as simply inevitable: in a time of globalization, we're told, border controls are pointless. Before considering the ethics of control measures we need to ask whether governments, including those of democratic countries, are capable of intervening effectively. Recent history shows that government intervention certainly can have a significant impact on migration. Take Germany, where generous asylum legislation allowed the number of refugees arriving to rise extremely rapidly, reaching 438,000 in 1992. After the laws were tightened up, the figure dropped dramatically to stand at 128,000 in 1995. Tougher asylum laws in the Netherlands, introduced at the start of the twenty-first century, had a similar effect. The number of asylum-seekers has fallen by between 50 and 75 per cent since the mid-1990s. Another example is the French approach to immigration from Algeria, making it progressively more difficult in the 1990s. The numbers quickly fell, especially after Tunisia and Morocco closed their borders.

Conversely, governments can have a decisive effect in attracting immigrants. This is clear from the number of guest workers who arrived in Northern Europe in the 1960s from countries like Portugal, Turkey and Morocco. Without support from governments in the countries that received them, the flow of migrant workers would never have started. In classic countries of immigration like Canada and Australia, governments have played an active role in attracting precisely the type of migrants they believed were needed. In many cases, Australia even paid their travel costs.

There's another sense too in which government decisions can have a significant impact. American researcher Myron Weiner concludes that 'much of the world's migration today is the result of the policies and actions of states that directly or indirectly encourage, induce, or force their citizens to leave'.[9] So while decisions at a national level are crucial in determining which migrants will be admitted, governments also have a huge influence on the decisions made by their own citizens to depart. Sometimes they may promote the idea of emigrating, as European governments did in the 1950s when they encouraged farmers to leave for Australia and Canada; on other occasions they may use threats and force, one example being the expulsion of the Asian minority in Uganda by President Idi Amin.

In some parts of the world outright expulsion is fairly common. In the Gulf states migration is strictly regulated. Temporary guest workers from the Philippines have far fewer rights than they would in the West; they are forbidden to start families and they have no prospect of a status that could lead to citizenship. The authorities there often refer to the European experience, which in so many cases saw a temporary stay turn into permanent residence, as one they have no wish to repeat. At fairly regular intervals, entire categories of guest workers are simply ejected.

The same happened to tens of thousands of Egyptian migrants in Libya in the 1980s.

Such measures are almost unthinkable in liberal democracies, where political interference in migration flows is constrained by constitutional norms, but this does not mean politicians are powerless in the face of mass migration. German political scientist Christian Joppke poses a rhetorical question. If immigration can no longer be controlled, why do states in the Middle East and South East Asia not do as the Western world generally does? Why don't they respect the rights of immigrants? He points out that the limited sovereignty of a liberal democracy is a self-imposed restriction. Pressure from the judiciary, which demands that the rights of migrants should be both respected and extended, has been the main obstacle to the many attempts by politicians to cut migration drastically.

In reality, Joppke says, after the economic crisis of 1973 all immigration was undesirable, but as a result mainly of interventions by constitutional courts like the Conseil constitutionnel in France and the Bundesverfassungsgericht in Germany, initiatives that would have put a brake on family reunion, for example, were blocked. These self-imposed limitations on sovereignty as a result of the separation of powers – in other words, the independence of the judiciary – cannot be taken to suggest that governments, as a result of globalization, no longer have any means of controlling their borders.

There's another sense too in which the actions of states can have a direct impact on the flow of migrants. Look at Haiti in the 1980s. It was partly because of the swelling flood of people fleeing the country that the US government decided to intervene militarily. This is not the only example of migration influencing international relations. The presence of Afghan refugees in Pakistan and of Palestinian refugees in Lebanon created tensions in those countries. Countless Palestinians were forced to leave Lebanon, since they were prolonging the civil war there.

In fact there are few large migratory movements in which governments have not been directly involved. Many of those who talk about the futility of trying to control mass migration undermine their own argument by talking scornfully at the same time about a 'fortress Europe' that's pulling up its drawbridges. The image of a fortress is at odds with that of powerless states unable to do anything to control immigration.

Controls are certainly needed, since there's every reason to assume that pressure to admit migrants will continue into the foreseeable future and indeed increase. The contrast between demographic trends in developed and underdeveloped countries is striking. While in some parts of the world populations are ageing, elsewhere a youthful surge is taking place. Meanwhile the gap in living standards between North and South is still considerable, and there's a constant demand for cheap labour. This contrast is at its most stark in countries like Mexico and the United States, or Morocco and Spain, where the two worlds meet at a common border.

A great deal is at stake. Along with measures to control immigration, the social compromise is up for discussion. The idea is gaining ground that with the rise of low-wage economies like China and India the prosperous world is being forced to give up much of its social safety net. In the West there's a clear conflict of interest that makes controlling immigration more difficult. The demand for cheap or even illegal labour is now a matter of global competitiveness, and this has created a shadow economy that affords its employees little protection. They're in a vulnerable position, at risk of becoming victims of exploitation of a kind we hoped had been eliminated after a century of emancipation.

Western governments reached deeper and deeper into the lives of their citizens over the course of the twentieth century. Concerns about interference aside, this represents progress towards greater civilization, in the sense that sickness, unemployment or old age no longer necessarily mean a descent into poverty. Nowadays, efforts to achieve equality are at odds with the liberalization of economies and the retreat of governments, which are steadily relinquishing the idea that society is malleable. This is to the detriment of parliamentary democracy, since citizens still have high expectations of their governments, despite today's reluctance to regulate economic life.

The credit crisis of the past few years has made the consequences of these developments startlingly clear; the deregulation of financial markets now confronts us with a question of confidence: to what extent can people rely on important institutions such as banks, or indeed their regulators? A lack of responsibility has led much-maligned governments to become caught up in a financial support operation the like of which the world has never seen. Twenty years after the fall of the Berlin Wall, banks everywhere are either being nationalized or going into receivership. No-holds-barred liberalism has undermined itself.

A further question arises. How much faith is it possible to have in national governments now that we're so aware of the impact of distant events? Some institutions have suddenly turned out to be far more vulnerable than anyone imagined. The effects will undoubtedly make themselves felt, since without strong institutions and a democratic culture able to straddle national borders, globalization will end in crisis and conflict.

It has happened before. On the eve of the First World War an optimism prevailed about the growth of economic interdependency that bears comparison with today's expectations. Those hopes were cruelly shattered. International trade collapsed. It took until some time in the

1970s for the world's economies to become as interwoven as they were prior to 1914; in fact between the wars there was a sharp decline in both international economic activity and migration.

Without shared democratic norms, neither a common market nor greater mobility will be possible in the long term. The beginnings of a backlash are already visible, with the rise of all kinds of populist movements born out of hostile responses to globalization. We've seen outbursts of discontent not just in the West but in Asia as well. In the late 1990s, against almost all expectations, an economic crisis erupted in the Far East where for decades economic growth had seemed boundless. A photograph from those days shows a group of students stamping furiously on a pile of ballpoint pens. The students were from South Korea, the pens from Japan. Their grim faces make clear this was not merely youthful indignation – it looks more like a magic ritual to ward off disaster. 'Buy Korean' was their slogan. Old accounts were being settled, since current accounts were not looking too healthy.

It's an image that captures the sense of powerlessness which overcame one of the much-praised economies of Asia when the financial markets suddenly threw a series of nations into a state of crisis. Powerlessness seeks redress. The anonymous forces that controlled the world market had to be given a face: Japan, concluded those Korean students; the Jews, the Malaysian prime minister was quick to presume; the Chinese, was the widespread belief in Indonesia, prompting acts of aggression against that minority; Westerners, many others cried, since the rescuers parachuted in by the IMF and the World Bank are generally white and unrelenting.

The globe is fragile, as the Korean students' pen-dance demonstrated. The internationalization of the economy can be jeopardized by violent conflict and social imbalance. The world market can't be left to its own devices; it relies on stable relationships, both national and international, which need to be regulated. It may often seem as if politics has lost out to the economy, but moments of public crisis prove otherwise. In short, the liberal utopia, in which peaceful international relations are an automatic result of shared trading interests, can be cruelly disrupted by national or ethnic conflicts.

Current agonizing over immigration should be understood against the background of tensions like these. Westerners are trying to find a new balance, but all too often they're told that because of immigration, which can't be controlled, the differences within countries are increasing even as the differences between countries decrease. If we accept this line of reasoning, then it would be a good idea to take a closer look at the consequences. Unlimited immigration means the contrasts that exist in the world at large will be seen in the West's major cities. As well as poverty and illiteracy, ethnic conflicts and religious extremism will permeate liberal democracies.

Some believe that the West's middle class can't survive without an underclass and that nowadays that underclass must be imported, since social advancement means cheap labour is no longer available within richer countries. Over past decades we've begun to anticipate where this could lead. The answer to the growing interdependence of nations surely doesn't lie in isolation; Europe is part of the world economy. But how wide can social and cultural divides become as a result of globalization before they start to destroy the trust citizens have in each other and in their representatives?

All the Colours plus Grey

Economic globalization and the immigration that accompanies it cry out for regulation. The pressure on Western societies is huge. As they face the despair of those seeking their fortunes in the prosperous regions of the world, receiving societies are coming up against increasingly vocal opposition to immigration. Surveys suggest that a majority of people in the member states of the European Union believe immigration should be more strictly limited. We see the same phenomenon in the traditional countries of immigration.[10] The Australian government has been trying to reduce the flow of new immigrants since the mid-1990s.

Those critical of more restrictive policies often point to a fundamental contradiction between the generally recognized freedom to leave one's own country and tight restrictions on entering someone else's. Globalization makes the discrepancy between freedom to depart and limits on access all the greater. Residents of the rich world can move around at will, but they think it more or less self-evident that residents of poorer countries should be confined as far as possible within the boundaries of their own regions. British economist Philippe Legrain calls this a form of 'global apartheid' and describes it as abhorrent and indefensible.

Limits on access don't usually apply to highly educated migrants, who are scarce and therefore welcome whenever shortages arise within their professions. Think of Indian computer specialists or doctors from the Philippines. Most arguments concern low-skilled workers and their families. They are seen as a burden on the welfare state and there's less optimism about the social advancement of their children than there once was. This has led most European governments to take steps to keep them out.

Yet there are those who advocate encouraging the migration of unskilled labour, for a variety of reasons. At one end of the spectrum people talk about safeguarding prosperity at home: there's a demand here; we need these people in order to maintain our way of life. At the opposite extreme people point to global inequalities, saying it's not so much a matter of demand for cheap labour as of supply, a result of the chasm between North and South. Free-market thinking and cross-border solidarity come together in a plea for more migration.

Let's look first at the economic incentive before turning to the moral argument. What does the receiving society have to gain from low-skilled migrants? In many European countries the results of post-war immigration are the main factor encouraging restraint. One Dutch study states: 'The net benefit of total immigration for an economy like that of the Netherlands is small in current circumstances, if not negligible.'[11] In Germany too there is growing scepticism about the costs and benefits of immigration. A recent report speaks of an 'unfavourable economic balance at present' and adds that it will only get worse 'if the status quo is perpetuated over the coming years'.[12]

As we shall see, in other countries too the economic yield of post-war immigration has been disappointing. The conclusion drawn from this finding by a government advisory body in the Netherlands is typical of the mealy-mouthed attitude that characterizes so much of current policy: 'As to the expectation of remaining a country of immigration, it is worth pointing out that this is a factual statement, not a statement about its desirability as an outcome.'[13] But politics is all about whether given developments are desirable or not. This kind of self-declared impotence has done more to undermine public acceptance of fresh waves of migration than to encourage it.

We cannot escape the question of what kind of immigration is desirable. The conclusions of another study are clear: 'For the labour market no positive effects of large-scale immigration are to be expected.'[14] This assessment takes account of Europe's experience with guest workers, people brought to countries including France, Germany and the Netherlands as a result of pressure from a business community that allowed itself to be guided by a need for cheap and eager workers. There were many unintended consequences, which are still making themselves felt. Guest workers started families, or reunited their existing families, so that today some 600,000 people of Turkish or Moroccan descent live in the Netherlands, that is to say 'ten times the maximum number of guest workers then working in the Netherlands at any given moment', as sociologist Han Entzinger writes.[15] In 20 years from now, both these ethnic communities will have doubled again, amounting to more than a million people.

Given the long-term consequences of labour migration, we need to look not just at the interests of business, legitimate though they are as such, but at the social costs that arise as soon as migrant labour is no longer needed, as was the case after the oil crisis of 1973. British demographer David Coleman sums up the expense involved in this kind of immigration: 'The total cost of the integration process, and of associated immigration and race relations business, the cost of meeting the special education, health and housing needs of immigrants, the net effects upon the education of ordinary [sic] children in immigrant areas, the permanent need to "regenerate" urban areas of immigrant settlement instead of demolishing them, issues of crime and public order, and the multiplier effect on future immigration.'[16]

Faced with pleas from various sides to allow in more low-skilled workers – the key terms being 'seasonal labour' and 'cyclical migration' – we need to ask ourselves whether the branches of business that rely so heavily on minimally educated and often illegally resident migrants have any future in the West. Take labour-intensive horticulture. Globalization means that fruit and vegetables from all over the world are available all year round. Why would rich nations want to compete with low-wage countries that are perfectly capable of supplying such products and would aid their own development by doing so? It's a thorny issue, but dependence on underpaid workers in countries with a significant agrarian sector raises a suspicion that this branch of business has no long-term future there. It would surely be better to anticipate the future than to resort to indefensible strategies involving subsidies and import tariffs, accompanied by illegal migration – quite apart from the high environmental costs of sustaining glasshouse cultivation, for example, in its current form.

The consequences of low-skilled migration can be problematic in the long term. For a start, this kind of migration reduces pressure on businesses to innovate. It prolongs the death throes of non-viable industries. This creates short-term job opportunities, but it's highly questionable whether it truly benefits the economy overall. Historian John Higham presents evidence that in America restrictive immigration laws from the early 1920s onwards necessitated greater investment: 'To the extent that the decline of immigration after the war encouraged capital investments in machinery, restriction probably stimulated the whole upward trend.'[17] Gérard Noiriel cannot escape the conclusion that in France the influx of low-skilled labour had a dubious effect on industrialization. It certainly helped to plug the gaps in heavy industry and agriculture, but at the same time it stifled innovation, the mining industry being one example.[18]

Another reason why the benefits accruing from migration often fail to meet expectations is that with permanent settlement the centre of gravity shifts from the active to the inactive. The first generation of guest workers is initially extremely productive, but the children, women and elderly who come to form an increasing proportion of the migrant community often bring social costs with them. A positive balance can easily tip over into a negative one as the years go by. The Turkish community in Germany illustrates this. In 1961, when 47 per cent of West Germans were in work, the figure for Turkish migrants was an astonishing 80 per cent, but by 1984 labour participation had swung round in favour of the indigenous population, with 47 per cent in work as compared to 45 per cent of Turks. Participation in the workplace by Turkish migrants continued to fall, until it stood at less than 40 per cent, half the rate of 30 years earlier.[19]

It's not so much that newcomers take jobs from the existing labour force. In a booming economy the existing population actually benefits as far as that goes, since activity by migrants creates new jobs, but American economist George Borjas has shown that current immigration, in the United States and elsewhere, exacerbates social inequality: prosperity flows away from employees, who are competing with immigrants, towards employers and others who use migrant labour. His succinct conclusion is: 'Workers lose because immigrants drag wages down. Employers gain because immigrants drag wages down.'[20] There are important choices to be made here. It all depends what kind of society we want.

There's a need to ask whether reliance on low-skilled migrants is compatible with a comprehensive welfare system. Immigration in the era of the welfare state is an unprecedented phenomenon. Never before have migrants been able to rely on a high degree of protection. The problem is not so much that generous social provision attracts migrants, since people don't take the risk of leaving hearth and home in order to live on state benefits. No, they come here to work and then get caught up in the welfare safety net. Whatever their original motives, this outcome is not a happy one, say Dutch researchers Han Entzinger and Jelle van der Meer: 'As a result of the coincidence of the open immigration society with the closed welfare state, forms of dependence arise that nobody actually wants and that can be costly too.'[21]

The incompatibility between a country of immigration and a welfare state has led some to conclude that migrants ought not to be allowed to claim social benefit payments until a certain amount of time has elapsed. Since 1996, immigrants to the United States have been eligible for welfare only after a legal residence of at least five years, although the law is not applied very consistently, while in Australia the period is two years, the idea being that migrants who do not have jobs must either survive independently or go back. If this restriction had been applied to guest workers in the past, however, the outcome would not have been greatly different. Most guest workers became unemployed only after 10–15 years of productive labour and would therefore have qualified for full welfare payments under this kind of system.

Some claim that new migration is unavoidable because Western societies are ageing and their social security systems will come under increasing pressure as a result. Demography, which concerns itself among other things with prognoses for future population trends, is a creditable but uncertain business. We have to live with that uncertainty, and it's true that an increase in the number of elderly people is bound to change the relationship between those aged 15–65 and the over-65s. The welfare state was built on the unspoken assumption that the ratio would need to be roughly 5:1, which is to say five people in work for every one person reliant on a pension, but already the ratio in Western Europe is 4:1 and over the coming half-century it will shift in the direction of 2:1. There will be fewer and fewer workers to support those dependent on them.

Pensions are therefore at risk, especially in countries such as Germany that have a pay-as-you-go system, meaning those in work pay to support the elderly in the expectation that their children will do the same for them. This 'contract between the generations' is premised upon a growing population, not one that is shrinking. Whereas only one in ten German women born in 1940 remained childless, one in three of those born in 1970 will not have children. By 2050 the proportion of people aged over 60 will have risen from its 1950 level of 14.6 per cent to 36.7 per cent, while that of the under-20s will have fallen over the same period from 30.9 to 16.1 per cent.

Demographers Michael Teitelbaum and Jay Winter correctly state that 'the coincidence of below-replacement fertility and large-scale immigration makes population politics an explosive issue'.[22] The term 'replacement fertility' simply refers to the fact that each couple must produce at least two children in order to replace itself. In a general sense, almost all developed countries have a fertility rate below the replacement value of 2.1, which means their populations will fall if there is no immigration. Fertility rates in Western Europe have dropped precipitately. If we compare the averages for 1950–5 with those for 1995–2000 we see a strong downward trend everywhere: in France from 2.73 to 1.76 children per couple, in Spain from 2.57 to 1.19, in Germany from 2.16 to 1.34, in Britain from 2.18 to 1.70 and in the Netherlands from 3.86 to 1.60.[23]

In the industrialized world, then, a demographic revolution is under way, and it is changing the population profoundly. One of the first countries to witness this phenomenon is Japan, where predictions suggest that between 2000 and 2050 the population will fall from 127 million to 105 million. In Western Europe too the trend is unmistakable. In Italy, for example, experts predict a fall in the same period from 57 to 41 million inhabitants. These figures are staggering.[24]

The combination of low fertility and high immigration means that new migrants account for a larger and larger proportion of any population growth developed countries can muster. In 1960 natural increase was responsible for roughly half the growth of populations in countries like West Germany, immigration for the other half. In 1990 practically all German population growth was attributable to immigration, and developments in other European countries show the same pattern. It is less true in the case of America: in 1960 one-eighth of US population growth was the result of immigration, and by 1990 this had risen to one-third. Figures for Canada are comparable to the US: in 1960 a tenth and 30 years later almost half its population growth was attributable to the arrival of migrants.[25] As for more recent trends, the European Union, with its 27 member states, saw a rise in total population of 2.4 million in 2007, taking it to 497 million, an increase of which 80 per cent was attributable to immigration.[26]

Behind moves in some countries to increase the birth rate, France being one example, lies a resistance to the colouring of the population. The slogan used by one German politician was quite explicit: '*Kinder statt Inder*', which roughly translates as: let's have more children of our own rather than importing computer specialists from India. That's not a sensible starting point when so crudely expressed, but the underlying questions have to be asked. What does a low birth rate say about the dynamics of a society? Must we simply accept that European societies are about to shrink, at least as far as their indigenous populations are concerned?

Whatever we may think about immigration, the cultural changes that low birth rates represent are unique. Never before have we seen a population shrink in peacetime. We can only speculate what the cultural consequences of an ageing population may be, but it's fair to assume that a less dynamic society will result. German demographer Franz-Xaver Kaufmann remarks that such a trend could easily lead to serious tensions, not so much between the social classes as between generations. There's a significant risk that demographic stagnation will be accompanied by economic crisis and that societies will become more inflexible. While globalization is placing increasing pressure on them to adapt, demographic decline is reducing their ability to do so.[27]

This revolution, which will have a profound effect on European lifestyles and on social stability in the near future, cannot be counterbalanced by migration from countries outside Europe. The United Nations institute charged with population prognoses presented detailed calculations in a report called *Replacement Migration* that shocked its readers when it was published in 2001. To keep the pressure of an ageing population at its present level until 2050, net migration into Europe would have to reach a total of 25 million a year – almost 50 times the present rate. Over a period of 50 years, some 1.3 billion migrants would be needed, double the population of Europe as it now stands, after which the problem of an ageing population would manifest itself again as the first of those migrants reached old age. More modest ambitions render up migrant numbers that are less astronomical but still problematic: merely keeping Europe's population stable would require a net total of two million immigrants a year. In short, the ageing of established populations can never in itself amount to an argument for permitting the immigration of unskilled workers on a large scale.

Furthermore, in attracting low-skilled migrants, rich countries would be ignoring their existing potential workforces of people with little in the way of higher education or training. The current and future expansion of the European Union to include countries further east, in due course perhaps Turkey among them, will release an enormous pool of cheap labour. This flow of newcomers, who after an initial transition period will be given freedom of movement, makes the call for immigration from outside the expanding union premature to say the least. The number of migrants from Poland who arrived in Britain as new citizens of the EU, to take one example, exceeded all expectations. Tens of thousands were expected; hundreds of thousands came.

Putting out another appeal for guest workers, even if we now call them seasonal workers, represents the line of least resistance. As we shall see time and again, the debate on immigration and integration confronts societies with their own failings. Importing cheap labour would be a way of sidestepping the problem of inactivity among a proportion of people of working age. This becomes clear from reading Emmer and Wansink, who rather unceremoniously write off the 1.5 million people in the Netherlands who are dependent on social insurance payments: 'A large proportion of those drawing state benefits are people who no longer have any chance in the labour market.'[28] Elsewhere they remark that it's not so much a question of a lack of opportunities as a lack of will: 'Dutch people feel themselves too good for such jobs, so without immigrants this kind of work is unaffordable.'[29] They have in mind the caring professions, and horticulture.

In that 'unaffordable' lies a recognition that it's not so much a matter of the indigenous population not wanting to do certain work as that this group will no longer work for the wages on offer. American researcher Thomas Sowell concludes that 'there are very few occupations that can be dispensed with entirely'. Were it not for immigration, 'many jobs would have been filled with natives at higher wage rates'.[30] In short, work such as cleaning is often performed by immigrants, but this doesn't mean that without migration there would be no cleaners. In countries like Japan, which has few immigrants, people pay more for certain services. Might it not be a good idea to remove the causes of inadequate participation in the jobs market before resorting to migrant workers?

Numerous economists insist that the increasing educational level of the population has created a shortage of low-skilled workers. But what about the second generation, the children of guest workers? Currently, half of all Turkish and Moroccan young people in the Netherlands leave school with only the most basic qualifications. Economist Arie van der Zwan is forthright: 'By making labour migration easier you are implicitly saying that our huge reserves of poorly educated and minimally integrated non-native residents now on welfare or in receipt of other social benefit payments will never find jobs. That is the tragedy of our major cities.'[31] Most Western European countries have considerable reserves of low-skilled labour, and those that haven't succeeded in creating work for their existing unemployed should have no illusions about the prospects for a new generation of migrant labourers.

This issue resonates all the more loudly when we consider that for every migrant, several relatives will arrive, meaning that limited labour migration can produce large ethnic communities within one or two generations. These long-term consequences are rarely taken into account. Given the problems of integration European cities face now, it would not be wise to opt a second time for large-scale immigration by people with little schooling. That would mean writing off many citizens prematurely, whereas in fact the social contract needs to be reassessed. A welfare state should confer obligations – a very different thing from bobbing on the currents of globalization.

Classic Countries of Immigration

In the debate about the economic benefits of immigration people invariably point to the classic countries of immigration: America, Australia and Canada. We are told that clearer demands are made of migrants there, with the result that they arouse far less opposition than in Europe. The comparison is certainly worth making, partly because it draws attention to the fact that in those countries too a fierce controversy is raging over the benefits of migration. The opposition to immigration they are experiencing bears comparison with the discontent felt in today's Europe.

The classic countries of immigration have all been through similar stages of development. The first obvious thing about them is that, when still sparsely populated, they were opened up by deliberate efforts to attract migrants. They all have a history of displacing and eliminating the original inhabitants, and their identity has been formed in part by the experience of the 'frontier'. One new generation of migrants after another has helped to conquer the land from nature, by laying railways, for example. In America, Australia and Canada, immigration was crucial to nation-building.

The immigration histories of these countries have other features in common. It's clear that their migrants came primarily from certain regions. In reality, and as a matter of policy, migration from Europe was given free reign until the 1960s, whereas much was done to dissuade people from other parts of the world from making the voyage. One of the first laws adopted by the Australian parliament after independence from Britain in 1901 was the Immigration Restriction Act, which specified that those coming to Australia must not be a burden on the public purse or on charitable institutions. This law, which remained in force until 1958, implicitly defined the White Australia Policy: coloured people were not welcome. This was never stated in so many words, but it was put into practical effect by means, among other things, of the 'dictation test', which Australian immigration historian James Jupp has called 'probably the most hypocritical invention in the long history of Australian immigration'.[32] It took the form of a 500-word dictation exam that enabled an immigration official to see whether a person could read and write. The test worked as a deterrent. It was clear to everyone that migrants from outside Europe had no chance. So they didn't come.

Like Australia, Canada applied racial criteria for many years in selecting its migrants. A government document from 1910 is quite explicit: 'It is the policy to do all to keep out of the country undesirables.' How were undesirable immigrants defined? 'Those belonging to nationalities unlikely to assimilate and who consequently prevent the building up of a united nation of people of similar customs and ideals.'[33] There was particularly strong opposition to Asian migrants. Time has caught up with the words of Premier Mackenzie King in 1947: 'Large-scale immigration from the Orient would change the fundamental composition of the Canadian population.'[34]

We will look at American immigration history in a separate chapter, but here we should note what has been called the 'love-hate relationship' between Americans and immigration. The United States began to impose restrictions at an early stage. At first, controls were fairly minimal and aimed mainly at preventing immigration from Asia – the Chinese Exclusion Act of 1882, for instance, which was not repealed until 1943. Around the turn of the twentieth century traditional migration from Britain, Ireland, Germany and the Scandinavian countries was overtaken by new immigration from countries such as Italy, Poland and Russia, and from the Balkans. In those years more broadly based opposition to immigration began to emerge, eventually leading to the 1924 Immigration Act, which attempted to consolidate the ethnic balance by favouring migrants from Western Europe and the Nordic countries. A statement by President Calvin Coolidge sums up the climate that prevailed at the time: 'There are racial considerations too grave to be brushed aside for any sentimental reasons. . . . The Nordic races propagate themselves successfully. With other races, the outcome shows deterioration.'[35] The 1924 legislation largely achieved its intended effect and it remained in force for many years.

Partly as a result of the Civil Rights Movement and criticism of colonialism, America relinquished these racial criteria bit by bit from the 1960s onwards, as did Canada and Australia. The consequences for the magnitude and the composition of immigration flows were spectacular. In 2005, 20.3 per cent of Australians were born outside the country, a slightly lower figure than in 2000 but still higher than for Canada and the United States, where the proportion of foreign-born residents is around 18.9 and 12.9 per cent respectively.[36] In Australia and Canada, Asian migration predominated from the late 1970s onwards. Today the proportion of immigrants to these countries who were born in Asia is around 40 per cent. The population of Sydney is now one-third Asiatic.

As well as immigration from Asia, America has seen a considerable influx of migrants from Latin America since the 1960s, more specifically from neighbouring Mexico. The assumption is now that by the middle of this century around a quarter of the US population will be made up of so-called Hispanics, a term that covers all migrants from the Spanish-speaking world. In Canada, Australia and the United States, European migration has fallen to around 10 per cent of newcomers. All three countries, once a product of British colonialism, are therefore slowly but surely breaking away from their origins. They have become nations that encompass more or less the entire world, although they receive relatively few migrants from Africa and the Middle East. This social transformation has met with resistance and everywhere there are clear signs of opposition to new migration.

It's often assumed that the classic countries of immigration have been making much clearer demands of people who want to immigrate than European countries have done up to now. In practice, rather less planning seems to have been involved, aside from the racial criteria we have already examined. In fact, only since 1967 in Canada and 1979 in Australia has much attention been paid to qualifications. With the abolition of Europe-oriented migration policies, other criteria gradually came to apply. In a sense these countries moved from one form of selection to another: economic criteria replaced ethnic criteria. The emphasis on economic usefulness intensified in the 1990s. If we look at three categories of immigrant – family members, those with skills to offer and asylum-seekers – then it's clear that in Canada there has been a strong shift away from the family and towards skilled labour. This is part of an attempt to tackle the swelling crisis of legitimacy surrounding migration, which now stands at more than 200,000 new residents a year. In the late 1990s Canadian philosopher Will Kymlicka described this crisis as follows: 'Canadians' former sense of confidence and optimism that our problems were manageable has been replaced with the feeling that things are out of control.'[37]

The same shift took place in Australia in the mid-1990s, but in contrast to Canada, total immigration fell to less than 100,000 a year. Australia, which according to Jupp has 'one of the most restrictive control systems of any democracy',[38] has used a points system for economic migrants since 1979, such that educational qualifications, age, knowledge of the English language and suitability for understaffed professions are central. There was a good deal of controversy about the way the system was implemented, mainly because a command of English soon came to weigh less heavily. Historian Geoffrey Blainey warned in the mid-1980s that while inadequate command of the language entails high economic costs, the social costs are even higher: 'confusion, loneliness, misunderstanding and prejudice'.[39] He expressed a belief that the reuniting of families was receiving undue emphasis, allowing too many uneducated migrants to enter the country. Such criticism was taken seriously and admission requirements were gradually tightened. The government also extended the period during which new migrants were denied access to welfare benefits from six months to two years.

Over the past few decades America has developed rather differently, although there too, since the new immigration act of 1965, migration has been predominantly about the formation and reunification of families. This accounts for some 75 per cent of the total. The United States differs from Canada and Australia in that it was not until the 1990s that it cautiously began to promote immigration by qualified workers and professionals, and it did so in addition to family-based migration rather than as an alternative to it. Along with ethnic interest groups, in America it's often religious groups who defend immigration by family members, as part of an effort to preserve traditional family values.

The important point here is that, aside from the past few years, in none of the classic countries of immigration have migrant labourers formed a majority of those entering. As a result, assessments of the economic importance of immigration over recent decades have been tentative. An Australian report from 1995, written before policy was steered in the direction of 'economic rationalism', states: 'Using immigration as a tool of macroeconomic policy is ineffectual . . . as it does not influence the main economic variables.'[40] According to Jupp, this is a fair summary of the debate in that country, and in Canada a government economic advisory body came to a comparable conclusion in 1991: an annual rise of 100,000 in the number of migrants would contribute little to the economy. Sociologist Peter Li sums up the main thrust of the Canadian study by saying that immigration has produced 'a moderate positive or neutral economic effect on Canada in the post-war period'.[41]

As to the economic benefits of immigration in the United States, the verdict of Borjas, who originally entered the country as a refugee from Cuba, is fairly outspoken. In his book *Heaven's Door*, which has become a classic, he analyses the waves of immigration seen in the 1950s, which included many well-educated Europeans and Canadians. Their arrival was beneficial, but the immigration of the 1970s and since, mainly involving low-skilled Asians and Hispanics, has been far less profitable. His carefully reasoned estimate suggests that 'the annual net gain is astoundingly small'.[42] Had the Canadian points system been applied to all immigrants to the United States, Borjas calculates, 40 per cent would not have been allowed in. Such a measure would have had widely divergent consequences for the different immigrant groups: of English migrants only 6 per cent and of Indian migrants 19 per cent would have been turned away, whereas 70 per cent of Portuguese and three-quarters of Mexicans would have found themselves refused entry.

In the classic countries of immigration, as elsewhere, there has been a fall in the educational level of immigrants and at the same time a rise in government expenditure, partly because of the relatively high cost of newcomers in state benefits and in educational initiatives for children who do not speak the language well. Whereas in America in 1960 migrants earned an average of 4.1 per cent more than people born in the country, this had been reversed by 1990, with immigrants earning 16.3 per cent less. In an assessment of two centuries of mass migration, economists Timothy Hatton and Jeffrey Williamson point to a discrepancy in performance on the jobs market between established residents and newcomers. The gap has certainly widened rapidly. It increased in the late nineteenth century too, but it became markedly greater in the half-century after 1950 than in the half-century after 1870. Since welfare payments are relatively modest, the number of migrants in work is higher in the United States than in most European countries. This is an important difference. Nevertheless, in the classic countries of immigration, as in Europe, a fierce debate is going on and a desire for restrictions on new immigration dominates public opinion.

In the same period a polemic has developed in the United States concerning primarily Mexican immigrants, many of whom are in the country illegally. Attempts to introduce legislation that would give official residence status to its estimated 13 million illegals have so far failed. Opposition among the public at large to the rapid growth in the number of newcomers, which we shall look at in more detail later, shows that there is nothing natural about openness even in a 'nation of immigrants' such as America claims to be. On the contrary, at various points in its history campaigns against immigration have arisen and restrictive laws have been passed. We are now witnessing a fresh episode of this perpetually recurring opposition.

One obvious conclusion is that, generally speaking, there is a clear preference for well-educated migrants. No fewer than 40 per cent of today's immigrants to Canada have academic training, although many are working below their level of competence, since the qualifications they earned in their own countries are not recognized. A wry joke says that Toronto has the best-educated taxi drivers in the world. The incommensurability of diplomas is a problem in Europe too; if no adjustments are made, the talents of highly educated migrants will go to waste.

The decision to permit more immigration isn't just a means to financial gain, it's a matter of identity. The essential question in the end is whether Europeans want to develop according to the pattern of countries like the United States, Canada and Australia. If they choose that option, will they regard the result as an improvement to their societies? Canada and Australia, with their highly organized immigration policies – think of the points system – might serve as examples to Europe. The relatively liberal policy of America, which admits a large number of migrants every year without requiring them to meet particularly strict standards for entry, seems less attractive. We'll return to the question of whether continuing to admit a vast number of newcomers, with first-generation immigrants accounting for 15–20 per cent of the population, is economically and culturally beneficial.

Migration and Development

Now that we've weighed up the economic case for encouraging immigration, we can turn our attention to humanitarian arguments. Recognizing that, on balance, European societies have little to gain by the arrival of large numbers of low-skilled migrants from developing countries, many of those appealing for more freedom to migrate choose a different starting point. It's not what the receiving society needs that counts, they say. Instead, they argue for the opening of borders as a way to improve the lot of the migrant. In their view, allowing immigration is a form of development aid.

A pamphlet called *People Flow* lays out this line of reasoning: 'It seeks to manage the movement of people by taking their needs and purposes as a starting point.'[43] The argument is based on a recognition that migration is transforming Western societies, but the authors add matter-of-factly: 'We propose "simply" to take this loss and try to turn it into a gain by letting go of an identity that has escaped us anyway.'[44] Their approach has the great merit of presenting a clear choice. If the narrowing of the gulf between North and South brings with it a relocation of poverty and illiteracy, then that's something we just have to accept. A choice made on this basis amounts to the moralization of migration.

The confusing thing here is that the practical consequences of these decisions based on humanitarian motives are the same as those of taking the economic self-interest of the richer part of the world as a starting point. As we have seen, some say that a prosperous middle class can't do without an underclass of low-skilled migrants to provide menial services. Moral principles can easily merge with self-interest. Multiculturalism and market liberalism have a great deal in common in that they both seriously call into question the value of the social compromise within the borders of Western countries. This is something Legrain makes explicit with his call to 'let them in', addressed both to devotees of the free market on the right and to internationalists on the left of the political spectrum.[45] In the immigration debate, traditional political boundaries become blurred.

Aside from the desirability or otherwise of this option for developed nations, the question arises as to whether such an approach would in fact help poorer countries. Many uncertainties surround the link between development and migration. The argument that emigration from developing countries amounts to a brain drain should certainly be taken into account. It's a cause for concern, at the very least, when 1,200 South African nurses come to the Netherlands, apparently because the Dutch feel such work is beneath them, while those same nurses are sorely needed in their home country. Ex-President Nelson Mandela of South Africa has complained about the departure of medical personnel. Over 70 per cent of the best-qualified citizens of the Caribbean and 60 per cent in the case of Gambia work in the richer regions of the world. The same goes for a quarter of highly educated people from Ghana, which has six doctors per 100,000 inhabitants, whereas countries like Britain and Canada have around 220.[46]

Castles and Miller write about Egypt, which sees most of its emigrants leave for Saudi Arabia: 'Labour emigration undoubtedly relieved chronic unemployment, but it also stripped Egypt of much needed skilled workers.'[47] Qualifications aside, it's usually the more enterprising who have the courage to set out for an unknown destination, people whose energies might otherwise have benefited economic life in their own countries. Their departure may amount to a safety valve for social tensions – a large population of frustrated young people can cause great unrest – but migrants take away with them much of a country's willingness to reform.

On the other hand, money flows back from migrant communities to their countries of origin in the form of what are known as remittances. Officially registered payments of this type amounted to 126 billion dollars in 2004 and their true extent is no doubt far greater. Important recipient countries include India, at 23 billion dollars a year, Mexico, 17 billion, and the Philippines, at 8 billion. In the case of Lebanon, payments sent home by migrants are equivalent to the country's entire export income.[48] In 2008, 32 billion euros were transferred in the form of remittances from workers in the European Union, of which 9.3 billion remained within the Union, while 22.5 billion went beyond its boundaries.[49] So for the countries of origin, considerable financial interests are bound up with migration. By any measure, as a worldwide phenomenon remittances far exceed official development aid. In 2001, registered money transfers alone came to 2.6 times the total amount given in aid that year.[50]

British economist Nigel Harris regards these payments as representing a huge opportunity and he stresses that opposition to immigration increases inequality in the world: 'Immigration controls in the developed countries impose very heavy costs on the developing countries.'[51] He presents calculations showing that as a result of the emigration of 2 per cent of the workforce of developing countries, a sum of between 40 and 50 billion dollars flows back to them annually. His conclusion: 'Perhaps the greatest opportunity for the eradication of world poverty lies in opening up the labour markets of the developed countries to workers from the rest of the world.'[52]

So there's a great deal to be said for the notion that migration is a form of development aid and far more effective as such than the activities of governments and aid organizations, because the money reaches families directly rather than having to be distributed by expensive aid workers or corrupt governments. All the same, there are those who question whether remittances really contribute significantly to development in poorer countries. Some would claim that money received from relatives in distant countries is not productively invested but instead mainly goes on consumer goods. Others, though, have demonstrated that money sent back to the countries of origin leads to children staying on longer at school, since they aren't called upon to start work so soon to supplement the family's income.

The discussion about the desirability or otherwise of migration from developing countries rightly places the gap between North and South at the centre of attention. It's often said that inequality in the world has increased enormously in recent years. Australian philosopher Peter Singer presents evidence suggesting otherwise. He points to a reduction in the difference in buying power between the poorest 20 per cent and the richest 20 per cent of the world's population. He also looks at life expectancy in developing countries, which by the turn of this century had risen to over 80 per cent that of the industrialized world. In 1960 it was considerably lower, at only 60 per cent of life expectancy in Western countries.[53] Still, however we weigh up the inequalities in the world, it's clear that the pressure to migrate is considerable, especially in regions with large differences in income that border each other, such as Mexico and the United States, or Europe and North Africa. Closing borders to the majority of low-skilled migrants and their families does bring other obligations with it.

The main issue here is not development aid – of which the total amount spent has now fallen to around a quarter of one per cent of the gross domestic product of the rich countries. The West's main responsibility concerns trade policy. Serious thought should be given to the need to open up Western markets and to adjustments that could be made to the international division of labour. No one wishing to ease the constant pressure to admit migrants can ignore the need to reduce European trade barriers, so that prosperity can develop elsewhere in sectors such as agriculture. Europe's horticulture is currently sustained by artificial means in every sense, whereas all kinds of fruits, vegetables and flowers would flourish far more naturally under, for example, the North African sun. The World Trade Organization has reported that the richer countries subsidize their own agricultural products to the tune of at least a billion dollars a day, more than six times the amount they give in development aid to poor countries.

Allow the products to come here, so that the people can stay there. Unfortunately even this is not as straightforward as it sounds. Opening up Western markets will not reduce migration in the short term. There are few things economists agree on concerning the connection between migration and development, but none of them doubts that in its initial phase economic progress would in fact lead to more migration. It's rarely the poorest who emigrate; they lack the financial resources to do so. British philosopher Michael Dummett writes: '[T]he first result of a serious attempt to relieve [a] country's destitution may be to increase, not decrease, the number of those who leave it for more prosperous lands.'[54] After migration from the countryside to the city comes migration to Western countries. This is demonstrated by emigration from the Chinese coastal province of Fujian, which has increased enormously with the rapid economic development this region is now achieving.

In the longer term, however, development is bound to result in reduced levels of migration. We see this in the European Union, where freedom of movement has not led to huge waves of permanent migration, despite the fact that before it expanded eastwards, differences in income between member states were as high as 300 per cent. Migration isn't triggered by absolute differences in prosperity but, to a far greater extent, by the lack of prospects people perceive in their own countries. If they see signs of durable progress at home, then eventually they'll be less likely to feel the urge to leave, even if the gap between people in poorer countries and citizens of the Western world remains appreciable for the time being.

All too often, those who focus on the relationship between immigration and development try to add weight to the moral argument by conjuring up visions of an inescapable threat. They emphasize not so much the unfairness of the situation as the impossibility of putting a stop to the great migration that is now underway. They point to demographic data. In 1990 the total world population was around 5.3 billion and average estimates suggest it will reach 8.5 billion by 2025. A full 95 per cent of this growth will take place in what used to be called the third world. Developing countries are experiencing a truly enormous increase, while the developed world struggles with declining growth or even shrinking populations.

These contrasting developments could in theory be evened out by a stream of migration from South to North. Historian Paul Kennedy understands the objections to such a massive shift in population but suggests that 'the imbalances in demographic trends between "have" and "have not" societies' probably mean we will see huge waves of migration over the coming decades'.[55] He is convinced the population explosion will have far-reaching consequences for the environment, not just in the countries affected but in more prosperous nations as well. 'The environmental issue, like the threat of mass immigration, means that – perhaps for the first time – what the South does can hurt the North.'[56] Kennedy predicts that developed countries will find themselves 'under siege' by millions of migrants if developing nations remain in the poverty trap.[57]

French writer and former government adviser Jacques Attali subscribes to the same diagnosis. 'Mass immigration from Africa, coupled with the flood of hard-pressed Eastern Europeans into Western and more prosperous countries, will prompt the construction of a new Berlin Wall, one that prevents people on the periphery from seeking their fortune in the centres of the affluent North.'[58] If nothing is done, then wars and violence will scar the periphery of the rich world. This is an appeal to enlightened self-interest. Western countries will have to intervene to create a fairer relationship between North and South, since through migration the South can cause disruption in the rich world. In other words, migration flows have increased the interdependence of the world to such an extent that the North will have to pay attention to the problems of the South to some degree, simply in order to avoid a 'state of siege'.

Attali and others who present such threatening scenarios do so for understandable reasons. They want Western countries to take a hard look at their responsibilities, if not on ethical grounds then for their own good. The resentment now spreading through poor parts of the world can't be held at bay for ever. A combination of moral considerations and fear of social insurrection was once the motivation for a redistribution of wealth between rich and poor within European countries. Why should such a redistribution not be repeated on a global scale?

In reality there haven't yet been nearly as many opportunities for poorer countries to put rich countries under pressure as some people claim. In any case, experience in major world cities like New York and Rio de Janeiro shows that extreme social differences can exist side by side. If rich neighbourhoods can shield themselves from poor neighbourhoods that lie within walking distance, then the rich 'districts' in the 'global village' surely can too. Migration undoubtedly creates new forms of dependency between North and South, but the Western world has innumerable ways of defending itself against the disruption these writers predict. In other words, we must take seriously the moral questions thrown up by immigration and not simply rely on self-interest to produce the right outcome.

Threatening scenarios and predictions of a 'state of siege' won't make attitudes any more open. Citizens will merely dig in their heels even more. The whole world pours into our living-rooms through modern media, and as a result too much is asked of us. A torrent of bad news weighs on our consciences, obliging us to act even though the opportunities to do so are limited. The claims made upon us by a morality that chooses to see the world as a community of fate can easily tempt us to reject all sense of obligation.

It's far harder to extend the range of our responsibility permanently than to arouse fleeting sympathy. How can we promote a growing consciousness of our vulnerability that translates into openness rather than self-isolation? There is an obvious need for protection against undesirable waves of migration and at the same time for progress towards a fairer system of world trade. Driving back protectionism in agriculture will be painful and the same goes for the cancellation of debts entered into on clearly defined terms. But there's no other way, if we want to reconcile a cautious immigration policy with a growing responsibility for the world around us.

A Morality of Mobility

The central question is: how can an open society exist in a world without borders? At first sight, this seems puzzling. Surely the fewer borders there are and the greater each individual's freedom of movement, the more open a society becomes? In reality that openness cannot be taken for granted and the rise of movements brandishing slogans like 'our own people first' or 'close the borders' are an early indication of this. Such slogans lead into an impasse and can never serve as guidelines for dealing with migrants or refugees. They do, however, make a problem visible.

There are two conceivable threats to the open society. One is the risk that the movement of peoples will exceed its ability to adapt, both socially and culturally. There are limits to what existing populations can and will accept, no one should have any illusions about that. The other risk is that the means by which immigration is controlled will be incompatible with the basic principles of a liberal constitutional state. Nobody wants to live in a country where they come up against police surveillance, identity checks and strict border controls at every turn.

Will the West succeed in finding a viable compromise between humanitarian obligations and concern about the pressures caused by migration? It must begin by refusing to see globalization as a natural state of affairs. We often hear that resistance to certain outcomes of the world economy is as futile as opposition to the weather. By extension there's a tendency to think it's impossible to influence the movement of people: legal or illegal, migrants will keep coming to the rich centre of the world from its poor periphery. The facts don't support such reasoning. This more intimidating side to claims about globalization must be challenged.

There's a need for a morality of mobility. If no way can be found of dealing with those cast adrift by world disorder after they arrive in Western countries – refugees, wandering adventurers, reunited family members and illegally resident foreigners – then any pretence at promoting a more or less equitable state of affairs outside the borders of the world's richest countries will be regarded as a smokescreen. The norms the West holds out to the world will be plausible only if they're evident in the way its societies work. The reverse is not the case: more rigorous forms of equality can be achieved within those borders than could conceivably be brought into being outside them.

Today's migration flows do indeed raise important moral questions.

Here we'll limit ourselves to the following dilemmas. Should states be permitted to refuse entry to citizens of other countries who wish to emigrate? How will it ever be possible to determine who is truly a refugee? And should a blind eye be turned to illegal migration or should everything be done to prevent it? These are all questions that haunt Western countries and often lead people either to avert their eyes out of indifference or to lose themselves in moralizing pronouncements.

First, let's look at the arguments of those appealing for open borders as a matter of principle, such as Michael Dummett. He claims there's a glaring contradiction in international law. The universal declaration of human rights states that everyone has the right to leave his country and return to it. At the same time, nowhere is it laid down that a general obligation exists to take in people who have left their home countries, unless they qualify as refugees. In other words, the choice to emigrate is a universal human right, but it runs up against restrictive immigration policies that still fall under the heading of national sovereignty. Dummett concludes that sovereignty must give ground, that the burden of proof ought to lie with countries wishing to exclude migrants: 'The principle of open frontiers ought to be accepted as the norm: a norm from which deviation can be justified only in quite exceptional circumstances.'[59]

The idea behind this argument is that indigenous populations do not have any special rights as compared to newcomers. What are the grounds for a 'right of the firstborn'? Why should a country belong to its inhabitants? The heritage of past centuries is for everyone to use to his or her advantage. Why should those who happen to live in prosperous and peaceful nations be able to claim a special right to that heritage? Are we not all newcomers to the countries into which we're born? This is reminiscent of proposals made in the past to impose an inheritance tax of up to 100 per cent. Why should children have a right to the wealth their parents have accumulated? By a simple analogy, why should the indigenous have a right to the wealth earned by their distant ancestors?[60] Having a particular place of birth surely cannot have any moral significance, Dummett argues. But this conflicts with the idea that society is based in part on a contract between generations. It's no surprise to discover that those who appeal for open borders talk only of rights; anyone who's dismissive of a society's historical dimension will lack a sense of the obligations that flow from it.

Every community exists by grace of its borders. They can have varying degrees of openness, but it's impossible to do without demarcation of some kind between residents and outsiders. American philosopher Michael Walzer emphasizes this point: 'The distinctiveness of cultures and groups depends upon closure and, without it, cannot be conceived as a stable feature of human life.'[61] He adds that members of a political community have a collective right to determine who will or will not be allowed in. Nation-states are internally inclusive, but towards the outside world they are exclusionary, or at least they do not adhere to the principle of equal treatment. If they did, then everyone who wanted to enter would be allowed in.

If states were to abolish all distinctions between their own citizens and others, there might be far more random exclusion and protection at a lower level. Walzer speaks in this context of a 'thousand petty fortresses'.[62] The first intimations of such a world can be seen in the rapidly growing phenomenon of 'gated communities', walled-off housing estates with their own private security services. We see similar signs of withdrawal in the attitudes of cities like Rotterdam and Malmö, where in various ways attempts are being made to give shape to a municipal immigration policy – for example, by banning all immigration, or all low-skilled immigration, for five years – because people don't feel their national governments are protecting them adequately.

Open societies aspire to be faithful to the democratic principles inherent in the notion of a social contract. This puts them in a position to argue for selective immigration policies. Myron Weiner recognizes that 'there is often a conflict between the moral obligations of governments to ensure the safety and well-being of their own populations and a more universal ethic that values the well-being of all humankind, irrespective of where people live'.[63] But this doesn't mean it's in any way improper for governments to be concerned about the consequences for their own populations of the extent and nature of migration flows. Weiner adds: 'A lack of generosity is not the same as immorality.'[64]

So if we measure the ideal of open borders against democratic standards, there are good reasons for allowing a distinction to be made between established residents and newcomers. Policies limiting entry for those who are not citizens are morally justifiable. This is not to say that states have no binding obligations towards people beyond their borders at all. The refugee issue shows that people in the West do accept this responsibility, however difficult it may be in everyday practice.

Anyone trying to determine whether an individual qualifies for refugee status inevitably stirs up a hornets' nest. How can we ever judge with any confidence a story told by a refugee? Moreover, it's fair to ask whether the Refugee Convention of 1951, which in many respects was grafted onto concerns about human rights under communism, is now out of date. Why should only those persecuted by their own governments qualify as refugees and not people who fall victim to civil wars or natural catastrophes? Why for example is famine not seen as a legitimate reason to flee?

There's little eagerness to start a debate about the Refugee Convention.

Some fear a reassessment would lead to more restrictions on asylum-seekers, while others fear their opportunities might be increased. So the status quo remains in force, even though everyone can see that it's lost much of its validity in our own era. The way it works now comes down to saying that everyone who manages to get into a more prosperous country – whether with the aid of people smugglers or not – and stand on his or her own two feet there for a while has a good chance of eventually being given official leave to remain. There's usually great reluctance to deport failed asylum-seekers. The preferred solution is to make the whole drama as invisible as possible by either turning people back at the border or deciding almost instantly whether or not they'll be allowed to apply for asylum.

Another dilemma arises from the fact that countries with a tendency to accept refugees may become accessories to oppression elsewhere. The support offered to refugees from Kosovo helped the Serbs in their efforts to drive out the Albanians. In the early 1990s Sadako Ogata, High Commissioner for Refugees, posed the following question: 'To what extent do we persuade people to remain where they are, when that could well jeopardize their lives and liberties? On the other hand, if we help them move, do we not become an accomplice to "ethnic cleansing"?'[65]

After a rise in the number of refugees in the 1990s, European policy became, generally speaking, more restrictive. In 1996 Canada granted refugee status to around 80 per cent of asylum-seekers from Sri Lanka, whereas in the same year Britain accepted hardly any applications for asylum from nationals of that country, despite basing its decisions on the same Refugee Convention.[66] European countries, and Australia too, have introduced countless measures aimed at stemming the flow of refugees. In Australia asylum-seekers were interned in appalling conditions in far-flung Woomera, and in August 2001 the government's stringent policy led to a refusal to allow the Tampa, a ship full of refugees, to moor at the coast. In response to international protests, the Australian government hurriedly reached an agreement with Papua New Guinea, which consented to take the stranded refugees in return for payment.

The humanitarian questions thrown up by the right to asylum are extremely problematic. If refugees are allowed to go through an often slow and lengthy procedure and spend years in reception centres, in many cases along with their families, then it becomes increasingly difficult to remove unsuccessful applicants from the community and send them back. There's an ethical dilemma here, since the more carefully the authorities weigh up whether or not to allow someone to stay, the smaller the chance they'll actually be removed from the country if the decision goes against them. Asylum policies turn refugees into illegals, with all the attendant consequences.

One telling example was the situation that arose in the Netherlands when the government tried to expel unsuccessful asylum-seekers from the country. There was widespread opposition. A campaign called '26,000 Faces' attempted to bring the refugees out of the shadows by depicting them as individuals. To take one example: 'Hazrat will be nine in two months from now. For as long as he can remember he's lived in centres for asylum-seekers. When he was three his parents fled the Taliban in Afghanistan. His entire family is now in the Netherlands. His grandparents and two uncles have refugee status but Hazrat's father does not.' The request for asylum was declined and the family ordered to leave the country: 'Hazrat is in year five at a Christian primary school and he prays every day. "I ask God to let me stay." He demonstrates how he prays, as a Muslim, his little hands open. "I never ask for anything else."'[67] Confronted by so many human tragedies, the next Dutch government to be elected eventually introduced an amnesty. The problem, however, is that every legislative change renders up new exemptions and raises the prospect that at any moment a fresh amnesty might be announced.

Finally, we need to look at the issue of illegal immigration. Its extent is of course hard to determine, but the number of applicants when amnesties are declared gives us some idea. In 1986 America offered illegals the opportunity to apply for residence permits. Almost three million people seized their chance, the majority of them Mexicans. This initiative did nothing to reduce the number of illegal residents. On the contrary, after the general amnesty far more migrants without permits arrived than before. The number is now estimated at 12–13 million.

In 1987 and 1998 Italy gave legal residence status to a total of 800,000 illegal immigrants. In 2004 Spain made a similar move and 700,000 people applied. In total, the number of illegal immigrants living in Europe is somewhere around eight million, and rough estimates suggest that between 500,000 and 800,000 are added to this figure annually. We are therefore talking about a considerable number of people. Partly because of the influx of illegals, the nations of Southern Europe, once a source of migrants, have become countries of immigration since the 1980s. In the case of Spain, the illegals are mainly from Latin America and they have fewer problems adjusting than other immigrant groups, since they already speak the language. But when a mass amnesty led to a huge influx of African illegals via the Canary Islands, the government became wary of too lenient a stance towards migrants without residence permits.

Some people believe that a generous attitude towards migrant workers will help to prevent illegal migration. The underlying idea here is that legal and illegal immigration are in some sense communicating vessels: when one column rises the other falls. But what does the enrolment of a computer expert from India have to do with a decision by someone from Senegal to cross the Straits of Gibraltar in a leaky boat? What does the recruitment of low-skilled migrants have to do with the people-smuggling that led to the death by suffocation of 58 Chinese illegals in the back of a lorry? Not much, as demonstrated by the ultimate country of immigration, America, which has a relatively liberal immigration policy and, as we've seen, a great many illegal immigrants.

Illegals have become commodities. The journey made by a woman called Quiru Liao has become typical of the kind of people-smuggling organized in China by criminal go-betweens with the revealing name of 'snakeheads'. 'For reasons that ultimately she alone knows, she borrows the money for the journey (150,000 yuan, well over €14,000) from the boss of a clothing factory whom she knows well. She pays half the cost of the voyage to snakeheads she found through local fishermen. In the harbour at Guangzhou she hides in the belly of a freighter. She spends four weeks at sea. The only place she's aware of the ship stopping during the voyage is Shanghai. One day the ship docks at Rotterdam. There, the smuggler says, pointing north, is Chinatown. She starts to walk It's the first time in her life that she's been outside Guangdong.'68 Quiru Liao is one of many millions of illegals and the reception they're given is lukewarm.

Governments are wavering uncertainly between the extremes of a general amnesty and a large-scale expulsion of illegals. This hesitancy is motivated far less by moral considerations than it might appear Everyone knows that illegals are extremely vulnerable; they can easily become trapped in a criminal milieu. One researcher has been seduced into calling this 'survival-criminality'. Quite apart from a reluctance to excuse crime in this way, there can be no justification for allowing illegality to flourish. Ultimately, that would be an attitude of 'let them rot in privacy', a decision to look the other way as long as they don't bother us. If we don't want to insist that the law must be enforced – and that certainly seems to be the position in most countries – then the only way out is to introduce general amnesties for illegal immigrants periodically One serious disadvantage of this is that it tends to encourage rather than deter people smuggling.

America clearly exemplifies the problematic nature of general amnesties. In the mid-1980s it reached a compromise: a 1986 law granted legal residence status to illegal immigrants while at the same time introducing tougher sanctions against employers who used the services of illegals. In practice, the second part of the legislation was not implemented, since the interests of agriculture in the south, for example, meant sanctions were resisted. Here again we see a marriage of convenience between those who want to leave illegals in peace for humanitarian reasons and employers acting out of blatant self-interest, no longer able to manage without labourers who will work for a pittance and who have no rights.

We could say the same of France, for example, where there's an obvious unwillingness to punish firms that employ illegal immigrants. Historian Patrick Weil writes that in the 1980s the authorities knew the whereabouts of illegal sweatshops in the textile trade, but the police and the labour inspectorate didn't intervene. 'They could therefore have been dismantled, but that did not happen, because there was a consensus among the various stakeholders that the law should not be applied.'[69] A blind eye is turned to illegality because it works as a lubricant, easing friction in the jobs market. The solution chosen in France consists not of a general amnesty but of individual amnesties that can be given to thousands of people a year without attracting attention, thereby avoiding serious political controversy.

Something essential is at stake here. The third world has been set adrift and it's anchoring itself to the first world. We can't hope to succeed in bridging the gulf between North and South to such an extent that the desire to migrate will decline in the near future, and perhaps migration can't be reduced in any other way either, primarily because the political will is lacking. Were the movement of peoples to prove uncontrollable, then it would be fairly safe to assume that disorder around the world would cause serious polarization in Western societies. This might then place a permanent strain on democracy.

The Citizens' Revolt

In recent years the Dutch have seen how the immigration impasse can lead to severe political shocks. It could be argued that this is simply a sign that the country has moved closer to the majority of its neighbours and is starting to look more like the European average. Denmark, Belgium, Switzerland, Norway and Austria are all relatively small countries in which populist parties have gained the support of a considerable proportion of voters over the past few years. But in larger countries too, including Italy and France, we've seen a similarly rapid growth in aversion to the established parties.

Political scientist Pippa Norris has investigated support for these parties across the Western world and she sums up the motives involved. First of all there's a fear of a loss of social status among vulnerable groups such as small-scale entrepreneurs, indeed even among low-skilled workers. Yet the habit of seeing these voters as losers in the process of globalization is no longer convincing. The better-off middle classes too have cast a large number of votes for parties with a populist message.[70]

Motives other than an awareness of occupying a weak position in society must therefore be important in prompting people to vote for parties like Vlaams Belang in Belgium and the Front National in France. These voters turn out to have less faith than average in the functioning of representative democracy, but Norris warns against interpreting this as purely a product of resentment. Their far from positive attitudes to the political system may be a result of unwillingness among the established parties to take account of their wishes. She points to another motive too, namely a perceived need to protect the home culture, the decisive factor being a dislike of mass immigration and the policies of multiculturalism that go with it. There's no straightforward connection between the number of migrants and the size of the populist vote, but it's clear that cultural 'protectionism' weighs even more heavily than a fear of sliding down the social scale.

Comparative research confirms that today's unease about democracy flows from a cultural rather than a social fault-line, although the two are of course related. It's surely food for thought that in a fairly relaxed and open society like the Netherlands, a citizens' revolt was able to spread so rapidly. After many years of economic prosperity, too. Within a few months, during the elections of 2002, a single politician with a programme opposing further immigration and favouring measures to strengthen public order became the second largest political force in the country. No one can say how far Pim Fortuyn might have got if he hadn't been stopped in his tracks by a violent act. Perhaps the novelty would soon have worn off, but as someone remarked: after such a death the novelty never will wear off.

This reversal in voter preferences demonstrates first of all the self-correcting potential of an open political system. Before loudly condemning these new movements, we would do well to understand their vitality as a democratic force. As Europeans come face to face with the frictions in society associated with large-scale migration, it would be more useful to interpret the rise of politicians such as Dewinter, Haider, Blocher and Le Pen as an invitation to critical self-examination.

There's no doubt these events are an illustration of how democracy is able to produce its own correctives, and that's a reassuring thought, but perhaps there's more going on here. Perhaps democracy is truly in danger in these times of globalization. In a succinct and uncompromising essay on 'the end of democracy', French writer and diplomat Jean-Marie Guéhenno explains the deeper background to the uncertainty: 'The year 1989 marks the end of the era of the nation-state.'[71] Since that year of revolutions, the market economy has been able to move ahead without restraint and it's clear to everyone that national governments and with them the grip that parliaments have on growing economic interdependence are weakening.

Why does the slow death of the nation-state mean the end of democracy as we know it? Guéhenno indisputably touches the core of the matter when he remarks that until now all forms of representation of the people have been tied to a clearly defined territorial base. In other words, democratic institutions are grounded in specific places. The logical consequence of globalization is that 'the solidarity of communities, which relies upon a shared territory, disappears and in its place temporary groupings emerge based on shared interests'. We are moving step by step into a 'post-political' world, he says, in which democracy falls away and is replaced by non-transparent networks that reach far beyond national borders.[72]

Against Guéhenno's vision of doom, it could be argued that he over-states the radical novelty of economic globalization, that in abruptly announcing the end of the nation-state he goes too far. But the increasing problems states are encountering in keeping order are part of a discernable trend. It's extraordinarily difficult to get a grip on the global problems that arise out of a combination of the population explosion, the destruction of the natural environment, the gap between rich and poor and the migration flows that result. This has provoked a hostile reaction in many liberal democracies.

A book by Filip Dewinter gives readers an idea of the thinking that goes on within a Flemish political movement called, at the time he was writing, the Vlaams Blok, and since renamed, after a politically motivated ban by the courts, Vlaams Belang. He appeals above all for a right to self-determination. Sustained migration, more than anything else, Dewinter writes, is at odds with the 'cultural individuality and identity' of Flanders – an extremely sensitive issue in itself, given the long domination of Belgium by its other, French-speaking region. 'After 170 years of the Flemish Movement, after more than a century and a half of the struggle for cultural emancipation, the essence of our nation is under threat once more.'[73]

A substantial proportion of the book is taken up by a sober assessment of the costs and benefits of recent immigration. The main difference between Dewinter's view and the beliefs of the parties at the political centre lies in his interpretation of cultural differences, which Dewinter, brandishing among other things the views of Samuel Huntington on the 'clash of civilizations', sees as unbridgeable. In his emphasis on cultural identity he is consistent: 'Foreigners continue to organize themselves as if still living in their countries of origin. From a human viewpoint this is understandable. People have their own identities and they want to preserve them.'[74]

The Belgian experience offers a clear lesson, he says: 'How can we expect to establish a multicultural society here with people and cultures from all over the world, when at the same time we are forced to conclude that not even the bicultural society of Flemings and Walloons can be run according to the normal democratic rules of the game?'[75] Dewinter claims the history of Flanders teaches us that societies with more than one culture will always produce a struggle for power: 'The French-speakers have tried to dominate and even to eliminate the Dutch language and the Flemish cultural heritage.'[76] Paradoxically, that traumatic experience is the key to his politics of integration. The foreigners in Flanders must be faced with a choice: 'assimilation or return'.[77] In his judgement, that is the only means the nation-state has of asserting its right to self-determination in the face of a growing number of migrants: 'The way in which nationality is hollowed out to become a free scrap of paper, the leniency with which the demands [sic] of illegals are met, the lack of the political will to tackle criminality among foreigners, the even greater lack of will and/or fear when it comes to defending the external borders of Europe: each and every one of these is symptomatic of a crisis of civilization.'[78]

To this populist challenge, which has been asserting itself since the 1990s, European elites have reacted with uncertainty, at first unable to think of any better solution than to declare these parties beyond the pale on grounds of racism. That was not a success. Subsequently, in countries including the Netherlands and Austria, there has been a decision to draw such parties into government, with the responsibility that entails, while in Flanders a *cordon sanitaire* was placed around the Vlaams Blok and in France around the Front National.

The same uncertainty can be seen in the work of Flemish commentator Manu Claeys. He is aware that the absorption of such a large number of migrants remains 'an experiment' and he has recommended among other things that 'citizenship must be sought halfway between the soul of the nation and the foreign culture'.[79] What exactly this would look like we are not told. He is clear about the Vlaams Blok, however. He advocates a ban on the party: 'Politicians should not flinch from admitting that a prosecution of a party of the extreme right is a political prosecution, since it is in the interests of society as a whole, even if it does confer martyrdom upon that party.'[80] This is the dilemma that has held Flanders in its grip for some 20 years. In that sense it is not alone.

The fact that immigration has become a major issue in the Western world is perfectly understandable. The image of a human migration that no one can stop has come to represent a worldwide disorder that is creeping closer and closer, creating division in a relatively harmonious society. If, as research suggests, a majority of citizens in the European Union are of the opinion that the limit to how many migrants their part of the world can absorb has been reached, then this amounts to more than simply saying 'no' to asylum-seekers, or to labour migrants, or to those seeking to build or reunite families. More profound feelings of insecurity and unease are being expressed, and they need to be taken seriously.

This has not happened enough. The democratic debate has always rendered up majorities reluctant to agree to large-scale immigration, but at the same time the outcome of the process of political compromise has often failed to reflect the majority view. According to Joppke, this is because the costs of immigration, such as downward pressure on wages or investment in remedial language teaching, are shifted onto society as a whole, while the benefits of immigration, such as cheap labour or the reuniting of families, accrue to specific groups. The clientism of immigration politics leads to a growth in immigration. Most of the rights that migrants now have were accorded to them not in the open arena of democracy but after agreement behind the closed doors of ministerial bureaucracy, or as a result of court decisions. This democratic deficit is provoking opposition.

Rapid demographic change in many Western European societies has caused a sense of alienation that can easily be exploited. In the past 10 years we have seen this happening all over Europe, and in Australia, for example. In his *All for Australia*, Geoffrey Blainey, the Australian historian mentioned earlier, criticized the taboo on the debate about the advantages and disadvantages of Asian migration to his country: 'The social tension does not stem primarily from the controversy. The social tension arises from an immigration programme that ignores public opinion.'[81] As a result, tolerance, which had actually increased after racial criteria were dropped from immigration policy, was being endangered: 'People are therefore entitled to inquire whether the distinctive character of their nation will remain if people from very different cultures are encouraged to come and, as far as possible, to maintain their own cultures.'[82]

Thinking about immigration and asylum is influenced far too much by the notion that it's uncontrollable. This self-declared powerlessness has far-reaching consequences for democratic culture. Anyone who pronounces himself no longer competent in such a vital area undermines the notion of citizenship. If people regard it as impossible any longer to have control over something as essential as the question of who should be allowed to stay in the country and who should not, then a call to 'close the borders' will never be far away. Such slogans lead nowhere, and they demonstrate the impasse that has grown up around immigration. The unspoken promise is that if only the authorities can be strict enough, the streets will again look the way they used to. This points back to a time when the presence of guest workers was easy to ignore. The fact that migrant workers suddenly had families and wanted to stay is something those who cling to a desire to 'close the borders' have not fully taken on board.

Europe is now a common market that allows freedom of movement. This increased freedom has brought new security problems with it. After the abolition of internal borders, the pressing questions Europeans are asking themselves now are: how can they protect their shared external borders? How can they combat cross-border criminality and terrorism in a Europe where everyone can more or less move around freely? And how can they prevent countries like Spain, Italy, Greece and Poland from becoming transit ports for illegal immigration? Each country currently pursues its own policy. Whereas in the Netherlands the government made a huge effort over several years to expel several thousand failed asylum-seekers – an attempt that was finally abandoned for reasons of both principle and practicality – Spain has unilaterally decided to grant residence permits to 700,000 illegals.

A consciousness is growing that now its internal borders have been abolished, patrolling the external borders is of crucial importance. Resistance to this is fairly strong, since border controls are still seen as the responsibility of individual nations. In 2005 an organization called Frontex was established, whose purpose is the 'coordination of intelligence driven operational cooperation at EU level to strengthen security at external borders'. The long-winded mission statement is not entirely reassuring, and it demonstrates what a loaded issue this is. Such worries add to the problems of legitimacy affecting the European Union, which is seen by many of its citizens, especially after its recent expansion, as a source of insecurity rather than protection.

The challenge Europe faces now is to defend its borders while remaining conscious of being part of a wider reality. Immigration is a continual reminder of poverty and deprivation in the wider world that can easily make unwelcome demands upon Europeans. How can they reconcile their responsibility for their own societies with the growing interdependence of the world? The way migration is dealt with is becoming a test of the resilience of democracy in an era of globalization.

4

The Netherlands: A Culture of Avoidance

As Others See Us

A society's reaction to the arrival of migrants reveals its strengths and weaknesses. In the case of the Netherlands, fierce clashes of opinion about newcomers over the past decade contrast with a pragmatic tradition of give and take. In fact its peaceful history is the country's most inviting feature; violent conflicts within its borders can be counted on the fingers of one hand. The Dutch have a talent for mediation and compromise.

This pursuit of pacification has a long history. From its founding in 1588, the Dutch Republic's regents succeeded in maintaining social peace without amassing all power at the centre or persecuting religious minorities – and this at a time when absolutist monarchies and religious conflict were setting the tone in Europe. The Republic was exceptional in many respects and contemporaries saw it as such. Numerous thinkers who suffered censorship in their own countries, including John Locke and Pierre Bayle, worked or published in Holland.

A connection is often made between this tradition of consultation and the battle with rising floodwaters. The Dutch had to cooperate or drown. Indeed, their earliest systems of democratic government grew out of the fourteenth- and fifteenth-century water boards. This was once called 'the democracy of wet feet'. The Dutch later came to describe their form of consultative democracy as the 'polder model' and if there is indeed such a model, then its origins lie in the bodies set up to control water levels. Increasing mastery of water led to a powerful sense that the world was malleable and could be regulated, a feeling reflected in the famously admiring comment 'God made the world but the Dutch made Holland'.

Dutch society has a great ability to blunt sharp edges. The desire to avoid conflict is undeniable, but the shadow side to this attitude generally escapes attention: the avoidance of conflict can all too easily lead to avoidance of a more general kind. The Netherlands lacks a culture of debate, whether in parliament, academic life or literature, since the life of the mind is permeated by that same sense of give and take. This has turned out to be a weakness in dealing with immigration.

Historian Ernest Kossmann once tried to define the nation-state. The nation, he said, is 'the continuous conversation we have with each other in our own language'.[1] But how can any conversation take off in a country that, in his words, is continually seeking a 'middle way'? The Netherlands is far less easy-going than many people think; in fact it's a relatively conformist country.

This became obvious in the 1960s. After 10 years of social conflict, the new norms were accepted to such an extent that many critics felt they had no option but to sit things out until events proved them right. Conservatives stood on the sidelines and there was no open debate. Those who thought differently were denounced or ignored. One of the country's most important post-war novelists, Willem Frederik Hermans, who had violated the cultural boycott of South Africa, was given to understand by the mayor of Amsterdam that he was no longer welcome in the capital. For a long time Dutch conformism was difficult to identify as such, since it presented itself to the world as free-and-easy liberalism. American historian James Kennedy has expressed his astonishment at this radical turnaround in the climate of opinion, which he explains as evidence of a desire for consensus. When broadly held attitudes are overturned, a large majority will fairly quickly fall into line. It happened in the 1960s and the same pattern can be discerned in the early years of this century. Open debate, with different ideas going head to head, is therefore remarkably rare: 'In such a culture opposing visions are not played off against each other, they follow one after the next.'[2]

The view of a relative outsider like Kennedy is revealing. The Dutch have a saying that translates literally as 'strange eyes compel', meaning that it sometimes takes a fresh pair of eyes to put things into perspective. An open society must be able to take on board critical or astonished observations by others. We often hear positive remarks about a tolerant country with a liberal drugs policy and an annual Gay Parade along its capital city's main canals, but a good many books have been published in recent years that present a contrary view. Their tone is by no means always flattering, as some of their titles demonstrate: *Het verdriet van Nederland* [The sorrow of the Netherlands], *Een vis verdrinken* [Drowning a fish], *Een land om bij te huilen* [A country to weep over].

For too long the Dutch have wallowed in their own tolerance when they ought to have listened rather more closely to critical comments like these. Some observations come up time and again, and a discussion has arisen about what's referred to as the 'moral geography' of the Netherlands. Many writers have addressed one question in particular: what is the effect on Dutch customs and mores of the concentration of a large number of people on such a small area of land?

Take a description of the country by French journalist Christian Chartier: 'The Netherlands is an astonishing accumulation of trifles, which have the subtle charm of a neatly maintained doll's house but at the same time explain why this country sometimes gives the impression of being rather restrictive.'[3] That image of an immaculate, somewhat scaled-down place is universally shared. So much so that one nineteenth-century traveller exclaimed in despair: 'There is bound to come a day when the foreigner travelling through the Netherlands suddenly feels an irresistible need for something tall, at which he can look up, for bends, across which his eyes can jump and wander, for forms that can inspire the imagination.'[4]

The rectilinear and uniform nature of the country strikes the visitor immediately and seems to characterize not only the exterior of the Netherlands but its interior life as well. All those asides about the flatness of the place. How strong is the urge for freedom, in fact, in a country that values consensus so highly? Chartier tries to unscramble the contradiction: 'Might this be the secret key to the Dutch ant heap? The herd mentality silently dictates behaviour and the tribesmen, despite liking to see themselves as anarcho-individualists, do nothing that could threaten the general unity.'[5]

The Netherlands is engaged in a perpetual quest for moderation. Extremes don't take root, as Anil Ramdas observes: 'The bourgeois mentality tolerates neither extremism nor eccentricity.' But Dutch moderation has contradictory results: 'It explains the paradoxical situation in which fanatical racists in the Netherlands have just as much difficulty penetrating the realm of middle-class culture as foreigners with non-standard cultural customs. Racists and foreigners alike deviate from the norm, from all that is ordinary, decent and fitting.'[6]

Precisely because of this tendency towards the mean, the much-praised tolerance of the Dutch has its limits, and we often encounter aspects of the country that call it into question. British cultural historian Simon Schama describes the 'mass devotion to purity' in the Dutch Republic: 'To throw a dead cat in the canal, to harbor an illegal immigrant, or to neglect one's duty of washing the pavement were all tantamount to delinquency – as if one had opened the gates to an army of infected marauders. Conversely, to be clean was to be patriotic, vigilant in the defense of one's homeland, hometown and home against invading polluters and polluted invaders.'[7]

Many observers have been struck by this reticence in the face of everything that comes from abroad. Portuguese author Rentes de Carvalho was extraordinarily bitter in his comments: 'But nothing, no one, no information at all will be strong enough to drive back the pernicious sense of superiority the Dutch person assumes as soon as he comes into contact with a foreigner who has the misfortune to have been born in one of those countries where the sun is the greatest source of income and who does not go about the place as a tourist.'[8] The Dutch are far less accommodating than they think they are. In daily life foreigners experience considerable pressure to assimilate.

Belgian writer Geert van Istendael issues a paradoxical declaration of love for his country: 'I love Belgium because it has none of the Dutch arrogance, self-satisfaction, tactlessness, aggression and blank incomprehension of everything beyond its own borders.'[9] This touches on an important failing. The self-image of a country that thinks of itself as having no borders often masks a lack of interest in what is actually happening abroad. Only those who know where the boundaries lie can try to reach beyond them. Another Belgian, Eric de Kuyper, who has lived in the Netherlands for many years, keeps bumping up against this concealed haughtiness too, in his own way: 'If I tell my non-Dutch friends the Dutch premier lives in an ordinary terraced house they don't get it. "How arrogant," they say. "What a display of false modesty!".'[10]

The Dutch spent many years convincing themselves that theirs is an easy-going country. They were not alone. The image of a tolerant Holland was often adopted wholesale abroad. All this has been called into question in recent years. Two political murders and the reactions to them have shattered a cherished illusion about the Netherlands in the rest of the world. Headlines like 'Hatred engulfs a liberal land' (*The Times*) and '*Haines raciales en terre de tolérances*' [Racial hatreds in a land of tolerance] (*Libération*)[11] heralded the end of a distinctly superficial reputation. In foreign coverage of those dramatic events, schadenfreude and fear jostled for precedence. People had often been annoyed by the pride of the Dutch and now that perpetually raised finger stuck in their throats. Magdi Allam, deputy chief editor of the Italian newspaper *Corriere della Sera*, who is Egyptian by birth, came to a devastating conclusion: 'Everyone now agrees that indifference camouflaged by tolerance has breathed new life into the colonial apartheid regime, based on the separation of races, in the heart of the motherland.'[12]

There were many who tried, as he did, to look behind the façade of Dutch society and who retrospectively shook off an excessively idealistic view of the Netherlands. The disillusionment, if nothing else, was clear. The recurring question concerned the meaning of tolerance. How could it have tipped over into indifference like this? British historian Jonathan

Israel offered a caustic diagnosis of the Dutch malaise. It wasn't so much the fundamentalists who presented a challenge to the country, he said; rather, it was the social elite, which had committed 'cultural suicide'. Having blatantly neglected its history, that elite had no right to complain about 'the sudden rise of a new barbarism and fanaticism'.[13]

The speed with which the established image of the Netherlands was overturned was remarkable. Further examples of intolerance followed in quick succession. The issue of whether or not Ayaan Hirsi Ali, a critic of Islam, should have her passport withdrawn was seen exclusively in that light. Author Mario Vargas Llosa, for example, denounced the way the government had acted: 'With the same clarity with which on other occasions I have applauded Holland for the reforms it has pioneered – euthanasia, de-criminalization of drugs, gay marriage – I now declare my disappointment at this shameful surrender on the part of government and public opinion in a democratic country against the blackmail of terrorist fanaticism. In recent times, moral courage and civic integrity seem to be sharply on the wane in the land of tulips.'[14] This view has stuck and today's commentators are mainly interested in confirming it, just as they once served up any example of unbounded tolerance they could find.

Over the past few years the failure of the Dutch 'model' has been postulated time and again. In France and Britain especially, events in the Netherlands were seen above all as confirming those countries' own beliefs about integration. Yet unease about the murder of Theo van Gogh remained. If even the Dutch, with their long tradition of moderation, had not found a way to get along with migrants, what hope was there for countries whose histories were far more deeply marked by conflict? This undertone came through particularly clearly in much of the German and Italian coverage, but it could be heard in other countries as well. As a German politician put it: 'The Netherlands is everywhere.' Whatever was happening among the Dutch, it should clearly be of concern to everyone.

Migration and Nation-Building

The Dutch for their part need to confront the image outsiders have of their country. In fact, they've no choice, now that so many new questions have been raised by the arrival of immigrants. Self-examination, embodied in the question 'Who are we now?', has become unavoidable. This in itself entails change, since for a long time that question was answered with a shrug. The Dutch always claimed, with apparent modesty, that they were unusual in not having an inflated view of themselves – but they sure did show off a lot about their aversion to showing off.

Meanwhile it's become clear that the denial of their own national identity was a cunning way of acting as a model for other countries to follow. After all, Holland was not like other nations, which tie themselves in knots worrying about who they are or, even worse, show insouciant pride in their heritage. There's a telling example of this attitude in an article by Kossmann: 'Why would we need to use pompous terms like national identity, heritage, mentality? A country like ours has no use for such rhetoric.'[15]

The stance of an elite that dislikes making things too explicit is understandable, since everyone knows that in a solid self-image lies the beginning of dogmatism. An emphasis on history can quickly become prescriptive; settling upon a national identity is often the easiest way of excluding certain groups. Long experience with conflict avoidance lies behind this resistance to words like 'heritage' and 'identity', but Kossmann's rejection of such notions is at the same time a sign of self-conceit: we don't need bombastic language; others apparently do.

None of this arose by chance. It's a result of the country's generally peaceful history. True, the turbulence that lasted for almost half a century between 1795 and 1830, from the Batavian Republic to the Belgian Revolt, was no small matter, and the German occupation and the loss of the Dutch East Indies both had a deep impact as well. A postwar slogan ran: '*Indië verloren, rampspoed geboren*' (roughly: the Indies' loss will bring forth chaos). Yet arguably the history of the Netherlands has taken a relatively harmonious course ever since it was recognized as an independent nation in 1648. It has generally been a haven in stormy surroundings. The Netherlands is one of the few countries in the world with undisputed borders. There are no minorities inside or outside its territory to call them into question, no independence movements like those of the Basques in Spain or the Flemings in Belgium, and no oppressed fellow-countrymen abroad comparable to the Hungarians in Romania or the Albanians in Kosovo. It is a 'satisfied nation' with little understanding for countries that suffer from far greater internal tensions. Dutch people are no different from anyone else, but the conditions that have created the Netherlands are different, which is to say they are generally favourable.

History therefore explains a great deal about this relaxed self-image, one that can easily topple over into self-delusion. A useful measure of the prevailing attitude is the way the Dutch treat their own language. In the early twentieth century, author Carry van Bruggen wrote in jest: 'There is nothing distressing or disconcerting about the thought that in a century or two Dutch will no longer be spoken. We haven't used towing barges or built step gables for a long time either. The attachment of the Dutchman to his language is of an order no higher than that of the Volendammer to his baggy trousers.' If Van Bruggen had been right, the Dutch would now have difficulty reading her prediction without an English translation.

There's a long tradition of such comments: 'What's so special about this language of ours?' Another example of an apparently open attitude is an essay by anthropologist Peter van der Veer called *'Nederland bestaat niet meer'* [The Netherlands no longer exists]. In his breezy polemic, he addresses the claim that Dutch culture has been absorbed into a transnational entity. A typical sentence runs: 'My prediction is that Dutch will meet the same fate as the Groningen speech of my youth – it will become a sentimental dialect.'[16] To him, the acceptance of English as a medium of communication looks like progress, since compared to the vast body of Anglo-Saxon writing, Dutch literature doesn't amount to much.

Despite these dismissive remarks, there is strength to be drawn from the combination of particularism and openness. About the advantages of having a distinct national language, Johan Huizinga wrote: 'It may hamper us in getting what we say across to the world, but it keeps us impartial, gives us our own mirror in which to capture an image of that which is foreign.'[17] We might debate just how impartial the Netherlands was or is, but there's a kernel of truth in what he writes, which comes close to saying that the nation amounts to a continuous conversation in your own language.

Downplaying the importance of a national language can easily spill over into a form of exclusion. What does such an attitude mean for the Dutch literature arising from migration? It's true that all important literature is world literature in the sense that authors have always borrowed from each other across borders, but anyone who's dismissive of his own language isn't going to bother finding out what questions are being asked by new writers about the prevailing self-image. Continental Europeans should be grateful to all those newcomers who have taken the trouble to add something to their literatures, to all those who have not decided they ought to concentrate on writing in English.

This self-negation has had perverse consequences, even for those it was intended to serve. Time and again people were told: it's not particularly important for migrants to learn to speak Dutch. In fact, education in their own language and culture was promoted, often with the argument that it would make learning a second language easier. There's nothing wrong with bilingualism – on the contrary, multilingualism is a vehicle of civilization – but in reality many migrants and especially their children command only half a language, being fully at home neither in the language of their country of origin nor in that of the place where they live. Whether or not they really become better at learning Dutch once they're fluent in their parents' language is an open question.

A lack of command of the official language makes entry into public life difficult. Languages involve conventions and manners, emotional nuances and references to the past. A person who doesn't speak the language well can't take a full part in society as a citizen. Many struggle with this handicap, which can be blamed in part on the nonchalant attitude of many Dutch people towards their mother tongue. French-Dutch commentator Sylvain Ephimenco had this in mind when he wrote: 'It is indeed hard to expect of newcomers that they will emulate with enthusiasm an indigenous population that enthusiastically repudiates its own identity.'[18] One telling example is a remark that appeared in the Dutch press a few years ago: 'Surely you're not going to bother Turkish children with the years '40–'45?' This casual attitude to history does nothing to help migrants become discerning citizens.

The self-image of a community of world citizens can be found in the work of countless academics who assume that the era of nation-states lies behind us. Yet although the media bring events from all over the world into our living-rooms every day, the majority of citizens still live in cultures that have developed in the context of nation-states. British anthropologist Ernest Gellner concludes soberly: 'For the average person, the limits of his culture are, if not quite the limits of the world, at any rate the limits of his employability, social acceptability, dignity, effective participation and citizenship.'[19]

For as long as the nation-state demarcates citizenship, we would do well to take proper care of existing institutions. Involvement in a society means understanding that something came before us and something will come after us. This too requires people to put themselves into perspective, but in a way that demonstrates genuine modesty by acknowledging they're part of an ongoing history.

That shared history ultimately creates a specific way of living together, which is not set in stone but subject to amendment by new religious groups or social strata. We need only look at Catholic emancipation or the rise of the Dutch working class. The same goes for migrants, who will undoubtedly help to shape the Netherlands as a nation, just as past newcomers influenced the self-image of Dutch society. European nations are now being invited to re-examine themselves. This creates uncertainty, yet the need to ask 'who are we?' can be felt all across the continent. That quest for a new 'us' – which applies to the migrant communities that have arrived over the past 50 years as well as to indigenous communities – will never end, since it must always remain open to the future.

It's important to ask whether immigration will be seized upon as an opportunity to contemplate a new 'us' or regarded as the end of any such concept. We should understand the nation as an 'imagined community', in the way anthropologist Benedict Anderson proposes. He rejects the image of a population group held together by blood and soil. It simply doesn't reflect reality. Instead, we should think of the nation as an imagined community, a human invention that's continually being reshaped, the product of concerted efforts over many generations.

The Netherlands is a clear example. Many years passed before the inhabitants of this country started to feel part of a national community. Geographers Hans Knippenberg and Ben de Pater write: 'The building of a nation – a mental development and therefore much more difficult to discern – lagged behind the building of a state. Many people who were Dutch citizens in a formal sense remained wholly or partly outsiders to the nation. Among them were some at least of the Catholic community, the lower classes and the residents of far-flung rural areas.'[20] Gradually, the country was linked together, by railway lines, for example, and the synchronization of clocks that train timetables necessitated. It was increasingly united in its mentality too. One new group after another became part of the 'imagined community', thereby transforming it.

That history is now being carried forward. With the arrival of large numbers of immigrants who are changing the country significantly, there's a pressing need for new voices to help reshape Dutch ideas about who they are in an era of globalization. As Jan and Annie Romein remark in *Erflaters van onze beschaving* [Legators of our civilization], 'Even in the established State, the Nation is still in the making.'[21] Integration is never complete, since new desires are continually becoming part of the imagined community. The country's second religion is now Islam and as a result its view of itself has been transformed. This is just one example of the many changes triggered by the arrival of people from all over the world.

Another is the appointment of Ahmed Aboutaleb as mayor of Rotterdam. The second city of the Netherlands is now led by a first-generation migrant from Morocco, a situation without precedent in continental Europe. Such a result would have been unthinkable had it not been for those heated debates about integration. At difficult moments, Aboutaleb has always been able to articulate tough questions aimed at native Dutch society, and he has not been afraid to confront his presumed following with thorny issues. In the pressure-cooker that is Rotterdam, developments have accelerated.

It's fascinating to see how the Dutch self-image has been challenged by large-scale migration over recent decades. In this chapter we'll examine a number of lasting characteristics of the way conflict has been avoided in the Netherlands. In looking at differences of opinion, it becomes clear that an imagined nation is always a divided nation. Whether it's a question of how the country has dealt with contrasting attitudes (tolerance) or with power politics in the wider world (neutrality) or with religious settlement (compartmentalization), all are forms of conflict avoidance.

Each of these approaches has influenced the way the Netherlands manages the issue of migration as a new source of conflict. At the same time, its traditions have inevitably been altered by those clashes, if only in that they were found wanting in various ways.

Of course Dutch political culture can't be summed up in a single word: avoidance. There are many ambiguities here. Tolerance literally means putting up with someone; a majority creates room for minorities in its midst. Endurance of this kind always implies inequality, since the space given to those we tolerate can always be taken away. Traditional Dutch compartmentalization (for which they have an untranslatable word, *verzuiling*, sometimes rendered as 'pillarization'), was a form of 'each to his own' that kept contrasting religious and ideological groups apart. Yet within the different compartments people were remarkably submissive. In their foreign policy, meanwhile, the Dutch have always tried to hold themselves aloof. As far as relations with the rest of Europe went, the Netherlands was a neutral country for many years, but of course the same did not apply in colonial politics. In the colonies interference was the norm and restraint rare.

Tolerance Is Not Laisser-Faire

How did these features of Dutch political culture affect the country's post-war dealings with migrants and how did its traditions change as a result? Tolerance is the most frequently used and abused word in the discussion of migration. Many people have forgotten the history of the concept in the Netherlands, where it originally meant turning a blind eye to things that were forbidden. One early example concerns what are known as 'conventicles', hidden churches where clandestine religious meetings and services were held. In Protestant Holland, worship by Catholics was banned, but it was tolerated as long as they didn't draw too much attention to their gatherings. This resulted in the building of churches that are indistinguishable from other frontages on the street side.

In our own time tolerance usually exists independently of any prohibition. The implications of the word now generally sound inviting: we must show respect for things that in the first instance seem strange to us; it's wise to suspend judgement, since if we're not too quick to apply our own norms, then understanding for the lifestyles and worldviews of others, including those of migrants, will grow. But the question is: Why should anyone show respect for those who can't muster any respect for people with whom they differ profoundly? Where do the limits of tolerance lie?

Of course this immediately raises another question: How tolerant has Dutch society actually been over the centuries? A whole gamut of critical remarks about the Netherlands suggests that its openness was rather more limited than its inhabitants believed. True, in the seventeenth century many Huguenots were allowed into the country, as were many Portuguese Jews, but there are plenty of examples of less accommodating attitudes. A famous play by Gerbrand Bredero, *The Spanish Brabanter* (*Spaanschen Brabander*, 1618), gives a wonderful impression of daily life in Amsterdam. Jan Knol, rather laughingly presented as a 'patriot', makes profoundly dismissive remarks about the German newcomers in the Dutch capital ('moffs and poops'), who were all said to live by begging: 'Yes, the Almshouse regents would feed them, / And twenty of our burghers' children would gladly show the way. / But our poor, they're too proud for that, / While moffs and poops are eels just bred to beg.'[22]

The Dutch need to re-examine their history. Many trace the origins of today's tolerance back to the seventeenth-century Dutch Republic. There is something to be said for this notion, certainly in view of the situation in other countries at the time, but we should bear in mind that the religious freedom of the period was fairly limited by today's standards. If we look at the separation of church and state in the seventeenth century, then it turns out to have been remarkably incomplete, if it can be said to have existed at all. It became permanently entrenched only with the 1848 constitution. The seventeenth century was a time of struggle between the principle of freedom of conscience, embraced at an early stage, and the notion of the Reformed Church as the 'public church' of the Netherlands. Although not an official state church, it received preferential treatment from the Dutch government. The title of a study by historian Enno van Gelder speaks for itself: *Getemperde vrijheid* [tempered freedom].

One lesson from this period is that the separation of church and state is intended not only to protect the state against interference by the church, but equally – and sometimes to an even greater extent – to protect the church against meddling by the state. Hugo de Groot (known to the world as Grotius) advocated the 'absolute sovereignty of the state'. A community can have only one supreme authority, so the church must be subordinate to the state, which is the guardian of the public interest. This idea was expressed in countless practical regulations affecting the churches. No meeting of the general synod could be held without the assent of the States General, which was not readily given. Similarly, prior approval by government was required for ecclesiastical appointments. Van Gelder summarizes the result by saying that the Reformed Church 'felt above all unfree'.[23]

If even members of the dominant church felt constrained by

government, how much more so minorities, such as Catholics and Jews? Catholic services were forbidden in all parts of the country, even after the end of the Thirty Years War in 1648, although they were tolerated in some places in return for a fee. Members of minority denominations, including Catholics, were banned from holding official government posts until 1795. There was freedom of conscience, but in general this did not mean permission to speak freely in public. Freedom was limited in other spheres of life too. Marriages between Christians and Jews were forbidden, for instance. Historian Piet de Rooy remarks: 'The extent to which sexual relations between Jews and Christians were discouraged is striking. Jewish men were not allowed to marry Christian women and they even forbidden to visit Christian prostitutes; they alone were systematically prosecuted for buying sex and severely punished.'[24]

The general conclusion can only be that while the seventeenth-century Dutch Republic was certainly ahead of the rest of Europe by the standards of the time, for many years the separation of church and state was controversial, and in practice it was not respected at all. This more realistic view of history matters in the Netherlands today, because norms are often held out to others as standards to be met without any awareness of just what an uphill struggle it was to establish them, and therefore without any real understanding of their fragility.

This historical digression is intended above all to indicate that tolerance as practised in the Dutch Republic should not be regarded primarily as a moral principle. Historian Arie van Deursen reaches a measured verdict: 'The famous Dutch tolerance therefore involved a fair amount of opportunism. This was in fact the reason for its considerable success. It was a typical product of Holland's pragmatic culture. Nevertheless, it undoubtedly included a principled element; the old instinctive aversion to restraint of conscience is institutionalised within it.'[25]

Nor should tolerance be too readily equated with individual liberalism. The toleration that typified Dutch society was exhibited by groups. It was not an individual accomplishment, let alone a widespread, general characteristic; it had to be organized and carefully sustained by rulers who were aware of the precarious nature of social peace in a country that was home to religious minorities. Another historian, Remieg Aerts, writes: 'The same civilized ideal that regarded tolerance as a virtue also encompassed modesty and decorum, in other words conformity to the established order and training in its conventions.'[26]

In recent decades this attitude has come to be regarded as a type of conformism that needs to be tackled. The pendulum has swung so far that tolerance is increasingly understood as a form of laisser-faire. This has its attractive sides, but the unwillingness to pass judgement on other people's beliefs and behaviour can actually undermine tolerance, allowing it gradually to subside into indifference. Those who demand nothing expect nothing. They have forgotten the words of Huizinga: 'However contemptible it may sound to anyone who feels zealous and brave, as a nation and as a state we are simply in a certain sense *satisfait*, and it is our national duty to remain so.'[27] In those words lie historical experience and wisdom, and above all the insight that relaxation requires effort. The satisfied nation needs continual upkeep and can never be taken for granted. There has been too great a tendency to think of Dutch society as invulnerable.

It's clear that in times of large-scale immigration tolerance is put to the test. Innumerable people have arrived in the Netherlands after growing up in unfree societies. Clashes with orthodox members of the Muslim community in particular are illustrative of the resulting uncertainty. Sometimes, conservative Muslims express beliefs that were commonplace some 40 years ago, but that doesn't make them any less disturbing in the here and now. This was clearly demonstrated by a case known to the Dutch as the el-Moumni affair. A Rotterdam imam at the An-Nasr mosque, who had been banned from preaching in Morocco because of his radical beliefs, caused a huge stir when he delivered a sermon in which he said of homosexuality, among other things: 'If this sickness spreads, everyone will be infected and that could lead to us dying out.' He did add that violence against homosexuals was unacceptable, but at first no one noticed that qualification. It then emerged that in earlier sermons he'd described Europeans as lower than 'dogs and pigs' because they permitted homosexuality.[28] The reactions were harsh; there were even calls in parliament for el-Moumni to be expelled from the country.

Suddenly a conflict had arisen between two minorities: Muslims and gays. This was rather confusing for those in the habit of regarding the oppressed as always in the right. How should we judge imams who preach intolerance for homosexuals? For a start, the same way as we judge the Dutch bishop who a few years ago described love between men as 'a neurosis'.[29] His statement caused immense indignation, but for understandable reasons no one called for his deportation. The same should apply to the imam.

The question keeps coming back: how tolerant should anyone be of intolerance? Of course those in authority don't need to settle every conflict publicly, but defence of the norms of an open society is one of the essential tasks of government. Faith in the self-regulating effect of democracy means restraint in the use of coercion and reliance on the power of words against words. So it's good that the Rotterdam imam was acquitted in a case brought against him for what he had said. A ban would only have driven religious beliefs like his, which are no doubt shared by countless Muslims, back underground.

It's not difficult to be tolerant among the like-minded. True toleration is all about dealing in a peaceful manner with profound differences of opinion. In other words, strict orthodox beliefs have their place in an open society. This way of maintaining social harmony is quite a different matter from living in a society in which everyone sticks to the multicultural etiquette, not daring to express a judgement about anything. A host of taboos can never serve as a basis for tolerance.

Governments are continually trying to avoid conflict, so they have a tendency to limit freedom of expression for pacification's sake. We saw this after the murder of Theo van Gogh, when the Dutch government suddenly dusted off an old law against blasphemy. Its attempt to placate the Muslim community should be recognized as an encouragement to the radicals, who can then say, 'See, we really are being insulted, the government itself says so.' The Dutch queen too, in her Christmas message, was trying to define the limits of freedom of speech when she referred to 'the sensitivities that can touch people at the very deepest level'.

Freedom of expression is ultimately limited by laws against incitement to violence, rather than by any sense of affront a person may have. It's not a matter of having a right to offend people – anyone who takes that as his starting point belittles his own motives. The point here is that criticism is often felt to be insulting, especially by deeply religious people who believe their God is immaculate. In many respects avoidance has turned out to be counter-productive as a way of ensuring peaceful coexistence. This doesn't imply endless freedom to do as you like – not everything that can be said needs to be said – but the Netherlands is changing. Cultural divides have deepened. In the future they'll lead to fiercer differences of opinion than they have in the past.

In many areas of life, avoidance is clearly being mistaken for tolerance. The fact that a few years ago only 37 per cent of Moroccan and 46 per cent of Turkish immigrants and their children were in paid work justifies the general assertion that in the name of tolerance an entire generation of migrants was written off.[30] Native or newcomer, it makes no difference: all have indulged in a form of nonchalance, and an endless reliance on welfare is one good example. This has not escaped the attention of migrants. Hafid Bouazza's verdict is harsh: 'People were exhorted to get themselves fired, since no Muslim should work for unbelievers; they were told to convert others and spend as much time as possible in the mosque. That was the famous "backache period," when many first-generation Moroccans took disability pay.'[31] Whether religion was the decisive factor here or laxity in enforcing the rules, or vague physical symptoms, the outcome is well known. A large number of migrants vanished into the margins of society, which had negative consequences not only for them but for their children too.

Tolerance has been eroded by lax law-enforcement, for which the Dutch have another untranslatable word, *gedogen*, an officially sanctioned form of permissiveness. It can sometimes be defended as a transitional phase between an outdated ban and future legislation. If abortion is about to be made legal, for example, then it may make sense to allow the practice even before the new law comes into force. In the Netherlands, however, such permissiveness often becomes permanent. Ignoring existing legislation over an extended period undermines faith in the rule of law, making society as a whole less free by openly giving sanctuary to those with the fewest scruples. Intolerance has nestled into the space left open by lax government. Tolerance cannot flourish in a climate of inequality before the law.

It should surprise no one that newcomers, many of whom come from societies with far stricter penal codes, are not impressed by this type of law-enforcement culture. Currently, around half the population of Dutch prisons is made up of people from migrant communities. Criminality is proportionately high among Moroccans and Antilleans, but in other migrant communities too, among Turks and Somalis for example, it's above average. The clash between different ways of imposing authority is characteristic of all migratory shifts from traditional to modern societies, but the uncertainty is reinforced in this case by the rather informal way the Dutch interact with those in authority.

Inconsistent application of the law has had unfortunate results. It's easy to understand the Turkish father who says angrily: 'You've messed my son up.' A Moroccan father who came to the Netherlands in the 1960s says the same thing in a slightly more roundabout way: 'It's not our fault, but more or less the fault of the government, which I think is far too mild. In this respect the Netherlands is an unclear country to me. There are enough rules, but there are all kinds of ways of getting around them. To be honest I don't understand this system at all.'[32] Of course, in the end it's the responsibility of parents and the children themselves to make sure they don't enter into a life of crime, but the Netherlands is indeed 'an unclear country', which doesn't help. Many of the classic countries of immigration, unsurprisingly, have societies that are much more rule-based.

The arrival of migrants has caused a certain notion of tolerance to founder. This may in fact assist society in moving forward, by forcing it to reconsider attitudes that have seemed self-evident but are no longer productive. It's impossible for a government that wants more than anything to avoid conflict to promote true tolerance, and newcomers can't work out where they stand in a society that gives in more often than it gives back. So the price of avoidance is paid by all. Tolerance is possible only in an open society, where opinions can collide freely and where at the same time everyone realizes that social peace requires observance of the laws of the land – and self-control, not to be confused with fear.

Organizing Islam

It's time to look at how the Dutch custom of compartmentalizing the beliefs of different groups (in other words *verzuiling*, or the existence side by side of different confessional pillars) influences the way migrants are treated, and at how the arrival of a new religion has made this tradition problematic. There was once an expectation that the integration of ethnic minorities would take roughly the same course as the peaceful reconciliation of religious groups in the Netherlands. Each 'pillar' would have its own broadcasting organization, its own trades union, its own schools and – why not? – its own sports clubs. As always, it would be a matter of accommodation, adaptation, give and take, negotiation and evasion. This traditional approach manifests itself above all as a boundless faith in elites, which are assumed not only to be willing to lead 'their' communities but also to be able to control their followers.

The coming of Islam to the Netherlands – after a long history of Dutch colonization of the largest Muslim country in the world, present-day Indonesia – took the form of the arrival of guest workers from Turkey and Morocco in the 1960s and '70s. Initially, there were few visible signs that a different religion was taking root. It was some time before money could be collected for the building of mosques and, in any case, only when guest workers brought their families to join them did religion assume a major significance in their lives. It's important to bear this history in mind when considering whether the old remedies still work in new circumstances.

The use of the compartmentalizing approach to enable the Muslim community to integrate into Dutch society was felt by many to be a logical continuation of an old tradition by new means. Sociologist Anton Zijderveld wrote in the early 1990s: 'Certainly for the Catholics, pillarization was the pre-eminent route to emancipation, allowing them to integrate into society while maintaining their own identity. Given this successful process of emancipation and integration, we should clearly call on the Muslims in our country to emancipate themselves via their own pillar and by so doing to integrate.'[33] He was not the only one to think this way.

So the reaction to the new religion took its lead from the past; many believed the old rules and customs of reconciliation would curb the new discord. But they were overlooking a chapter called 'Sense of national solidarity' in a classic book by Arend Lijphart. The conclusion he comes to in his assessment of the Dutch political system is as follows: 'The strength of Dutch nationalism should not be exaggerated, but there can be no doubt it exists.'[34] All those pillars supported one and the same roof, which explains why religious and ideological 'apartheid' never degenerated into violent conflict.

Attempts to settle religious disputes peacefully actually contributed to a sense of solidarity. Many historians have made a connection between the nation's division into different 'pillars' and Dutch nation-building. It's interesting to note that in the late nineteenth century the beginnings of compartmentalization coincided with the rise of strong cultural nationalism. Differences in beliefs and attitudes fell within a shared history, were kept in check by a broadly accepted constitution and could be debated in a single language.

The Dutch now find themselves with a new religious community in their midst, and this time history, language and the constitution can't be assumed to serve as ties that will mitigate division. In the past it was possible to find shared points of reference. This was not always obvious. In his lecture *Het vergruisde beeld* [The shattered image], Jan Romein describes an argument about how the Dutch Revolt should be interpreted. He is typical of writers on the subject in emphasizing the differences to such an extent that he fails to notice the common ground, which to him is self-evident. The conflicting beliefs he writes about relate to a major historical event, the revolt against Spanish rule, which, although subject to various interpretations, is seen by every school of thought as of essential importance in the emergence of the Dutch nation. In an era of migration it becomes harder to fall back on a shared history.

We have already looked at the significance of language. The extent to which the Dutch underestimate the command of a common tongue as one of the essential sources of mutuality available in their fragmented country is remarkable. Just look at the problems faced by countries like Belgium and Canada, which are still struggling, many years after independence, with the existence of two linguistic communities in a single nation-state. In the Netherlands today, the Dutch language cannot be taken for granted as a shared vehicle, given many immigrants' limited proficiency in it.

Finally, we should be clear about the fact that the Dutch constitution is a product of conflict mediation. Article 23, which says that schools founded by religious communities will receive state funding, is one example. The compromise over education was the outcome of a history to which all religious and secular movements had contributed, so it could be used as a basis for settling future conflicts. Nowadays, Muslim appeals to the right to found their own schools are a bone of contention, since they were not involved in the conflict appeasement that produced this constitutional provision.

In other words, there were specific conditions that prevented disputes between the pillars of Dutch society from degenerating into civil war, conditions that are not automatically in place to help reconcile current religious differences. A shared history can no longer be taken for granted, a shared language requires more effort to sustain than it once did, and the constitution is no longer seen, either by the established population or by newcomers, as a framework for solving contemporary problems. The age-old way of living together in peace will not automatically work in entirely new circumstances. It will have to be reinvented.

There's another sense too in which traditional Dutch conflict resolution through pillarization no longer works. The Muslim community is far less internally cohesive than the Catholic and Protestant communities were. One significant new element is the existence of ethnic divisions: in daily life a Turkish Muslim has little contact with a Muslim from Morocco or Surinam, even though they may run into each other on a pilgrimage to Mecca. Zijderveld recognized this problem: 'For purposes of pillarization, religious identity must be able to transcend ethnic differences. Pillars cannot be constructed on an ethnic basis.'[35] It has indeed proven extremely difficult to create a Muslim consultative body and almost impossible to bring together diverse Muslim groups that are organized along national lines. The Muslim broadcasting organization, which had blocks of time on the public networks, recently broke up as a result of profound differences of opinion.

This pattern is familiar from the history of immigration in America. It was a long time before Irish, Polish and Italian Catholics, for example, began attending the same churches. Their initial impulse was to worship in congregations of their own nationality. The church was, among other things, a means of breathing fresh life into the everyday customs of the country of origin on foreign soil, so the social significance of American migrant churches was at least as great as their religious significance. Something similar applies to Muslims in the Netherlands and other European countries. Perhaps eventually their ethnic differences will fall away, but there is no sign of that as yet.

As well as significant ethnic division, the one-sided social composition of the Muslim community is clear for all to see. The pillars that once made up Dutch society were themselves socially mixed, each including both business leaders and common labourers. The socially weak position of Dutch Muslims is of course a result of the low social status of the original guest workers. Migrant labourers are by no means a reflection of the population of their countries of origin; rather, they are a specific group, mostly drawn from poor rural districts. It's no surprise to find that

Muslim schools are almost entirely populated by children whose parents have little schooling. This has prompted a Protestant politician to remark that this type of school threatens to become 'a prison of poverty'.[36]

One of the problems within the Muslim community in the Netherlands is the weakness of its elites. There are simply too few well-educated people, especially in the first generation. The model of pillars, with their fairly authoritarian leaderships, relied upon powerful elites. Perhaps these will be produced by the children of the migrant generation, but one of the striking things about members of that second generation is their lack of any explicit ambition to take charge of the communities to which they're assumed to belong. On the contrary, members of the second generation often want to free themselves from their fellow countrymen or fellow believers, finding such associations too constraining. Moreover, it's precisely the most liberal Muslims who are least likely to organize. Those who set themselves up as leaders of the Dutch Muslim community, a few exceptions aside, represent conservative forces.

Commentator August Hans den Boef concludes: 'Integration via the mosque means integration within religious communities that are divided along national and regional lines and led by their conservative male segments, which largely consist of people from rural tribal cultures who have little education. In Dutch Muslim communities most children attend black schools, or Islamic schools that are an extension of the mosque.'[37] He believes the emphasis on the mosque as an instrument of integration – a minaret among the pillars – not only leads to a decline in 'social cohesion within the city as a whole, it reinforces social control within Muslim communities'. He is right to speak of communities, emphasizing the plural. Plainly there is no such thing as 'the' Muslim community. It's not a cohesive entity with its back turned to society but a group of believers that's deeply fragmented along ethnic, generational and religious lines, composed of people trying to find their way in strange surroundings. It's the weakness rather than the presumed strength of the Muslim segment of society that presents a problem to those in search of a compromise.

Here we come up against another important difference between the old, compartmentalized Dutch community and efforts to create a society based on the same model in our own time. The traditional 'pillars' represented religions that had existed side by side for many years and had been forced to defend themselves against sometimes stinging criticism. We can by no means be certain that Islam will succeed in claiming a place for itself as a minority religion in a liberal and secularized society, if only because Islam has always been in a majority or even monopoly position in the countries of origin.

A nation that enjoys freedom of religion can make room for Islam only on condition that the vast majority of Muslims accept their duty to defend that same freedom for people with whom they fundamentally disagree. This attitude is lacking in many mosques, where the principles and institutions of liberal democracy are questioned and in some cases rejected. Governments have looked away for a long time, not wanting to cause conflict. On this point too Hafid Bouazza injects a note of urgency into his criticism: 'If Muslims get their sense of superiority from anywhere then it is from the fact that they have been able to play so many tricks on these Dutch people and been patted on the head in return.' His sombre conclusion: 'I foresee an infernal split in this small but miraculous country.'[38]

In most countries of the Islamic world, with the important exception of Turkey, Islam has never needed to prove itself in open confrontation with other religions or secular beliefs. Muslims in the West tend to have difficulty facing up to criticism of their faith. Too often they adopt the stance of victims, looked down on by the society around them. How often do we see criticism of religion stamped as racism? It isn't, of course. The religious choices made by Muslims and others are subjected to exactly the same kind of criticism as Catholics faced in the 1950s. Criticism of religion, however narrow-minded it may sometimes be, should never be confused with ethnic or racial prejudice.

Research shows that in general young Muslims in the Netherlands have the same views about democracy as their counterparts in the rest of the population. Only when it comes to freedom of expression do significant differences emerge: no more than a small minority of Turkish and Moroccan young people are in favour of press freedom if it means a religion can be ridiculed.[39] This is another indication that the integration of Islam by the pillarization route will be less easy than it was in the case of religions required to hold their own for many years in open rivalry in a democratic environment.

During the rapid secularization of Dutch society over recent years, the divide between the worldview of the average Dutchman and the faith-based outlook among Muslims has only increased. Comparative studies demonstrate that few countries have detached themselves from God so quickly and radically as the Netherlands. It therefore seems strange that in a landscape where the confessional pillars are rapidly disappearing, the Muslim community is being invited to form a pillar of its own. As a liberal politician once remarked: a Muslim pillar would make a rather lonely impression in a flat Dutch landscape in which all the other pillars have disappeared. It is a vivid image.

Finally, pleas for a Muslim pillar neglect the fact that Islam in the West is developing as part of an international climate of conflict, with radicalization of a kind that has already led to violence in Europe and America. The vast majority of Muslims in the Netherlands undoubtedly want to live in peace, but at the same time many are personally affected by the conflict between political Islam and Western society. There's a real danger that with the arrival of so many Muslims in Europe the conflict in the Middle East will be brought to cities elsewhere. Already, in Antwerp, Lyon and Amsterdam, for example, the tension between Moroccan and Jewish communities is palpable.

Islamophobia and anti-Semitism are often seen as expressions of one and the same worldview. The underlying thought is: 'We know how history turned out; what happened to the Jews might happen to the Muslims tomorrow.' Geert Mak has written by way of warning: 'I walked along the Weesperstraat in my own city, a bleak thoroughfare of office blocks. I visualized the same street two generations ago, a busy, narrow, popular shopping street similar to the Utrechtsestraat. All those people who walked around here were murdered, eighty thousand in Amsterdam alone, and it all started with language, with words, with slogans like "national", and "pure", and "them" and "us". May we please remember that?'[40]

His concern is understandable, but raking up this tragedy and making connections with our own time only obstructs the debate about Islam. There's no indication that a reaction against the presence of Muslims in Western society is emerging that in any way resembles what happened to the Jews. Although there are certainly groups that wish to deny Islam a place here – and which must therefore be powerfully contradicted – there are opportunities to build mosques and schools, and many Muslims exercise their right to vote either passively or actively. The comparison with the fate of the Jews reinforces many people's sense of victimhood, which is something that must not be allowed to happen.

A few days after the murder of Theo van Gogh, Ahmed Aboutaleb (at that time an Amsterdam alderman) gave an unambiguous speech in the El Kabir mosque: 'There is no place in an open society such as the Netherlands for people who do not share the essential core values of that society. All those who do not share these values would be wise to draw their conclusions and leave. We cannot accept that anyone among us demands that we respect his views and at the same time is not prepared to respect the views of others.'[41]

To equate criticism of Islam and its more radical believers with anti-Semitism is to ignore the acts of terror that have taken place, on 11 September 2001 and since. They fuelled unease about Islam enormously. In the streets of Amsterdam a murder was committed that caused great social unrest, on a par with reactions to the murder of a young black man called Kerwin Duinmeijer in August 1983. There is therefore a context of violence, one without any parallel in the history of the Jewish population of the Netherlands in the 1930s. After the attacks of 2004 on commuter trains in Madrid, Sylvain Ephimenco called upon moderate Muslims to speak out more clearly: 'Asking for a verbal response from Muslims is not the same as demanding that the innocent exonerate themselves from crimes others have committed. It's a matter of active participation in the struggle against blind violence, a conscious act of opposition to the dark forces that have broken into the house of Islam.'[42] Indeed, why was it so quiet and why did we hear only protests in support of Hamas on Dam Square in Amsterdam?

The radicalization we've seen involves rancour towards the Jews, something that's unfortunately all too tangible, despite many well-meaning attempts at rapprochement. We must never mistake earnest criticism of the state of Israel for anti-Semitism, but neither should we forget that the letter Mohammed Bouyeri left on the body of Theo van Gogh included an anti-Semitic tirade. If Muslims distance themselves from that, living together will be easier. No collective guilt falls to Muslims for the violence committed by a few in the name of Islam, but that violence does confer on them a special responsibility to oppose radicalization in the circles in which they move.

New questions have arisen, and dividing society neatly into 'pillars' won't help in finding the answers. The Muslim community has certain specific characteristics that make it quite different from the religious and secular communities of the past. Moreover, the Netherlands has changed. Secularization has continued. As we shall see, it's possible to seize upon the arrival of Islam as a way to start a discussion about what is left of 'pillarization'. In a time characterized by large-scale immigration, social peace in the Netherlands cannot simply be perpetuated using the old methods.

Postcolonial Lessons

Lastly, a long tradition of neutrality in international politics has affected the way the Dutch deal with ethnic communities. Neutrality was for many years the means by which their country avoided becoming involved in international conflicts, the 1930s included. Of course it's possible to see in this the inherent interests of a small nation, one that has nothing to gain from power politics. But that neutrality was also the source of many illusions, as a marvellous statement by leading Dutch politician Johan Rudolf Thorbecke from 1830 illustrates: 'Dutch Politics, itself free of the lust for power, is the most equitable judge of the lust for power in others.'[43]

What arrogance, we immediately think; it sounds like an early version of '*Nederland gidsland*' ['The Netherlands, model country'], a 1970s slogan. The words 'itself free of the lust for power' were written in the first half of the nineteenth century, when the Dutch colonial empire, despite some shrinkage, was still of considerable magnitude. It reveals a split in the Dutch self-image: on the one hand, a vulnerable country on the European continent at continual risk of being overrun by nations like France and Germany, and, on the other, a colonial power, which in establishing and maintaining its rule over the Dutch East Indies and Surinam took little heed of the norms it brandished as an example to others.

Historian Henk Wesseling writes that 'long-drawn-out wars such as those the Dutch fought against Aceh, Bali and Lombok were pursued unscrupulously'.[44] A soldiers' song from the time of the Aceh war of the 1890s goes: '*Roeit uit dat gebroedsel, verneder die klant / Met Nederlands driekleur 'beschaving' geplant*' ['Wipe out that vermin, humiliate their nation / Plant in them the Dutch tricolour that brings civilization']. That was the dominant mood of the military campaign in the far off East Indies. It emerged only fairly recently that Hendrikus Colijn, later to become prime minister of the Netherlands, was an officer serving in the Lombok expedition at the end of the nineteenth century and that under his orders atrocious killings took place. His biographer quotes from a letter sent by Colijn to his wife: 'I've had to gather together 9 women and 3 children, who begged for mercy, and have them shot dead there and then. It was unpleasant work but there was no other way. The soldiers relished spearing them with their bayonets.'[45] His letters contain not an inkling that the colonial wars might be unjust.

In a more general sense too we can say that the Netherlands has had great difficulty in facing up to its colonial past. The wars fought between 1945 and 1949 in opposition to Indonesian independence are to this day referred to as 'police actions'. This seems an extraordinarily veiled term for a conflict that went on for years and claimed around 100,000 lives among the native population. No less telling is the fact that, until recently, the Dutch were extremely reluctant even to acknowledge the anniversary of Indonesia's declaration of independence on 17 August 1945.

This evasiveness in dealing with colonial history shows through in the treatment of ethnic minorities in the post-war Netherlands. Many of the migratory movements that followed the Second World War had their origins in decolonization. In the 20 years after Indonesia became independent, most members of the 'Indisch Dutch' community were forced to leave. This meant that for the first time in its history the Netherlands was faced with a considerable ethnic minority in its midst. Many of the 300,000 who settled in the Netherlands after the war of independence of

1945–9 thought they knew exactly where they were going, but they were disappointed by the country they encountered in everyday life. Although the Dutch did not welcome these migrants, they did feel bound by promises made. Their country – like France and Britain, as we shall see – was hostage to its colonial past. In his history of this wave of migration, Gert Oostindie concludes that 'in all cases there was social and political opposition in the Netherlands to extensive postcolonial migration, sometimes embedded in statements that would strike us as racist, but the most essential point is that in none of the three cases was the right of acknowledged citizens of former Dutch colonies to settle in the Netherlands ultimately removed. All postcolonial migrants therefore had the same civic rights and duties as other Dutch people.'[46]

Despite this formal equality, the ambivalent attitude of the receiving society left its mark. 'Indisch Dutch' immigrants met with little in the way of Dutch goodwill and many felt treated as second-class citizens. Author Tjalie Robinson observed: 'We're a bunch of stand-in Dutch who aren't part of the most important patterns of life here and indeed understand bugger all about them.'[47] They were seen as a separate group by those they lived amongst, and indeed felt more comfortable within their own circles. That feeling would last for many years; some say it remains true for the first generation even today.

The loss of the East Indies was a heavy blow for many, especially the 10,000 or so Moluccans who never truly said goodbye to their homeland but dreamed of returning to an independent Ambon. As time went on, that hope faded and their growing frustration was expressed in a series of violent campaigns. Moluccan terrorism in the Netherlands in the 1970s – especially the hijacking of a train and the simultaneous holding hostage of a school class – made clear that the colonial past was not about to disappear of its own accord.

Initial incomprehension can be excused to some extent in light of the hardships of those immediate post-war years. Everyone was concentrating on the future after the privations of wartime and they had no desire to look back. If it had been a little more open to the experiences of these first post-war migrants, Dutch society might have been rather better prepared for what was to follow. There would have been more understanding for the sense of loss that is an aspect of all migration, especially when departure is not a matter of choice. In his 1954 novel *Vergeelde portretten* [Yellowed portraits], Rob Nieuwenhuys describes the repatriated. 'Thousands live as they do in The Hague alone: East Indies emigrés and the uprooted. Some sit aimlessly at windows, looking out at the wet streets and bare branches and thinking of their plantations of fruit trees and melati bushes, of flowerbeds and palms. They are homesick, with pangs of longing for *their* East Indies, and they say to each other: "A shame things ended this way; it used to be so good there."'[48]

Immigrants from the former East Indies were a lasting reminder of a lost war no one any longer wished to think about. They carried a stigma, since the Dutch looked back with increasing shame at 300 years of colonial rule. Those who embodied that time found themselves on the wrong side when the historical balance was made up. As a result a fault-line appeared and many important memories of the colonial period, the manner in which Islam was handled in the East Indies for example, passed into oblivion.

In the mid-1990s, sociologist Jacques van Doorn published a study of how the colonial heritage makes itself felt in the way minorities are treated in the Netherlands. He speaks of indecisive manoeuvring 'between the Western civilizing mission and a well-intentioned respect for the indigenous culture'.[49] He sees the same wavering between the pursuit of assimilation and the recognition of cultural differences in post-war policy towards minorities: 'It's no exaggeration to say that government policy in the East Indies accentuated cultural pluralism to a greater extent than the policies of other colonial nations, and that the Dutch government now does more than the governments of other countries of immigration to support ethnic communities.'[50]

Despite this continuity, it's clear that in the 1950s the policy towards those repatriated from the East Indies was focused on assimilation, whereas later policy towards minorities can be summarized as 'integration with the retention of identity'. The settling of accounts with centuries of paternalism and oppression in the colonial period was undoubtedly one reason for the evasive attitude towards migrants who came to the Netherlands from the 1960s onwards. The Dutch could not have taken leave of the white civilizing mission more wholeheartedly.

Edgar du Perron's memories of a childhood in the East Indies, as described in the 1935 classic of Dutch literature *Het land van herkomst* (published in English the same year as *Country of Origin*), convey cautious criticism of colonial relations: 'Even my parents never questioned the fact that in many respects the Javanese are more appealing than Europeans. But even now I don't believe that they are superior in every respect and that, therefore, it's our duty to be sympathetic to every Javanese. All I know for sure is that if I ever go back to their country, I will have infinitely more sympathy and attention for them than I used to have.'[51] What in Du Perron's case was a still hesitant reconsideration of the issue became in the 1960s an increasingly vehement condemnation of the colonial past.

This became all the clearer after the arrival in the Netherlands of a second group of postcolonial migrants, the Surinamers, who emigrated after their country became independent in 1975. Some 350,000 now live in the Netherlands and, with their arrival, the colonial past was dredged up once again. At their insistence, bitter memories are gradually penetrating the collective consciousness. The slavery memorial erected a few years ago in Amsterdam is one highly visible example.

Migration from former colonies changes a country's self-image and it can make that society more open. In any case, the Dutch could not simply go on polishing up the seventeenth-century Golden Age in the hope that everyone would be dazzled by it. The shadow side of that renowned era demanded attention; their view of the Dutch Republic had to expand to include not just the great masters with their brushes but the slave masters with their whips.

To anyone who allows all the agonizing over slavery to sink in, it's clear that historical insight reveals the fragility of civilization. Historians talk of a moral deficit and describe how the Netherlands played a pioneering role in the rise of slavery and the slave trade. When the Dutch stopped trading in slaves in 1807 it was not by choice but because Britain enforced a ban. The question of why the Netherlands abolished slavery relatively late, in 1863, whereas Britain and France took that step in 1834 and 1848 respectively, remains a source of discomfort. Oostindie offers one explanation: 'The lateness of abolition by the Dutch can be explained by the absence of a strong anti-slavery movement in the Netherlands. And by tight-fistedness: the issue of compensation was complicated.'[52] He's referring to slave-owners who were compensated for their losses; the slaves themselves were left with nothing but their hard-won freedom, generally in appalling circumstances.

There were those who did voice opposition and press for the abolition of slavery at an early stage. One example is a treatise about the slave trade published in 1793 by Hendrik Constantijn Cras. His position was clear: 'All people, whichever region of this earth they inhabit, however different they may be in the shape of their bodies, the colour of their skin or the capacity of their minds, however diverse in the stage of civilization reached, they all have the same nature as ours and the excellence of that nature must extend to them a guarantee that they will not be subjected to anyone's arbitrary rule against their will, far less degraded to such a level that others can enter into agreements and bargains over the buying and selling of them as they do over animals and inanimate things.'[53]

We must be aware of this history in its full magnitude. The monument and the annual commemoration represent not just division but a shared investigation. It's not easy to come to terms with slavery, and the effort to do so can slip into insincerity. People who grow up in the Netherlands with a feeling that they can derive rights from the sufferings of past generations and therefore have no sense of obligation towards the society that caused those sufferings are above all doing themselves and their children a disservice. Being nourished by the past is quite different from being consumed by it.

Is there a chance that a new 'us' might emerge, bringing together the heirs of colonial rule and the descendants of slaves? Many say not. How can we build a bridge between perpetrators and victims? But for how many years can the sins and sufferings of earlier generations be handed down? How long do they remain a living experience and when do they become a borrowed one? For how long will we emphasize difference and when does it become possible to transform yesterday's horrors into today's moral strengths?

The history of Dutch colonization and the migration that flowed from it are part of a story that must be passed on to future generations. A failure to revise traditional views of the past and the ways we memorialize it will not only devalue historical knowledge, it will gradually cause narratives about that past to lose their significance. We would be wrong to commemorate slavery out of a need for self-pity or self-chastisement. It's essential to make clear that in Dutch history too, civilization and barbarism overlap.

Identity and Openness

The upshot of this brief exploration of Dutch political culture is that the temptations of avoidance have not gone away. The strength of a country with a long peaceful tradition shouldn't be underestimated, but we would do well to ask whether the means by which that peace was preserved are as effective now as they once were. Compartmentalization is no longer a useful response to the emergence of a new religion; in fact, more should be done to question the legitimacy of the confessional pillars of Dutch society, which continue to exist to some degree in a secular age. Tolerance must be redefined and above all liberated from the indifference with which it has become too much identified. Finally, we must learn to see that behind a façade of neutrality lies a colonial history whose legacy is at best confusing.

The old answers are inadequate and they've thrown the country off balance. Dutch elites feel insecure, since the space in which they operate is being profoundly changed by globalization. The social and cultural divides that need to be bridged are wider than they once were and it's clear that any attempt at integration under these circumstances can easily lead to restrictions on freedom. The ideal of an open society must not only be articulated more precisely, it must be defended with greater sensitivity to the fragility of all such ideals. This is essential, since the words of Huizinga still apply: 'It is not our own merit but a benevolent fate that has spared us the causes and consequences [of rampant nationalism].'[54] The phrase 'not our own merit but a benevolent fate' is particularly thought-provoking. We have already looked at the comparatively comfortable circumstances that enabled the Dutch to have a relaxed national consciousness.

In times of mass immigration, there's a risk that societies will grow more rigid and inward-looking. The Netherlands needs to come to terms with the prognosis that by 2050 around 30 per cent of its population will consist of migrants and their descendants. Bearing in mind that such predictions are tentative, if we add the third generation, then by the middle of this century perhaps as many as four out of ten of its inhabitants will have their origins in post-war immigration. The standard Dutch surnames will be increasingly scarce. The image of the 'average' Dutchman will have changed beyond recognition in the space of a century. This is a delicate matter, and it doesn't take much imagination to see a danger that some parts of the population will turn their backs on that new reality.

Current demographic change cannot be evaluated in isolation, since it's embedded in a process of globalization that undermines many other certainties as well. We're living through a transition period; institutional façades look the same as ever, but behind them a great disengagement is taking place. A recent study revealed what at first seems a peculiar picture of the state of the nation. The attitude of most of those questioned could be summarized as 'things are going fine with *me* but badly with *us*'.[55] This unease about societal issues is by no means limited to the Netherlands. It can be felt right across Europe.

Many are looking for a certain idea of the Netherlands. The word 'certain' is ambiguous of course. It suggests predictability, whereas everyone knows there can never be any guarantee of certainty while the world is in such turmoil. In an open society insecurity is a permanent feature, if unevenly distributed. Some people are doing well as a world economy emerges. Others are in danger of becoming the losers. There's nothing inevitable about openness in a time of globalization.

Although borders are clearly losing their significance, we continue to talk about changes to communities each of which has an ongoing and recognizable history. Will it in fact be possible to re-imagine our national communities? Amsterdam historian Niek van Sas thinks it will: 'The Netherlands is busy reinventing itself again. As at earlier critical moments, like the periods around 1800 and 1900, its reinvention once more takes the form of a dialectic between particularism and openness.'[56] The established order is creaking under the strain and there's little certainty as to what will replace it, but Van Sas believes this is nothing new.

That sounds more reassuring than it actually is, because particularism and openness don't necessarily go together. The reconciliation of these ill-assorted goals assumes favourable circumstances, along with a good deal of self-confidence and regular maintenance. The Netherlands, convinced it had history on its side, accepted immigration with apparent ease. This explains the attitude of its elites, which believed that 'a country like ours' should not lose itself in self-reflection, in examining its own identity. The notion that foreigners could disrupt their way of living together simply did not occur to them.[57]

The Netherlands is less and less able to screen itself off from turbulence in the wider world. When the Kurds' struggle for independence spills over into Dutch cities, events in Turkey have repercussions there, as was demonstrated by the attack on the Kosedag family in The Hague in 1997, in which a mother and five children died. The same applies now that Islamist terrorist networks have a foothold in Dutch Muslim communities. Author Ian Buruma reaches a similar conclusion: 'Although Theo van Gogh was Dutch and was killed by a Dutch citizen, in the end this is not just a Dutch story but a Middle Eastern one imported to the heart of Europe.'[58]

Faith in the familiar patterns of adjustment and compromise has clearly declined. Does current uncertainty about what's often regarded, explicitly or not, as the characteristic feature of the Netherlands go some way to explain why it's becoming less open to the rest of the world? Seen from this perspective, the debate about the integration of migrants is one focal point in a far more general quest that has produced appeals from all sides in recent years for 'the passing on of the core values of the constitution', as a parliamentary commission put it. This could be a change for the better if it means a new balance can be found between attempts to contemplate objectively the questions raised by contact with other cultures and a need for self-assurance, an understandable response to a turbulent world.

A reassessment of this kind arouses powerful emotions, which are no less understandable. The emphasis on identity can easily lead to the exclusion of people or ideas that are felt to be foreign. At the same time, the neglect of a cultural heritage can produce a less cohesive society, one that no longer has citizens but merely consumers. Society as a marketplace or meeting point may be an attractive metaphor to some, but it would be a rather barren outcome to a national history spanning centuries.

An example of this search for a new balance between heritage and openness is the debate that arose over plans to renovate the most important art gallery in the Netherlands, the Rijksmuseum. The building required substantial repairs, but, as a result, the contemporary significance of this national symbol, which dates from the nineteenth century, came up for discussion. Contrasting attitudes went head to head. On one side people argued that in a world without borders no embodiment of a national culture or history can be anything more than an anachronism, that these days there's no such thing as a coherent story a museum can tell. Typical of this view were statements like 'The myth of the nation and nationalities sounds less and less convincing' and 'The Rijksmuseum should no longer advertise itself as the "National Treasure-House"'.[59]

Opposed to this repudiation of national identity as a future context for the Rijksmuseum were many who believe that identity should be its starting point. Their reasoning is that in a globalizing world contemplation of specific cultural histories will increase, since so many people are looking for shelter and for something to cling to. This produced statements such as: 'The grand gesture, even that of the building itself in all its glory, emphasizes the importance we attach to our cultural heritage' and 'A national museum must have the ambition to develop a clear vision in response to the sensitive question: What is the specific, characteristic identity of Dutch culture?'[60]

Is it possible to unite these two views of the museum? At first it seems not, since the relativism of one is all but diametrically opposed to the self-affirmation that the other hankers after. Words like 'pride', 'heritage' and 'identity' are hard to reconcile with 'hot air', 'myth' and 'elitism'. Yet it must be possible to overcome these antitheses and to see the questions asked so obtrusively as we deal with our past as an invitation to take that past seriously in a contemporary sense. This is illustrated by the ways in which the colonial era is dealt with today. Why would we need to commemorate slavery if the history of which the trade in human beings is part had lost all significance?

A cultural transformation is under way that perhaps has to do with the secularization of society. Interest in the past has become a non-religious way of maintaining a connection between the living and the dead. Perhaps that's the reason the need for a historical consciousness is growing. Van Deursen expresses it in his own way: 'History is about love for our fellow man. Love does not end in death. This is why we must continue to pay attention to the past, not because it makes us any better. If it does so as well, then that's a bonus.'[61] In a time when the religious world-view has lost much of its eloquence, a return to history is perhaps the best way to establish a 'contract between the generations'. One indication of this is the growth of interest in genealogy. People increasingly feel a need to discover a connection with those who went before them. This could be seen as a sign of nostalgia, but another conclusion is possible: the desire to get to grips with the boundary between life and death has found secular expression in a cherishing of the past. The point has been made more succinctly: 'Without God nothing remains but history.'[62]

Out of these discussions have come initiatives that will lead to the building of an entirely new museum elsewhere, dedicated to national history, and to the compiling of a 'canon' of key events in that history for use in schools. Some see their fears realized, believing that with such a museum and such a canon a one-sided view of history will become generally accepted. Others recognize an opportunity to elicit self-critical opinions about the past, thereby contributing to an open attitude that always keeps an eye on the future.

The work of no less important a Dutch author than W. F. Hermans can be taken as demonstrating that a knowledge of literary history will not necessarily lead to patriotic bombast. In one of his novels, published in 1949, the protagonist says: 'Every Dutchman detests Holland. That is our cardinal national characteristic.'[63] He scoffs at this dismissive attitude, but at the same time he baldly declares that the quality of Dutch literature is mediocre, beginning with the famous Joost van den Vondel. No literary canon exists, since there haven't been enough achievements to fill one. In truth, all important writers criticize the nations that produced them. Hermans is far from alone in that. Attention to the literary past cannot easily be turned into a form of cheap self-affirmation.

Time and again we're called upon to put into words the things that bind us and the things that divide us. Citizenship has to do with a willingness to contribute to the wider surroundings. That effort will be made only by people who are convinced they're part of a continuing history, since what is citizenship in the end but the insight that something has gone before us and something will come after us? We cannot prevent a rancorous turning away from the outside world by neglecting the past, only by reflecting upon it. Heritage and openness should not be experienced as opposites; instead we should always be looking out for new ways to combine them.

Today's unease about democracy is different from that of the 1960s. Then people worried about the freedom of the citizen, whereas now they tend to feel impatient about a perceived lack of security. Anyone seeking an explanation for increased aggression in public places has to consider the one-sided emphasis on rights over past decades. The space demanded by each individual has grown enormously and every violation of it is experienced as a personal insult. The emphasis on individual freedoms has its dark side, as we have seen.

Behind the conflict over integration lurks an uncertainty that has descended upon the Netherlands as a whole about the norms deemed desirable. The murder in The Hague in 2004 of deputy headmaster Hans van Wieren by a Turkish schoolboy revealed a more general shortcoming. It was rightly observed that this murder should be seen against a background of growing aggression in the classroom. Murat D, the boy convicted, is the product of a society struggling to decide how authority should be exercised. That's not to say he was a passive victim – an exception was made in his case that allowed him to be tried in an adult court – but the conclusion drawn on various sides was that aggression is threatening to become commonplace.

Change is now in evidence; people everywhere pine for 'social control'. Wherever you look, whether in psychiatric institutions or housing corporations or schools, attempts are being made to tackle intimidating behaviour and to formulate rules of conduct. People have become suspicious of the habit of turning a blind eye, which is seen as symbolizing a time of indiscriminate tolerance. After so many years in which individual autonomy was given priority it can do no harm to talk once more about our dependence upon one other.

The open society can't be taken for granted. There are plenty of examples of despotism and intolerance in Dutch history. The challenge is to pass on the story of a community without turning our backs on the outside world. A good place to start may be the formulation offered by Jan and Annie Romein that we looked at earlier: 'Even in the established State, the Nation is still in the making.'[64] In that idea lies an invitation to migrants and their children as well as to the rest of society. The conflict surrounding newcomers may prompt a reassessment of the meaning of citizenship in an interdependent world. Clearly, avoidance is not the answer in a time of immigration.

5
European Contrasts

From Emigration to Immigration

Unlike Americans, Europeans do not regard immigration as an important part of their history. Indeed, they generally ignore the fact that over the years millions of people have arrived from beyond their borders. The contrast can be explained. The story Americans tell about their origins and development is woven around the idea of their country as a 'nation of immigrants'. In our part of the world migrants have not played such an important role in the formation of nation-states. For a long time migration in Europe was seen as the exception to the rule.

This self-image is open to challenge, since the crossing of borders has in fact been an essential part of European history. Gérard Noiriel points out that in the interwar years the percentage of foreigners was greater in France than it was in America.[1] The scale of immigration into France in those years may have been exceptional, but migration has been significant all across Europe since early modern times. Dutch historian Jan Lucassen has studied seven distinct patterns of migration in seventeenth- and eighteenth-century Europe. In total, some 300,000 migrant workers were on the move every year, often travelling hundreds of kilometres. Tens of thousands left the poorer mountainous regions of the Massif Central, the Pyrenees and the Alps to head for Paris, and Irish migrants fanned out eastwards across Britain in considerable numbers.

Much has been written about the *Hollandgänger*, Germans who travelled to the wealthy coastal provinces of Holland and Friesland where they helped with haymaking or the heavy labour of cutting peat. Conditions in the 'peat colonies' were tough, with 16-hour working days and high mortality rates from disease. German migrants worked in

Dutch cities as well, as servants or maids, or were employed in merchant shipping and the Dutch colonial army. This particular type of migration peaked in the second half of the eighteenth century, with some 40,000 *Hollandgänger* arriving annually. Jan Lucassen and Rinus Penninx conclude: 'For centuries past, large numbers of newcomers have been coming to the Netherlands, perhaps more than to any other country in Northwestern Europe.'[2]

In the nineteenth century, too, many people left their homes in search of a better life. The large population of Italian migrants in France is one obvious example, as are the many Irish and Poles who moved to other European countries. It says a great deal that the lives of their compatriots in America have been far better recorded, although the deficiency has been rectified to some extent in recent years.

There are early examples of refugee movements too, border crossings that were not a matter of choice. In the sixteenth and seventeenth centuries the new arrivals were mainly communities expelled for their religious beliefs, probably the best known being the half-million French Huguenots persecuted by French Catholics. These were highly skilled people, and cities in the Netherlands competed to attract them, partly by offering tax breaks. Later displacements were increasingly political in nature. Many people fled Poland as a result of the revolutions of 1830–1 and 1848, and most could count on a fair degree of sympathy. The Russian Revolution produced colonies of exiled and impoverished aristocrats in Berlin and later in Paris.

There is another way in which great historical events turn people into migrants. Take the exchange of populations in the 1920s when the Greek inhabitants of Turkey and the Turkish inhabitants of Greece, a total of more than two million people, were forced to move to their 'own' countries. The British diplomat who negotiated this ethnic cleansing was well aware of the moral catastrophe that population transfers represented, describing them as 'a thoroughly bad and vicious solution, for which the world will pay a heavy penalty for a hundred years to come'.[3] Another low point was the expulsion of the Sudeten Germans from Czechoslovakia after the Second World War, which troubles relations between Germany and the Czech Republic to this day.

These are merely a handful of examples from a long history of flight, expulsion and deportation that assumed unprecedented proportions in the post-war period. The number of people displaced by the Second World War has been estimated at 50–60 million. It would not be overstating the case to describe the twentieth century as the 'century of the refugee'. Saskia Sassen has concluded that these refugee movements were partly a product of nation-building, which meant not only that people moved across borders but that borders moved across people.

The founding of new states turned majorities into minorities overnight, like the Germans who suddenly found themselves living in a newly independent Poland.

Migrant labourers and refugees helped to make Europe what it is today, so we should examine this aspect of European history more closely. Which developments are still ongoing and where do the discontinuities lie? In this chapter we will look at the three most important countries in Western Europe – France, Germany and Britain – and make a series of comparisons. Are we witnessing a gradual convergence of ideas on the subject? What impact does the current agonizing over migration have on the process of European integration?

First a quick and inevitably rough sketch of immigration over the past two centuries, focusing mainly on two discontinuities and two rather more enduring aspects. In the nineteenth and early twentieth centuries Europe was the jumping-off point for a vast intercontinental migration that saw a net total of around 45 million Europeans move, mainly to the New World. After the Second World War the flow changed direction, and Northwestern Europe in particular, then Southern and later Central Europe became the destination for a growing number of migrants. This represents a great historical reversal. Another change concerns the role of the state. Klaus Bade is among those who suggest that the First World War marks a turning point. For most of the nineteenth century governments were reluctant to become involved in migration issues, but the end of the Great War signalled the rise of state intervention. Governments were suddenly eager to exercise more influence over the movement of people across borders.

The main reason why Europeans were set adrift in the nineteenth century was the transition from an agrarian to an industrial society, which produced a flow of people from the countryside into the cities. The rationalization of agriculture, along with the inability of cottage industries to compete with factory production, caused a dramatic decline in employment in rural areas. The countries that were first to industrialize were also the first to see large numbers of citizens leave for distant lands; Britain is a prime example, later followed by Germany. The same rule applies to regions that industrialized earlier than others: northern Italy initially led the way; emigration from the south began later.

Industrial expansion went hand in hand with astonishing population growth. Around 1700 Europe's population stood at roughly 115 million and a century later it had risen to 185 million. Then the truly explosive growth began. The first half of the nineteenth century saw a rise of 43 per cent, the second half 50 per cent. On the eve of the First World War there were 468 million Europeans, even though some 45 million had emigrated.

An influential work by Spanish philosopher José Ortega y Gasset, *The Revolt of the Masses* (1930), makes continual reference to this population explosion. The author stumbles over his fellow citizens everywhere: 'Towns are full of people, houses full of tenants, hotels full of guests, trains full of travellers, cafés full of customers, parks full of promenaders, consulting-rooms of famous doctors full of patients, theatres full of spectators, and beaches full of bathers. What previously was, in general, no problem, now begins to be an everyday one, namely, to find room.'[4] This enormous volume of humanity placed a huge strain on society, and the migration of millions to the New World functioned as a safety valve.

Europeans poured out across the globe, but most went to America and later to Canada, Australia or New Zealand. Argentina and Brazil were important destinations as well, especially after the United States implemented a much more restrictive policy towards European immigrants in the 1920s. Ireland, Poland and Italy were among the main countries of origin. Between 1876 and 1976, no fewer than 5.7 million Italians left for America and even more, 12.6 million, for destinations within Europe.

History is repeating itself. With a similar population explosion and depopulation of the countryside taking place outside Europe, considerable flows of migration towards the old continent have developed over the past half-century. Europe once sent its excess population to settle abroad and now many countries in what used to be called the third world are doing likewise. Having been a point of departure, Europe is now the destination for many migrants. In a sense this is a reversal of what happened in the previous century. Migratory patterns in our own time have a great deal to do with our colonial history; Europeans, uninvited, interfered in other societies for centuries and now millions of inhabitants of what were once European colonial possessions have moved to their former motherlands.

Europe's immigrants can be placed under four main headings. First there are the postcolonial migrants, such as the Surinamers who now live in the Netherlands, the Pakistanis in Britain, the Algerians in France and the Angolans in Portugal. The old colonial relationships had often prepared them for what to expect. Many already spoke the language of the old-and-new country. Then there were the workers brought to Europe in years of rapid economic growth, especially the 1960s when the number of migrants living in the European Economic Community doubled from 3.3 million to 6.6 million.[5] Up to a point they too were from former colonies, like the Moroccans who moved to France. Their presence turned out to be permanent and with them came a third category of migrants, family members, who now form the largest category of immigrants in most Western European countries. Lastly, Europe has seen the arrival of a large number of refugees. This group is the most nationally diverse and relationships with the receiving countries are the least clear-cut. A sense of humanitarian duty towards refugees is the decisive factor and in countries like the Netherlands we now see rapidly expanding communities of people from, for instance, Iraq, Afghanistan, Iran, Somalia and Vietnam. Germany is home to a relatively large number of people from former Yugoslavia.

This transformation of a continent of emigration into a continent of immigration brings us to another important discontinuity, namely the increasing tendency of state governments to steer migratory movements. The First World War marks a break with the liberal optimism of the turn of the twentieth century, when cross-border economic traffic increased enormously and people were extremely mobile. In the years before the Great War there were no passport controls. The few that had been in force were abandoned – France, for example, abolished its passport requirement for entry in 1874 – and hundreds of thousands of migrants moved back and forth in an unregulated European labour market. Many Italians worked in France, Poles in Germany and Irish people in Britain, and then there were the Belgians and Poles in France and the Dutch and Italians in Germany. It was generally a situation of laisser-faire, entirely in accordance with the spirit of the times.

It would nevertheless be a distortion of history to say that governments of the period left migrants entirely to their own devices. In 1889 relatively liberal naturalization laws were introduced in France, but in 1913 Germany opted for more restrictions on access to state citizenship. Britain passed an Aliens Act in 1905, making it easier to deport undesirable foreigners. Wars repeatedly made aliens into suspected fifth-columnists of some kind. All German males living in Paris at the start of the Franco-Prussian War in 1870 were ordered to leave the city within three days, and between 1894 and 1906 France expelled some 1,600 immigrants on suspicion of anarchism, in response to the murder of President Sadi Carnot by an Italian anarchist in June 1894.

Yet despite these earlier interventions it remains true to say that the influence of governments on the movement of individuals increased significantly in the years after the First World War. The immediate cause of this change was the economic crisis, which motivated governments to protect their own populations, often by preventing the entry of too many migrants in times of unemployment and economic downturn. Germany introduced a practice called *Inländervorrang*, meaning that priority was given to the indigenous population. In France, entire professions were closed to migrants, despite an otherwise fairly open immigration policy that remained in place until 1932 and which we will look at shortly. The time of free 'proletarian mass migrations', as Sandor Ferenczi calls them, was over. Restrictions were placed on access not just to Europe but to the United States and emigration from Europe to America reached its lowest level for a century.

After the Second World War the development of welfare states, which guarded citizens against the consequences of illness, unemployment and old age, necessitated an even greater degree of control. As more rights accrued to citizenship, access to it became more significant. Equal treatment for those within a nation's borders was predicated upon *un*equal treatment *at* the borders. It was impossible to allow open access to societies that were becoming complex welfare states offering an unprecedented degree of protection to their populations.

Twentieth-century nation-building made the boundaries between natives and foreigners more clear-cut. The sharpening of the distinction can be seen as the price paid for an increase in citizens' rights. Immigration historians concentrate primarily on the problematic side of the break with nineteenth-century liberalism and most are critical of state influence on migration flows. Sassen's view typifies this attitude: 'Although immigrants and refugees at various times reached significant numbers and were seen as "others" even if European, the experience of "invasion" and flows that are out of control do not seem to have been dominant images until the aftermath of World War I. The formation and strengthening of the interstate system brought to the fore questions of border control and nationality. . . . The will to regulate and to "nationalize" all spheres of activity marks this new era in the history of the state.'[6] Bade too is dismissive in his judgement of what he sees as a dual strategy of inclusion and exclusion. He underestimates the fact that efforts to make people integrate are a natural result of state support, which protects residents but inevitably excludes non-residents, protecting those inside while creating obstacles for those outside. The welfare state is an important contributory factor in generating opposition to immigration in our time.

When migrants were thrown out of work en masse after the economic crisis of 1973, their above-average reliance on welfare payments undermined arguments for more immigration. Migrants were still arriving, however, since one of the paradoxical consequences of the economic crisis was that their communities settled in for good. At precisely the point when the oil crisis put an end to Europe's need for migrant labourers, guest workers brought their families to join them and their stay became permanent. The reunification of families not only made immigrants more visible, it also altered the balance of cost and benefit. The original guest workers had been young men at the height of their productive powers, but as soon as they brought their families to join them the proportion of children, women and the elderly in immigrant communities increased.

Early Opposition

Alongside these major changes, certain patterns are repeated throughout the history of European migration over the past two centuries. Clearly, migration within Europe has almost always been of greater magnitude than immigration from the rest of the world, and opposition to migrants emerges time and again. As Leo Lucassen has shown, the newcomers of the nineteenth century were hardly welcomed with open arms. There were riots in 1852 when the residents of Stockport near Manchester attacked Catholic migrants from Ireland, and several people were killed in violent attacks against Italian migrants in the salt mines of Aigues-Mortes in 1893. Countless incidents like these illustrate the uneasy relations between natives and newcomers.

Between the mid-nineteenth century and our own time there were several major migration flows and the three most important countries of origin within Europe were Ireland, Poland and Italy. Migration from these countries continued in the twentieth century, although in the case of the Irish and Italians the numbers fell significantly in the 1970s. Polish migration has increased since the fall of the Berlin Wall in 1989, an indication that the iron curtain shielded Western Europe from migration from the east.

Sassen emphasizes the limited scale of international migratory movements. 'Both emigration and immigration always encompasses only a small fraction of a country's population.'[7] This is certainly true of the receiving nations, but when it comes to the countries the migrants left behind, her assertion is disputable. The extent of emigration from Ireland and Italy was truly immense. As we have seen, 12.6 million Italians left for other European countries and millions more crossed to the New World. The scale of Irish emigration in relation to the population as a whole was even greater. In 1914 two-thirds of all people born in Ireland lived elsewhere.

It is interesting to consider whether these countries benefited from emigration on such a scale. Sassen thinks not: 'But it is clear that for Italy and Ireland, even if now they receive immigrants, the fact of two centuries of labor exporting was not a macroeconomic advantage.'[8] Most research into migration looks at the phenomenon from the perspective of the migrants and says little about the consequences for their native countries of their departure, although we are often reminded that migrants tend to be relatively enterprising and that their emigration deprives a society of reformers and entrepreneurs.

Let's examine for a moment the extent of Italian, Polish and Irish migration.[9] Looking just at the Italians who moved to France, it becomes clear that before the First World War the numbers were well into the hundreds of thousands: 63,000 Italians were registered as French residents in 1851, and 419,000 in 1913. Whereas in 1850 the Belgians were much the largest immigrant group in France, by the turn of the twentieth century the Italians had overtaken them. They were active mainly in the building trades and as seasonal workers in agriculture. In cities like Nice and Marseille they made up around 20 per cent of the population.

The scale of migration out of Poland was astonishing as well. Between 1870 and 1914 around two million Poles emigrated. Along with economic misery, the population was having to endure foreign rule. Since the late eighteenth century Poland had been divided up between the three great powers that bordered it: Prussia, Austria-Hungary and Russia. From the Prussian-held region a huge number of Poles left to work in the expanding mining industry of the Ruhrgebiet in western Germany, especially in the years between 1890 and 1910. On the eve of the First World War the presence of some half a million 'Ruhr Poles' was recorded, and in towns like Bochum, Gelsenkirchen and Dortmund they made up around 20 per cent of the population. In a juridical sense the Ruhr Poles were not immigrants, since until 1918 they were citizens of the German Empire, but in a socio-cultural sense they are a clear example of an ethnic minority.[10]

Finally, Ireland was a disaster area, where the famine of the 1840s (known as 'the hungry forties') claimed countless victims and forced many to flee abroad. Between 1845 and 1855, 2.1 million people left the island, the majority bound for America. While neighbouring countries were experiencing demographic growth, the Irish population declined sharply. Estimates suggest that between 1840 and 1914 a total of some five million Irish people moved to England, Scotland and Wales. The numbers peaked between 1841 and 1861, when half a million crossed to cities like Liverpool, Dundee and Glasgow, where they made up around a fifth of the population.[11]

Lucassen has compared these three migrant groups in an attempt to answer the question of whether the integration of today's migrants from Turkey, Algeria or the Caribbean really is much more problematic than the challenge of absorbing the Irish, Italians and Poles around 100 years ago. His general conclusion is that we have a tendency to see the past in a positive light and the present in a negative one: 'Many elements that are considered crucial stumbling blocks on the road to integration of present-day migrants, . . . such as a threatening religion, homeland politics, transnational ties, (low) social status, and criminality are not as new as we might think.'[12]

His research shows that integration was actually more difficult in the past; the three immigrant communities moved up the social ladder much more slowly than we tend to assume. Although details about the second and third generations are extremely scarce, his considered judgement is that social advancement was limited. The Poles and the Irish in particular had great difficulty extricating themselves from a life in the underclass. The Italians did rather better, a result Lucassen attributes to the relatively inviting attitude of the French government, as demonstrated by more liberal naturalization laws.

These turn-of-the-century migrants aroused considerable opposition. Lucassen presents evidence that the sense of threat many people feel now was just as acute a century ago, when the migrants in question came from other parts of Europe. He identifies three sources of conflict between the three specific groups we have looked at and the countries in which they settled. In France it was mainly a matter of social tensions. The Italians were seen as strike-breakers and as cheap workers who put downward pressure on wages, which is of course true to some degree of all labour migration. There were frequent conflicts, on several occasions leading to violent attacks on Italians, known as '*chasse à l'Italien*'.

Such tensions were palpable in the mining regions of northern France. A series of articles in the socialist daily *Le Reveil du Nord* gives a vivid impression of the mood on the eve of the First World War. There are complaints about migrants who come to earn a bit of quick money: 'The instability of many foreigners is a notable fact. The Germans, the Italians, the Austrians are the most nomadic. . . . They save their little pile of coins, denying themselves everything in order to save the sum they have dreamed of collecting. Then they say goodbye to the mine.' This tendency to avoid spending anything had its consequences: 'The need to save . . . forces the foreigner to lead a sordid life. Spaniards, Italians, Turks, Germans, Austrians present the signs of the blackest misery and the most disgusting filth. What a striking contrast to our French miners, whose concern about cleanliness is such that they wash in their tubs on return-ing from the mine and do not come out before having "freshened up".'

The newspaper, aimed at a readership of local French labourers, is perturbed not only by the nomadic lifestyle of the guest workers of a century ago, but by the crimes they are said to commit: 'The arrival of these strangers has coincided with an upsurge in brawls and violent incidents. It is not unusual after eight in the evening in mining country to hear shots fired. . . . Take a look in the public courtrooms of mining regions. People with exotic silhouettes can often be seen sitting in the dock. . . . Thefts increase; company guards dare not intervene in certain cases for fear of cruel reprisals.'[13]

Social tensions certainly affected Irish and Polish immigrants, but they were compounded by religious differences. Catholic migrants were not at all welcome in overwhelmingly Protestant England and Scotland.

Serious conflict erupted in the years after 1851, when the Catholic epis-
copal hierarchy was restored by the Pope, but religious riots were not
confined to that decade. There was great hostility towards the illiterate
and religiously rather conservative Irish, which on the Irish side led to an
increased consciousness of what they as a people had in common.

The combination of nationalism and Catholicism had enormous
cohesive power for most Irish migrants, with the exception, naturally, of
the Protestants among them, who identified with Britain. This helped to
create political organizations such as the Irish Nationalist Party, which
held seats on Liverpool City Council for several years. But as Irish historian Gearoid O Tuathaigh remarks: 'The dominance of the "national
question" in Irish immigrant political behaviour severely retarded,
indeed almost entirely precluded, significant Irish participation in domestic British politics for the greater part of the nineteenth century.'[14] Irish
nationalism, coupled with a deep aversion to Catholicism, did indeed
arouse fierce opposition.

Alongside all this, the social impact of migration created unease in
the native population. Immigrants competed mainly at the bottom of the
labour market and therefore depressed wages. The notorious description
of Irish immigrants by a youthful Friedrich Engels in his *The Condition
of the English Working Class in 1844* speaks for itself: 'For work which
requires long training or regular, pertinacious application, the dissolute,
unsteady drunken Irishman is on too low a plane. To become a mechanic,
a mill-hand, he would have to adopt the English civilization, the English
customs, become, in the main, an Englishman.' Engels feared that the
English working class would be adversely affected by the presence of
immigrants: 'For when, in almost every great city, a fifth or a quarter of
the workers are Irish, or children of Irish parents, who have grown up
among Irish filth, no one can wonder if the life, habits, intelligence, moral
status – in short, the whole character of the working-class assimilates a
great part of the Irish characteristics.'[15]

The history of the Poles in the Ruhrgebiet renders up another example
of social and religious differences compounded by a conflict of loyalty.
Germans greatly feared Polish nationalism. Under Bismarck, Germany
waged a fierce cultural battle with the primary aim of Germanizing the
Polish-speaking population. Priests were ordered to use the German
language and required to pass an exam in German literature and
culture. Some issues are older than we think. Exactly the same demands
are now being made of Islamic leaders in countries like France and
the Netherlands.

Polish immigrants were greatly distrusted, as demonstrated by the
increasing involvement of the police, who tried to nip nationalism in the
bud. In 1896 Heinrich Konrad von Studt, Oberpräsident of the Province

of Westphalia, gave a clear impression of the mood of those years: 'If nothing is done to stem further political developments, the time will no longer be far off when the Poles will be elected onto their own separate local councils with a majority that will give them dominance on the Municipal Council. . . . Under such circumstances that movement could become, in unsettled times, a threat to public order.'[16]

Such suspicions had unintended consequences, just as they had in the case of the Irish: nationalism in Polish migrant circles only increased and one expression of such sentiments was the establishment of a Polish miners' union. The existing social democrat and Christian trade unions did not treat Polish immigrants as equals, because of what the historian Christoph Klessmann calls their powerful 'national loyalty'. He goes on: 'For their part the Catholic Poles could rarely overcome their deep-seated reservation towards the "German socialists". Despite the class position shared by German and Polish workers, the national question therefore formed an obstacle that was hard for either side to overcome.'[17]

We can examine this kind of social, religious and nationalistic conflict partly with an eye to the present day. There are innumerable parallels between historical and contemporary migrations, and past conflicts confirm the general impression that immigration always leads to clashes. Conflict should be seen as part of the history of integration and clearly the most explosive situations arise when social tensions are combined with religious or national division. Take the riots in Marseille in 1881, when smouldering resentment towards Italians erupted in the context of an international dispute between France and Italy over Tunisia. When returning French troops entered the French port city, people in the crowds that had turned out to watch claimed they'd heard disapproving whistles coming from the Italian Club. A violent reaction ensued. In widespread rioting that continued for two days, Italians were hunted down. Three people died and some 20,000 Italians left the city in the aftermath of the disturbances.[18]

Such incidents demonstrate that international conflicts can have direct consequences for relations between immigrant groups and native populations. It therefore takes little imagination to see the risks posed by the combination of integration problems affecting Muslim communities in the Western world and a flaring up of hostilities between the West and political Islam in the Middle East. International tension of this kind can lead to conflicts of loyalty in migrant circles as well as to suspicion in majority communities, which regard every sign of protest as a warning of treachery to come.

The underlying suggestion in Lucassen's work is that the frequency of such confrontations down through history means today's conflicts are nothing out of the ordinary. This emphasis on historical continuity is perfectly legitimate as long as it doesn't create a nonchalant attitude of 'all's well that ends well'. In the long run, a settlement is generally found, but the fact remains that problems of adjustment can be persistent and intense. Although history teaches us that every integration process is accompanied by conflict, this is not to say that a harmonious outcome is guaranteed under present circumstances. There is considerable uncertainty, as the story of post-war immigration in France, Germany and Britain makes clear. All three countries are experiencing profound changes in the composition of their populations, and everywhere the traditional answers are proving inadequate.

Republican Answers

France's immigration history is characterized first of all by exceptional demographics. Almost a century earlier than in other European countries, a rapid drop in the number of births caused the population to shrink – in a deeply Catholic country at that. This says a great deal about the discrepancy between religious doctrine and real life; it seems Catholic teaching about marriage and reproduction did not fall on fertile soil. These extraordinary circumstances forced the country to resort to immigration at an early stage, so that it could continue to industrialize in the second half of the nineteenth century. Migrants were sought mainly in neighbouring countries such as Italy and Belgium, but many more came from Poland and Portugal.

The composition of the population is not the only unusual thing about France; its political principles mark it out as well. After the Revolution of 1789, for all the tragic oppression and violence that followed, it aimed to set an example as a modern nation based on the principle of equality. The French republican tradition is similar to that of America with its 1776 Declaration of Independence. Both countries see themselves as the bearers of universal ambitions. Yet in contrast to America, the revolution in France initially resulted in a more divided nation. Efforts to establish the republican ideal as a shared horizon only really took shape in the final quarter of the nineteenth century.

France's immigration history therefore begins at the intersection of two developments: demographic decline and the rise of republican thinking. Demographic stagnation was at odds with its lofty ambition. Noiriel speaks of the paradox of a 'completed' nation with a shrinking population.[19] Ironically, while France was building a colonial empire, the population back home could be sustained numerically only by immigration. Sooner or later colonialism and immigration were bound to influence each other.

Let's look more closely at French immigration history before moving on to ask how republican ideals influenced the integration of the country's many newcomers. From the late nineteenth century onwards there was an urgent need not only for foreign workers but also for soldiers. At the start of the twentieth century France signed agreements with countries including Italy and Belgium, and with the lands that became the independent states of Poland and Czechoslovakia. A considerable number of immigrants arrived between 1920 and 1930 alone – in total more than a million newcomers were registered in that decade.[20] The Société Générale d'Immigration was set up in 1924 to guide the flows of migration in a favourable direction, assuming responsibility for selection and medical examinations, and for organizing transport and regulating the distribution of groups of migrants across the companies offering to employ them. This is similar in every respect to the post-war history of guest workers.

After the Second World War the situation was not significantly different. Once again France was struggling with a demographic deficit that could be resolved only by immigration. Within the Haut Comité de la Population a debate raged about the numbers required. Political and economic incentives overlapped, but they were not identical. Considerations of power politics led to persistent efforts to expand the population, whereas economic demand for migrants fluctuated according to market trends. Weighing up these interests, France settled on a target figure of one and a half million migrants for the five years beginning in 1945.

An interesting debate ensued about how to select immigrants. Georges Mauco, a leading figure in the Haut Comité, was an advocate of the American model, which distinguished between migrants according to ethnic origin. Based on the assumption that certain groups would assimilate far more readily than others, he wanted to exclude migrants from North Africa and Asia. Mauco's recommendations, which were taken up by President de Gaulle, include this assertion: 'It is necessary to limit the entry of Mediterranean and oriental people. They have changed the population structure of France profoundly over the past half-century.'[21] In his discussion of this episode, historian Patrick Weil emphasizes the contradiction between the republican ideal of equality and the proposed ethnic selection of immigrants. In the end, the ethnic guidelines did not pass into law. After intervention by the Conseil d'État, all references to the selection of immigrants were removed.

Decolonization was to be the next test of the equality principle. Like Britain, France was ensnared by its own colonial ambitions, with the ultimate outcome that from 1947 onwards Algerians were officially categorized as French citizens and therefore had a right to freedom of movement between the colony and the motherland. Because of this commitment the colonial question had a major impact on the politics of immigration, as illustrated by the words of a young parliamentarian of the time, Jean-Marie Le Pen, the future leader of the populist Front National. During a debate in 1958 he remarked: 'What should be said of the Algerians is not that they have need of France but that France has need of them. ... I contend that there is nothing in the religion of Islam that, from a moral point of view, prevents a believing or practising Muslim from becoming a full French citizen. ... I conclude: offer the Muslims of Algeria entry and integration into a dynamic France.'[22]

From the moment the influx began, France tried to dissuade Algerians from coming, but the country was hostage to promises made, and after decolonization it had a struggle on its hands to impose any restrictions at all. Not only did French leaders try to reduce the number of immigrants, they were worried about the rights accruing to them. Their presence was supposed to be temporary and their attitudes were closely monitored. During the struggle for Algerian independence, Algerian immigrants were denied the right of association for many years. When in the 1970s they were finally granted permission to organize, it was the Algerian government that raised objections, since it feared they would find their own voice and anticipated political problems. Weil points to an incentive to sustain the flow of migrants while at the same time restricting their rights, an incentive shared by entrepreneurs, the government of the country of settlement and the government of the country of origin.

The 1950s and '60s were decades of large-scale labour migration, but after the economic crisis of 1973, France stopped recruiting workers from abroad. Virtually all Western European countries made the same decision. At that point there were 3.5 million foreigners in France, the largest groups being 750,000 Portuguese and a roughly equal number of Algerians, half a million Spaniards, slightly fewer Italians and a quarter of a million Moroccans. One might say that until the mid-1970s immigration into France was primarily a Mediterranean affair. Clearly, geographical proximity was of crucial importance to post-war as well as to pre-war migration flows.

As in surrounding countries, the effect of the decision to end migration to France was counterintuitive. While there was no longer any economic need for migrants, the reuniting of families and, not long afterwards, the formation of families became major factors, bringing millions more migrants to France. Of all European countries, France made the most tenacious efforts to send them back, especially the Algerians. Beginning in 1978, it negotiated with the Algerian government to arrange for the return of the 800,000 Algerian migrants who at that point did not have

French nationality. Parliament decided that 120,000 migrants would be returned annually, by force if necessary. Countless diplomatic agreements and economic support measures later, the French concluded that their efforts had run into the sand. The Algerian government was deploying a combination of diplomatic delaying tactics and appeals to the former colonizer's sense of guilt.

Those years saw innumerable attempts to regulate family reunification and family formation, but intervention by the courts showed such rights to be inviolable. The Algerian government, incidentally, was not at all happy to see families reunited, since it meant the permanent settlement of migrants in France and therefore a reduction in transfers of money to the home country. Also, and not without cause, it predicted that the children of migrants would slowly become estranged from Algerian culture. The accuracy of this prediction was demonstrated in a way no one had expected. France and Algeria agreed that young people with dual nationality should undergo national service in their parents' country. It soon emerged that the Algerian army was experiencing great difficulty with young recruits who had grown up in France and were in many respects both unwilling and unable to adjust to the traditional practices of the Algerian armed forces.

Once the realization finally dawned that it was illusory to expect migrants to return and that attempts to limit family reunification had failed, France began working on improvements to their social and legal position. From the early 1980s onwards, restrictions on further immigration were coupled with policies designed to promote integration. The same happened in Britain and Germany, but ideas about integration differed between the three countries. The republican equality principle and resistance to the formation of ethnic groups were crucial to France's efforts to merge newcomers into society.

We need to look more closely at the history of republican thinking in order to understand the strengths, and indeed the weaknesses, of that tradition where it relates to the position of migrants. The lost war with Prussia of 1870–1 was followed by an age of modernization. France continued to centralize and the state was increasingly seen as the embodiment of an emancipatory ideal. Victory over the powerful regional orientation of its citizens and the adoption of a standardized language that steadily supplanted regional dialects were important steps towards the creation of the modern French nation. From this perspective, France's 'crucible' was initially a means not so much of assimilating newcomers as of absorbing Bretons, Basques and other population groups into the French state.

Schools were crucial to these efforts to unify and assimilate. Education became compulsory for French children in 1882, beginning with those aged 6–13. For the children of migrant families, the rule applied only from 1936 onwards. The state school, as defined by Jules Ferry, Minister of Education when the Act was passed, is a familiar concept in France. As well as handing down knowledge, it was explicitly intended to create citizens who would identify with the republican ideal and therefore free themselves from group cultures, whether regional or foreign.

The main focus of republican thinking was a belief that each new generation must pay its debts to previous generations. Everyone is born into a world shaped by the efforts of those who have gone before; all newcomers, whatever their backgrounds, are presented with a legacy. Clearly this debt cannot be repaid to former generations; instead it imposes a duty on everyone to make an effort to help the community. Awareness of this was hammered into the citizens of France: 'The right of one is the duty of another.'

Large-scale immigration in the late nineteenth century meant that migrants helped mould republican thinking. France did not really see itself as a nation of immigrants; rather, as sociologist Dominique Schnapper puts it: 'Unity was professed, sought and valued all the more as reality became more diverse.'[23] In this sense immigration reinforced republican thinking. The French nation was multiform in a cultural sense, but it strove to bind its diverse beliefs and lifestyles into a common project.

This concept of citizenship brought with it liberal ideas about the naturalization of newcomers, and access to French nationality became easier. The first major legislation dates from 1889. Its inspiration was twofold. First, a relaxation of the conditions for naturalization was prompted by a need to maintain the number of conscripts. Without new Frenchmen there was a risk the army would decline in strength, and irritation had arisen about migrants who'd resided in the country for years but could not be called up for military service. The second explicit aim of the new naturalization laws was to prevent the formation of 'foreign nuclei' (*noyaux allogènes*). Even at this early stage there was a fear of segregation and of the consolidation of ethnic groups. It's interesting to note that towards the end of the nineteenth century the French government actually started encouraging immigrants to reunite their families or to create families by marrying women from their home countries, since the nomadic lifestyle of Italian migrants was regarded as incompatible with efforts to integrate them. Members of the Italian migrant community had a strong tendency to return to their native land. Bringing a wife and children to join you is indeed a form of permanent settlement.

The thinking behind naturalization shifted away from an emphasis on blood relations towards a stress on an individual's place of birth. In other words the *ius sanguinis* was replaced by the *ius soli*. The *ius soli* already had a long history. The connection between nationality and territory had been recognized before the French Revolution, which introduced the new criterion of blood relations in determining a person's nationality. In the sixteenth century the emphasis on links with the soil had meant subjugation to the ruling prince, but by this point, at the end of the nineteenth century, a person's place of birth had gained a more emancipatory significance.

There were limits to the elevation in status brought about by naturalization, however, since the new French did not have the same rights as established citizens in every respect. They were not eligible to vote until they had resided in France for 10 years, and from 1934 onwards all kinds of obstacles were thrown up to prevent naturalized French people from joining professions such as the law and medicine. This distinction between the native and the naturalized was of course a fundamental violation of the republican ideal of equality. At the time of the Vichy Regime it would lead to the reversal of naturalization for many thousands of Jews. This is one more argument against ever placing such limitations on citizenship; naturalization should be an irreversible step that dissolves all distinctions in law between newcomers and the indigenous population. Only in the late 1970s and early 1980s were all restrictions on naturalized French citizens finally lifted.

Although the past few decades have seen fierce arguments about whether all children born in France to foreign parents should automatically be accorded French nationality, the principle of *ius soli* has never again been seriously contested. The underlying idea is that a lasting stay on French soil ensures people absorb local habits and customs. School-aged children in particular are drawn into the history of the republic, which they increasingly experience as their own history. So much for the theory. Nowadays people are beginning to wonder whether that is still the way it works. The self-confidence of the French has been visibly eroded.

Ever since the early 1990s, Dominique Schnapper has been convinced that integration is in full swing: 'The massive fact, confirmed by all the research, is the acculturation of children schooled in France who come from migrant families and their willingness to integrate.'[24] Others question whether such a willingness exists and see the periodic outbursts of violence in the *banlieues* since the early 1980s as indicative of a far broader alienation. There is much more going on, says philosopher Jean-François Mattéi. The crisis in the *banlieues* 'shows us the failure of the French social model and of the pretence of being a cultural exception'.[25]

The malaise many migrants find themselves in goes right to the heart of the equality model of the republican state. It's not hard to understand why, after the umpteenth riot on France's urban housing estates, people in authority prefer to stick within the confines of a social issue and avoid

of citizenship and what it means in practice on urban housing estates. The republican model has lost some of its power to bind people together, but in France there are not many workable alternatives as yet. Here and there appeals can be heard for the introduction of positive discrimination in some form and the allocation of public subsidy for the building of mosques.

France is now reconsidering its unique position. The Europeanization of the country is experienced as a painful adjustment, but there is no other way out of the current impasse surrounding immigration. This is equally true of other countries where similar difficulties have arisen. It would be to the advantage of all if that self-examination were accompanied by a sharing of experiences across borders, starting with the country with which France allied itself in its efforts to make the unification of Europe a reality after the war: Germany. It would then become clear that a lack of self-confidence can be found elsewhere too, despite the fact that historical experiences have affected relations with post-war migrants in diverse ways.

Foreigners After Genocide

However much Germany wants to see itself as a normal country, there's no escaping a sense that it's not entirely normal, if only because the word 'normal' is so often heard. Germany's history is actively present in heads and hearts, including those of the post-war generation. There can be no denying that the proximity of its terrible past under Hitler makes it an exception. No other country has engaged so conscientiously and persistently with the most damning aspects of its own history, the results of a racial worldview, and Germany's dealings with immigration have been powerfully influenced by the settling of accounts with that past.

Since the unification festivities at the Brandenburg Gate, if not before, two views of the future of the nation have stood in opposition. On one side are Germans who long for the country's normalization. Finally a line can be drawn under its wartime history. Germans have given sufficient account of themselves. On the other side are those who believe that because of Auschwitz the Germans have more or less forfeited their right to self-determination; a people capable of plumbing such depths can no longer be left to its own devices. Only if Germany is irreversibly bound to Europe will it have armed itself adequately against a return to the past. Normalization versus mistrust – the same feelings about Germany switch back and forth outside the country as well.

In the turbulent years that followed the fall of the Berlin Wall, the stance of those who looked upon the new Germany with trepidation seemed justified when a series of attacks took place on centres for asylum-seekers. In those outbursts of the early 1990s several people were killed. German migration expert Christian Joppke calls the wave of violence 'the most serious domestic crisis' Germany has had to deal with in the post-war period.[30] The violence began in the former East Germany, when crowds in Hoyerswerda and later in Rostock-Lichtenhagen cheered as centres for asylum-seekers were attacked by extremist right-wing youths. This series of violent incidents and especially the inability of the police to come up with a convincing response brought back memories of the unstable Weimar Republic. The arson attack in Mölln in which a Turkish family died and violence towards foreigners in Solingen produced outrage across Europe and further afield.

After the attacks there was heightened suspicion, as illustrated by books such as *Wird Deutschland wieder gefährlich?* [Is Germany becoming dangerous again?] by Jewish author Ralph Giordano. He describes how for over a year 'at the heart of Europe ... an area of near-lawlessness' existed.[31] He does not believe the old demons have returned to Germany, but still, what will happen when the generation that can remember the war is no longer around? Could it be that 'efforts to shake off the dark episode in German history will find particularly fertile soil? Such a break with the history of National Socialism would amount to a re-entry of the "*Auschwitzlüge*" through the back door.'[32] Is there really a slippery slope such that the desire for normalization inevitably leads, via suppression of the memory of recent history, to outright denial of the holocaust (the *Auschwitzlüge*)? Every attempt to bring about a balanced relationship with the past risks accusations of disavowing that past. And every debate about asylum and migration in Germany becomes tangled up with what happened during the war.

One of the country's young authors, Bodo Morshäuser, has shrewdly exposed this attitude as unsustainable. He describes the shadow boxing between 'national pride' and what he calls 'negative nationalism': 'Why is it impossible for many people to accept that others are proud of their origins? And why do those others have to say that they are proud? Their statement derives its effect from the backgrounds of all those who are ashamed to be German.'[33] During the period of violence against foreigners, demonstrators marching in Berlin appealed to immigrants: 'Don't leave us alone with the Germans in this country.'

Over the border in the Netherlands, many people shared these suspicions. A million Dutch citizens sent postcards expressing their 'fury' after the attacks in Mölln and Solingen – the assumption being that the majority of Germans would not have been able to reach a comparable conclusion on their own behalf. No one wanted to acknowledge what lay behind the crisis surrounding the right to asylum in Germany. For a start, the country had the most liberal asylum laws possible. The famous Article 16 of the post-war German constitution states in four words, without any proviso at all: '*Politisch Verfolgte geniessen Asylrecht*', meaning that anyone suffering political persecution has a right to asylum in Germany. Those who drew up the article were aware of the consequences of such an open formulation, but they regarded the clause as penance. Joppke writes that the German constitution is in fact quite extraordinary, since the first seven articles place universal human rights above any duty to German citizens. The rights of the individual are paramount and those rights are guaranteed irrespective of nationality.[34]

Daniel Cohn-Bendit and Thomas Schmid, both of whom were responsible for integration policy in Frankfurt in the early 1990s, point out that 'enforced generosity' as laid down in the constitution is a contradiction in terms, since generosity has to be a voluntary gesture. Openness cannot be decreed by law.[35] Housing asylum-seekers in small towns and in problem districts within major cities had the opposite of the intended effect. It's undeniable, they write, that through 'the presence of asylum-seekers – in already disadvantaged areas in particular – the quality of life for residents can decline appreciably'.[36]

This proved true in the years that followed German unification. The direct cause of the asylum crisis was the size of the influx of migrants and asylum-seekers. Between 1989 and 1992 the recently united country had to deal with around three million. The fact that the asylum crisis coincided with the years of unification was the result of a number of factors. In some ways it was coincidental, in others not. The coincidental aspect was that floods of refugees were produced by, among other things, the civil war in Yugoslavia, but of course it was no accident that many went to Germany. They chose it because of its generous asylum laws. Add to this the streams of other newcomers from Eastern Europe and it becomes clear that migration was placing an increasing strain on Germany and that this was a contributory factor in hostile reactions to it.

After the attacks in Mölln and Solingen there was great embarrassment. Everything that people had come to believe in recent years was suddenly up in the air again. The agonizing of Germans about Germans is still going on, and of course migrants have not failed to notice. Necla Kelek writes about the 'nature conservancy' (*Naturschutz*) under which Germany places everything that is culturally different. She criticizes the vicious circle of 'misplaced tolerance and silence as an expression of solidarity' among those aware of abuses in minority circles.[37] Given all the post-war evidence of good behaviour, it should indeed be possible for Germans to address immigrants in their own country with rather more candour.

They would have to start by taking stock of the complicated history of immigration in Germany over recent decades, which involves two very different groups of newcomers: the ethnic Germans who poured eastwards after the war and the guest workers who arrived from countries like Italy and Yugoslavia and later from Turkey. The contrasting treatment of the two groups can be understood only by looking at the extraordinary history of divided Germany, since the West German constitution imposed a special duty towards those of German descent who found themselves living outside the borders of the Federal Republic. They were allowed immediate access to citizenship, whereas guest workers and their families were given only very limited opportunities to acquire German nationality. The obligation to accommodate the German diaspora was not a dead letter: quite the reverse. Between 1945 and 1989 the country absorbed 14 million ethnic Germans. In the year the Wall fell, around a quarter of the German population had its origins in this form of immigration, whereas only around 8 per cent was without any German ancestry.

A substantial proportion of those 14 million were what were known as *Heimatvertriebenen*: ethnic Germans who had lived in Eastern Europe, often for many generations, and who were no longer welcome there after the war. Their expulsion went unmentioned for many years; Germans were perpetrators, not victims. German historian Guido Knopp describes how the so-called Sudeten Germans were expelled by brute force after the liberation of Czechoslovakia. The first step towards their expulsion was the introduction of white armbands with a large N on them (for *Nemec*, the Czech word for German), which they were forced to wear. Not long afterwards, families that in many cases had lived in Bohemia for centuries were driven out. They left all their possessions behind, if they escaped being killed. This form of revenge was accepted by the Allied powers.[38]

Stories like theirs explain why Germany's nationality laws could not be changed until after 1989. The division of the country into East and West meant that the duty towards ethnic Germans elsewhere was beyond dispute. Only after unification were quotas placed on this group, which in recent decades has been arriving mainly from the former Soviet Union. Currently, no more than 225,000 such migrants are admitted each year.

At the same time the conditions for acquiring German nationality were changed. While in most European countries and in America official residence for five years is sufficient to qualify a person to apply for citizenship, in Germany a reform of the law reduced this period from ten years to eight. The children of migrants, if they were born in Germany, do now have much easier access to state citizenship. This step was unavoidable, since the results of the nationality law were becoming steadily more grotesque. Descendants of the Volga Germans, for example, who often did not speak the language and lacked any understanding of the country they were moving to, were immediately recognized as citizens, whereas the children of Turkish migrants, born in Germany, were categorized as foreigners. Until 1990 no more than 1,400 non-German migrants were naturalized annually. One consequence was that the civil service, where employment is open only to holders of German passports, had always been off-limits to immigrant job applicants.

Germans generally saw post-war labour migration as a temporary phenomenon, as did the new arrivals, who clung to the myth of return for far too long. The provisional nature of their presence, compounded by the fact that it was virtually impossible for them to become German citizens, contributed significantly to the sense of alienation in the large Turkish community. Research by Wilhelm Heitmeyer shows that no fewer than three-quarters of young Turkish people polled agreed with the statement 'we can never feel like Germans because we don't belong'.[39]

The recruitment of guest workers began in the late 1950s, but it was boosted by the building of the Berlin Wall, which sharply reduced the number of migrants from the east. Workers from the south were needed to sustain the country's astonishing economic growth. The first agreements were made with Italy, Spain, Yugoslavia, Portugal and Turkey. By 1955, 80,000 guest workers were living in Germany, and by 1959 their numbers had risen to 160,000; in 1961 there were 500,000, in 1966 1.3 million, and by 1973 there were 2.6 million. In the 1960s between 500 and 600 labour exchanges were engaged in attracting willing and cheap labour to the dirtiest and toughest jobs in the country, often in metalworking and construction.

Cohn-Bendit and Schmid comment that the recruitment of guest workers was the lazy way out. The arrival of foreign labour undoubtedly contributed to a delay in badly needed innovation. This is the most commonly expressed criticism of the labour migration option: downward pressure on wage levels enables enterprises using outdated means of production to sustain their output, although usually for a limited period. When rationalization is finally implemented, as it was in the car industry between 1980 and 1985, a loss of jobs results, mainly affecting foreign employees. These authors are right, by the way, to say that the term 'guest worker' has 'a totally unbearable undertone of generosity', since this type of labour migration could equally well be regarded as a form of 'foreign development aid for Germany'.[40] At least, they're correct as far as the first few decades are concerned. The economic balance of labour migration has since tipped the other way and the benefits are declining before our eyes.

After the economic crisis of 1973, in Germany as in France, there were attempts to reduce immigrant numbers, but as elsewhere the newly restrictive policy actually prompted people to make the decision to stay. Generally speaking, efforts to persuade guest workers to return came to nothing and the same can be said of moves to limit family reunification. In 1981 this led to a political crisis. Over the preceding three years almost half a million family members had arrived, mainly from Turkey. The government stated frankly that Germany felt no responsibility for the children and grandchildren of the original migrants. As in France and Britain, politicians were sensitive to growing opposition to continued migration, but the courts set themselves up as liberal defenders of the constitution.

One important exception in the German case concerns the right of migrants from outside the European Union to vote in local elections. In contrast to countries like Sweden and the Netherlands, Germany refused to go down this route. The same is true of France, where in 1981 the idea of introducing a right to vote in local council elections was briefly entertained but then abandoned. This means there is a distinction between migrants from countries within the European Union, who do have such voting rights, and migrants from outside the Union. Constitutional expert Josef Isensee has presented several arguments in support of his belief that giving non-naturalized migrants the right to vote is a bad idea. It devalues state citizenship, since it means naturalization confers few exclusive rights. It also means creating a distinct type of citizen, since unlike the indigenous population, migrants can retreat from the consequences of their own voting decisions by returning to their countries of origin. He regards a migrant's right to vote as 'freedom without responsibility'.[41]

Despite its outcome, the debate surrounding the rights of migrants demonstrates that guest workers had increasingly converted their temporary stay into permanent settlement, as reflected in the famous dictum of the Swiss writer Max Frisch: '*Man hat Arbeitskräfte gerufen, und es kommen Menschen*' [We called for workers, and we got people]. The composition of migrant communities changed. The Italians, initially the largest group, were replaced by Turks, who at 2.5 million now comprise by far the biggest migrant community in Germany.

Much has been written about the Turkish community. Of the more critical writers, several stand out, among them Necla Kelek and Bassam Tibi. Both believe that in the majority of cases the integration of Muslims in Germany should be regarded as a failure up to now. They say there's a significant risk that society will split into a series of 'parallel communities', separate ethnic enclaves that have little contact with the wider environment. In several of these niches – most famously in Hamburg – the attacks of 11 September 2001 were prepared.

Tibi comes originally from Damascus, and he makes no secret of his disappointment about various features of the receiving society, but he directs his main criticism at the aloof or even dismissive stance of many Muslims and the naive reaction of gullible Germans, often with a Protestant background (*Deutsche Gutmenschen*), who try to compensate for the past by embracing all things foreign. Germans renounce their own identity while going out of their way to protect the identities of migrants. Tibi claims there's insufficient awareness of the fact that the individualism of the European Enlightenment tradition can easily come into conflict with the attitudes many migrants exhibit: 'In Islam there is for instance no concept of individual identity.'[42] A clearer orientation is needed in Europe, Tibi writes. In cases of conflict, basic Western values should take precedence over those of Islam.

The increasing importance of Islam in the lives of guest workers should also be seen in the light of family reunification. With the arrival of their wives and children, men were reminded of their duty to defend their families against what was seen as a hostile environment of lax morals. The guest workers became Turks and the Turks became Muslims, and this was not simply a result of how they were seen by the Germany majority society.

Kelek has written extensively about family relationships in the Turkish community, relationships that make it all the more isolated from German society. The practice of importing brides is flourishing. Girls are 'sold' and Germany itself, with all its opportunities, is the real bride price. Often given in marriage at an early age, they lead an utterly isolated existence in their new country. Most are kept out of sight so that they inconvenience the men as little as possible and cannot tarnish the family's honour. Kelek paints a sad picture, saying that for many girls human rights simply do not apply. She's equally worried about the sons, since no one has taught these 'lost boys' to question their fathers' authority, to be critical in their dealings with people in positions of power. There's no culture in which they can seriously learn about their own responsibilities; they simply submit to the orders of the family.

Kelek passes harsh judgement on parents who refuse to recognize that they need to prepare their children for life in a new environment. Why don't they send their children to kindergarten, where they'd come into contact with other children and learn the language through play? Instead they opt for the Koranic school. Her conclusion is: 'Anyone who, having lived in Germany for 30 years, still presents Turkey to the children as their true home and brings them up according to the maxim "*en büyük türk*", the Turk stands above all others, discredits his own path in life as a mistake.'[43] After all, why would anyone choose to live in surroundings they profoundly despise? It's an attitude she illustrates with a remark by one of her interviewees: 'We've got everything here, we don't need the Germans.'[44]

Almost all studies show that nationalism in the Turkish community is strong, despite the fault-lines that divide it, such as the ethnic distinction between Turks and Kurds, the political distinction between Kemalists and Islamists and the religious distinction between Sunnis and Alevis. It's a fragmented community, but one in which a clear majority of parents and children have explicit religious and nationalistic beliefs. Heitmeyer's research reveals attitudes that do not belong in a liberal democracy. Two-thirds of young people questioned, for example, dismiss adherents of other religions as unbelievers, more than half believe Islam is superior to other faiths and a quarter endorse the use of violence in defence of Islam. The powerful nationalism that Heitmeyer encountered as an accompaniment to this religious stance is discomforting, given his respondents' rejection of the majority society and indeed of other minorities.

In attempting to explain the findings of his research, which was carried out in the mid-1990s, well before 9/11, Heitmeyer says among other things that many young Turkish people have low self-esteem and Islam has the effect of raising their status. Many of the children have little in the way of educational qualifications and their ambitions have not been realized. It doesn't help that the majority population persists in an attitude that sees young people who were born and brought up in Germany as foreigners. He makes a connection between a prevalence of extremist beliefs and 'modernization's losers', who are present in above average numbers in migrant communities.

Heitmeyer is one of many who warn against the development of parallel societies, saying that most of the Turkish community has isolated itself from the majority population. He adds: 'The necessary recognition of the Turkish population group as a normal part of society has a "downside" in that it involves a more critical attitude towards that group.'[45] This remark shows once again that it's still difficult to carry out this kind of research without immediately being accused of stigmatizing others.

Quite apart from the country's traumatic history and the specific issues surrounding Muslim communities, the entire debate about immigration and integration in Germany has been heavily loaded for another reason. The country is struggling more than most with the effects of an aging and shrinking population. The indigenous population now has a fertility quotient of 1.2, which is low even by European standards, certainly compared with, for example, more than 1.8 in the case of France, which, as we have seen, was faced with demographic decline even in the nineteenth century and introduced corrective measures long ago.

Hans Magnus Enzensberger sets the fear of population shrinkage beside the fear of too much migration. We are continually hearing that 'the boat is full'. An odd image, he says, in the sense that the native inhabitants draw a comparison that makes them seem like 'boat people', in other words refugees, but odder still in that, according to demographic trends, the established population is aging and therefore declining. 'The idea that at one and the same time too few and too many people are living on the same territory causes panic – a form of suffering that I would propose calling demographic bulimia,' he comments sarcastically.[46]

Yet the two questions that lurk behind this psychological disorder – namely, how should we deal with a shrinking population and how much immigration can we handle? – are real enough, all the more so in combination. The population is aging and changing colour at the same time. Population growth in Germany is entirely attributable to immigration. Moreover, the origin of migrants is increasingly diverse. As in other countries of immigration in Europe, the resulting unease is tangible and it's seeking a political voice.

Author and politician Peter Glotz wrote a sombre account of the issue even before German unification. He detected deep fears of *Überfremdung* in the population, in other words a loss of identity through immigration, and warned against an 'all too relaxed liberal cosmopolitanism'.[47] Decades later, populism has still not really broken through in German political life, in contrast to many of its neighbours, but the possibility hangs in the air, especially in the former East Germany. The debate about immigration remains circumspect, but it has produced a number of important adjustments, for example to the naturalization laws. The issue that lies behind all this – how to deal with both a shrinking population and growing immigration – has yet to be resolved.

Taking Leave of Empire

The shadow of history hangs over post-war immigration in Britain too, but a history of a very different kind – that of decolonization. The unforeseen arrival of colonial migrants went hand in hand with a proclaimed farewell to an imperial illusion. Profound changes to Britain's role in the world set in motion a stream of new Britons from the West Indies, West Africa and the Indian subcontinent. From the start, the debate about the place of the 'coloured minorities' in British society was part of a broader search for a new place for Britain in the world.

Not that people were quick to reach the conclusion that the end of the British Empire was at hand. Even when many colonies were granted independence in the decades after the war, Britain tried to pursue its worldwide role by other means. Indian independence in 1947 led to the founding of the Commonwealth, a loose agglomeration of countries that had once been part of the British Empire. The laws on British nationality introduced in 1948 described every citizen of the Commonwealth as a British subject and provided for their freedom of movement as a logical outcome of that status. So, in theory, any resident of India or Jamaica could settle in the 'motherland'. Of course they were not expected to do so, but the principle of equal treatment for all 'subjects' was essential to the dream of a continuing British role in an era of decolonization.

This is the irony of the post-war immigration debate in the United Kingdom, which is comparable to the French experience in the sense that again it was the most determined defenders of the imperial tradition who tried longest to uphold the right of people from the former colonies to settle in Britain. In the mid-1960s journalist Elspeth Huxley wrote: 'Here crops up, again, the image of the mother who has sent forth her sons and mustn't slam the door in the face of any who want to come home.'[48] It was precisely that enduring memory of the worldwide mission of the British that unintentionally encouraged the permanent settlement in the motherland of so many migrants from the colonies. In this sense the 'multiracial' nature of Britain is to some extent the result of an inadequate grasp of reality on the part of those who tried to hold on to the imperial idea long after it had passed its sell-by date.

The beginning of this type of immigration is symbolically marked by the arrival of the SS *Empire Windrush*, which docked at Tilbury on 22 June 1948 with more than 400 West Indian passengers on board. A considerable proportion of them had fought for Britain during the war, some as RAF pilots, many as ground staff. They arrived in the motherland with high expectations, regarding their trip in a sense as 'going home', a voyage to the country whose praises they had sung every day as school-children. Sam King, from Jamaica, remembers: 'So your whole outlook was British oriented, because they rule. The schoolbooks, the missionaries and everything was the British mentality. You could not be good on your own. Your good was not good. Your good had to be British.'[49]

They were so favourably disposed towards the motherland that ultimate disappointment was inevitable. The cold shower came quickly. The arm's-length reception they received was particularly shocking to those who had fought alongside the British and been welcomed affectionately at that time. How come they now found not the slightest sign of gratitude? Then there was the question they were continually being asked: 'When are you going home?'

Migration brought the 'Windrush generation' another disturbing but salutary experience. In the colonies they'd come into contact only with the British elite – if they had any contact with the upper echelons of society at all – but in daily life in British cities, still peppered with bomb sites, they clashed with the working classes. The shock of seeing a white woman sweeping a station concourse was incalculable. They'd never seen

English people working with their hands. An encounter with an illiterate white man would shatter a long-cherished illusion.

V. S. Naipaul, who arrived from Trinidad a few years later, would always remember his disillusion at the motherland of his dreams: 'So I grew to feel that grandeur belonged to the past; that I had come to England at the wrong time; that I had come too late to find the England, the heart of empire, which (like a provincial, from the far corner of the empire) I had created in my fantasy.'[50] In search of a centre that no longer existed, the young Naipaul retained a burning ambition, as he reported to his father: 'I have got to show these people that I can beat them at their own language.'[51]

But no one was truly eager to welcome him and the government reacted less than invitingly to the arrival of the first immigrants. In Parliament, the minister responsible declared he had been unpleasantly surprised by the *Windrush* and ordered an investigation into who was to blame for the influx of migrants: 'The arrival of these substantial numbers of men under no organised arrangements is bound to result in difficulty and disappointment.'[52] In retrospect, such concern about a few hundred immigrants seems disproportionate, but this was in the context of the immediate post-war years, when there were significant shortages and therefore a compulsion to leave nothing to chance. His response is still regarded by some as understandable.

Whatever the case may be, those uninvited migrants met not only with coolness but with hostility, especially in the impoverished districts where they ended up. Forms of segregation in neighbourhoods and schools soon emerged and the newcomers were conspicuously avoided in everyday life: 'When the bus fills up and you find you're the last one to have somebody beside you, then you know something is wrong. You say to yourself: come on, be yourself, be strong,' Tryphena Anderson recalls.[53]

Despite opposition, a surprising number of these early immigrants – most of them young single men – entered into mixed marriages. West Indians in particular had a strong tendency to marry British women. Reactions from the community were fiercely antagonistic, as mixed couples remember. They were ostracized. 'White people would never speak to you. As they used to pass you, they used to spit. It was terrible.'[54] Fantasies about the sexuality of black men knew no bounds, and women were the prize in a contest which was also about access to homes and jobs. On the lowest rungs of the social ladder battle commenced over the place immigrants were to occupy. There was a high level of interference by others in the community. Michael Banton describes the reactions: 'The coloured people in Stepney and elsewhere allege that individual police officers go to great lengths to try to separate the women from the men when opportunity arises.'[55] Although he also looks at the stereotypical image migrants had of the average Englishman, Banton is forced to conclude that the greatest obstacle to integration was the hostile attitude of white people towards coloured immigrants.

There were attempts to deter potential migrants. One intriguing example is the BBC series *Going to Britain?* (1959), used by the British government to inform potential migrants, from the Caribbean for example, but at the same time to discourage them. In the inimitable BBC English of the day, the commentator asks: 'Are you prepared for this kind of cold climate with its icy winds, its sleet and snow?' This particular episode continues, far from invitingly: 'Whenever you are inclined to get angry when a person is staring at you, remember that English people are ignorant of your ways and habits. From the time you start to live in England it is as if a sea of white faces is always around you.'[56] The warning words had little effect.

Calls for more restrictive laws therefore grew, but as long as the number of 'coloured' migrants remained relatively small, a succession of governments declined to introduce new legislation. Until the early 1960s non-white immigrants made up no more than one-quarter of one per cent of the population. There was much talk on the subject in the mid-1950s, but in the end nothing was done. It was not until 1961 that the Commonwealth Immigrants Bill was introduced, aimed mainly at regulating immigration by 'unschooled' migrants, the unspoken assumption being that the main effect would be to limit the number of non-white newcomers.

There was a profound fear of the sort of trouble America was experiencing, with black ghettos and race riots. In light of the images coming out of the American South in the 1950s, this seems hardly surprising. As early as 1919 there had been racial conflict in a number of British port cities, with five dead and many more injured. In 1958 the powder keg ignited in both Nottingham and London's Notting Hill, as groups of white youths, cheered loudly by bystanders, looted and trashed coloured districts.

After the Notting Hill riots, a number of Conservative MPs introduced a motion aimed at limiting immigration. One of them, Martin Lindsay, explained the background to their initiative: 'We all know perfectly well that the whole core of the problem of immigration is coloured immigration. We would do much better to face that and to discuss it realistically in this context. . . . We must ask ourselves to what extent we want Great Britain to become a multiracial community.' They faced fierce criticism from all sides, even though Lindsay tried to distance himself from discriminatory attitudes: 'One of the difficulties about discussing this problem is that we are all a little scared of being thought to be illiberal. . . . I could not find any excuses whatever for anyone who believed in a colour bar in any community where black and white have to co-exist. That, however, is altogether different from changing the nature of a community.'[57] Few at Westminster were convinced by his argument.

British historian Ian Spencer argues that, if anything, the riots delayed the passing of new laws, since the government did not want to reward the rioters. But there remained a concern that large groups of migrants would cause social conflict.[58] The official justification for the laws that were eventually passed lay in 'the strains imposed by coloured immigrants on the housing resources of certain local authorities and the dangers of social tensions inherent in the existence of large unassimilated coloured communities'.[59]

Innumerable commentators, such as Clifford Hill, claim to have identified a spurious argument in this fear of social conflict. Britain has never had a mature policy on the issue, he claims, because 'politicians have always been glancing over their shoulders at the racial attitudes in the country and have allowed these to influence their immigration policy'.[60] The essential question, however, is: Should governments take account of the possibilities and impossibilities surrounding integration when confronted with choices surrounding immigration? Surely they ought to consider not only the migrants involved, but also the attitude of the receiving society. That would seem to be the natural starting point in a democracy.

Other interests and principles counterbalanced the fear of racial tension. Successive governments were apprehensive about the repercussions that restrictions on immigration might have for their relationships with the countries of the commonwealth. An end to freedom of movement would seriously detract from the legitimacy of efforts to perpetuate Britain's global role. This was an anxiety voiced again and again in government circles. As we have seen, it was precisely the more conservative advocates of empire who felt a need to defend postcolonial migration.

Alongside these 'imperial' interests, the principle of equal treatment weighed heavily. Historians often point to the hypocritical attitude of a series of British governments, which outwardly condemned discrimination while behind closed doors actively reining in 'coloured' migration. Many would have liked nothing better than to limit the number of colonial migrants, regarding their arrival as problematic, but it was a long time before governments took steps to do so and one reason for the years of hesitation was a reluctance to trample too casually on the principle of equal treatment. A cabinet memorandum from the 1950s sums up the thinking nicely: 'There is no effective means of stopping this influx without legislation. . . . There could be no question of seeking such power to deal only with coloured people.'[61]

The multiracial Britain that emerged was the product of such considerations. Spencer claims that the composition of the British population would have been fundamentally different had the government intervened in the mid-1950s. When restrictive laws were introduced in the early 1960s, they prompted an influx of immigrants who wanted to get in before the borders closed, the so-called 'beat-the-ban rush'.[62] It was self-perpetuating or chain migration that eventually created an urgent need to implement the new law. The opposition, with Labour leader Hugh Gaitskell as its main spokesman, argued against the bill in the parliamentary debate of 1961. He too was concerned primarily about numbers: 'It is, in my opinion, an utter and complete myth that there is the slightest danger or prospect of millions and millions of brown and black people coming to this country.'[63] When he spoke those words there were around a quarter of a million Caribbean, African and Asian immigrants in Britain. Twenty years later they and their descendants numbered 2.1 million, by 1995 the figure had risen to 3.2 million and today it stands at over 4 million. When the Labour party took power, incidentally, not long after the 1962 Commonwealth Immigrants Act was passed, it reversed its policy and tightened up the immigration laws considerably.

Even before this, the trade unions had been struggling with an angry white membership; they could not afford to be too generous. In the backs of union leaders' minds, American tensions between white and black served as a warning. After the London riots of 1958, for example, a report about districts where many migrants had taken up residence states: 'In these places, settled communities have had their established way of life disturbed by the superficial imposition of alien patterns of behaviour. The significant word is "alien", not "black" or "inferior".'[64]

The rapid growth in the number of migrants from former British colonies leaves no room for doubt that the new immigration law of 1962 was less draconic than is often assumed. The level of immigration remained fairly constant in the years that followed, at somewhere between 30,000 and 50,000 a year. The new legislation actually marked the start of multiracial Britain rather than its end.

How is this possible? Ian Spencer offers various explanations as to why, in his view, the immigration laws produced the opposite of the intended effect.[65] The long lead-in time of the new law accelerated the influx of new migrants. In the two years before it was adopted and came into force, the black and Asian population doubled. The law opened up opportunities for family reunification and family formation, and it was interpreted generously, so Asian immigrants in particular invited their families to join them. In any case, the 1962 legislation was not particularly restrictive, since there were still opportunities for educated migrants to come to Britain. In the years that followed, restrictions on immigration were further tightened by governments of every stripe. The final legislative change was the British Nationality Act of 1981, which replaced the 1948 law. This meant saying farewell to the old broad definition of the British subject. The collapse of the empire had been internalized and illusions about the Commonwealth abandoned. British citizenship was brought into line with European norms.

The British example once again demonstrates that a relationship exists between immigration and integration, since along with the introduction of more restrictive laws, a Race Relations Act was passed to combat discrimination. As time went on, hand in hand with measures to regulate immigration further, anti-discrimination legislation was given a broader remit and its implementation made more coercive. Since the mid-1970s Britain has had a Commission for Racial Equality, which recently became the Commission for Equality and Human Rights. The new name is a sign of a change in attitude; people are now concerned about all forms of discrimination and no longer want to place a special emphasis on racial exclusion.

The Commonwealth Immigrants Act by no means silenced the debate about non-Western immigration. The line taken by the prominent Conservative politician Enoch Powell in the late 1960s created a particularly fierce storm of reactions. It was a speech he gave in Birmingham in April 1968 that caused the biggest fuss. Classicist Powell painted an apocalyptic picture of racial conflict, commenting: 'It is like watching a nation busily engaged in heaping up its own funeral pyre. . . . As I look ahead, I am filled with foreboding. Like the Roman, I seem to see "the river Tiber foaming with much blood".' It would go down in history as the 'rivers of blood speech'. A *Times* editorial accused him of preaching a 'new tribalism', but there was considerable support for his ideas among the population as a whole. When the Conservative leader sacked Powell from the shadow cabinet, dockworkers demonstrated in his support.

Reading the text from a contemporary viewpoint it's clear that he was primarily putting himself forward as a spokesman for a silent majority of ordinary citizens whose voices were being ignored. He tells of a meeting with a man in his constituency, who thinks that within 20 years 'the black man will have the whip hand over the white man'. Powell comments: 'Here is a decent, ordinary fellow Englishman, who in broad daylight in my own town says to me, his Member of Parliament, that this country will not be worth living in for his children. I simply do not have the right to shrug my shoulders and think about something else.'[66]

His words still echo, and they will always resurface in the collective memory when serious riots break out, as they did in the early 1980s in Brixton, among other places, and again in the 1990s and since. It was the second generation of Caribbean and Asian young people who rebelled, refusing to resign themselves to frustrations over high youth unemployment, school drop-out rates and continuing discrimination. The children reacted differently from their parents. As Mike and Trevor Phillips put it: 'The difference in the generations was that Caribbean migrants in the late fifties and sixties were usually willing to take the potential for racial conflict out of the situation. For instance, when kids reported that they were being discriminated against at school, parents would typically reply with an exhortation to work harder or see protest as some cover for laziness.'[67]

A slogan of the first generation, 'come what may, we're here to stay', certainly expresses determination, but it also implies a subcutaneous fear that sooner or later the day might come when they would have to leave. It was a long time before that fear subsided – 'Enoch Powell terrified us' – but the new generation finds its parents' or grandparents' slogan simply incomprehensible: What do you mean 'here to stay'? Where else could we go? This is where we come from, isn't it?

With the permanent settlement of migrants and their descendants, strikingly diverse developments took place within and between the different migrant communities. As in many other European countries, there was soon a strong polarization between a new middle class and a sizeable underclass. Ziauddin Sardar sees a growing identification with Britain among the children of the original migrants, of which he is one: 'My generation was part of a full-blown dress rehearsal. We were British – but there was always this unease, a slight uncertainty, some hesitation in seeing ourselves as truly, fully British. . . . The new generation of Asians are the real thing. They are as naturally British as eating Balti. They have changed, and are changing, their own communities, constantly reinventing themselves while remaining the same.'[68]

His optimism is not equally valid across the spectrum. Of the various communities in Britain the Indians are doing the best by far, better even, on average, than the white population, whereas things are going less well for the descendants of Caribbean migrants and of those from Pakistan and Bangladesh. Not only do clear differences in economic performance exist between different groups, cultural preferences are diverse too. At an early stage Michael Banton discovered a correlation between resistance to integration and the degree of cohesion within the various communities. He writes of a series – Sikh, Pakistani, Somali, West African, West Indian – each of which has less internal coherence than the one before and therefore a greater willingness to be part of the wider environment. He also detects in this sliding scale 'the extent to which European influences have disrupted the culture of the country of origin'.[69] This view is generally shared. Caribbean migrants had a weak identity and were very much oriented towards British society, whereas, at the other extreme, Pakistanis generally tried harder to hold on to their own traditions.

Sardar too remarks on the degree of segregation in cities like Bradford and Oldham, which is very high by European standards. In a sensitive portrait of the 75,000 Pakistani migrants in Bradford, he shows that practically all have their origins in one particular region, Mirpur. Their social life in their new country is still dominated by clans, known as *biradari*. These represent networks of mutual aid, but they also control everything members do. Despite his optimism about new generations, Sardar is forced to conclude that 'this tradition comes with consequences. It is not only charitable solidarity that was revitalized in different circumstances, but the pernicious and inhumane aspects too.'[70] He is thinking of honour killings, which occur at regular intervals, but he is also referring to forms of radicalization, to which young people of Pakistani origin seem particularly susceptible.

The image the British have of themselves as a successful multicultural society is not entirely convincing. Its most striking feature is the preoccupation with racial differences. Frequent use of terms like 'multiethnic' and 'racial equality' gives an outsider the sense of a distant echo from an imperial past. The attention paid to ethnicity may have been given a positive spin in a concept like 'multiracial', but in essence it's simply the same old over-estimation of the significance of skin colour.

A slightly arrogant assessment of British society as a model to hold up before others is a feature common to past and present. Sometimes it would be nice to hear more of the mild scepticism of Elspeth Huxley. In the mid-1960s she wrote a series of journalistic articles about the new migrant communities. In her conclusion she sums up the half-hearted attitude of her compatriots: 'Immigration is like a wet day. We don't really *want* it to happen, but know it's good for the gardens, and anyway, we can't stop it, so might as well make the best of things. And once we've got it, we must be fair. The newcomers must be treated decently: no incipient ghettos, segregation, colour bar – in theory at least.'[71]

As in the immediate post-war years, there's a discrepancy between the self-image of Britain as the 'motherland' and the realities of everyday life. Now as then, for example, the image London is keen to present to the world belies the considerable ethnic tensions that still exist in Britain today. Furthermore, it's rarely pointed out that British multiculturalism is accompanied by an island mentality. Unlike most continental countries, Britain clings anxiously to its borders.

Under the surface, just as much violence is brewing as in many other countries, perhaps even more. The race riots of recent years in cities including Bradford and Birmingham, and especially the bomb attacks on the London underground of 7 July 2005, have seriously damaged Britain's self-confidence. More and more critical voices are making themselves heard, connecting the growing segregation and alienation of Muslim communities, in particular, with multiculturalism. One example is a partly autobiographical book by George Alagiah, which includes numerous sobering observations about the separate lives lived by immigrants and the rest of the population: 'If these findings can be extrapolated, they give the lie to one of the most commonly accepted views about what happens to immigrant communities – that they become more integrated with every new generation.'[72] He concludes that the fostering of ethnic differences must give way to an emphasis on shared citizenship.

At the External Borders

This exploration of immigration in the three most important countries in Europe suggests that all models have been found wanting. So it's no surprise to find that doubts have set in everywhere. After all, the social reality in Malmö, say, does not differ greatly from that of Bradford, Marseille, Rotterdam or Frankfurt. Thinking in terms of models contributes to the tendency for experiences to remain locked in behind national borders. In France people are happy to talk of the failure of 'the Dutch model' or 'the British model'. This is simply a way of saying: what's going on there proves we're right, or at any rate doesn't apply to us. Yet it must be possible to make shared experiences in Europe visible to all, as the first step to finding a way forward.

It begins with a recognition that problems surrounding immigration and integration cannot be viewed in isolation. Adrian Favell remarks that ethnic minorities in each country are the 'symbolic vessels for larger issues concerning . . . national unity and social order'.[73] We have only to look at Flemish, Scottish and Basque nationalism to see these other forces at work, putting the old nation-states of Europe under pressure from within at the very time when immigration is raising difficult questions about their identities. More generally, as we have seen, the debate about integration is part of a search for the meaning of citizenship in a highly individualized society.

Despite diverse traditions, attention everywhere is beginning to be focused on citizenship. Joppke and Morawska characterize this reversal of thinking as 'a turn away from multicultural and postnational perspectives toward a renewed emphasis on assimilation and citizenship'.[74] This attitude has become central to European thinking, but it exists elsewhere too; even in Australia, a classic country of immigration, thinking is moving away from official multiculturalism. Attitudes have shifted. Whereas the emphasis used to lie on cultural differences, the quest for social integration is now the main concern.

Everywhere we see similar pleas for a more self-conscious way of dealing with democratic traditions. The vulnerability of an open society in a time of large-scale migration is becoming more broadly recognized. In Britain especially, the disenchantment is palpable. A 2001 Home Office study known as the Cantle Report offers a clear description of how communities are growing apart, showing that Pakistani young people in particular are developing in ways that are undoubtedly problematic. The compilers of the report declare themselves unpleasantly surprised by 'the depth of polarisation of our towns and cities'. The lives of residents from different communities 'often do not seem to touch at any point, let alone overlap and promote any meaningful interchanges'.[75]

Thinking has not stood still on the other side of the English Channel either. In France, after the riots in the *banlieues* that made the malaise of many migrants and their children visible once again, the debate on integration is in full swing. The government has gone so far as to establish a ministry responsible for 'immigration and national identity', a linkage that illustrates the insecurity involved in the quest. Meanwhile, in Germany too, in the context of new laws on labour migration, a great deal of thinking is going on about how to include newcomers and their children. Everywhere, we see an emphasis on integration, the aim being to keep diversity within the bounds of liberal democracy.

With the abolition of internal borders in the European Union there are signs of some convergence of views on integration. How far this will go is uncertain. It's doubtless true that some form of European citizenship would make integration easier, since it would have a great deal more to offer than national citizenship. Here lies one essential difference between Europe and America. The United States is a continental power with which immigrants can easily identify, whereas independent European countries have less to offer newcomers. It makes a good deal of difference whether a Turkish migrant is asked to become a Dane or an American, since the English language is a passport to the world, whereas Danish or Dutch are not – quite apart from the size of Turkey in comparison to the smaller nations of Europe. Until talk about European citizenship becomes a reality, it will be harder here than in the United States to give immigrants a sense that their horizons are expanding.

We have to be realistic. It will be a long time yet before Europe is in a position to qualify as a truly transnational society. There's profound disagreement about how to establish a common language alongside the national languages. A shared public life and therefore a lively democracy are simply impossible with the language barriers that currently exist. Only when it becomes natural for people to work, marry, engage in debate and pay taxes across national borders will we have any chance of creating a transnational citizenship.

Sociologist Abram de Swaan refers to 'expanding circles of identification' which in theory can include the whole of mankind. Yet he is forced to conclude that such supra-national identifications are fragile.[76] It's possible that in the future Europe will offer opportunities for such a broader identification, but getting to that stage will be a lengthy process. The quest for European unity now finds itself in deep water for this very reason. Societies are being profoundly changed by immigration – in several member countries one in four, perhaps one in three, of all residents will be migrants or the descendants of migrants by the middle of this century.

Besides this, European countries will need to open up to each other over the coming decades. This dual task of integration is raising questions about national identity everywhere and we could well see majorities turning against the outside world. European societies are going through a delicate process of change that is forcing them to rethink the fundamentals of an open society. Self-examination is under way and it requires a Europe with the ambition not so much to replace national sovereignty as to facilitate the continued existence of its member countries as robust democracies under the rule of law and as welfare states. The hope is that European cooperation will go some way towards absorbing the shocks of world disorder.

This makes a shared immigration and asylum policy essential. Sassen argues that migratory movements from specific countries have a beginning and an end: 'Migrations do not assume the form of invasions; they did not in the nineteenth century when border controls were minimal or nonexistent, and they do not today.'[77] Yet it is by no means certain that without border controls the current migration trends from south to north and from east to west would not take the form of a vast movement of populations. In a world made far smaller by mass communications and where differences in prosperity are so visible, it seems improbable that migration would regulate itself without interference by states.

What began as a common market has expanded in just a few decades into a large union offering considerable freedom of movement. The right to settle in other member states was put in place at a time when there were no longer any mass migration flows within the European Union. Where they did threaten to occur, as the Union expanded eastwards for instance, transition periods were laid down for new members. With the abolition of internal borders, citizens of each member state have gained the freedom to settle in whichever of the others they choose. That freedom means that the countries of the EU have a natural interest in knowing who is being allowed in and exactly which laws govern naturalization. No agreement has yet been reached as to what the consequences of this increased freedom of movement ought to be for legal migrants who have lived in countries of the Union for many years. Exactly what rights do they have?

With the expanding geography of immigration in Europe, more and more countries are being forced to cooperate. Nations like Spain, Italy and Greece, once countries of emigration, have been transformed into countries of immigration in the past 10–20 years. Central European nations too, such as the Czech Republic, Hungary and Poland, will be increasingly affected by worldwide migration. They are perhaps still seen as places people leave from, but within the next decade they will find themselves becoming recipient countries. Migration from south to north will interconnect with migration from east to west. Klaus Bade points out that two-thirds of migrants in Western Europe now come from the east and only a third from the south.

All this migration reminds us that Europe is surrounded by turbulent regions and its aspiration to be and remain a secure community means it must formulate answers to the increasing problems on its external borders. Anyone looking at the geographical position of America and comparing it to Europe can only conclude that the Pacific, with its growing economies, China in particular, presents far more opportunities than the Mediterranean region, where Europe is faced with a band of countries stretching from North Africa via the Middle East to the former Soviet Republics, practically all of which are stuck in a deep malaise.

If we take stock of these crisis areas on the borders of Europe, then the remarks of former Dutch prime minister Jan Peter Balkenende seem inadequate: 'It isn't "us" against "them". Not "Europe versus the United States" or "Europe versus the Islamic world". Europe must not cordon itself off against others but against the ghosts of its own past.' Certainly, we must not close our minds to the outside world, but we do have to protect ourselves against problems that arise, of which radicalization in Islamic countries is one of the most worrying. This requires a more focused awareness of the dangers threatening democracy. Balkenende was right to say: 'The Union as a defensible community under the rule of law has a moral charisma in the world.'[78] But Europe's defensibility depends upon creating a community with a common border, which is impossible without a common approach to immigration and refugee flows.

The creation of a union that can take care of its own security needs would be a radical break with the past. European history is imbued with war and the memory of war. It's not hard to find evidence to support the suspicion that wars are of all times and all places, a core feature of human society. All borders set residents against outsiders. The formation of groups all too often carries within it the germ of violence of a kind that grew to unprecedented proportions in the era of nation-building, when entire populations were mobilized in devastating wars.

The First World War brought an end to the belief in progress that characterized the long nineteenth century. As Paul Valéry famously said: 'We civilizations now know ourselves mortal.'[79] After that war, nothing would ever be the same again; doubts about the values of liberal culture increased and were compounded by the ending of the civilizing mission to the colonies that people had assigned themselves. In the final volume of Pat Barker's First World War trilogy, images of a hospital for wounded soldiers are interspersed with notes in the margins of an anthropological study into the habits and customs of a primitive tribe in a remote region of Polynesia, which is still practising headhunting. The anthropological question – what is the difference between the killing in the trenches and the bloody rituals of a primitive tribe? – becomes an indictment of the hypocrisy of the British Empire, which allows the mass slaughter of the Somme to continue and at the same time tries to stamp out ritual killing in its colonies, condemning it as uncivilized behaviour.

It would be too easy to fall into a state of cultural pessimism, as many have done and still do, based on the countless examples of barbarity in European history. True, Europe's past is full of war and oppression. At the same time, over the last half-century it has determinedly reasoned against the inexorability of fate. By trial and error, it has launched nothing less than an attempt to realize Immanuel Kant's vision of 'eternal peace'. The liberal hope of the years prior to 1914 is now being carried forward by other means. Nevertheless, the bulk of history weighs against this belief in human malleability and it is well worth giving further thought to the fundamental conflict between these two visions of the world.

6

The Cosmopolitan Code

The Colonial Trap

With its great voyages of discovery and the building of colonial empires, Europe made a decisive contribution to global cohesion. The heirs to Columbus and Magellan were undoubtedly driven by curiosity and the pursuit of profit, but they also had a civilizing mission. The racial and religious motives behind that mission can be criticized on all sorts of grounds, but the fact remains that few cultures managed to escape it entirely. Ever since, the world has been bound together by a discordant network of relationships.

It all began with the seizure of the North African coastal town of Ceuta in 1415, a Spanish enclave in Morocco to this day and now a transit point for desperate migrants looking for a backdoor route into Europe. Next the New World and soon afterwards the Far East were opened up by a long series of voyages of discovery. Successful navigation across the oceans meant that scattered empires could be formed. Conquest had previously been limited to neighbouring regions. The voyages of discovery created connections that literally spanned the globe.

This major historical change was set in motion by a small number of European countries that between them covered no more than 1.6 per cent of the earth's surface. The British Empire stands out in every respect; at its peak Britain's worldwide possessions amounted to a quarter of the earth and its population. It still seems astonishing that eight European countries – Portugal, Spain, France, Britain, the Netherlands, Belgium and later Germany and Italy – managed to subjugate such a large part of the world for more than three centuries. In 2000 the United Nations had 188 member countries, of which no fewer than 125 were former colonies.

Pride comes before a fall. In the space of a few decades the conquest of centuries was reversed. Once a source of self-assurance, colonial history became the cause of deep uncertainty about the significance of European culture. The experience of the First World War trenches had already delivered a huge blow to Europe's self-confidence, and after the publication of Oswald Spengler's *The Decline of the West* (1918–22) Europe's downfall was commonly depicted as inevitable. The development of civilization was now conceived as cyclical, each flourishing period followed by decline. The loss of overseas territories reinforced that impression.

Yet the shock of decolonization had a beneficial effect. European integration would have been unthinkable without that experience. The crucial initiative that brought European countries together was taken by former colonial powers, such as France and Belgium, which saw the integration of the old continent as a means of checking their own decline. Only when they stood alone did they begin to see each other as neighbours. This helps to explain why Britain was so slow to join the European Community. It continued to cherish the illusion of imperial grandeur even when, after Indian independence in 1947, there was less and less reason to do so.

The loss of power in the world led to self-examination in another sense too. British historian Arnold Toynbee was keen to emphasize the limited horizon of the colonial worldview: 'The paradox of our generation is that all the world has now profited by an education which the West has provided, except the West herself. The West to-day is still looking at history from the old parochial self-centred standpoint which the other living societies have by now been compelled to transcend.' That self-satisfied attitude could not last, since 'sooner or later, the West, in her turn, is bound to receive the re-education which the other civilizations have obtained already'. He wrote these words in 1948 and we can see his prediction as having since been borne out by post-war immigration.[1] As a young Pakistani man in London wrote on a banner years ago, cutting a long story short: 'We are over here, because you were over there.' Europe touched the world and as a consequence it is now being touched by the world.

The one-time colonizers' ability to adapt is currently being tested in precisely the way Toynbee regarded as desirable. The elites that once commanded a civilizing mission have become so uncertain that they no longer have any clear understanding of their cultural heritage. Who are we – given the moral depths of the colonial period – to judge others? Immigration forces us to think again about the fundamentals of our societies. The coming decades will show whether the shock is being absorbed productively.

A good deal of uncertainty about the role of European culture and religion existed even during the colonial period. Take the famous missionary and explorer David Livingstone. In late 1857 he spoke about the situation in India after a revolt against British rule: 'I consider we made a great mistake, when we carried commerce into India, in being ashamed of our Christianity. . . . These two pioneers of civilization – Christianity and commerce – should ever be inseparable.'[2] Formulated in this way his conclusion amounts to a call to his countrymen: profit and principle must go hand in hand in raising people up. It seems the importance of religion could not be taken for granted.

Livingstone was right in saying that in the first century and a half of its existence, the East India Company had not made any effort to convert people to Christianity, preferring religious tolerance for the sake of its own trading interests. The British Empire was for a long time little more than a loose network of trading posts. Its fairly detached government had no ambition to alter native ways of life but was guided mainly by the profit motive. That changed in the course of the nineteenth century, when a civilizing offensive was launched, driven mainly by moral conviction. This too had its positive side. Opposition to slavery, inspired by religious and humanist beliefs, gained momentum and ultimately won out over economic interests. In 1807 the slave trade was banned and Britain deployed its navy to ensure that no more human beings were shipped out from the West African coast.

The campaign against slavery was accompanied by a revival of missionary fervour in the colonies. The abolitionist movement favoured the conversion of heathens. In his biography of David Livingstone, entitled *Victorian Superman*, British historian Niall Ferguson shows how the two motives were bound up together. The civilizing zeal of the young missionary was sorely tested as he watched an attempt to convert the natives end in a drinking spree. He noted in his diary, with unintentional irony: 'A minister who had not seen as much pioneer service as I have done would have been shocked to see so little effect produced by an earnest discourse concerning the future judgement.'[3] Livingstone eventually chose to take his leave of missionary work, throwing himself and his unbounded energy into the exploration of the African interior. What followed became a children's adventure story.

Livingstone's uncertain quest in India is representative of what was happening on a far larger scale. Anyone reading about European colonialism will be struck by a succession of unintended consequences. It's a tale of improvisation. What began as a scattering of trading posts in Asia and the New World developed by fits and starts into a system of foreign rule that aroused its own opposing forces and was eventually destroyed by them. The gradual penetration of the interior from coastal regions has been deployed as a metaphor often enough; the European powers became increasingly enmeshed in a colonial enterprise whose balance of profit and loss was not at all easy to determine.

What still looks in retrospect like a conscious strategy of domination, progressing step by step, was in reality a piecemeal project. Only in the course of the nineteenth century do we see a slow transition from an informal to a formal empire and not until the early twentieth century were the Dutch East Indies truly subjugated and moulded into a single political entity. The same went for the British colonies. The main factors prompting the British to consolidate their spheres of influence into colonies and protectorates were French expansion in Africa, Russian advances in Asia and Germany's colonial policies from the latter years of Bismarck's rule onward. Even so, the British sought compromises with local rulers and respected traditional ways of delivering justice. India, with a population of 250 million, was administered by just a few thousand British civil servants and it always had a complex combination of diverse forms of government with varying degrees of autonomy.

How can we explain the enormous imbalances of power that enabled European countries to rule such a large part of the world? After all, empires are of all times and all continents, so why did modern colonialism not originate in the Arab world or in China? In the Middle Ages those regions were far more advanced than Europe, but they failed to recognize the importance of voyages of discovery. Many have said the reason was primarily cultural. Whereas the Arab world and China were generally inward-looking, Europe developed a huge fascination for things beyond its own conceptual universe.

One telling example is the Chinese decision during the Ming dynasty to curtail a series of important voyages made by Admiral Zheng-He in 1405–33. In those years, at least seven expeditions were undertaken in the seas around what is now Indonesia and in the Indian Ocean. The decision to abandon this venture was inspired by financial considerations, but it was also a symptom of the politics of seclusion. Historian David Abernethy concludes: 'Europe had the will as well as the capacity to reach China. China had the capacity but not the will to reach Europe.'[4] Deliberate disengagement could not have come at a worse moment. As China withdrew, Europe was beginning a long series of conquests.

A number of researchers have looked at why Europe had an urge to explore, rule and exploit the world when others did not. In his search for an explanation, American historian David Landes goes back to the fragmentation of political power after the fall of the Roman Empire. Coercion was less effective than on other continents, since authority was widely dispersed, making control more difficult and leading to the emergence of independent city-states, which became the crucible of capitalism and democracy. Serfdom was abolished in Western Europe in the fifteenth century.

Tensions between earthly and spiritual powers were another reason why it was impossible to control society from a single centre. The authority of religious rulers was finally curbed, but only after a long struggle. They lost control of scholarly work. The split within the Christian church known as the Reformation caused a crisis of authority, and the individual relationship with God that Protestantism encouraged cleared the way for more democratic forms of government.

German sociologist Max Weber believed that the emergence of Protestantism was a decisive event in the rise of modern capitalism, which went hand in hand with colonization. Landes comments: 'The heart of the matter lay indeed in the making of a new kind of man – rational, ordered, diligent, productive. These virtues, while not new, were hardly commonplace. Protestantism generalized them among its adherents, who judged one another by conformity to these standards.'[5] He goes on: 'It gave a big boost to literacy, spawned dissents and heresies, and promoted the skepticism and refusal of authority that is at the heart of the scientific endeavor.'[6] As a result, large developmental differences grew up within Europe; much of Eastern Europe remained excluded from the revolution of the mind, and even the original pioneers of discovery – Spain and Portugal – were left behind, since for religious reasons they shut themselves off from the new way of thinking. Figures for illiteracy demonstrate the sharpness of the contrast: by 1900 only 3 per cent of people in Britain were unable to read or write, whereas in Spain the percentage was 56 and in Portugal 78. A similar distinction existed between North and South America.[7]

Cultures differ historically in their degree of scientific and technological development and in their receptivity to advances made by other countries, but large discrepancies in economic productivity do not mean that those differences are permanent, let alone innate. Japan, for example, has made Western progress its own to a great degree since the mid-nineteenth century. Other countries have been slower and many are underdeveloped in a technological sense to this day.

Landes seeks the key to European expansion in what he calls 'the invention of invention', meaning the spread of unrestricted research. He points to the development of mechanical clockwork as one example, and to printing, seen in the Muslim world as blasphemous. In Istanbul the Jews and Christians had printing presses while the Muslims did not. For many years the prospect of a printed Koran was unthinkable: 'Islam's greatest mistake . . . was the refusal of the printing press, which was seen as a potential instrument of sacrilege and heresy. Nothing did more to cut Muslims off from the mainstream of knowledge.'[8]

The greatest puzzle is why China, ahead in a technological sense for so long, was not responsible for the most important scientific breakthroughs. Most commentators attribute this less to religion than to state control. Discoveries such as gunpowder, the compass, porcelain and paper were not taken further, whereas the military applications of gunpowder, for instance, were eagerly seized upon in Western Europe. This illustrates the fact that individual freedom lies at the heart of the scientific and later the industrial revolution: freedom from church authorities, the liberation of the peasants, the breaking of the exclusivity of guilds, the abolition of tolls, freedom of settlement – they are all examples of increases in spiritual and physical mobility, which in many parts of the world came about only much later. These were the reforms that made possible the unprecedented power of the West.

Expansion was driven by what Abernethy describes as an 'explore-control-utilize syndrome'.[9] He writes: 'Imperial expansion and scientific/technological innovation share an underlying logic.'[10] Knowledge and power were inextricably linked; the will to discover and the will to govern went hand in hand from the start. Public institutions, private entrepreneurs and religious groups reinforced one another, Abernethy writes, in 'a triple assault on other societies: on indigenous institutions of governance, on long-standing patterns of generating and distributing economic assets, and on ideas and values that gave meaning to life'.[11] A combination of nation-building, urban capitalism and Christianity made expansion possible and at the same time territorial expansion strengthened the economic growth of Western Europe and its political and religious institutions.

The consequences can still be seen every day in the former colonies. It's possible to think of countless examples: demographic patterns were deeply affected by the near or even complete extermination of the native inhabitants and by slavery; the model of the nation-state imposed long ago is still in place and colonial borders have usually remained unchanged; the language of the former colonizers is more often than not still the official tongue; the spread of Christianity into innumerable regions is another legacy of colonialism; and the concept of economic development has taken root in the former colonies, whatever obstacles may have been encountered in practice.

How should we take stock of the colonial era? The combination of the profit motive and public-spiritedness – think slavery and hospitals – makes a straightforward verdict both impossible and undesirable. Henk Wesseling is critical, but at the same time he rejects the idea that the severity of colonial exploitation explains anything about the relative success or failure of states in our own time. India and Indonesia were subjugated for centuries but are better off today than, for example, Ethiopia or Afghanistan, which escaped colonization. Weighing up the economic consequences of colonialism is difficult. Which criteria should we apply? Some would emphasize the deep chasm between rich and poor in the world and blame systematic exploitation for underdevelopment today. Others point to economic development in the colonial era and conclude that the average income of the indigenous inhabitants increased. The rise of a well-educated native middle class was a precondition for the anti-colonial movement that heralded the end of foreign domination.

Still, its contribution to progress does nothing to mitigate the moral catastrophe that colonialism also represented. Wesseling describes the dark side: 'The slave trade was not only immoral from a contemporary point of view, it had indisputably negative effects on the demography of West Africa, while slavery in the New World had permanent or at least very long-term negative consequences for the slaves and their descendants.' He also points to the genocide that was perpetrated in colonial times. 'The annihilation of the Herero in south-western Africa is the most vivid example.'[12]

A recollection of the low points of colonial rule should be part of our historical consciousness. If anything shows that the open society represents a fragile norm of civilization, then it is colonial history, with its genocide and its trade in human beings. The humanist ideal the West has wanted to present to the world since the American and French revolutions was blatantly betrayed.

'Enlightened' Racism

The conflict between self-declared principles and colonial practice has prompted both self-justification and self-criticism over the years. Justification of imperial rule usually took the form of a racist worldview that envisioned a fixed hierarchy of cultures, with those of white Europeans at the top. Self-criticism ultimately led to cultural relativism, which assumes as a matter of principle that all cultures are of equal value. In societies that now include so many migrants from former colonies, it is important to understand each of these two contrasting outlooks in the context of the other. After all, accusations of racism are still a prominent feature of criticism of Western society; feelings of superiority among whites are still said to be the norm.

In the late 1950s, in his now famous *The Colonizer and the Colonized*, Tunisian writer Albert Memmi portrayed the psychology of colonial relations. He showed how colonial subjects were in a sense placed outside time, no longer seen as shaping their own histories. The route to full citizenship was blocked, which destroyed the social dynamic. Under normal circumstances generational conflicts would find an outlet in social reform, but the colonial situation prevented access to positions of responsibility. Cultural expropriation – the fact, for instance, that education was geared towards the motherland and delivered in the language of the colonizer – divided local populations, with people increasingly feeling like outsiders in their own countries.

One option for those affected was to take the route of complete identification with the culture of the distant metropolis in the hope of being absorbed into the community of the colonizers. But all too often this was accompanied by self-loathing and ultimately it led nowhere, Memmi writes, since the route to true assimilation was barred. It would have undermined the colonial relationship. This was another reason why there was no real will to make a success of conversion to Christianity: a shared religion would be too much of a threat to the colonial hierarchy.

Memmi describes the mediocre quality of colonial elites and says the discrepancy between the privileges enjoyed by the colonizers and their accomplishments cried out for justification. The theory of racism provided the answer. It would be a mistake to think that colonial expansion flowed from a worldview that saw white civilization as the indisputable apex of history. In fact the opposite is closer to the truth: voyages of discovery led to dominion over a large part of the world that then needed to be justified. Contact with other cultures forced colonizers to reflect upon the place of their own civilization.

Classic racism, as it arose in the eighteenth and nineteenth centuries in Europe and America, offered an explanation. The theory is not hard to summarize: humanity is divided into races that have internal as well as external characteristics; the morality and culture of the various racial groups are directly linked to their biological features. Furthermore, the races – the most commonly distinguished are the Caucasian (white), the Negroid (black) and the Mongoloid (yellow) – exist within an immutable hierarchy, with white civilization at the top, followed by the Asiatic peoples, and at the bottom the Africans and their descendants.

In our day, racism is equated with ignorance, but when it first emerged it was a generally accepted worldview with a scientific basis. Little by little, the desire to investigate nature and to record observations created a belief that humanity too could be classified all in its diversity. Using increasingly precise methods – such as that endless measuring of skulls – distinct races were charted.

The doctrine of racial inequality can be seen as a product of the scientific attitude disseminated by the Enlightenment. Indeed, great philosophers such as David Hume, Immanuel Kant and Voltaire all believed there was a hierarchy of races, even though that belief was at odds with their philosophical principles. Hume, an opponent of slavery, comments in *On National Characters* (1741): 'I am apt to suspect the negroes . . . to be naturally inferior to the whites. There never was a civilized nation of any other complexion than white, nor even any individual eminent either in action or speculation.' A little further on he sneers: 'In Jamaica, indeed, they talk of one negroe as a man of parts and learning; but 'tis likely he is admired for slender accomplishments, like a parrot, who speaks a few words plainly.'[13]

Similar views were expressed by the founder of modern liberalism, British philosopher John Locke, who in the second half of the seventeenth century wrote about the colony of Carolina: 'Every freeman of Carolina shall have absolute power and authority over his negro slaves, of what opinion or religion soever.'[14] This was not simply a defence of slavery; it meant that should any of them convert to Christianity it would not affect their status as slaves.

It would be easy to come up with a whole raft of such statements, showing that the greatest minds of early modern times, almost without exception, had a racial view of the world. It was a product of those voyages of discovery that brought Europeans into contact with 'primitive' peoples. How could the differences, especially in technological development, be explained? Surely not by external factors alone?

Another question occupied many minds. How could it be that so many profoundly different peoples had emerged from one act of creation? Christians were torn between the biblical creation story and their increasing difficulty in believing that the different races had a common origin. The religious dogma of a single creation (monogenesis) was incompatible with the scientific notion of multiple creations (polygenesis). Voltaire – in contrast to Kant, incidentally – was drawn to the notion of polygenesis, if only as a way of treading on the church's toes. The debate raged in the Netherlands too, but there powerful religious convictions meant that arguments in favour of polygenesis were consistently quashed. In the mid-eighteenth century a Dutch scholar called Camper even went so far as to ask whether the first human might perhaps have been brown or black: 'Whether Adam was created black, brown, tawny or white, his descendants must of necessity, as soon as they were spread out across the wide earth, according to the way the land, the particular foods and sicknesses differed, have changed their colours and shapes.'[15] In short, in his view racial differences were a product of the highly contrasting environments in which people lived.

With the arrival of Darwin's theory of evolution, the controversy was settled. Natural selection explained how such diverse races could have arisen from a single source and why one race had adjusted better than another to the circumstances in which it found itself. Darwin's *On the Origin of Species* is subtitled *The Preservation of Favoured Races in the Struggle for Life*. The application of his theory to society – later known as social Darwinism – was a natural step and one the great scholar did nothing to discourage.[16]

In a later book, *The Descent of Man* (1871), Darwin looked at racial issues in more detail. He was convinced the races differed in their emotional lives and indeed their intellectual capacities. In a section entitled 'Natural Selection as affecting Civilized Nations' he leaves no room for doubt that efforts to protect the weakest in society will result in the degeneration of the race. The struggle for existence, which only the most vigorous peoples will survive, must not be alleviated. Nothing must be placed between mankind and its suffering. Darwin was an opponent of poor relief and of institutions for the mentally ill: 'There should be open competition for all men; and the most able should not be prevented by laws or customs from succeeding best and rearing the largest number of offspring.'[17]

He is aware that a rejection of social legislation is reason for discomfort: 'Nor could we check our sympathy, even at the urging of hard reason, without deterioration in the noblest part of our nature.'[18] It was impossible to deny that modern society, despite poor relief, had developed extremely successfully during the nineteenth century, but Darwin was perturbed by its leniency: 'Thus the reckless, degraded, and often vicious members of society, tend to increase at a quicker rate than the provident and generally virtuous members.'[19]

It's important to realize that judgements concerning the colonial world at this time were embedded in seemingly enlightened notions about the struggle for existence. Historians have pointed out that the conditions in which slaves lived were not much worse than those of workers in Europe's major cities in the late eighteenth century and the early years of industrialization that followed. Average life expectancy among the urban proletariat was low. Dreadful living conditions were recorded by Jacob Riis even at the start of the twentieth century. His photographs show immigrant populations living like rats in damp cellars and in firetrap apartment blocks without sanitation. The struggle for existence was merciless indeed.

What went on inside the borders of the home country could easily be perpetuated in the colonies. The civilized nations' struggle to subdue the 'barbarians' was therefore predictably short. 'Viewing such men,' Darwin remarked, 'one can hardly believe that they are fellow-creatures, and inhabitants of the same world.'[20] The civilizing mission, the so-called 'white man's burden', was based on this social-Darwinist vision. 'You may roughly divide the nations of the world as the living and the dying,' said British prime minister Lord Salisbury at the height of British expansionism. It was clear to everyone on which side the dying was happening.[21]

In the second half of the nineteenth century, out of a not altogether coherent combination of racial classification, evolutionary theory and research on heredity, racism emerged as a worldview with a scientific foundation. Up until at least the 1920s and '30s it was the usual way of understanding the world. One consequence was a deep aversion to racial mixing, since it would surely bring about the decline of civilization. In this sense the ideology of apartheid was presaged long before it was given a name.

Racism was more, incidentally, than simply a matter of colour. The different national groupings in Europe were regarded as racial as well. Europeans were usually divided into three races. In the late nineteenth century they were referred to as the Nordic race – the pinnacle of civilization – and below it the Mediterranean and Alpine races. A commission of the American Senate adopted this way of thinking, describing the Dutch as 'the Englishmen of the Continent'. Racism was not just a question of white versus black but of white versus less white. The then widely respected Madison Grant complained about the new migrants from Europe who were not of the Nordic race: 'The new immigration ... contained a large and increasing number of the weak, the broken, and the mentally crippled of all races drawn from the lowest stratum of the Mediterranean basin and the Balkans, together with the hordes of the wretched, submerged populations of the Polish ghettos. Our jails, insane asylums, and almshouses are filled with this human flotsam and the whole tone of American life, social, moral, and political has been lowered and vulgarized by them.'[22]

Racism was part of a far broader pattern of discrimination and inequality. Eugenics, specifically the forced sterilization of the social underclass, was regarded as a perfectly acceptable means of dealing with misfits and at the same time reducing pressure on the elites. Those who embraced such beliefs in the 1920s and '30s, with their fear and loathing of the masses, include some of the most prominent writers of their day. Aldous Huxley, having made approving reference to the steps being taken in Hitler's Germany, challenges the critics of such measures: 'We may ask mystical democrats how they expect democratic institutions to survive in a country where an increasing percentage of the population is mentally defective.'[23] Control of 'barbarians', so characteristic of the colonial worldview, was being practised robustly within the territories of the ruling nations.

The Value of Cultures

Cultural relativism emerged as a reaction to colonial abuses, and especially the racial arrogance contained in the arguments used to justify
them. Its most important theses can be summarized as follows: cultures
do not have biological roots but are acquired by learning, so it's wrong
to connect race with culture; there's no evolutionary progression from
primitive to civilized forms of society and we're mistaken whenever we
think in terms of a hierarchy; the judgements people make are linked to
their cultures and therefore biased from the start.

These ideas were originally formulated, with a good many reservations, by anthropologist Franz Boas, but step by step his students took
cultural relativism to a more radical conclusion. It's to the lasting credit
of Boas, who came to prominence at the beginning of the twentieth
century, that the racist worldview was knocked off its scientific pedestal.
The idea that cultures have a racial foundation and that the races can
be arranged in an immutable hierarchy from high to low is hardly ever
taken seriously these days. Racism in its scientific manifestation has been
marginalized.

Boas begins with a cautious suggestion for further research: 'If a close
relation between race and culture should be shown to exist it would
be necessary to study for each racial group separately the interaction
between bodily build and mental and social life.'[24] But if this endeavour
proves unsuccessful, as it inevitably will, then we must study the different cultures without reference to biological characteristics. Boas believes
environmental factors are far more important than racial differences: 'In
short, historical events appear to have been much more potent in leading
races to civilization than their innate faculty.'[25] He cites an example from
migration to America, which offers 'ample proof showing that the racial
position of an individual does not hinder his participation in modern
civilization'.[26] He can see no reason to assume that the black population
is incapable of developing; indeed, he believes that were it to be treated in
an equal manner to the white population, then the performance of both
groups would very likely be comparable.

Looked at in this way, racism can be regarded above all as a 'narcissism of small differences'. The similarities in physical make-up between
the racial groups are many times greater than the distinctions between
them, for all our relentless attempts to squeeze people into racial categories. There's generally more variation within racial groups than across
racial dividing lines, and a 'greater lack of cultural values than that found
in the inner life of some strata of our modern population is hardly found
anywhere'.[27]

With these observations Boas breaks the connection between race and culture. At the same time he criticizes the idea that in primitive societies we're looking at what amounts to a childlike stage of humanity. History should not be seen as a transition from social simplicity to social complexity; Western societies are highly developed from a technological point of view, but technology is not to be taken as the measure of all things. The languages and religions of primitive peoples cannot be dismissed as simple, and the same goes for family structures, which are often extraordinarily complex. Nevertheless, Boas clings to the notion of progress. Primitive societies are far more wedded to habit. As civilization advances, opportunities for critical investigation of traditions increase. The number of people for whom we feel responsible has grown enormously; members of primitive societies identify with comparatively small groups.

Boas's followers drew more radical conclusions. Melville Herskovits rejects all suggestion of evolution, since as soon as we adopt the evolutionists' stance we are led inexorably to a belief in a hierarchy of cultures. He therefore criticizes any belief in progress: there are no stages leading from 'primitive' to 'civilized' culture; such a view is little more than prejudice, a way of seeing our own culture as an end point and arranging all the other cultures according to their proximity to our own norms. In order to banish this hierarchy of cultures we must acknowledge that all judgements are of their time and place. The quest for universally valid norms will get us nowhere, since all morals are embedded in specific traditions, which are non-transferable outside their own cultures. As Herskovits puts it: 'Cultural relativism is a philosophy which, in recognizing the values set up by every society to guide its own life, lays stress on the dignity inherent in every body of custom, and on the need for tolerance of conventions though they may differ from one's own.'[28]

This tendency within anthropology has an explicit pedagogical goal: a recognition of the relativity of all morality will encourage politeness and respect in our dealings with people of other cultures. The defeat of ethnocentrism in Europe and America is therefore seen as a contribution towards the peaceful coexistence of different cultural groups. Boas speaks of 'a higher tolerance than the one we now profess'.[29] Herskovits for his part talks of the 'social discipline and 'mutual respect'[30] that anthropology will be able to instil in people if at its heart lies a recognition of that 'dignity inherent in every body of custom' of which he writes.

Sometimes this line of thought is extrapolated even further. In some cases the study of other societies has actually led to a reversal of the hierarchy, such that the 'noble savage' represents a higher form of civilization that the supposedly civilized West. Barbarians, as Montaigne knew, are people who see others as barbarians.[31] There is of course a contradiction here, since even if we reverse the ranking of civilization and barbarism, as soon as any ranking is laid down, relativism has been rejected.

Boas's school of thought has great merit, but its weaknesses are no less significant. Whereas biology was once seen as decisive in explaining human behaviour, culture is now regarded as all-embracing. This form of determinism carries within it a similar risk of a closed worldview. If people correspond to the cultures to which they're presumed to belong, then what remains of human freedom? Anthropologist Ton Lemaire puts his finger on a sensitive spot: cultural relativism is actually 'racism in reverse', with a no less 'conservative outcome' than its opposite.[32] Relativism is shaped by that which it hoped to defeat.

So despite its historical significance and noble intentions, the verdict on cultural relativism cannot be a favourable one. Acknowledging the fateful power of tradition doesn't so much defeat ethnocentrism as confirm its inevitability. Bias is democratized, as it were; everyone has a right to his own prejudices. No escape is possible, since we are all trapped in our own partiality. In this sense relativism is a form of conservatism; if we take the force of custom as a starting point, cultural innovation becomes hard to conceive. A critical morality, by contrast, aims to put cultural traditions up for negotiation in the name of universal values.

Here the inner contradictions of relativism emerge. If we are all tied to our own traditions, how can the colonial claims of European powers ever be challenged? What makes the cultural relativists themselves immune to the general rule they posit in saying that everyone is a prisoner of the beliefs and habits of a specific place and time? Lemaire puts it this way: 'On the one hand Herskovits denies that it is possible for humanity to have a value-free, non-culturally-determined standpoint, whereas on the other hand he wants to practise a non-culturally-determined, objective, value-free anthropology.'[33] Relativism fails to take full account of the fact that people can rise above their own cultures and assess them critically.

Franco-Bulgarian philosopher Tzvetan Todorov points to yet another paradoxical habit of cultural relativists: familiarity with something from their own history makes it acceptable when they see it in others.[34] In connection with Islam it is often said that condemnation of homosexuality is part of Western history and therefore liberals shouldn't take such exception to it. Not only is this to regard one's own history as the measure of all things despite a professed relativism, it is also to forget that a critical attitude to tradition is precisely what made the moral advances of the past few decades possible.

If we reject the concept of universal morality, on what basis will we ever be able or willing to condemn anything? Female circumcision, the immolation of widows, honour killing, cannibalism, slavery, infanticide, witch trials – they are all culture-specific practices that clearly do not have and should not have universal legitimacy. No wonder authoritarian regimes all over the world are more than happy to appeal to relativism as a way of staving off interference, which they usually describe as 'meddling in internal affairs'. The silence of cultural relativists in the name of the 'dignity inherent in every body of custom' is not innocent. It can easily degenerate into complicity in human rights violations.

Relativism seems to deny the possibility of moral progress. Hirsi Ali writes about traditional family culture: 'The individual is completely subordinate to the collective. Every child is socialized into the culture of shame, in which concepts of honour and disgrace are central. Values such as freedom and individual responsibility play no part at all in this way of thinking.'[35] Although we are aware of all the problems of individualism, a culture that stresses the importance of self-determination represents moral progress compared to a culture in which birth into a specific class or caste, or with a particular skin colour or gender, determine the entire course of a life.

Since relativism denies the possibility of progress, it undermines any notion of development. It therefore fundamentally rejects the idea of developmental cooperation. What do we mean by development if there's no such thing as underdevelopment? Although there may be countless domains of social and spiritual life in which the ideal of progress is meaningless, without it we are at the mercy of the gods. According to the relativist, there are no shared aims for diverse cultures to strive after. In that case, how can we cooperate? A dialogue between cultures presupposes the possibility of rising above the cultures to which we belong in order to judge other cultures and our own.

Anthropologist Claude Lévi-Strauss, in many ways an advocate of relativism, was aware that 'what countries that are "insufficiently developed" reproach other countries for in international assemblies is not that they are Westernizing them but that they are not giving them the means to Westernize quickly enough. . . . It is pointless to try to defend the originality of human cultures against those cultures themselves.'[36] He wrote this in 1952, but in the intervening years countless people have brushed aside precisely this insight in their efforts to defend 'the originality of societies' whether or not it means bowing to authoritarian, even murderous practices.

Relativism might be an appropriate creed if cultures were still separate and unconnected, but in an interconnected world we cannot say, for example, that the ban on child labour must be upheld in our own country but we'll continue to trade with countries that have no objection to it. We can't work together in international organizations without both asking and listening to questions about breaches of human rights.

Quite apart from its moral ambivalence, relativism falls short as a description of a world in which relations between different cultures have developed to the extent they have now. Ruth Benedict, another follower of Boas, says explicitly that the 'untouched' cultures, those that exist in 'comparative isolation', are a kind of laboratory for anthropologists. These are the circumstances in which cultural patterns can best be studied.[37] Hence the conservative tendency in cultural relativism. Its origins lie in the study of comparatively isolated cultures and it's hard to apply to our increasingly interconnected world.

This is especially true of contacts between cultures as a result of migration. What cultural relativists cannot comprehend is precisely the alienation that invariably affects those who start a new life elsewhere. Cultural habits that had a function in a traditional rural society – such as the custom that the eldest son inherits all his parents' property – are inappropriate in the major cities of post-industrial countries. We don't need to make value judgements in order to recognize this.

Cultural relativism, which understands conservatism better than change, does not offer a good description of the consequences of the migration process for those involved. As well as falling short in its descriptive powers, relativism is a dead end in the prescriptive sense. Migration brings very different traditions into close proximity. Society needs a number of shared norms if people's contrasting backgrounds are not to lead them into violent conflict. To take one example, the tradition of forced or arranged marriage must not escape critical scrutiny, however much we emphasize the 'dignity inherent in every body of custom'. Migration forces choices upon us. It is indeed best thought of in the way it was once described: as a 'brutal bargain'.[38]

Beyond Multiculturalism

This critical discussion of the ideas of Boas and his school helps to identify the contradictions inherent in multicultural thinking, which in many respects represents a continuation of cultural relativism by other means. For many years multiculturalism set the tone, to such an extent in fact that the notion of a multicultural society was taken for granted. A reversal in thinking can now be seen everywhere. After more than 20 years of debate in the Western world, the tenets of multiculturalism are slowly being abandoned. We are moving in the direction of a renewed emphasis on the ideal of shared citizenship.

Before enumerating the various problems with the notion of a multicultural society, something needs to be said about its history. The first systematic exposition of a multicultural philosophy comes from American author Horace Kallen, who emerged in the 1920s as a fierce critic of the doctrine of the 'melting pot', speaking out against its forceful agitation for the 'Americanization' of the immigrant. His appeal reads like a precursor to what would later become a widely held view, namely the notion of society as an aggregate of cultural minorities. 'For in effect the United States are in the process of becoming a federal state not merely as a union of geographical and administrative unities, but also as a cooperation of cultural diversities, as a federation or commonwealth of national cultures.'[39]

Under the influence of decolonization, a multicultural way of thinking that elaborates on this opposition to the 'melting pot' revealed itself first in America, then in Europe. If taken merely to suggest that worldwide migration produces multifarious societies, then there's little to be said against it. It's broadly accepted nowadays that such a society must create space for everyone by, for example, adjusting laws about the disposal of the dead or by opening prayer rooms, to allow for the rituals engaged in by Hindus or Muslims. The marking of religious festivals of one kind or another can be seen simply as a reaching out of hands.

Beyond this emphasis on the kind of pluralism that in theory characterizes every open society, and beyond the practical adjustments needed to make room for new religions and lifestyles, a more drastic idea has arisen. It has to do with the belief that society is made up of more or less autonomous cultural communities, which ought to be recognized in a whole range of areas including the administration of justice, education and the jobs market. Will Kymlicka, who advocates a mild form of multiculturalism, acknowledges that those who defend it as an idea have little to say about the limits of diversity.[40] As a result of this inadequacy, the tendency to see society as a patchwork of ethnic communities has aroused opposition.

The term 'multiculturalism' refers to a wide range of approaches and it's easy to get caught up in a war of words. One person will have a very different idea from another about exactly what it means. The work of British political theorist Bhikhu Parekh and sociologist Tariq Modood represents what Modood describes as a 'self-critical' and 'moderate' multiculturalism.[41] Although my criticism of the concept is mainly aimed at what might be called strong multiculturalism, even in its more moderate form it places the emphasis on groups to an extent that goes beyond the empirically justifiable and the normatively desirable. The Parekh Report's description of Britain as a 'community of communities' is problematic, as is the notion that diversity is a concept of the same order as equality and freedom.

Recent books such as Modood's *Multiculturalism. A Civic Idea* have

taken into account much of the criticism of the strong or broad interpretation of the term. Modood writes, for example, that 'to speak of
the recognition or accommodation of minority identities is not necessarily to advocate the reproduction of the past or customs from far-off
places'.[42] Yet many of the practical applications he writes about, such as
appeals for bilingual teaching, single-sex schools and new housing stock
for large families, point towards the retention of culture.[43] He also has a
habit of combining ethnicity and religion by writing of 'ethno-religious
groups' and 'ethno-religious minorities'. This too tends towards conservatism, since there is a permanency to religious groups, whereas ethnic
identifications usually diminish from one generation to the next.

Modood is certainly aware of variety within ethnic groups and of
change as a characteristic of all cultures, yet he appeals for 'the building of group pride' without asking whether or not it is compatible with
variety and change.[44] He regards pride with justifiable suspicion when
expressed by majority cultures but embraces it in minority cultures. In
other words, multiculturalism, even at its most moderate, places more
emphasis on heritage than on openness, whereas the important thing
now is to explore the productive tension between the two. This tendency
towards cultural conservatism, which cannot be defended in either its
descriptive or its prescriptive form, shows that a new paradigm is needed.

To summarize, multiculturalism in its strong or immoderate form
tempts us to partition people off into ethnic categories in the name of
cultural pluralism. Based on 'integration with the retention of identity',
respect for others has in practice meant hampering people's freedom
to shape their own lives, with the ultimate result that customs such as
honour killing, which claimed many victims, have been ignored for years.
We should defend the kind of open society in which all traditions are subjected to critical examination, as opposed to the conservatism of group
cultures. In this sense multiculturalism is a 'first-generation philosophy',
a way of thinking that belongs to avoidance and is now giving way to a
phase in immigration history in which conflict features large – as does,
increasingly, accommodation.

Amartya Sen is decidedly not an adherent of multiculturalism. He
quotes Gandhi, who was quick to oppose what he called 'the vivisection
of a nation', meaning a division into its cultural or religious compo-
nents. Sen asks himself where we got the idea that the coexistence of an
array of cultures in close proximity will be peaceful in nature. Without
a shared foundation, no meaningful exchange is possible and instead we
become caught up in permanent miscommunication or worse. An open
society should afford plenty of room for disagreement, but without a
minimum of common ground disputes cannot be productive, whether in
an economic or a democratic sense.

A small but telling example concerns how we deal with performance in school. Canadian sociologist Peter Li points out that researchers
always compare the progress of migrants' children to the average for the
indigenous population.[45] He claims that the use of such benchmarks is
a concealed attempt to assimilate them. It does indeed seem logical that
a multicultural society would let go of shared norms. Why should the
school performance of the native population be the standard measure? In
debates about education, we have seen a temptation to compare children
primarily with their parents, but this fails to address the question of what
they need to succeed in the workplace. After all, they are not competing
within their own communities – they need to be able to hold their own
in society at large.

Another shortcoming of multiculturalism is its underestimation of
modernity as a shared horizon. It's simply not the case that all cultural
manifestations are appropriate to a post-industrial society. In a service
economy, cognitive and social skills are of great importance and selection takes place more than ever on the basis of socio-cultural capital.
Kymlicka writes: 'A modern economy requires a mobile, educated, and
literate workforce, and standardized public education in a common
language has often been seen as essential if all citizens are to have equal
opportunity to work in this modern economy.'[46] Unless a society exhib-
its some degree of cultural cohesion it can neither produce nor sustain a
modern economy.

The redistribution involved in many kinds of social provision is
another reason why cohesion is essential. Kymlicka lays considerable
emphasis on this point: 'The sort of solidarity required by a welfare
state requires that citizens have a strong sense of common identity and
common membership.'[47] Experts on immigration are suspicious of
national borders as a way of excluding people, but they seldom look at
the positive side. The history of the liberal nation-state is a history of
social rights and cultural emancipation that would be impossible without
external borders.

The history of migration teaches us that survival strategies which
work well in one environment may be dysfunctional in another. Take the
example of the extended family, so essential to societies without social
welfare provision. In such environments, having a lot of children is the
only way to guarantee a carefree old age, but in modern societies families in which three generations live together are increasingly rare. The
offspring of migrants tend to have far fewer children than their parents,
in fact their families are not much larger than those of the population in
general. This brings with it a different family culture. So not only does
multiculturalism have its weaknesses in a normative sense, it also fails
as a description of integration processes down through the generations.

Another objection concerns what is perhaps multiculturalism's most curious feature, namely that it does not attribute any explicatory value to culture. All cultures are equal, we're told, so they can't be used to explain disparities between ethnic groups in socio-economic outcomes, say, or in crime figures. Explanations in terms of class, on the other hand, are extremely popular. Multiculturalism celebrates cultural difference and is happy to discuss anything else as long as cultures are spared all criticism.

In a balanced assessment of 'culture and inequality', anthropologist Hans Vermeulen criticizes this unwillingness: 'The cultural dimension is important in studying social mobility among immigrants and their offspring. But cultural patterns should wherever possible be understood in relation to prior structural circumstances.' He describes, for example, the changing attitude to education in Turkish families. 'It involves more investment in the educational careers of the children and less in the old social obligations in Turkey.' A greater emphasis on education also changes relationships within the family. Daughters, for example, are given more freedom outside the home.[48]

There are plenty of other instances of cultural preference that cannot be reduced to class differences and have an impact on the severity of disadvantage. In the end everyone is free to choose which elements of a cultural heritage he or she will adopt or decline to adopt, but migrants are shaped by the habits and customs of their countries of origin. Leaving their native lands changes them, if only slowly, as is often the case, and their cultural preferences have an influence on the social opportunities open, for example, to their daughters.

Yet another objection is that multiculturalism cuts receiving societies loose from their history. It's a conservative concept from the newcomers' point of view – after all, they're expected to cherish their traditions – but from the point of view of the established population it entails profound change, since it requires the setting aside of many prevailing customs. Multiculturalism doesn't explicitly recognize any obligation arising from achievements made by the receiving society through considerable efforts over many generations. It silently accepts this inheritance while at the same time rejecting any suggestion of continuity as merely a way of excluding migrants and their children by regarding them as people who are not part of a shared history and who therefore cannot identify with it.

Recall the telling statement from a Dutch researcher: 'Surely you're not going to bother Turkish children with the years '40–'45?' Why shouldn't children whose parents were born in a village in Anatolia be put in a position to learn about a crucial episode in Dutch history, the Nazi occupation, so that they have a chance to influence the way in which the memory of those events is shaped?

A step further and we see how the denial of a collective memory which newcomers could share fits neatly with a sense of revulsion among orthodox Muslims, who believe their children shouldn't be bothered at school with lessons about the persecution of the Jews. It starts with an enlightened idea – let's look beyond the boundaries of national history – and ends in a form of self-censorship. Once we stop feeling we're part of a continuing history, every attempt to draw upon the past in a way that's open to all as a matter of principle will fail. Surely broadening the historical picture – for example by paying more attention to the history of migration – implies a belief that the stories we tell about our countries remain significant. There's no need to choose between a black history and a white history. As historian Arthur Schlesinger said, children must learn to see the arrival of Columbus both through the eyes of those already there and through the eyes of those who sent him off on his distant adventure.

Another, final objection is that, taken to its logical conclusion, multi-culturalism leads to an undesirable legal pluralism. This occurs when on the basis of a recognition of the equal value of cultures, 'distinct' communities are given the right to live according to their own authority and their own laws, even if their legal institutions deviate from prevailing judicial practice. There are innumerable problems with this approach. When is a community truly 'distinct'? What demands are to be made of it? Are group rights binding on anyone judged to belong to that group, or can an individual decide whether or not to be counted as a member?

Here it's illustrative to look at attempts to absorb *sharia* law into the Canadian legal system. This application of multiculturalism seems fairly logical. Why shouldn't Muslims be able to resolve issues such as divorce through mediation within their own circles? That was the thinking behind the change in Ontario, but the results were highly problematic. Who will defend the position of women within the Muslim community? Can there ever be any guarantee that a spouse will submit to such mediation voluntarily?

There have been comparable controversies in other countries. In 2006 a verdict by a German court caused a huge stir. Arguing that in 'Moroccan culture' violence within marriage is customary, a judge in Frankfurt turned down an application for divorce submitted by a German woman of Moroccan origin who had been abused by her husband for many years. In her final decision the judge referred to verse 4:34 of the Koran, which states that Muslim men are permitted to beat disobedient wives. Necla Kelek commented that the judge had adopted precisely the argument of traditional Muslims, who believe there is an inner world and an outer world. They argue that in the private domain, which includes marital relationships, Islamic law applies and the German state must not come between man and wife.[49]

In the Netherlands too a development was under way that would have created more space for cultural diversity in the field of law, as described in a study by two Dutch lawyers: 'Attitudes to "separate development" are now much more positive, both in the realm of policy and politics and among spokespeople for the communities involved. The claim to their own separate law and a separate legal position is thereby given a completely different social significance.'[50] That was a decade ago. Now the balance has shifted and responses to pleas for separate development are far less compliant.

In sum, the main weakness of the notion of a multicultural society is that it is oriented towards the past, as its most common definition suggests: 'integration with the retention of identity'. This formulation was introduced with a view to the eventual return of migrants to their native countries. Education in their own language and culture was judged necessary to ensure that children didn't become divorced from their countries of origin and have great difficulty adapting when they returned. The migrants stayed, but so did the idea of 'integration with the retention of identity'. As a result, migrant communities were above all seen as diasporas, which is to say groups that continued to focus on what they had left behind.

This approach not only underestimates the changes thrown up by the transition from one society to another and the generational dynamic that results, it also falls short in a normative sense, since it ignores the shared norms any modern economy and democracy needs to enable it to compete productively and resolve conflicts. In the absence of shared laws, shared public holidays, generally recognized standards of success at school, a level playing field for job interviews and historical references understandable to all, the room for meaningful differences of opinion shrinks and the room for misunderstanding grows.

Prejudice Weighed

This criticism of the multicultural worldview has consequences for the way we look at prejudice. Broad concepts such as xenophobia, which colour much of contemporary literature about immigration, are a way of focusing on a social phenomenon as mainly a question of guilt. The answer is plain and simple: the majority must learn to open up to minorities. Who would deny that? We come upon far too many examples of hostile or even aggressive attitudes towards newcomers among the established population.

What makes this outlook one-sided, however, is that only the majority is confronted with its prejudices, whereas in reality migrants are not without firmly held opinions of their own. What should we make of the relationship between Creoles and Hindustanis from Surinam, between Arabs and Berbers from Morocco, between Turks and Kurds – in short between majorities and minorities within migrant communities? And what about the opinions Antilleans hold about the Dutch, Algerians about the French or Pakistanis about the British? The still limited number of mixed marriages tells a story of ethnically motivated prejudice and that story too must be told. Alagiah concludes: 'It's true that there is a strong and visceral strain of racism amongst some Asians that is rarely, if ever, confronted with the same vigour that is reserved for white racism.'[51]

Anyone who advocates an open society should see every claim to superiority on the part of one ethnic group over another as an unfounded tradition. Adherence to shared norms always necessitates an investigation into the prejudices of our own communities, without waiting to see whether others are prepared to do the same. The revolving door of self-righteousness results in an eternal 'after you' in which the first step always has to be taken by somebody else.

The opposite of the self-examination we need is an uncritical embrace of what we regard as our own communities, also known as ethnocentrism. The term was first used by the American sociologist William Graham Sumner in his book *Folkways* (1906), where he describes ethnocentrism as 'this view of things in which one's own group is the center of everything, and all others are scaled and rated with reference to it. . . . Each group nourishes its own pride and vanity, boasts itself superior, exalts its own divinities, and looks with contempt on outsiders.' In the same context Sumner introduces a distinction between 'in-group' and 'out-group'.[52]

It's possible to read his study as an early expression of cultural relativism: everyone is simply a prisoner of the beliefs and customs of his own culture. In other words, we are all creatures of habit, and questions of good and evil are meaningless when applied to our moral standards, since the criteria by which we distinguish between the two lie in those moral standards themselves: 'Everything in the mores of a time and place must be regarded as justified with regard to that time and place.'[53] For centuries, Europeans regarded torture as a natural part of the judicial process, and in colonial New England countless witch trials were held. In his own time too, says Sumner – a time apparently so critical of traditions – it's almost impossible to hold a rational discussion on matters such as private property, parliamentary democracy or monogamous marriage.

Values are the driving force behind social selection. They determine what is normal and what is abnormal, who is well adjusted and who is not. This kind of selection is ruthless. It's all about who best conforms to the dominant values. So there's little connection between success and merit. Sumner has no illusions: '[Most people] are conservative. The great mass of any society lives a purely instinctive life just like animals.'[54] No attempt to enlighten the masses will ever come to anything. Whatever freedom may mean, no one can disregard the morals with which he grew up.

Lévi-Strauss interprets the inward-looking mentality in a similar way as a 'normal, even legitimate attitude, in any case inevitable'.[55] He believes identification with specific norms and values within a group is required to make it partly or wholly impervious to other groups. This relative inability to communicate is the price that must be paid to preserve a community's values; cultural self-preservation is impossible without ethnocentrism.

According to this anthropological approach, prejudice is unavoidable, and since it's a universal trait this goes for majorities as well as minorities. Yet the degree to which groups and individuals have fixed opinions varies greatly. Some are more prejudiced than others. In short we need more research into relationships between different groups and into the character traits of individuals who are biased in their opinions, to a greater or lesser degree. Both ways of looking at prejudice – we might call them the sociological and the psychological approach – have proven their worth.

Sociologist Norbert Elias lays the emphasis on interaction between the established and the outsiders. In the 1960s he compared two white working-class neighbourhoods in a British city to see how they differed in their degree of prejudice. Ethnic factors were not significant and neither were socio-economic differences. The only distinction between the two groups was that in one the residents had lived in the area for generations, whereas the neighbouring district was inhabited by people who had come to live there relatively recently. 'Without regard to this diachronic group dimension, the rationale and meaning of the personal pronoun "we" which they used with reference to each other cannot be understood.'[56]

Differences in length of residence create power differentials: 'Because they had lived together for a fairly long time, the old families possessed as a group a cohesion which the newcomers lacked. . . . And this integration differential substantially contributes to the former's power surplus.'[57] Thinking in terms of power relations is important, because inequalities affect the images that groups have of each other and the likelihood that those images will gain broader acceptance. Elias shows that the target group has the tendency to adopt the very same prejudices: 'These newcomers themselves, after a while, seemed to accept with a kind of puzzled resignation that they belonged to a group of lesser virtue and respectability, which in terms of their actual conduct was found to be justified only in the case of a small minority.'[58]

It's always disturbing when people accept the unjustified verdict that others pronounce upon them, but Elias underestimates the importance of self-criticism within groups, whether the established or outsiders. He tends to see the problematic behaviour of some in the outsider group purely as a reaction to the attitude of the established: 'How far the shame of outsiders produced by the inescapable stigmatisation of an established group turns into paralysing apathy, how far into aggressive norm and lawlessness, depends on the overall situation.'[59]

Elias's theory explains a great deal about the history of, for example, the Irish and Germans in America, or Caribbean migrants in the Netherlands. Those communities were indeed absorbed into society within a few generations. It's surely relevant to note that the former outsiders began to be regarded as belonging to the same group as the established as soon as new outsiders arrived. With the coming of the Italians and Poles, earlier migrants suddenly became 'old' immigrants. The same can be said of postcolonial migrants in the Netherlands, who were thought of as outsiders right up to the point when guest workers and their families from Morocco and Turkey became a visible part of society.

Old antagonisms can be driven out by new antagonisms. Enzensberger sums up this phenomenon in an image to which everyone can relate, that of a train compartment.[60] A passenger sitting alone in a carriage experiences the first person to come in as an intruder, making room for him with visible reluctance. When they are joined by a third passenger at the next station, a degree of solidarity immediately develops between the former opponents. Both scowl at the new outsider, whose arrival has disturbed the balance. The initial opposition between established and outsider is swept away by the fresh intruder. The pattern that emerges here applies on a far larger scale between ethnic groups.

Earlier migrants often react with just as much hostility as the original inhabitants to the arrival of newcomers. 'Full means full' is not a sentiment exclusive to the white majority. The history of migration can be envisioned as a slowly expanding circle of established residents, such that each new group gains a place within the image a society has of itself. As we shall see, Catholic migrants were far from welcome in Protestant America, and the same went for ethnic communities from Eastern and Southern Europe. A century later those religious and ethnic groups had been absorbed into a new 'us' that was less exclusive than before. The community of the established in America and Europe is growing still.

Which is of course not to say that all prejudice vanishes into thin air as time goes by. Elias is being rather optimistic when he writes: 'What one calls "race relations", in other words, are simply established-outsider relationships of a particular type.'[61] There are plenty of examples to the contrary. Anti-Semitism has turned out to be a persistent phenomenon and the same is true, although in a different way, for problematic relationships between black and white in the Anglo-Saxon world. The idea that ethnic relations are not much different from relations between the established and outsiders is too limited.

The sociological way of addressing the issue is in need of further input from psychology. Why does one person in a given group exhibit so much more prejudice than another? There are two classic studies, both concentrating primarily on personality traits: *The Nature of Prejudice* (1954) by American social psychologist Gordon Allport, and a study by German philosopher Theodor Adorno and his team that looks at the authoritarian personality, called *Studies in Prejudice* (1950). Both were written at a time when experiences with Nazism and Fascism were fresh in the memory. The fear of a repeat of those horrors clearly shows through.

Allport examines at length the distinction between prejudice and rational verdicts about groups. He writes that investigations into differences between groups must continue, because otherwise it will be hard to distinguish between justified and unjustified generalizations. Not every generalization is a prejudice. People need to categorize things if they are to bring order to the chaos of everyday life. We often need to anticipate unprecedented circumstances, and since we can't judge each and every case on its own merits, we have to fall back on previous experience and the judgements we've formed as a result. This is a normal way of proceeding, although of course it can easily spill over into unjustified prejudice. There are real conflicts of interest too, which must be distinguished from bias. When a strike is broken by low-paid immigrants, for example, tensions and conflicts naturally arise, but these are not necessarily a matter of bias, however readily prejudices may come to the fore at the same time.

Allport's most important claim is that preconceptions often stem from personality traits in those who pass judgement, rather than having very much to do with the characteristics of the groups concerned. This is demonstrated clearly by the way negative verdicts on different ethnic or racial groups often coincide. Generally speaking, a white person who cannot abide Jews will not be particularly well disposed towards the black population. Blatantly contradictory views about specific population groups are another sign of a prejudiced personality. Allport took note of the following conversation: 'Mr. A: I say the Jews are too much alone; they stick together, and are clannish. Mr. B: But look; in our community there are Cohen and Morris on the Community Chest, several Jews in the Rotary Club and Chamber of Commerce. Many support our community projects . . . Mr. A: That's just what I was saying, they're always pushing and elbowing their way into Christian groups.'[62]

Allport recognizes a type of personality that he calls prejudiced and contrasts it with the more tolerant personality. Their cognitive processes differ markedly, he contends. The prejudiced or authoritarian person, as Adorno describes this type, has a tendency to see sharp dichotomies, to make few subtle distinctions and to have a rigid approach to reality. Prejudices are functional. They help those with insecure personalities to maintain a favourable self-image, and they help people to convert frustrations about their own lives into aggression against other groups, whether in word or deed. Allport believes insecurity is the key to understanding prejudice: 'In order to avoid hurt and achieve at least an island of security it is safer to exclude than to include.'[63] This is not merely a matter of upbringing, since insecurity may increase considerably in times of great social change that affect a person's social status.

Like Adorno, Allport also points to the role of religions. Rather reluctantly he concludes that 'individuals having no religious affiliation show on the average less prejudice than do church members'.[64] The explanation for this, he says, lies partly in the fact that religions absorb the cultural traditions of groups: 'It is the prevalence of ethnocentric interpretations of religion that alienates many tolerant people from the church.'[65] Much of today's discussion about Muslim communities in the Western world relates to this intermingling of their religion and the culture of their countries of origin.

One of the more problematic conclusions of these studies aimed at finding psychological explanations is that as character traits prejudices are stubborn. Indeed, they're so much part of a personality that relinquishing a prejudice would involve a profound change to the whole 'emotional economy'. This conclusion overlooks the fact that prejudices are often born of conformism and not always particularly deeply rooted. Developments in many countries since the 1960s, America included, show at the very least that a new conformism can arise, a new norm that, for example, condemns discrimination against the black population, even if it remains true to say that old habits die hard.

If we are to break the cycle of prejudice, then self-criticism is essential, not just among the majority but among migrants and their children. Allport concludes that 'ethnocentrism may be higher among minority groups than among the dominant majority'.[66] This has indeed been confirmed by research on the black population in America and the Turkish community in Germany. Like Elias, however, he regards such prejudice as primarily a defensive attitude. The formation of clans is a result of exclusion. He has little to say about bias in minority circles towards other minorities, or about bias that cannot be attributed to hostility on the part of the majority.

With his study in hand we have to go a step further, since factors that contribute to the formation of prejudice can often be found to an above average degree in migrant communities. Ethnocentric traditions are often prevalent in their countries of origin, and this is compounded by the fact that their children are generally brought up with greater respect for authority. The strong emphasis on family is accompanied by distrust of society. Furthermore, the majority of migrants have had relatively little education, which makes them more likely to exhibit prejudices. Add to this the insecurity that inevitably results from migration and the stronger religious ties that go with it, and all the ingredients for an 'authoritarian' personality come together. Although we should not see the prejudices of the majority as cancelled out by those of minority groups, it's far too simple to regard the 'my own people first' of the minority purely as a reaction to the 'my own people first' of the majority.

How are we to respond to all this? In many European countries there's a growing rift between members of elites, who increasingly regard themselves as world citizens with a vested interest in a transnational society, and people who lead lives far more firmly tied to a specific place. There are many indications that in a society which emphasizes ethnic differences, majorities too may start to see themselves as ethnic groups. Surely white is a colour? Such declarations of loyalty present a real danger at a time when everyone is in search of an identity of his or her own. We have to break the vicious circle of prejudice. The first step is to salvage the ability to reach critical judgements about our own traditions.

World Citizens in the Making

We need to move beyond criticism of the colonial worldview and set off in search of a contemporary cosmopolitanism. Relativism must be given a place, but it should never be allowed the final say. Universalism is essential, since it holds open the possibility of reaching a critical verdict on norms that are generally accepted within a specific community. We have to resist the temptation to embrace traditions uncritically, but at the same time we must reject any concept of world citizenship that fails to relate to a community for which a person can feel responsible. It's proving increasingly difficult to reconcile a cultural heritage with openness to the world, two things that seem to be drifting apart in the richer nations.

Our world is becoming both larger and smaller, bringing people closer together and pushing them further apart. The astonishing mobility of capital, information, goods and people is making societies not only more involved with each other, but more permeated by each other. At the same time the aversion to integration and cultural mixing is increasing and people are withdrawing into their shells. World citizenship is a remote prospect for most. The central question here is what a contemporary cosmopolitanism ought to look like.

Polish-Canadian writer Eva Hoffman emphasizes the fact that the conditions for world citizenship have changed: 'Whereas cosmopolitanism used to defend itself against the narrow-mindedness of provincialism and nationalism, nowadays we are trying to use it as an antidote to the superficiality of globalism and life as social nomads.'[67] She sees a 'new betrayal' by intellectuals in 'the denial of the desire for meaningful attachment'.[68] Which returns us to the question: What form should an open society take in a borderless world?

There's a great deal to be said for the attempts that have been made in our own time to expand the community with which a given individual can identify – just as long as it's a matter of deepening responsibility, rather than a flight from obligation of the kind that's all too much in evidence everywhere. The current blurring of borders presents more opportunities for self-interest than for serving the needs of communities. The notion of world citizenship may help to expedite enlightened ways of living together, but it has its dark side. French philosopher Jean-Jacques Rousseau knew this: 'Distrust those cosmopolitans who go to great lengths in their books to discover duties that at home they regard as beneath them. Such philosophers love the Tartars to avoid having to love their neighbours.'[69]

A useful observation, particularly now. Many people are trying out a comfortable identity as citizens of a global village in the making without asking themselves whether the pursuit of a world without borders is not all too often a way of ignoring those close to them. The festive embrace of the global village is offset by urgent questions about the conditions for citizenship of a city and a state. In defiance of a readily professed openness towards the world, our heritage retains its significance.

In his autobiography, Austrian writer Stefan Zweig presents a wry exploration of the illusions surrounding the concept of the world citizen. He tells of how he was exiled. After a long wait on the 'petitioners' bench' it dawns on him exactly what the difference is between having the right to a passport and being granted a residence permit. 'Often in my cosmopolitan reveries I had imagined how beautiful it would be, how truly in accord with my innermost thoughts, to be stateless, obligated to no one country and for that reason undifferentiatedly attached to all.'[70] Now he knows better and speaks of 'that terrible state of homelessness'.[71]

Elsewhere he writes that emigration 'disturbs the equilibrium'. His book could be read as an account of the disenchantment of a world citizen as he slowly discovers the unspoken conditions of his mobility at a time when being uprooted is no longer the result of a free choice but is brought about by force of circumstance. His life story invites a study into the often misunderstood notion of world citizenship.

We come upon a similar grappling with cosmopolitanism in the work of French philosopher Alain Finkielkraut. At first, the targets of his indictment were those who glorify what is theirs at the expense of the things we hold in common. He clearly opted for a form of universalism. In his recent books, however, he explains the risks of exactly that option: faith in humanity turns out to be as easily abused as the cherishing of a birthplace. He now refuses to choose between the resulting alternatives: 'Detachment or attachment. Openness or heritage. Tolerance or loyalty.'[72]

By combining the two rather than opting for one or the other we can avoid an impasse. We should value the crossing of frontiers in the knowledge that borders are an inalienable part of our lived reality. We need to contemplate cultural differences instead of denying they exist. People are not prisoners of their origins, but each individual existence has to be embedded in something. It's a matter of seeing a heritage not as prescriptive but as a prerequisite for independent action. Freedom, after all, needs a context.

A true cosmopolitan tries to embrace that tension between the local and the universal. This is surely rather different from believing in a worldwide market of ideas, each of which can be appropriated or rejected at will. How can we envision and revise our own cultures in the light of those of others? When we try to make comparisons we find ourselves forced to lower our sights. It's not easy to find a way into a foreign culture, even that of a neighbouring country. Anyone who tries to fathom the often implicit references in a novel originally written in another language immediately runs into difficulties. The reader is required to transpose him- or herself, and that requires effort. As T. S. Eliot rightly observed: 'Though it is only too easy for a writer to be local without being universal, I doubt whether a poet or novelist can be universal without being local too.'[73]

Surely the attitude that many adopt is a strange one. They claim to be greatly interested in other cultures and regard the rejection or brushing aside of their own culture as a gesture that underlines that interest. But only those who are conversant with their own cultural traditions can move beyond them; only those who understand that boundaries exist can overstep them. In the end we learn by comparison. We get to know ourselves better by examining that which is foreign. Detachment and attachment, heritage and openness, loyalty and tolerance: these attitudes belong together and if they're decoupled a precarious balance is upset.

Finkielkraut describes his own stance: 'The cosmopolitan is distinguished by the fact that he does not regard it as dreadful but as salutary to be put to the test by the other, the stranger: the other, that which he is not, over whom he has no hold.'[74] Were all borders truly dissolved, there would be no outside world any longer. He therefore passes stern judgement on self-declared citizens of the world: 'They couple the tribal practices of introverted groups with the moral condemnation of their own hearth and home. . . . A person without a navel is a person who advocates unbounded human rights, but an abominable citizen.'[75]

The weakness of cosmopolitanism lies in the fact that the ambitious 'everyone is in principle responsible for everything' can easily degenerate in practice into 'nobody is any longer responsible for anything'. This was tragically illustrated by the peacekeeping operations in Yugoslavia and Rwanda. Where no direct security interests are involved, it's easy to look the other way. Even the aim of making the international community live up to a collective responsibility to prevent genocide – surely a moral minimum – seems extraordinarily difficult to realize.

We are looking for words that bridge the gap between the local and the universal, for a world citizenship that connects with its own lived environment. Philosopher Kwame Anthony Appiah tells of a life lesson he received from his father, who was born in Ghana: '"Remember that you are citizens of the world." He told us that wherever we chose to live we should endeavour to leave that place "better than you found it".'[76] His father thereby made clear that even those who settle somewhere temporarily can leave something permanent behind, or rather, ought to want to leave something permanent behind. He describes this idea as 'rooted cosmopolitanism'.

The concept of the world citizen is in the first instance a European legacy, but the source of humanist ideals need not discredit them in the eyes of non-Europeans. When the Universal Declaration of Human Rights was drawn up it was deliberately not given a philosophical basis. It may have been conceived according to the European tradition of individual rights, but no cultural grouping can repudiate its norms. They are applicable to all countries, including those in which they were originally formulated. One example here is of course decolonization. The revolt against the colonial powers was led by elites educated in the West, who used the modern vocabulary of self-determination and human rights. There is no escaping the paradox: resistance to European colonizers took place in the name of ideals that originated in Europe.

We must learn to distinguish between the origin and the spread of ideas. Just as the classics in music, architecture and literature are appreciated far from their countries of origin, so the democratic revolutions of America and France can be seen as a universal heritage that has broken free of its sources. Singaporean diplomat and scholar Kishore Mahbubani writes: 'For 500 years the West has been the only civilization carrying the burden of advancing human knowledge and wealth. Today, it can share this responsibility.' And he adds: 'It should also celebrate the clear spread of Western values in the rise of Asia.'[77] The applicability of human rights is not limited by their European background. Whatever we may say about Asian values – with their emphasis on collective duties rather than individual entitlements – there is no real alternative to the code of human rights.

British author Timothy Garton Ash advocates a transition from the idea of the West as the embodiment of '*the* free world' to that of '*a* free world' that covers far more regions of the globe. He sees it as an historical opportunity: 'Isn't it better to accept that the West, in going so far beyond its historic self, also ceases in some important sense to be the West?'[78] This is an important question now that democracy has spread so far across the globe. We can join Garton Ash in talking of the 'post-West', just as long as we realize that there are as yet few institutions that can give any real substance to this commonality of interests among the world's democracies.

The rights of man are essential to any society, but they do not encompass culture in a general sense. For that reason we should never speak of a hierarchy of cultures. What is the point in comparing Spanish and Turkish literature in such a way, or Western and Asian architecture? Within Western culture too, questions of this type are nonsensical. Is Schopenhauer a better philosopher than Socrates? Should we see Stravinsky as superior to Schubert? What could statements of this kind mean? There are many domains of social life where questions about progress or hierarchy are meaningless. It therefore means little to say that Islamic culture is backward.

There is only one way to prevent criticism of ethnocentrism – which elevates specific traditions to the status of universal truths – from degenerating into a cultural relativism that rejects universality in the name of particular preferences. Anyone choosing to defend a civilizing mission is himself part of that mission; norms held up as an example to the world will inevitably come back to haunt those who disseminate them. The civilizer must become civilized – that duty is unavoidable if we want to continue to defend universalism. It's unhelpful to speak of the superiority of Western civilization, since an open society relies on a capacity for critical self-assessment.

What we are eager to defend must be understood as a history of trial and error. Anyone hoping to impress upon others the importance of equal rights for men and women will do well to realize first of all that these are norms that came into being only after considerable resistance had been overcome. Precisely because they are such recent and incomplete achievements, they must be protected against the hostility of those who wish to undo them.

No regime can any longer entrench itself behind its own borders. Even the most authoritarian governments feel forced to justify themselves on the basis of generally accepted norms, whether or not they repeatedly violate them. The effects of worldwide openness undoubtedly contribute to this. We live in what has been called an 'emotional democracy'. The decline of indifference towards injustice wherever it occurs in the world can certainly be seen as moral progress. Aloofness is increasingly difficult to sustain.

Nevertheless, the colonial past casts its shadow across every intervention. In our own day some speak with enthusiasm of 'democratic imperialism', which they say should be the guiding principle for activist politics around the world. It stands in contrast to the 'multicultural aloofness' that draws a quite different conclusion, namely that because of the abuses of the colonial period, Western values have largely lost their appeal. Whatever we may conclude about European domination, it's clear that the attitude we adopt towards the colonial period is of great significance for the way we act today.

The imperialism that regarded the dissemination of its own civilization as a mission violently broke through the walls of other cultures and brought them into contact with each other without their consent. This combination of power and principle has produced a guilty conscience, which reveals itself in the notion that it's impossible to pass judgement across cultural boundaries. An attitude of this kind means opting for detachment: who are we to judge, let alone interfere? Samuel Huntington has been wrongly criticized for deriving an American imperialism from the 'clash of civilizations'. In fact he does the opposite. He rejects the claim that Western countries have a right to intervene outside their own cultural realms. He sees his clashing civilizations in the light of cultural relativism and his analysis amounts to an invitation to stand aloof from interaction between civilizations. Further clashes are exactly what he wishes to avoid.

Universalism and aloofness do not go together. This conclusion is far from innocuous. Many see the new interventionism – in Kosovo, Afghanistan and Iraq, for example – as a continuation of the old colonialism by new means. People have quite rightly asked whether such a thing as 'democratic imperialism' is possible, or whether the use of force inevitably corrupts all moral intentions. A heedless rush to defend human rights everywhere can easily lead to a deepening of the gulf between 'the West and the Rest'.

Even those who advocate greater involvement in human rights issues elsewhere may well question the notion of humanitarian intervention, which ultimately amounts to warfare. Is the militarization of morality sensible, or is it a way of continuing colonial history by other means, with all the profound contradictions that involves? The idea that humanity must be placed above sovereignty – which is to say that third parties can intervene in a country in the name of human rights – has problematic consequences to say the least. Canadian essayist Michael Ignatieff puts it like this: 'Human rights is increasingly seen as the language of a moral imperialism just as ruthless and just as self-deceived as the colonial hubris of yesteryear.'[79]

What remains is the conclusion that these rights must be defended globally. This will be possible only once universalism has absorbed the experience of colonialism and digested it. All pertinent questions thrown up by cultural relativism should be taken into account, but to relinquish democratic impatience would be to betray the open society as an ideal. It would surely not be credible to swear loyalty to our own democracies and exhibit indifference to democracy elsewhere in the world. This universalism creates obligations. Plainly Western countries cannot withdraw from the modern world order, which they have created, whenever it suits them. There is no longer any way out of the colonial trap.

7

The Rediscovery of America

The Colonists' Creed

America is regarded as an exception by the rest of the world and it sees itself as a country with a unique destiny. Central to this self-image is the idea that ever since independence it has been a 'nation of immigrants'. Every American has a story of departure and arrival somewhere in his or her family history. The United States is both the most powerful country of our day and the most cosmopolitan, drawing people from all points of the compass. This melting pot of migrants has increasingly come to represent all the peoples of the world, and it has acquired a global scope.

The image of a 'nation of immigrants' is often held up as a reproach to Europe, a continent bound by its own traditions. Whereas Americans can look back on a proud history of accommodating immigrants, Europeans have proven incapable of successfully integrating those who have arrived since the Second World War. Not wanting to acknowledge that their countries too are gradually becoming nations of immigrants, they refuse to absorb the lessons of American history.

This reproach is hard to ignore, if only because we hear it so often. The most obvious answer, and the least interesting, is that Europe is a collection of nation-states with many centuries of history behind them and therefore cannot be compared with America. Immigration into Europe took off only after nation-building had reached an advanced stage, whereas on the other side of the ocean the arrival of migrants was woven into the story Americans told about themselves. The contrast is undeniable and its impact on attitudes towards immigration impossible to ignore.

It's far more interesting, however, to take the comparison seriously and to look in more detail at the American experience. It soon becomes clear that the self-image of a 'nation of immigrants' masks several of the country's essential characteristics. These have to do with aspects of American history that may contain valuable lessons for European countries. Experiences on the two continents have a great deal more in common than is often supposed. Conflicts surrounding immigration in contemporary Europe resemble the opposition frequently faced by newcomers to the United States.

What does it actually mean to say that America regards itself as 'a nation of immigrants'? The focus of attention is usually the enormous diversity of its migrant populations, but what is the 'nation' that holds all this diversity together? For an answer, we need to look back to the origins of the United States. American history begins not with immigration but with colonization, which is a different thing altogether, not only in that it involved the displacement and annihilation of the indigenous inhabitants, the 'Indians', but because there is a considerable difference between colonists and immigrants. Samuel Huntington stresses the distinction: 'Settlers leave an existing society, usually in a group, in order to create a new community. . . . They are imbued with a sense of collective purpose.'[1] Immigrants do not create a new society: 'Migration is usually a personal process, involving individuals and families, who individually define their relation to their old and new countries.'[2] Whereas colonists create a society of their own, immigrants become part of an existing society.

In 1776, the year of the Declaration of Independence, around four million people lived in America, 700,000 of them slaves. Of the white population, 80 per cent was British, the remainder overwhelmingly German or Dutch. At the time of the first federal census in 1790 around 100,000 Americans had Dutch roots, the majority of them residents of New York (formerly New Amsterdam). The number of today's Americans who have Dutch ancestry has been estimated at about four million.[3] Research shows that around 50 per cent of contemporary Americans are descendants of the original colonial population, including the slaves, while the other half have their origins in later immigration. The description of America as a 'nation of immigrants' is therefore literally half true. Moreover, between 1820 and 2000 the proportion of the population born abroad was never more than 10 per cent, except for the years between 1860 and 1910, when the proportion of migrants reached 13–15 per cent, which is comparable to present-day figures.[4]

'Before immigrants could come to America, settlers had to found America,' Huntington concludes.[5] The society the immigrants encountered had a number of well-defined characteristics. The original population was almost exclusively Protestant, the main exception being the colony of Maryland where many Catholics lived. Intense religious feeling set the tone. Early Americans can be described as dissidents within Protestantism, which was itself a form of dissidence. Those who came to America had often belonged to persecuted minorities in their own countries. Its religious heritage helped to shape America's democratic ideals. Individualism, moral fervour and opposition to hierarchy made the country what it is today.

Out of that culture and out of the Enlightenment, America developed a creed in which the main emphasis lay on the fundamental equality of all men and on individual liberty. Religious tolerance was hard to achieve in a country with conflicting religious passions, but nevertheless it was an essential feature of the new republic. The separation of church and state did not mean the marginalization of religion, rather it was a way of guaranteeing freedom of worship. America has always had a mainly Christian population and a secular government. Even before Independence, Voltaire and other Enlightenment thinkers wrote in praise of religious freedom in Pennsylvania, for instance, although in the colony of New Amsterdam there was rather less freedom of worship. Peter Stuyvesant, governor from 1647 to 1664, refused to allow the Lutherans to found a church of their own and placed restrictions on the activities of Quaker missionaries. He also limited the rights of Jews. Only under pressure from the West India Company – which had several major Jewish investors and advocated tolerance for commercial reasons – was this stance moderated.

The separation of church and state was an important achievement of the 1787 constitution, which avoided any reference to a higher power. Thomas Jefferson said that a 'wall of separation' must be built between church and state. The first article of the 1791 Bill of Rights states that America will have no established religion, while article six of the US Constitution makes clear that no religious test will ever be required of anyone wishing to hold public office. The latter provision was heavily criticized in some quarters, but it remained unaltered.

The idea of a land without precedent was set down in *Letters from an American Farmer* by John de Crèvecoeur, an immigrant from France, written shortly after America became independent. 'Here individuals of all nations are melted into a new race of men, whose labors and posterity will one day cause great changes in the world.'[6] (The term race was then used mainly to indicate a people or a nation.) Truly prophetic words, at least as far as the influence of America in the world is concerned, but we may well ask whether reality has lived up to that faith in a new kind of human being.

The situation at the end of the eighteenth century did not match De Crèvecoeur's hopes. Nation-building was a slow process in America, in fact it was only really in the second half of the nineteenth century, in other words after the Civil War, that a true sense of being one nation developed. The opening up of the country by means of the railroad was crucial in this respect, although the impact of the telegraph should not be underestimated. Because of America's sheer size, which makes it more a continent than a nation, local and regional identities were still strong a century after independence. Only when communications improved could a real national identity emerge. As poet James Russell Lowell observed in the aftermath of the Civil War: 'It is no trifling matter that thirty millions of men should be thinking the same thought and feeling the same pang at a single moment of time, and that these vast parallels of latitude should become a neighbourhood more intimate than many a country village.'[7]

The expansion westwards was particularly conducive to integration. American historian Frederic Jackson Turner emphasized this point: 'In the crucible of the frontier the immigrants were Americanized, liberated, and fused into a mixed race.'[8] The great mobility of Americans helped mould them into a single nation. Even today their tendency to move within their own country exceeds that of the population of any country in Europe, let alone mobility across European borders. The new states out west promoted national unity in another way too. They had not existed as independent entities before independence but were called into being by the new America, so their identification with the nation as a whole was stronger than that of some of the existing states, which focused on their own independence. The arrival of increasing numbers of migrants from countries other than Britain further weakened ties to the old country and made it easier to create an American self-consciousness.

The extent to which America defined itself in opposition to Europe at an early stage is striking; the terms 'New World' and 'Old World' speak volumes. The ideal of equality, with the great opportunities it presented to immigrants, was seen as a huge improvement on attitudes in the class-ridden societies of Europe. The promise that anyone with sufficient determination could build a better life encouraged newcomers to identify with America. Historian Merle Curti writes that even during the eighteenth century 'the belief in the degradation of the Old World and the mounting fame of America had become widespread'.[9] Europe stood for absolutism and doctrinal dogmatism, whereas America wanted to serve the democratic ideal. It became a refuge for all the persecuted of the earth. Its mission to embody a new world is essential to any understanding of America, especially as a 'nation of immigrants'. It was a broadly propagated mission which, for all its problematic aspects, helped to hold all that ethnic diversity together.

It's no coincidence that America's openness to immigrants increased in periods when it was intensively involved with the rest of the world and decreased in times of isolationism. The idea that America could reshape the world in its own image went hand in hand with a confidence that immigrants would be assimilated. 'We are the Romans of the modern world – the great assimilating people,' wrote Oliver Wendell Holmes.[10] By contrast, there were periods, between the wars for instance, when America held aloof as far as possible from the rest of the world and immigration was kept to a minimum.

Involvement in two world wars contributed enormously to the integration of migrant groups. There were many conflicts of loyalty, one example being the crisis experienced by the German community in America during the '14–'18 war, which we will look at later. Another concerns the Japanese community during the Second World War. The fate of the Japanese who were living in the United States in those years has rightly been described as one of the low points of recent American history. After the attack on the US fleet in Pearl Harbor, many were picked up and interned. Despite such excesses, it was that war more than anything else that brought the country together. Few people realize that hundreds of thousands of American troops of German extraction and a large number of Italian-American soldiers fought in Western Europe. However seriously their loyalty may have been questioned before the war, little remained of that distrust by the time it ended.

For the black community too, both world wars represented great strides towards emancipation. Initially, many regiments were still segregated, but even so, the sight of black Americans bearing arms was a slap in the face to those who persisted in seeing them as second-class citizens. Precisely because the struggle against Nazism and Fascism was motivated by a rejection of racist thinking, the gap between America's civilizing ideals and everyday practice became increasingly obvious. Racial segregation in the South could no longer be justified. The campaign for civil rights for the black population was given a huge boost by the war.

Irrespective of the internal tensions created by America's involvement in a range of conflicts elsewhere, generally speaking its world role increased the tendency of its citizens to identify with their country, which seemed to have a special mission. The national pride forged by those interventions is undeniable, and worldwide opinion polls consistently place Americans at the top on a scale of patriotic sentiments. The powerful emotions aroused by the attacks of 11 September 2001 illustrated the country's faith in itself, and the destruction of the World Trade Center claimed the lives of people with extremely diverse backgrounds. The building was a symbol not just of the capitalism so hated by some, but of an unparalleled ethnic diversity.

The notion of America as embodying the entire world is an inspiration to many migrants. One telling example is that of General John Abizaid, who at the turn of this century was the highest-ranking American soldier at Central Command, which covers the Middle East. The son of a Christian Lebanese-American father, he speaks fluent Arabic, attended a university in Jordan and specialized in the Middle East when he continued his studies at Harvard. Careers like his exemplify America's status as a world power, and the role migrants and their children can play in it.

The self-image of America as the world in a nutshell, as a country without precedent, as the one and only 'nation of immigrants' makes it hard to distinguish self-interest from principle in its foreign policy. A display of power that cloaks itself in moralizing rhetoric provokes fierce reactions from the rest of the world, but in presidential speeches we can still recognize the America that aspires to be a beacon, however unpopular and thankless a task that may be. 'At some point we may be the only ones left', said Bush Jr shortly after 9/11. 'That's okay with me. We are America.' Indeed, the words of Oliver Wendell Holmes still ring true a century later: America is the new Rome. In our day too it's a country with an almost irresistible power of attraction.

Nevertheless the place of America will change over coming decades. In *The White Tiger*, Indian novelist Aravind Adiga describes the rise of an entrepreneur in Bangalore. The novel takes the form of an open letter to Chinese premier Wen Jiabao. In the margins of his story we read: 'White men will be finished within my lifetime. There are blacks and reds too, but I have no idea what they are up to – the radio never talks about them. My humble prediction: in twenty years' time, it will be just us yellow men and brown men at the top of the pyramid, and we'll rule the whole world. And God save everyone else.'[11]

This might stand as a witty summary of the content of a good many academic bookshelves. We continually hear predictions that the centre of gravity of the world economy is slowly but surely shifting eastwards. The combination of irresponsible borrowing and two vastly expensive wars have undermined America's position in the world. Kishore Mahbubani has accentuated the point: 'It is futile for the 12 percent of the world's population who live in the West to imagine that they can determine the destinies of the remaining 88 percent, many of whom feel newly energized and empowered.'[12] The question for America is how to deal with this relative loss of power.

In the Melting Pot

The melting pot has become the most enduring image of the great experiment that America undeniably represents. As early as 1845, Ralph

Waldo Emerson spoke of the desire to 'construct a new race, a new religion, a new state, a new literature, which will be as vigorous as the new Europe which came out of the smelting-pot of the Dark Ages'.[13] This is a notion reflected in America's motto, E *pluribus unum*, out of many one, a unity born out of a multiplicity. By multiplicity, of course, the founders primarily meant the 13 colonies that formed the United States, but later the phrase acquired the additional meaning of a 'nation of immigrants'.

The notion of unity in diversity contains an irresolvable tension that is the source of America's dynamism. One moment the emphasis is on unity, the next on diversity. Both can be interpreted according to the thinking of either the Enlightenment or Romanticism. Unity can be seen either as a democratic ideal of mixing and blending or as an organic national character that excludes certain groups from the start. The same goes for diversity. It can be seen either as the kind of pluralism that should be part of any open society or as a collection of groups that exist side by side and put their own ethnic origins first.

The melting pot idea is the interpretation closest to Enlightenment thinking, since it regards America as a blend of old cultures that are the raw material for a new culture. It was the British playwright Israel Zangwill who in 1908, in his play *The Melting Pot*, conveyed this metaphor to a broad audience – meeting with great enthusiasm, incidentally, from the then US president, Theodore Roosevelt, who attended the opening night. The play itself, the slightly saccharine story of a Jewish boy and a Christian girl who fall in love, is not an outstanding artistic achievement – it's too didactic for that – but it did turn out to be an effective way of making a point.

The melting pot has become part of the image Americans have of their country. In the Ford factories of the 1920s it even became the basis for an elaborate public ritual. On the stage stood an enormous cauldron with the words 'Ford English School Melting Pot' emblazoned on it. At the back of the stage was a cardboard steamship out of which came the immigrants, holding signs that indicated their countries of origin. Then the factory's English teachers approached, bearing enormous spoons and calling out 'stir, stir'. On cue the scruffy immigrants of a moment ago came walking out of the melting pot as neatly dressed Americans, holding the stars and stripes.

The period 1865–1960 can be seen as the high tide of assimilation, and although on closer examination that century can be broken down into periods with contrasting climates of opinion, the fundamental tone was that of a conscious effort to absorb newcomers into their new country. In the early years of the twentieth century a large popular movement grew up in support of the 'Americanization' of immigrants. Some have seen this as cultural conformism, while others would say that successful immigration depends upon pressure to assimilate. Historian John Higham emphasizes the movement's dual nature: it involved both an explicit desire for social reform and nervousness about a lack of loyalty among newcomers. In theory these democratic and nationalistic impulses clash, but in practice they often turned out to reinforce one another.

The initial impetus towards a deliberate integration of newcomers came from social reformers. At first they had not been particularly concerned about the fate of immigrants. 'The progressives of the early twentieth century were unafraid, but in general they were also indifferent and aloof', Higham writes.[14] This soon changed. The discovery that a growing number of migrants were illiterate led to the founding of night schools offering lessons in the English language. The first of these opened in 1901 in New York, in 1903 in Chicago and in 1904 in Detroit. In that same period the first research was carried out into the deplorable living conditions endured by immigrants in New York and in 1912 former president Roosevelt denounced 'the fatal policy of indifference and neglect which has left our enormous immigrant population to become the prey of chance and cupidity'.[15]

This increasing sense of urgency gave rise to the North American Civic League for Immigrants, an organization founded in 1907 that is generally seen as the start of the popular movement for the Americanization of migrants. We should take a close look at this movement, since it gained a good deal of experience that is of particular relevance to all those in European countries who are now urging the integration of newcomers. The history of the League sheds a great deal of light on both the productive and the problematic aspects of this democratic impatience.

The movement for Americanization was fuelled first of all by unease about the vulnerable position of immigrants, people unable to take a full part in society because of their inadequate command of the language. They were victims of much exploitation and abuse. Frances Kellor, a key figure in the movement, said that in retrospect a lack of protection by the federal government had forced migrants back into their own circles and made them dependent on what she described as 'racial solidarity'.[16] The result was a society in which the established population and newcomers had hardly any contact with each other: 'America is a country which is just awakening to the fact that it is not a nationality but a mixture of nationalities.'[17]

From the start, the League was a coalition of social reformers, teachers, concerned intellectuals and representatives of the business sector. This last group regarded the rapid assimilation of immigrants as a convenient way of disciplining the workforce. Businessmen like Henry Ford were at the forefront; English became the compulsory language of Ford's employees. There was all the more call for such rules when strikes and unrest broke out in 1912–13. The chairman of the League concluded that 'none of these incendiary movements would have the sinister form which makes them dangerous, had it not been for the mishandled non-English-speaking population'.[18] After the Russian Revolution, in particular, the fear of the red peril grew.

The movement strove for a rapid identification with the principles and institutions of American society (assimilation), for the learning of the language (education), for resistance to the concentration of migrant groups in poor urban districts (distribution), for a rapid decision to acquire American nationality and education that would prepare people for citizenship (naturalization) and for improvements to immigrants' living and working conditions (protection). It was truly an ambitious undertaking, which received a powerful stimulus from the growing threat of war and developed into a crusade that could boast strong approval among the population at large.

When the First World War broke out there was increasing emphasis on national unity. Kellor was aware of the danger that national conflicts in Europe would spark violence between migrant groups in America: 'Isolated as we are from the foreign born groups we are likely to assume that they, like ourselves, are immune from foreign influences.'[19] How could Americans prevent Germans, Hungarians, Austrians, Turks and Bulgarians, all of whom were at war with the Allied forces, from laying claim to the loyalty of their compatriots in America?

Americanization steadily became an integral part of the war effort, placed at the service of plans for general mobilization. In 1915, Independence Day, the Fourth of July, was turned into an Americanization Day under the slogan 'Many Peoples, But One Nation'. A year later that motto was changed, significantly, to 'America First'. The war in which America was now becoming involved called for undivided loyalty. The movement leading the way named itself One Hundred Per Cent Americanism, with all the intolerance inevitably attached to such a high dose of patriotism.

There were plenty of attempts at coercion. Some states demanded that all schoolteachers should be American citizens; other states forbade education in any language but English. A bill was introduced into Congress that would have provided for the deportation of immigrants who failed to declare within three months that they wanted to become American citizens. Many such resolutions were quashed by judges or blocked by the House of Representatives, but they demonstrate the risks of the campaign for Americanization. Despite all this, Higham, who describes the lapses in detail, concludes that the movement was ultimately based more than anything else on an invitation to the immigrant: 'It turned part of the new fears of foreign influence which came out of the war into a positive program of emancipation rather than a wholly negative one of exclusion.'[20]

French sociologist Denis Lacorne is of the opinion that what began as an opportunity quickly became an obligation: 'Assimilation was no longer a choice freely made, an attractive hybridity or a love story, as Zangwill imagined it, but a conformism brutally imposed by those who believed they possessed the truth about America. Americanization "to the full hundred per cent" broke through the boundaries of private life in the name of an Anglo-Saxon concept of efficiency in the workplace, moral rectitude and modernity.'[21] Seen in this light, Americanization has a great deal in common with the civilizing offensive undertaken in so many European countries in the early twentieth century. Ideas about the education of the masses went hand in hand with pressure to conform, which did not stop at the front door. In the European 'offensive' too, social engagement and fear of conflict reinforced one another.

Frances Kellor's approach unites these two motives; social welfare and national discipline are inseparable in her thinking on integration. She consistently advocates assimilation, but she develops the idea with far more subtlety than her later critics would have us believe. What are the underlying principles of the citizenship of newcomers? She names recognition, reciprocity and participation, in that order. Prejudices entertained by the established population have stood in the way of a due recognition of migrants and their role in American society. Racial barriers must be removed and economic life is the place to start, but this is not the full story, since the immigrant has paid too little attention to the achievements of American society: 'He has come to know the dollar far better than he has the man.' In many cases the migrant has been heard to express superficial criticism of a society he did not help to build and therefore cannot fully fathom: 'He has often mistaken liberty for license and duties for privileges.'[22]

Reciprocity imposes a duty on the established population as well, since everyone must aspire to live up to the same norms. Take the example of the chairman of the largest trade union, Sam Gompers, who wrote in a letter to the League that if workers at the United States Steel Company were expected to embrace American ideals, then factory managers must at least make an effort to comply with those ideals in their dealings with workers. Kellor writes that this demand lies at the heart of all integration: the norms that are held up before newcomers will make no impression on them unless they are taken seriously by the country's longstanding inhabitants.

Regardless of any moral verdict on the desirability of assimilation, it's useful to ask whether the melting pot image accurately describes

America's historical development. In the early 1960s, in their classic *Beyond the Melting Pot* (1963), sociologists Daniel Nathan Glazer and Patrick Moynihan drew an unambiguous conclusion, dryly remarking that 'the point about the melting pot is that it did not happen'. Migrant groups with diverse backgrounds were not absorbed into a greater whole. They remained clearly distinguishable. In the 1960s ethnicity was still of enormous importance to large migrant communities like those of the Italians, Irish, Puerto Ricans and Jews of New York.

Yet ethnicity is not what we often imagine it to be, namely a residue of old traditions and customs that have proven hard to let go. Rather, ethnic groups are a new social fact. Glazer and Moynihan write: 'Ethnic groups then, even after distinctive language, customs, and cultures are lost, as they largely were in the second generation, and even more fully in the third generation, are continually recreated by new experiences in America. . . . A man is connected to his group by ties of family and friendship. But he is also connected by ties of *interest*. The ethnic groups in New York are also *interest groups*.'[23]

Moreover, although it is true that after a while the nationalist dimension of ethnicity fades, this is far less true of the religious dimension: 'Religious identities are strongly held by New Yorkers, and Americans generally, and they are for the most part transmitted by blood line from the original immigrant group.'[24] This explains why, despite the fact that intermarriage between national groups increased as time went by, there were remarkably few marriages between different religious groups. Catholic, Protestant and Jewish melting pots developed. The arrival of Muslims may well create a fourth melting pot.

Since Glazer and Moynihan published their book, time has not stood still, and certainly as far as Americans with European backgrounds are concerned there are increasing signs of fusion. According to the most recent census figures available (2000), more and more people do not identify with any specific ethnic community but simply call themselves Americans. Among the descendants of nineteenth-century immigrants from Europe, bonds with the countries of origin can be said to have steadily weakened. We might even conclude that America is as yet the only place where European integration has been truly successful.

Historians Leonard Dinnerstein and David Reimers think that, on the whole, assimilation still works. They claim that those who advocate the preservation of a way of life orientated towards their countries of origin cannot offer nearly enough to keep their children away from mainstream American society. Youth culture alone is far too attractive.[25] The immigration of people from many parts of the developing world is too recent for us to reach an unambiguous verdict on their fortunes in America, but Asian Americans are increasingly entering into mixed marriages and therefore, as with other immigrant communities, the boundaries separating them from the outside world are starting to fall away.

Opposition to Immigrants

The history of immigration in America is not a simple success story. It's also a tale of ethnic conflict and of opposition to newcomers. Immigrants – a total of 66 million over the past two centuries – were by no means always welcome. Historians who have studied American immigration are broadly in agreement. In all the familiar accounts, we come across statements like: 'For most of their history, Americans did not hold favorable views of immigrants.'[26] Or: 'The immigrants came with high hopes, and although in some places they got on well, in general they were unprepared for the coolness with which so many Americans received them.'[27] The notion of America as a 'nation of immigrants' conceals a long history of opposition to immigration.

The doubts felt by one of the founders of the republic, Benjamin Franklin, about the feasibility of making German immigrants integrate, as expressed in his 'Observations Concerning the Increase of Mankind' (1751), are well known. In the final decades of the eighteenth century, immigration from Germany got into its stride and Germans formed around a third of the then quite small population of Pennsylvania. Franklin questioned the willingness of migrants to adopt the language of their new country and believed great moral disparities existed, as well as a lack of political loyalty. He feared Germans would become 'so numerous as to Germanize us instead of our Anglifying them, and will never adopt our Language or Customs, any more than they can acquire our Complexion'.[28] These are fundamental concerns that arise in all debates about migration and they demonstrate that current differences of opinion in Europe represent a continuation of that historical pattern rather than a radical departure from it. Reactions do not differ so very greatly after all between the Old World and the New.

Sociologist Aristide Zolberg describes how, right from the early days of independence, arguments raged about how much immigration was desirable and of what kind. It's interesting to note that his interpretation of the disputes surrounding immigration diverges from a commonly held belief of the past few decades that sees the call for the influx of newcomers to be stemmed as a means of venting other frustrations. He writes that anyone who believes immigrants are merely scapegoats 'minimizes the rationality of the behavior of groups and classes with respect to the consequences of immigration'.[29] Large-scale migration always tests a country's social and cultural compromise. It's a 'legitimate source of concern' rather than a symptom of 'paranoia'.[30]

Zolberg talks of 'the perennial dialectics of American immigration politics'.[31] Mass immigration provokes opposition from the existing population, which in turn prompts immigrants to mobilize. Generally speaking, those with a vested interest in the arrival of immigrants, mainly employers in search of cheap labour, have won out against opposition to newcomers. This has produced a relatively open immigration policy. There were three periods in which the call for strict limits to be set became very loud indeed: the mid-nineteenth century, the years between 1880 and 1920, and the early 1980s to the mid-1990s. Zolberg links these reactions to peaks in the level of immigration. The timing of opposition from large majorities of longstanding residents is never a matter of chance.

Let's look more closely at these episodes. Protests against immigration were heard as early as the 1830s. There was Samuel Morse, for instance, the man who invented telegraphy. His proposals sound familiar to a contemporary observer: immigration controls to prevent penniless new arrivals becoming a drain on the public purse, the denial of voting rights to recent immigrants, and an extension of the period that individuals would need to reside in the country before they could become citizens. He also advocated the founding of publicly funded schools to counteract the influence of Catholic ideas on young people.

Morse's suggestions turned out to be a portent of much fiercer opposition to immigration. In the mid-nineteenth century the Know Nothing movement emerged. It arose out of the Supreme Order of the Star-Spangled Banner, a secret society whose members were sworn to silence, which probably explains the sobriquet 'Know Nothing'. The movement had a considerable following in many states and it was responsible for organized opposition to Catholic immigration in particular. The background to this development was a sharp increase in immigration in the period 1845–54. In that 10-year period almost three million migrants arrived in America, more than the total for the preceding seven decades.

Not only had the extent of immigration increased, it had changed in character as well. Newcomers from Ireland and Germany in particular were more likely to be illiterate, and there were far more Catholics among them. People suspected that a conspiracy by the Vatican lay behind this new wave of immigration. Although the Catholic population was modest in size, many were fearful of a demographic shift that would undermine America's Protestant culture. Protestantism was seen by the Know Nothings as a guarantee of individual liberty in their country and they regarded the hierarchical Catholic Church as the epitome of despotism. Catholics were suspected of block voting in elections, whereas the Protestant vote was split between different parties.

This criticism did not arise out of thin air. Catholic bishops were making an unprecedented show of missionary zeal in these years. They attacked the public schools, opposing, for example, the use of the Protestant King James Bible in education. Not only did Catholics found their own schools, there was increasing pressure to have them financed by the state. 'Are American Protestants to be taxed for the purpose of nourishing Romish vipers?' asked the *Philadelphia Sun*.[32]

In his history of the Know Nothings, Tyler Anbinder writes that their aim was not so much to reduce the level of immigration as to impose restraints on the political role of immigrants. They were convinced that, for electoral reasons, the governing parties, far from caring about new-comers as such, were corrupting the political process by naturalizing large numbers of them shortly before elections, purely so they could vote.

In the end the Know Nothings failed to alter the requirements for citizenship. They had proposed that a period of no less than 21 years ought to pass before a migrant could put in an application. That period was justified by reference to native-born Americans, who had to wait until they were adults, in other words aged 21, before they were entitled to vote. The idea was that the migrant must first be 'nationalized', in effect made to identify with his new country instinctively, before he could be naturalized.

Despite this failure, the Know Nothings gained a considerable following. The movement had more than 100 representatives in Congress within a few years of its founding in 1850, as well as eight state governors and the mayors of cities including Boston, Philadelphia and Chicago. President Lincoln was outspoken in his response. Referring to the words of the founding fathers, he wrote: 'As a nation, we began by declaring that "all men are created equal." We now practically read it "all men are created equal, *except negroes*." When the Know-Nothings get control, it will read "all men are created equal, except negroes, *and foreigners, and Catholics*".'[33]

Yet the situation was more complicated than that, since the Know Nothings in the North were vehemently opposed to slavery, which they saw as a form of oppression comparable to the despotism of the Catholic Church. One particular bone of contention was the compromise reached with the southern states, which obliged the North to return escaped slaves. A famous case was the arrest by an Irish militia in Boston of the runaway slave Anthony Burns, which led to fierce anti-Catholic protests. It is understandable, Anbinder writes, that historians have been reluctant to mention the bigoted Know Nothings in the same breath as the admirable advocates of the abolition of slavery, but the movement nevertheless 'displayed a precision and sophistication equal to that of other antebellum reform movements'.[34]

Let's look in more detail at the considerable hostility aroused in the course of the nineteenth and early twentieth centuries by the arrival of Irish and German immigrants. Later we'll examine opposition to the 'new' immigration from countries including Italy and Poland. These are interesting examples for several reasons. For one thing, they demonstrate that clashes between the established and outsiders often have social and religious aspects. They also show how immigration can create wrenching conflicts of loyalty. It's fascinating too for Europeans to see that the emigration of their compatriots in earlier times aroused such intense emotion.

The level of Irish immigration was high, as illustrated in a marvellous book by Oscar Handlin about the mainly Irish immigrants who came to Boston in droves from 1840 onwards. By 1850 some 54,000, out of a population of a mere 140,000, were Irish. The overwhelming majority were poor peasants who had fled famine and arrived destitute. Living conditions for this new underclass were appalling. Packed together in slums, without sanitation, the Irish immigrants quickly fell victim to epidemics of cholera, tuberculosis and other diseases eradicated elsewhere in Boston long before. Life expectancy was low. It was said that an Irish immigrant lived for an average of 14 years after arrival – or, more accurately, managed to survive that long by hook or by crook.

Handlin writes of a great divide between Irish migrants and the society around them: 'For a long time they were fated to remain a massive lump in the community, undigested, indigestible.'[35] The causes of this unwillingness to live together were not just economic, but cultural and religious too. The deeply traditional Catholicism of the Irish was far removed from the relatively liberal Protestantism of most Bostonians. The Irish had a fatalism born of experience, an attitude diametrically opposed to the prevailing sense of progress. They were against all reforms, whether the abolition of slavery, rights for women or the introduction of publicly funded schools. The contrast could not have been greater, and the Anglophobia the Irish brought with them for understandable reasons certainly did not help to bridge the gap. So hostility towards Irish immigrants was in essence the result of a conflict between a reform-minded majority and a traditionalist minority. It does not take a great deal of imagination to see in the Catholic Irish of the nineteenth century the Muslim migrants from Morocco or Pakistan of the twentieth.

The history of the Boston Irish can be evaluated from a number of different perspectives. First of all, it's clear that their integration was ultimately successful, since eventually little hostility would surround what had once been regarded as irreconcilable differences. But seen from another angle, their story shows that migration can disrupt and divide an urban community for many years. Look at how long it took before a Catholic president could be elected. During his campaign for office, John F. Kennedy was repeatedly forced to underline the fact that his loyalty lay with America and not with the Vatican. Even a century and more after the first Irish immigrants arrived, it still did not go without saying that a descendant of theirs would one day hold the highest office in the land.

It wasn't only the Irish who provoked hostility; the Germans too were far from welcome. In the century of mass European immigration (1830–1930), some six million Germans moved to America, the majority before 1890. Until the 1930s, German migrants and their children were the single largest immigrant group. In 1900, 31.4 per cent of newcomers were from Germany. The proportion then fell sharply, but in 1930 it still stood at 17.7 per cent. Around the turn of the twentieth century, New York, with its half-million German-born residents, was known as the world's second largest German city. The Germans were the first substantial immigrant group to arrive from continental Europe, later followed by Scandinavians, Italians and others.

John Hawgood divides the history of German immigration to America into three periods. First, from 1830 to 1855, there was the time of the 'German Idea', with plans to form a German state in America modelled on New England. A serious attempt was made to give Missouri, Wisconsin and Texas a predominantly German culture by means of mass immigration. 'Its aim was to keep the German element in its new environment racially and culturally distinct', Hawgood says.[36] The idea was to create a distinct German territory and German economic activity. It had no chance of success, this pursuit of a 'New Germany' on American soil, but it indicates how powerfully opposed German immigrants were to absorption into American society, which they regarded as culturally inferior. 'They struggled harder than perhaps has any other immigrant group in the United States of America, at any time.'[37]

When it became clear that efforts to create a territorial barrier against assimilation had come to nothing, all the more energy was invested in the creation of a psychological barrier designed to preserve German culture, even though this often meant foregoing economic opportunities. This second phase in the history of German immigration ran from 1855 (the failure of the New Germany project) to 1915 (with increasing pressure on German Americans as a result of the First World War). It was the period of hyphenation, of the emergence of a group known as the German-Americans. Hawgood writes: 'Germans in America between 1855 and 1915 lived not in the United States but in German-America.'[38] They formed a counterculture known as *Deutschtum*. Many clashes resulted, especially over prohibition and Sunday observance, which did not much suit German immigrants.

The centres of resistance to pressure from American society were the family, the school, the church and the press. German immigrants successfully blocked compulsory English-language education in Wisconsin and Illinois. This defensive attitude was not simply a matter of preference, it was a reaction to efforts to force migrant communities to adapt. As Hawgood sees it: 'The greatest influence in bringing the Germans into politics was undoubtedly the Nativist movement. . . . In many ways this is the greatest tragedy of German-America.'[39] It was a vicious circle. German-Americans looked down on the society around them and that society did not hold them in particularly high regard.

Against this background it's easy to understand why the First World War brought an end to hyphenation. A choice had to be made between Germany and America; there was no longer any place for German-Americans. This marks the start of the third period of German immigration history, in which German-Americans ceased to exist as a distinct community. Appeals by the German-American Alliance for a neutral stance on the war in Europe were felt to indicate a lack of loyalty. 'The time has come for the American people to end hyphenism,' said President Woodrow Wilson. Education in the German language was an immediate target, but it did not stop there. Everything that smacked of German culture was attacked, even in the field of classical music, with a campaign to oust Karl Muck, conductor of the Boston Symphony Orchestra. The German-language press disappeared, the Lutheran Church switched to holding services in English and countless Germans Anglicized their names. Assimilation was forced upon them and it was successful in the sense that, after 1918, the Germans were barely recognizable as a community.

The collapse of the German-American ideal after the First World War makes painfully clear that considerable tensions can arise between migrant groups and their host societies when international armed conflicts break out. Concerns about their loyalty can have dramatic consequences for migrant groups should they have any doubts about which side to choose, but the reaction of the receiving society, which in such circumstances soon tends to imagine itself faced with a fifth column, can have a profound impact too. The history of the German-Americans demonstrates this vividly. There is no reason at all to dismiss their experiences as irrelevant.

The Golden Door Shuts

The Know Nothing movement was swept away by a larger conflict, the Civil War, in which countless immigrants on both sides proved themselves loyal citizens on the battlefield. After a period of reconstruction and economic prosperity, opposition to immigration resurfaced at the end of the nineteenth century. Above all, there was opposition to the arrival of Catholics, of anyone assumed to be a revolutionary, and of supposedly inferior southern and eastern Europeans. Higham sums up the mood: 'Typically they trembled at the Roman challenge to American freedom, rallied to the defense of the public school system, and urged limitations on immigration and naturalization.'[40]

Higham believes that opposition to further immigration was spurred not just by periods of economic crisis during the 1880s and 1890s, but by the completion of the colonization of America, the closing of the frontier. The sense of a 'closed space' expressed itself in a diminishing faith both in social mobility and in assimilation as a natural process. Another important factor in creating this growing opposition was a radical change to the level of immigration around the turn of the twentieth century and to the composition of the immigrant population. The numbers rose rapidly – in the first decade of the twentieth century 8.8 million new immigrants were registered – and their countries of origin were different. The old immigration from England, Ireland, Germany and the Scandinavian countries was outstripped by what became known as 'new immigration' from Italy, Poland, Russia and the Balkans.

One of the leading thinkers behind the campaign for limits to be set to immigration was Henry Pratt Fairchild, a professor of sociology in New York, whom we have come upon before in this book. His *Immigration*, published in 1913, is a fascinating mishmash. He explicitly distinguishes between 'race' as a biological fact and 'nationality' as a cultural phenomenon, but in his discussion of the problems surrounding immigration he tends to conflate the two. His approach is to draw a clear dividing line between 'old' and 'new' migration and in doing so he distinguishes between European racial groups. Simply put: yes to Swedes and Brits, no to Italians and Poles, who were regarded as inferior peoples.

It's interesting to note what Fairchild has to say about assimilation. Races can be mixed, although that isn't something he advocates, but nationalities cannot be forged into something new. The notion of the melting pot is a fallacy. Nationalities have an inherent cohesion. 'There is no such thing as a composite language, a blended religion, or a mixed moral code.'[41] Fairchild gives an example: either you should hit your wife or you should never hit her. We cannot say that on Mondays, Wednesdays and Fridays you are permitted to do so and on other days you should keep your hands to yourself. Give and take is not the solution. What does it mean, anyhow? 'While we were going to meet Italy half way in some particular we would be moving further away from Denmark, and when we were trying to accommodate ourselves to Hungary we would be destroying our unison with England.'[42] People from Northwestern Europe were racially the closest to existing Americans and therefore a brake should be put on the arrival of migrants from other parts of the old continent, Fairchild insisted.

As early as the final decade of the nineteenth century, opposition to the 'new' immigration began to grow. There were appeals for stricter conditions to be placed on naturalization, and with the founding of the American Protective Association in 1887 and the Immigration Restriction League in 1894 these took the form of calls for the introduction of a literacy test. Every immigrant aged 14 or over would have to be able to read and write. This proposal was blocked three times by presidential veto and finally introduced during the First World War, 25 years after it was first submitted. Even then, in 1917, the president of the time, Woodrow Wilson, made one final attempt to prevent the resolution becoming law.

It turned out to be extraordinarily difficult to change the immigration laws. How can we explain this? Higham concludes that interests and principles became intertwined: 'Immigration was one of the cornerstones of the whole social structure, and a cosmopolitan ideal of nationality was woven deeply into America's Christian and democratic heritage. The stone could not be dislodged or the ideal renounced with ease.'[43] This social structure was defended most consistently by employers, who had a vested interest in a high level of immigration, since it kept wages low and guaranteed a flexible workforce. Workers of different nationalities could easily be played off against one another.

The trade union movement defended a different set of interests, although with a fair amount of hesitancy. Organizations such as the American Federation of Labour had many migrants among their members and felt bound by principles of social justice, so the unions were initially rather unresponsive to pleas for limits to be set, but their attitudes gradually changed and they started to support the campaign against further immigration. By excluding foreign labour, they were hoping to achieve greater economic security for their members.

As we have seen, the First World War was a turning point. It became possible to introduce measures that had previously met with resistance and laws were passed with the aim of limiting immigration drastically. The wartime mood is illustrated by the re-establishment of the Ku Klux Klan in 1915, an organization originally formed to oppose the emancipation of the black population in the South during the years of reconstruction after the Civil War. In those days the Klan had preached white supremacy as opposed to national unity, which it regarded as the oppression of the American South by the North. Now the Klan had become a distinctly nationalist movement that put itself forward as the defender of Anglo-Saxon tradition and therefore admitted only native-born Protestants as members. In 1923 Klan membership reached its peak at little short of three million, after which an equally rapid decline set in as a result of infighting.

In these years laws were introduced that placed strict limits on the influx of migrants from Europe. Asia had been targeted long before. With the Chinese Exclusion Act of 1882 almost all immigration from China was banned and the route to naturalization blocked. Not until 1943 were Chinese people once again permitted to become US citizens. The campaign against Japanese immigration had also begun at an early stage, especially in the case of the so-called 'picture brides', women brought to America by Japanese migrants solely on the basis of photographs. Once again the history of immigration in America suggests remarkable parallels – European countries are struggling to deal with comparable forms of arranged marriage today.

The laws introduced in 1924 to control the migration of Europeans to America took the form of a strict quota system. Ethnic groups in America, as measured by the 1920 census, were to be allowed to increase by no more than 2 per cent a year as a result of immigration. The bulk of available places went, as intended, to the British, Irish and Germans, while the Poles and Italians were given a raw deal. This meant that after the mass immigration of 1880–1920, America was more or less closed to outsiders for a long period. The level of immigration fell drastically in the years 1924–65. The figures speak for themselves. Whereas in the period 1901–10 a little under nine million migrants were admitted, that number fell to just over half a million in 1931–40. The economic crisis had a severe impact, of course, but restrictive immigration laws were undoubtedly responsible for part of the drop in the figures, and most of the new legislation remained unchanged until 1965.

All kinds of questions might justifiably be raised about the climate in America in those years after the First World War, but too many assessments of the 1924 Act neglect the fact that America's controls on immigration helped to create a new equilibrium. Dinnerstein and Reimers, who are critical of opposition to immigration, cannot avoid this conclusion: 'As a result of the immigration laws of the 1920s, the nation had achieved a general balance of ethnic groups.'[44] Historian Philip Gleason too, after criticizing the racist undertone of the new laws, concludes that 'once restriction had been accomplished, Americans could afford to relax about national unity'.[45]

The new law also brought about a considerable change to the relationship between generations within ethnic groups. In 1910 around 15 per cent of the population was foreign-born; in 1970 a mere 5 per cent.[46] After several decades of strict limits to immigration, first-generation migrants were no longer a significant factor in American life. Then the country returned to a more liberal policy and by 1996 the proportion of the population born elsewhere had reached 10 per cent once again. High levels of immigration mean that experiences in the country of origin remain hugely significant, tending to complicate integration, whereas tighter restrictions reduce the influence of new migrants, with the result that ethnic groups are more quickly absorbed into the society around them.

The third wave of opposition to immigration – after those of the mid-nineteenth century and the turn of the twentieth – lies only just behind us. In the mid-1990s, America, like Canada and Australia, experienced fierce arguments between advocates and opponents of immigration. Alongside doubts about the economic contribution made by new migrants, the main stimulus to debate was a commonly held belief that illegal immigration was out of control. In 1996 the number of illegal immigrants in America was estimated at 5 million, with annual growth of 275,000. In other words, the illegal population of the United States was predicted to reach about 8 million within 10 years. In fact the rate of increase was twice that and by 2009 there were around 12–13 million illegal residents in America.

Reimers has reconstructed this latest debate about immigration and he concludes that much of the legislation of the 1980s and 1990s can be seen as 'catering to a variety of interests, business, ethnic, national, religious and legal'.[47] The degree to which established groupings have formed alliances of convenience with the aim of maintaining the level of immigration is indeed remarkable. One telling example was the joint attempt by a particularly liberal senator, Ted Kennedy, and a distinctly conservative one, Orin Hatch, to remove from the 1986 law all sanctions against employers who hired illegal migrants.[48] Similarly, a motley array of people now oppose the introduction of national identity cards that would make it possible to put in place more effective controls on illegal residence.

In the early 1990s, a widespread campaign against immigration, especially of the illegal kind, emerged in California. More than 40 per cent of America's immigrants live in California or Texas, so it's no surprise to find that opposition is concentrated in those two states. A citizens' movement succeeded in having Proposition 187 adopted in a referendum, winning 59 per cent of votes cast. This piece of legislation would have disqualified illegals and their children from public services including education. It was later declared invalid by the Supreme Court, but it did lead Congress to introduce stricter immigration laws in 1996, which among other things prevent migrants from applying for a wide range of public provisions in their first five years of legal residence.

The conflict surrounding these most recent changes to the law is instructive. The original intention was to reduce legal immigration to the level of the 1980s, at around 300,000 new immigrants a year. An intriguing coalition emerged to create the lobby that stood in the way. It was only to be expected that it would include ethnic groups, especially Latin Americans, but opposition from the Catholic Church and fundamentalist Christian organizations, which put themselves forward as defenders of family migration, was rather less predictable. Not without reason, they regarded migrants as exemplars of traditional family values. Representatives of the business sector also fought against limits on immigration; as ever, they did not want the stream of cheap labour to dry up. In short the issue of immigration makes for strange bedfellows. This explains why the latest struggle to restrict immigration failed at the final hurdle.

In America a deep divide has opened up between public opinion and official policy. Not a single opinion poll since 1945 has shown a majority in favour of the relaxation of immigration laws. In fact, since the early 1980s there has almost always been majority support for a reduction in the number of immigrants. A survey carried out in 1990 – when new legislation was introduced that had the effect of raising the number of migrants admitted to the country by a third – showed that only a very small proportion of those questioned were in favour of more immigration, whereas almost half wanted precisely the reverse.[49]

This gap between political negotiations over immigration legislation and trends in the public mood is striking and it continues to cause periodic outbursts of discontent. The 'golden door' to America is still open, having been left only slightly ajar for many years, but once again differences of opinion about the desirable level of immigration have come to the fore. Resistance to the current rapid increase in the number of illegals is so powerful that their status cannot easily be regularized. In the ultimate country of immigrants, immigration does not go unchallenged.

The Lingering Shadow of Slavery

To think of America as a 'nation of immigrants' is to gloss over another essential aspect of the country's history. Slavery, which grew enormously in the first half of the nineteenth century, does not fit with the country's self-image. However much born out of need, immigration is ultimately a free choice. The forced shipment of millions of Africans cannot be compared to it in any way, and, unlike slavery in European history, the trade did not happen in a distant colony but in full view of all Americans. It had a far more direct impact on society as a whole and in some ways this remains true right up to the present day.

Slavery is of all times and all places. The ownership of human beings was common in ancient Greece, in African societies and in the Muslim world. The reproach that slavery flows from a racist view of the world is therefore historically incorrect. In Africa it was the usual custom for tribes defeated in war to be led away as slaves. In Islamic countries the trade was widespread and slavery was abolished there only relatively recently. It is rarely mentioned that the year in which America freed its slaves, 1863, coincides almost exactly with the year in which Russia freed its serfs: 1861.

The unique feature of slavery in America is the wrenching conflict to which it led, and this has everything to do with a profound contradiction between the trade in human beings and the principles on which the new republic was explicitly founded. It has often been pointed out that the authors of the Declaration of Independence of 1776, with their 'all men are created equal', established a principle they intended to live up to only in part. One of those founding fathers, Thomas Jefferson, was a slave-owner, as was the first US president, George Washington. The interests of the southern states – where the majority of slaves were held – were diametrically opposed to the principle laid down in the Declaration of Independence.

Slavery was crucial to the founding and shaping of the United States – so much so that a history of the black population is in many respects a history of America. The past few years have seen an increasing emphasis on the significance of slavery. Historian Ira Berlin, for example, writes of 'the extent to which slavery was woven into the fabric of American life'. From the earliest days of the colonies, 'slavery shaped the American economy, its politics, its culture, and its most deeply held beliefs'.[50]

The arrival of 20 Africans in Jamestown in 1619 is generally seen as the beginning of the Atlantic slave trade. In the first half of the seventeenth century, slavery coincided with the rise of the plantations, where the main crops were initially tobacco and sugar. In the nineteenth century cotton predominated. Most worked on the plantations, but there were slaves in the cities too. They did domestic chores and generally enjoyed better living conditions.

In a major history of black America, John Hope Franklin writes that each colony dealt with slavery in its own way, as demonstrated by the contrasting examples of Georgia and Pennsylvania. Whereas in Georgia slavery boomed and soon involved the majority of the population, in Pennsylvania there was opposition to the practice from the start. Within a few years Pennsylvania had made the import of slaves subject to taxation and in 1750 the trade virtually stopped. This was a result not just of humanitarian concerns but of a fear that the presence of too many slaves would disturb social relations. In Virginia, the colony with the highest number of slaves, this same concern soon led to stringent legislation designed to limit the slaves' freedom of movement severely. Franklin comments that there was a conflict in people's minds between the economic value of the black population and the threat to social stability it posed. The profit motive usually won out, but this did not reduce the fear of a slave uprising.

In 1741 panic in New York sparked an explosion of violence against the city's black inhabitants. After a break-in at a merchant's home and a series of arson attacks, anger among whites soon became targeted at the slaves, of whom more than 100 were found guilty at an improvised trial: 18 were hanged and 13 burned alive. A number of poor whites were also convicted for what had seemed like an attempted uprising. There were several such eruptions of panic and violence, indicating the great unease that accompanied slavery.

It was the struggle for independence from Britain that truly laid bare the inner contradictions of slavery. How could the image of colonists oppressed by their mother country be reconciled with the thraldom of hundreds of thousands of people in America itself who had absolutely no rights? A passage laying all the blame for slavery at the door of the King of England, which Jefferson tried to have adopted as part of the Declaration of Independence, was a distortion of history. It foundered because representatives from the South refused to accept its inclusion.

The drafting of the Declaration of Independence is a fascinating story in its own right. How could the general principles of equality and freedom be reconciled with slavery? One of the ways in which Jefferson evaded the issue was by refusing to include the word 'property' in the definition of inalienable rights, replacing it with the much broader 'pursuit of happiness'. A right to property would have been understood as a defence of slavery. Slaves were, after all, considered to be possessions. Nor is there any reference to slavery in the constitution. The compromise with the slave-owners was a practical one and not formally recognized.

Slavery therefore continued after independence. In his *Democracy in America*, Alexis de Tocqueville devoted the longest chapter by far to the lamentable fate of the Indians and the Negroes. He opposed the institution of slavery, both in his own country and elsewhere, in the name of human freedom. 'Plunged into this abyss of troubles, the Negro barely feels his misfortune. Violence has made a slave of him, the habit of servitude has made his thoughts and ambitions those of a slave.'[51]

Whereas the British abolished slavery in 1833, America did not follow suit until 1863. Franklin writes that 'ironically enough, America's freedom was the means of giving slavery itself a longer life than it was to have in the British empire'.[52] This line of reasoning has been pursued by lawyers Alfred and Ruth Blumrosen, who argue that the American rebellion against British rule was motivated in part by a fear in the southern states that the British might intervene to end slave ownership. Anxiety on this point increased markedly after the verdict of a London judge in 1772 that upheld the claims of the slave James Somerset, who had escaped during a journey to England. In passing judgment Lord Mansfield called slavery 'so odious' that it could not possibly be justified on either moral or political grounds. His statement was soon relayed to the American colonies, where slave-owners feared for their property since in theory their slaves could walk away on the basis of this finding by a British court.

The interests of the northern and southern states may have coincided when it came to independence, but that did not defuse the explosive charge attached to slavery. With great difficulty, a compromise was reached as to how the population of the South should be counted for the purpose of determining the number of delegates each state was entitled to send to the House of Representatives. Counting slaves as part of the population was seen by the northern states as a recognition of and encouragement to the slave trade. In the end the two sides agreed that each slave should be regarded as equivalent to three-fifths of a non-slave. It would be hard to find a more cynical expression of the moral and political confusion surrounding slavery. The numbers involved were large. Despite high mortality among slaves, in states including Georgia, South Carolina and Virginia they represented between 40 and 50 per cent of the population in 1800.

The compromise reached over slavery ran counter to the basic principles of the young republic. With the ideal of equality enshrined in the Declaration of Independence, the seeds had been sown for the Civil War that would divide the nation so deeply almost a century later. Jefferson's agonizing – later in life he became an increasingly vehement opponent of slavery – demonstrates that from the start Americans were divided on the issue. It was a matter of time. The conflict would have to be resolved one way or another. As well as dividing the races, slavery pitted white against white, ultimately to the extent of civil war.

The black-and-white image of slavery is incorrect in another, perhaps more surprising sense. Berlin points to the existence of black slaveowners: 'In slave societies, nearly everyone – free and slave – aspired to enter the slaveholding class, and upon occasion some former slaves rose into the slaveholders' ranks.'[53] This was far from common, but nevertheless slavery could also pit black against black. The history of black slave-owners has received little attention, for understandable reasons, but the publication of The Known World by black author Edward P. Jones broke the silence. He tells the story of the rise and fall of Henry

Townsend, a black slave-owner: 'We owned slaves. It was what was done, and so that is what we did.'[54]

The Civil War put an end to slavery. The emancipation of all slaves was declared in 1863. The effects of this proclamation on soldiers in the northern army were problematic. Curti comments: 'Although the Proclamation inspired patriotism in the abolitionists, it dampened the enthusiasm for the war in countless soldiers and civilians. Many humble folk who earned their livelihood by manual labour feared that the freedmen would become economic competitors.'[55] In New York that year there were riots against conscription, lasting several days. The black population bore the brunt; many were lynched.

The North's rather half-hearted attitude to the black population is further illustrated by Abraham Lincoln's initial refusal to accept freed Negroes into the federal army. Throughout the war he continued to believe in the eventual return of the black population to Africa. In August 1862 he said to a delegation of black Americans: 'Your race suffer greatly, many of them, by living among us, while ours suffer from your presence. . . . In a word we suffer on each side. If this is admitted, it affords a reason why we should be separated.'[56]

The Civil War left deep wounds that were slow to heal. The emancipation of the slaves certainly did not mean that black people would henceforth be treated as equals. During reconstruction, especially in the southern states, legislation was introduced that severely limited the rights of the black population and established segregation along racial lines in every conceivable field. Far from putting an end to prejudice, freedom tended to widen the racial divide. Even where blacks were initially given a chance to vote, a combination of legislation and terrorization quickly made it impossible for them to do so. The blatant contradiction between the founding principles of the republic and the exclusion of a tenth of the population was not resolved. 'The great test of America's democratic tradition is the acceptance of the Negro with other minority groups into the mainstream of American life,' John Hope Franklin wrote.[57]

At the turn of the twentieth century Booker T. Washington was a leading figure in the black community. His was a gradualist strategy, taking one careful step at a time to avoid provoking whites in the South in any way. He did not appeal for the granting of civil rights. It was far too soon for that. First the black population must be systematically trained to become useful artisans and industrial workers. Washington succeeded in setting up a series of educational institutions and through a network of white philanthropists he became extremely influential. In his autobiography he writes: 'I think, though, that the opportunity to freely exercise such political rights will not come in any large degree through outside or artificial forcing, but will be accorded to the Negro by the Southern white people themselves.'[58]

His strategy was increasingly controversial, since it did nothing to improve the situation in the South, especially after a verdict by the Supreme Court in 1894 that presented a legal justification of segregation using the now notorious formulation 'separate but equal'. Washington's critics claimed that the route of extreme caution – the condescending charity of his financiers being painfully obvious – amounted in practice to the acceptance of the notion that the black population was inferior and that racial segregation was not in itself a problem. They believed that giving up the struggle for political power, for genuine civil rights and for higher education would mean relinquishing their self-respect.

There was a wish to be absorbed into mainstream society and at the same time an awareness that this was not really possible. Rarely has the desire to become part of America been described with so much compassion and suppressed rage as in *The Souls of Black Folks* by W. E. B. Du Bois (1903). He begins by posing a question: 'How does it feel to be a problem?'[59] He then goes on to describe how two worlds, divided by colour, have grown apart: 'Despite much physical contact and daily intermingling, there is almost no community of intellectual life or point of transference where the thoughts and feelings of one race can come into direct contact and sympathy with the thoughts and feelings of the other.'[60]

Their exclusion, and the contempt with which blacks were treated, created a split personality. This could certainly be overcome, but not by giving up one half or the other. Du Bois attempts to explain the Negro's position: 'He would not Africanize America, for America has too much to teach the world and Africa. He would not bleach his Negro soul in a flood of white Americanism, for he knows that Negro blood has a message for the world. He simply wishes to make it possible for a man to be both a Negro and an American, without being cursed and spit upon by his fellows.'[61] Du Bois wanted more than simply vocational training for the black population; he aimed to foster a black elite which he called the Talented Tenth.

His essay reads as a lengthy plea for even-handed reconciliation: 'I should be the last one to deny the patent weaknesses and shortcomings of the Negro people; I should be the last to withhold sympathy from the white South in its efforts to solve its intricate social problems.'[62] Anyone who calls to mind the realities of the South with its lynchings and its segregated restaurants, buses and toilets will appreciate the almost implausible generosity of these words.

Yet 30 years later the writer had become an advocate of segregation. What happened? In the life story of Du Bois, who was one of the founders of the National Association for the Advancement of Colored People (NAACP), which had both black and white members, we see all the contradictions of failed integration. He died at the age of 94, on the eve of the march on Washington in the summer of 1963, when Martin Luther King gave his most famous speech. Years earlier Du Bois had given up his US citizenship and emigrated to Ghana.

Why, despite all his early anger about segregation, did he 'return' to Africa? Having long since lost faith in equitable integration, he came to the conclusion that black segregation was the only answer. The diagnosis arrived at by the later Du Bois is bitter. The ideal of integration had come to nothing; even Franklin Roosevelt's New Deal ignored the needs of black people. His Talented Tenth was threatening to drift away from the mass of the black population. Nothing remained to black people but to make a virtue of necessity and build up a separate economic, political and cultural life of their own. They should no longer rely on the benevolence of white liberals, no longer wait for acts of charity. They must take their fate into their own hands.

The words of the later Du Bois, full of rage and frustration, say it all: it's a myth that in the North there's no racial segregation, at best it differs from the South only in degree. The higher a Negro wants to climb, the more pitiless his exclusion on grounds of colour. Segregation is an evil, but at the same time there is no escaping it. 'Without it, the American Negro will suffer evils greater than any possible evil of separation: we would suffer the loss of self-respect, the lack of faith in ourselves, the lack of knowledge about ourselves, the lack of ability to make a decent living by our own efforts and not by philanthropy.'[63] His followers were shocked.

The background to this loss of faith provides sufficient explanation. The exclusion and humiliation of the black population are part of a history that can never be undone. We cannot ignore that legacy, since its consequences are obvious for all to see, even in our own day. How can people interact open-mindedly with such a past to look back on? Nevertheless, fostering racial differences is a dead-end route, since it only increases the divide and makes mutual trust impossible. There can be no productive interaction in a society that sees everything in terms of colour. The conflict between the ideas of the young and old Du Bois has never been resolved. It was to return in the clash between King's pursuit of integration and the separatism of Malcolm X.

We have all seen dramatic images of the civil rights movement, which eventually led to the Civil Rights Act of 1964. Announcing the passage of the legislation, President Johnson said of the black American: 'He has called upon us to make good the promise of America. And who among us can say we would have made the same progress were it not for his persistent bravery, and his faith in American democracy.'[64] The most important judicial step had been taken in 1954 with a Supreme Court decision that went against segregated education. At long last the 'separate but equal' doctrine introduced by the Court in 1894 had been renounced, as a result of the simple but penetrating insight that segregation always brings inequality with it. The images are indelibly printed on the memory of an entire generation: the university student James Meredith, who had to be escorted to and from classes by federal marshals, and the governor of Alabama, George Wallace, who personally stood in the way to prevent black students from registering at the university.

That 1954 court decision was only the first step towards genuine integration, since segregation continued in everyday life much as before, even in many schools and colleges in the North. The problem of ghettos is still a pressing one all these years after the granting of civil rights. This is a story of broken promises, of laws that were never observed, of exclusion justified by religion and a great deal more besides. It's easy to conclude from these developments that democratic principles are of little consequence.

Yet other things may strike us too: an ideal of citizenship will always make prevailing exclusion problematic; general principles of equality have their own eloquence and demand to be realized. These are the central themes of Gunnar Myrdal's book *An American Dilemma* (1944). The issue of race is in essence a moral one, he writes. 'The Negroes are a minority, and they are poor and suppressed, but they have the advantage that they can fight wholeheartedly. The whites have all the power, but they are split in their moral personality. Their better selves are with the insurgents. The Negroes do not need any other allies.'[65] In other words, the qualms of the majority will suffice.

A subtle paternalism lurks within this attitude, of course. The problem of the blacks was ultimately the problem of the whites, and the experiences and potentials of black people were passed over by Myrdal as by so many before him. The inner conflict had to be resolved by whites and the responsibility for improving the lot of the black population therefore lay largely with them. In the years of the civil rights movement, when black activists and white liberals walked hand in hand, that dilemma seemed to have been resolved. But the ideal of shared citizenship would soon be unmasked as hypocrisy.

Affirmative Action

Du Bois's change of heart turned out to be the harbinger of a far broader shift in attitudes. At the point when important civil rights finally became a reality, many in the black community lost any hope of integrating, or even the desire to do so. In their wake, some migrant communities too began laying the emphasis on their own identities. From the 1960s onwards the old adage that America was a 'nation of immigrants' was often interpreted as an acknowledgment of unbridgeable cultural differences. In many ways what had begun as a time of hope and reform in the name of a shared ideal of civil rights changed course to become a celebration of ethnic identity.

Philip Gleason describes how the mood has shifted again and again. Periods in which universalist interpretations of American identity predominated were times of self-confidence, whereas periods of particularism, whether construed as religious, racial or ethnic, point to a lack of faith. The 1960s and '70s were indeed marked by a crisis of confidence, low points being the Vietnam War, the Watergate scandal and race riots in many major cities. The democratic ideal of America was dismissed as insincere and many responded by withdrawing into subcultures.[66]

The revival of ethnic thinking should be seen against this background. Important examples are the revision of school textbooks and the introduction of positive discrimination in the jobs market, known as affirmative action. In education a form of multiculturalism was advocated that went far beyond drawing attention to forgotten aspects of American history. The introduction of the Ethnic Heritage Studies Program Act in 1974 sparked a divisive debate that in many ways is still going on. In the battle over the curriculum some starkly contrasting visions emerged as to what might suffice to hold the 'nation of immigrants' together in our own day.

The more radical champions of multiculturalism in the black community aimed to replace a Eurocentric curriculum – described by Molefi Kete Asante as 'killing our children, killing their minds' – with an Afrocentric one. Black children were said to have been estranged from their origins, underperforming in school as a result. There was talk of a lack of 'self-esteem and self-respect' that could be resolved only by an education that recovered the alleged continuity in their past. As Asante puts it: 'There exists an emotional, cultural, psychological connection . . . that spans the ocean.'[67] African Americans were urged at the very least to think back to the place from which they once came.

Earlier generations had rejected such Afrocentrism out of hand. In the nineteenth century black leader and former slave Frederick Douglass commented: 'No one idea has given rise to more oppression and persecution toward the colored people of this country than that which makes Africa, not America, their home. It is that wolfish idea that elbows us off the side walk, and denies us the rights of citizenship.'[68] There is indeed a tragic side to the Afrocentric plea to black Americans to cut themselves off from their surroundings: get back to where you came from, you don't belong here. James Baldwin too turned against this way of thinking: 'The Negro has been formed by this nation, for better or worse, and does not belong to any other – not to Africa, and certainly not to Islam. . . . To accept one's past – one's history – is not the same thing as drowning in it; it is learning how to use it.'[69]

This is not at all to say that the reinterpretation of American history serves no purpose. We need only recall the words of Arthur Schlesinger: 'Let our children try to imagine the arrival of Columbus from the viewpoint of those who met him as well as those who sent him.'[70] But a critical investigation is a quite different matter from an education that aims to bolster ethnic self-esteem. The rewriting of American history has huge consequences and it leads to a belief that every shared history is a distortion. After all, it's impossible to tell a story that will satisfy both 'victims' and 'perpetrators'. Schlesinger expressed his concern and apparently he was not alone, since in 2000 Congress unanimously passed a resolution to increase investment in the teaching of American history.

The pursuit of bilingual education, for Hispanics in particular, is an extension of attempts to make the teaching of history a tool for consolidating ethnic groups. Education in the child's mother tongue took off in the 1980s and '90s, but as in many European countries it is now in retreat. There have even been calls for a constitutional amendment that would make English the country's only official language. In seven states such a rule has been introduced on the basis of referendum results. Of all the referendums held on the subject of strengthening the position of English and opposing bilingual education, only one has been lost – an indication that the mood has changed, especially in states with a large number of Spanish-speaking immigrants.

These and other initiatives are manifestations of an underlying conflict about the nature of American society and especially the concept of assimilation. Will the United States remain faithful to its basic mission of forging a new people with a wide variety of ethnic backgrounds, or is it on its way to becoming a patchwork of closed-off ethnic communities, as Horace Kallen envisaged? Will the individual route to citizenship continue to be given priority or will group rights gain the upper hand? Within the civil rights movement lies a seemingly irresolvable tension between these two approaches.

Affirmative action attempts to provide an answer. It is based on a belief that formal equality is insufficient to overcome a historical legacy of inequality. All those centuries of slavery and racial segregation cannot be consigned to the past unless the victims are given preferential treatment in the here and now. This applies to access to education, jobs in the public and private sectors, and the awarding of government contracts. As President Johnson said in 1965: 'You do not take a person who, for years, has been hobbled by chains and liberate him, bring him up to the starting line of a race and then say, "You are free to compete with all the others", and still justly believe that you have been completely fair.'[71]

Originally advocated as a temporary and targeted measure to help African Americans, this approach has grown since the 1970s to become a system of positive discrimination for all minority groups, and it has acquired a permanent character. Since the 1990s, if not before, a great debate on the subject has raged in America, and it's far from over. This is a dispute from which Europe has much to learn, since here too similar ideas and measures have been introduced, if in a less rigorous manner.

What are the grounds for affirmative action? Is it indeed a possible answer to patterns of exclusion that are still in place? Classic racism may be losing some of its power, the argument goes, but racism still exists in hidden forms. A well-known researcher in the field, Thomas Pettigrew, writes: 'Racism is typically far more subtle, indirect, and ostensibly non-racial now than it was in 1964, during the full swing of the Civil Rights Movement. Consequently, detection and remedy have become much more difficult.'[72] Racism is now the outcome of anonymous processes of selection and exclusion – sometimes called 'institutional racism' – rather than individual preferences or aversions. It's not the intentions of the employer that matter; we need instead to look at outcomes. The assumption here is that all groups are equal and cannot be distinguished in terms of talent. All ethnic groups should therefore be represented in all walks of life according to their share of the population, once all hindrances have been removed. The under-representation of minorities in specific occupations or specific educational institutions is therefore attributable to discrimination.

This prompts the question: is it in fact true that cultural differences have no effect on schools and the jobs market? The history of Asian immigrants demonstrates that although discrimination can lead to low performance in education and in economic life, it is not the whole story. Asians have faced exclusion in American history, yet they have on the whole been relatively successful. Moreover, the existence of a black middle class proves that African Americans are not condemned to live in the underclass. Escape is possible.

No one would want to deny that the history of segregation has left deep scars, but in parts of the black community in America, Thomas Sowell says, cultural patterns have emerged that make social advancement difficult. The large number of one-parent families, for example, is not simply the result of a history of discrimination. It's a phenomenon that was far less pronounced half a century ago, in a time when discrimination was taken for granted in large parts of society. In 1960 three-quarters of black families had two parents; the figure is now only

40 per cent. The fact that so many people have become trapped in the lifestyle of the underclass is more than simply an expression of poverty or exclusion.

Meanwhile, special measures in education and employment are now being demanded by innumerable ethnic groups that have no connection with the history of slavery and segregation. This has eroded the justification for such approaches, and the proponents of affirmative action all too often forget that there are people who pay the price. No small number of white and Asian Americans have seen their access to the better universities blocked despite good academic results. Wherever one is helped, another is disadvantaged. In the 1990s and since, this has created considerable resentment, helping to fuel opposition to immigration. As the result of a flurry of court decisions, affirmative action is now on the wane.

The battle surrounding the Eurocentric curriculum and positive discrimination demonstrates that considerable uncertainty has arisen in America over the past few decades as to what it means to be a 'nation of immigrants'. Many of its critics feel that the idea of assimilation was brought into disrepute as soon as large-scale immigration resumed in the mid-1960s.[73] Decolonization brought a new wave of immigrants, but that same decolonization aroused considerable doubts about the value of Western culture. The same happened in Europe; mass immigration from all over the world was accompanied by a wholly new perspective on integration.

Samuel Huntington, in his book Who Are We?, gives a clear impression of the disquiet this cultural reversal is causing. He describes the triumph over racial and ethnic interpretations of the nation's identity, and the creation of a multiethnic and multiracial society in which people are judged on their merits, as America's greatest achievement. There is a danger that this accomplishment will be lost, Huntington contends, especially given the mass immigration of Spanish-speakers, who will soon form the largest minority group in America. He sees this type of immigration as unusual on several grounds. The enormous difference in prosperity between the two sides makes the shared border between the United States and Mexico unique in the world and this has led to unprecedented levels of illegal immigration. Never before has one group of newcomers been as dominant as the Mexicans are now, making up a quarter of all immigrants in the 1990s. (As we have seen, this is not entirely true. The Germans, for example, once made up an even larger proportion of the total immigrant population.) Then there is the regional concentration of these new migrants, which Huntington claims is equally unprecedented.

He concludes that all these factors have changed the dynamics of integration considerably. His assertions have attracted a good deal of criticism, but the impression that Mexican immigrants and their descendants are not rising up the social scale at the rate that might have been expected is confirmed in a comparative study of the second generation of Mexican-Americans by Alejandro Portes and Rubén Rumbaut. They identify 'low aspirations and cumulative disadvantages' and conclude that performance in school remains poor. They see a 'downward assimilation' taking place in this group, meaning an adjustment to the most deprived social milieus. But they place the blame for these outcomes in part on a history of contempt for Mexican immigrants: 'The results are not hard to discern in the spectacle of the impoverished barrios of Los Angeles, San Diego, Houston, and other large southwestern cities.'[74]

Demographic predictions suggest that Hispanics will make up around a quarter of the American population by 2050. Spanish has become America's de facto second language. From 2001 onwards President Bush held his weekly radio address in Spanish as well as English: 'Mi Casa Blanca es su Casa Blanca.' Not long ago Mexican demonstrators in Chicago made clear that they are well aware of this: 'Today we march, tomorrow we vote.' Such is the history of America, says Zolberg. Mass immigration provokes resistance among the established population and this hostility in turn prompts migrants to mobilize. In short, conflict of this kind is not about the repudiation of shared citizenship, it's part of the history of integration and participation. The number of Mexicans taking US citizenship has increased hugely, as has their participation in elections. In that sense Huntington's pessimism about their unwillingness to become part of American society is premature, in fact his critics are right to point out that 'contrary to popular opinion Mexican-Americans acquire English in ways similar to previous immigrants and, according to at least one important measure of assimilation – conversion to evangelical Protestantism – are likely ahead of all other immigrant groups except Koreans'.[75]

There are historical parallels, and they include the recurrent uncertainty about the future of America as a 'nation of immigrants', which is palpable in our own time. The emphasis currently lies on the millions of illegal aliens among them, who, incidentally, are simply included in the figures used to determine the number of members from each state in the House of Representatives. Today's increasing sense of uncertainty also has to do with the continuing high rate of influx of legal migrants since 1965, unprecedented in American history, which as we have seen has always alternated between a raising and lowering of barriers. This consistently high level of immigration changes the relationship between the generations and with it the character of ethnic groups.

In Europe we are witnessing a comparable trend. The uncertainty with which the Old World has reacted to the arrival of migrants from all regions of the globe is not so very different from the insecurity that is a feature of the long history of immigration to the New World, with all the conflict it has entailed. It's actually quite surprising that the two continents, so closely linked by a shared history of immigration, exchange ideas on the subject relatively rarely. There are so many shared principles and experiences, so many shared interests and family histories, that it seems logical to make comparisons.

The challenge of controlling the US–Mexican border, for example, has a great deal in common in many respects with problems surrounding illegal immigration from the Mediterranean region. In both cases a contest is under way between migrants and border guards, one that's claiming an increasing number of victims and causing growing unease among local populations. The generally fruitless attempts by America to handle both legal and illegal migration more effectively – a failure attributable mainly to a lack of political will – contain plenty of lessons for European countries. The fiasco surrounding two important reforms is particularly instructive. The Immigrant Reform and Control Act of 1986, which was intended to combat illegal residence by dealing more harshly with employers while regularizing the status of around three million illegals, achieved only the latter. A revision of the Act ten years later, which among other things excluded migrants from certain forms of social welfare, produced few results. The Act was soon pared back drastically under pressure from interest groups.

Recurrent conflicts over migration have ultimately made the idea of America more inclusive. Each of the periods in which opposition to immigrants was uppermost had a different focus. With the Irish it was a question of whether Catholics belonged in America, with the Italians and Poles it was all about ethnic differences, and with the Mexicans it's to a large degree a matter of holding on to English as the official language in the face of pressure to recognize Spanish. America is overcoming more and more of its original religious and racial limitations on the concept of citizenship, but it's unlikely to go so far as to embrace official bilingualism.

The election of Barack Obama has brought America closer to its own principles and changed its image in the world. Of course it is troubling that 50 years after segregation was formally abolished the election of a black president is celebrated as a major breakthrough. A sense of relief can be heard in the enthusiasm of many white Americans and Europeans: at last a line can be drawn under a shameful history; never again the 'white man's burden'. But the past cannot be shaken off so easily. President Obama is not the final endpoint of the long history of emancipation, but a milestone within it.

Part of his attraction – especially for many white voters – is that

Obama is a relative outsider to the bitter history of black America. As the son of a Kenyan immigrant and a white woman from Kansas, he is far from the embodiment of slavery and the segregation that followed. His life story is that of an immigrant's child, and furthermore the product of a mixed marriage. In his autobiography he writes that he sometimes found himself talking dismissively about 'white folks' and at such moments 'I would suddenly remember my mother's smile, and the words that I spoke would seem awkward and false'.[76]

America is a compelling experiment as a 'nation of immigrants', for all the qualifications we need to set beside that rather rosy self-image. It's increasingly a country that embodies all of humanity, now that people from continents other than Europe have come to make up such a large share of its population. Zolberg is hopeful, ending his history with the words: 'Immigrants who feel welcome rarely set out to destroy their new home.'[77] Indeed, there are no examples in America of migrant communities that have caused endless social disruption. Clashes have been fierce nonetheless. Immigration doesn't just bring about more immigration, it provokes opposition among a large segment of the existing population.

In this sense it's important to rediscover America. Behind the slogan 'a nation of immigrants' lies a history of avoidance, conflict and accommodation. The slogan has obscured the fact that the welcome given to newcomers has never been unconditional. Along with openness, America has been through lengthy periods in which its doors were closed. A country of unprecedented diversity, it nevertheless has a long history of assimilation, the aim of which was to forge the many into one. The failed integration of a considerable proportion of the black population has divided America particularly deeply. Strictly speaking, slavery and racial segregation are not part of the history of immigration, but their legacy influences the way in which America deals with ethnic differences to this day. Migrants have ultimately created a great world power, which as a 'nation of immigrants' is held together by a potent sense of mission. These are the lessons of the history of America, and they are both instructive for Europeans and of great value to contemporary Americans.

8

The Divided House of Islam

Islam and Imperialism

There's no escaping it any longer. Every day, certainly since that bolt from the blue, we're confronted by violence in the name of religion, in the name of Islam. It shrinks our world, turning the global village of our dreams into a beleaguered city.[1] This makes it increasingly hard to look at Islam without thinking of fundamentalism and terror, increasingly hard not to see the Muslims within our borders as part of a worldwide community of faith that's in a deep state of crisis.

We're assured from many sides that Islam is 'a religion of peace' that preaches tolerance and respect. At the same time pictures roll across our screens of Muslims who say they're engaged in a 'holy war'. The fact is that all monotheistic religions have both peaceful and violent traditions. Their scriptures support the image of a loving God but no less the image of a vengeful God. In our time Islam is at the centre of a global conflict, but we should not forget that great diversity exists within the Muslim community, nor that Christianity too has a history of violence.

American political scientist Carl Brown criticizes both the way Islam is presented in the West and attitudes to the West in the Islamic world: 'The one constant element in Muslim–Western relations throughout the centuries is that of religious suspicion and politico-military confrontation.'[2] This is unique, since the West does not have such tense relations with any other faith. The religions of the East are simply too far away and they have not sought political confrontation. The clash between Christianity and Islam has everything to do with the geographical proximity of the Middle East. Moreover, both are monotheistic religions with a universal mission. There's a lot to be said for the idea that this age-old conflict arises as much out of what the two religions have in common as out of their differences.

Their confrontation has a long history, shaped in part by the crusades and the way they're kept alive in our minds. It says a great deal about the contemporary Arab self-image that those confrontations long ago – the crusades began in 1096 and ended with the expulsion of the Franks from the Holy Land in 1291 – still figure so large in the collective memory. This equating of the West with imperialism and colonialism, the self-image of Islam as the eternal victim, is a rather one-sided view of history, and a way of evading responsibility.

Muslim interventions in Europe, by contrast, culminating in the seizure of large parts of Spain and southern Italy (eighth century), the Battle of Tours-Poitiers (732), the sack of Rome (846), the fall of Constantinople (1453), the conquest of the Balkans (sixteenth century) and the sieges of Vienna (1529 and 1683), contribute hardly anything nowadays to the image of Islam in the Western world. Nevertheless, up until the early eighteenth century the fear in Europe was considerable. The relief that followed the Treaty of Karlowitz in 1699, which many historians regard as the start of a new era in political relations between the two sides, was correspondingly great.

Italian historian Franco Cardini describes the centuries of pressure from Islam as a 'violent midwife' to Europe.[3] The contrast gave rise to self-definitions and self-images. Initially, the battle against Muslim armies was not considered a religious conflict, but this changed in the mid-ninth century after the looting of St Peter's in Rome and the killing, for refusing to convert to Islam, of the 'Martyrs of Córdoba', 48 Christians in the Iberian peninsula, which by then was almost entirely under Muslim control.

That memory now has little significance, except in Spain, where during one debate a journalist with the quality newspaper *El País* remarked that it was perfectly clear what the Muslims were up to. This was still quite some time before the fateful 11 March 2004, when four trains were blown up in the Spanish capital and some 200 people killed. He believed we were witnessing an attempt to reverse the Reconquista of 1492, when Muslims were driven out. In Austria too the historical clash with the Muslim world still works its way through into public life. The siege of Vienna by the Ottoman armies was a turning point in the country's history.

These two nations aside, it's clear that the old conflict with Islam has little effect on the way Europe looks at current tensions. The balance of power has changed and the influence of religion is declining. Critical commentary on the crusades goes back a long way. Take the 1882 Dutch classic by C. Busken Huet, *Het land van Rembrand* [Rembrandt's country], in which the crusaders are ridiculed as culturally inferior: 'Familiar with no other forms of building than those of the ungainly or wretched abbeys of Bloemhof and Rozeveld, Moorish architecture fills them with a sense of wonder they would like to put into words. Yet they are still too much bushman of the North to be able to venerate that which they do not understand. Their Christianity and race hatred makes them see the work of the Devil in the artistic creations of the Mohammedans.'[4]

European countries and the Muslim world differ significantly in the way they deal with the past. The direct connection made by quite a few Muslims between the crusades and the modern-day imperialism of Europe and America obscures several essential historical episodes. Crucially, Islam coincides from the start with a history of colonization and imperial conquest. On the subject of Indonesia, for example, V. S. Naipaul remarks: 'Islam and Europe had arrived here almost at the same time as competing imperialisms.'[5] He describes how non-Arab peoples were colonized twice over, twice alienated from themselves. The cultural influence of Islam was profound: 'Converted peoples have to strip themselves of their past. It is the most uncompromising kind of imperialism.'[6]

Not that Western expansionism is cancelled out by that of Islam, but we should be aware of both. The notion of 'competing imperialisms' seems exactly right. Colonization by Islam was just as much a matter of cultural domination, slavery, violence and abuse of power. Slavery, for example, was provided for at length in Islamic law. The trade was not abolished in the Ottoman and Persian empires until the early twentieth century, in Egypt even later, in 1923, and in Iraq in 1924, while anti-slavery laws were introduced in Yemen and Saudi Arabia as recently as 1962. Even today we hear reports of slavery in African countries such as Sudan.

Muslim reformer Fatima Mernissi concludes bitterly that the Islamic struggle for equality was turned on its head: 'So we see that Muslims, beginning in the seventh century, could have started elaborating laws that would have realized the Prophet's dream of an egalitarian society. But it was not until the twentieth century that with much anguish – and under pressure from the "immoral infidels," otherwise known as the colonizers – they renounced slavery.'[7]

Islam as a victim of the imperialism of others, Islam as underdog. It's a rather cursory way to summarize centuries of expansionism. At the very least we should recognize that the Muslim world has always aspired to create states. History has left its mark. Islam and Christianity have contrasting views on the relationship between church and state. In the Christian tradition, which took shape politically only after a full three centuries of battle and persecution in the Roman Empire, we find a doctrine dealing with the relationship between spiritual and earthly powers: 'Render therefore unto Caesar the things which are Caesar's; and unto God the things that are God's' (Matthew 22:21). No matter how the relationship between holders of worldly and spiritual power changed – from open conflict to close cooperation, from subordination to domination – a church hierarchy existed throughout, with institutions of its own.

From the outset, Islam, by contrast, developed hand in hand with a rapidly expanding empire. The state was Islamic from its inception and therefore had little need of separate religious structures. Islam has no 'church' in the sense familiar to us. The less hierarchical way in which the *ulema* (religious scholars) are organized makes an institutional confrontation between church and state such as arose in Christian Europe virtually impossible. The history of the Islamic world is characterized by a separation of state and society rather than church and state. The main features of its political culture were subordination and resignation.

Pointing to the Islamic world's expansionism does nothing to justify the often barbarous methods by which the European powers tried across two centuries to gain a foothold in the Middle East, but it does give us the context. In his study of the crusades, Amin Maalouf describes the differences between the belligerents from an Arab perspective. He portrays their history with considerable sympathy for the Muslim point of view, yet he concedes that whereas in Europe the crusades heralded a long period of prosperity, the Arab world had entered a period of decline even before hostilities began. Maalouf speaks of 'long centuries of decadence and obscurantism'. He goes on: 'Assaulted from all quarters, the Muslim world turned in on itself. It became over-sensitive, defensive, intolerant, sterile – attitudes that grew steadily worse. . . . Henceforth progress was the embodiment of the "other". Modernism became alien.'[8]

The nostalgia of many Muslims for their Golden Age refers not just to a quest for religious purity and originality, but to a desire for imperial greatness. Abhorrence of the West is not a rejection of the imperial idea as such; rather it reflects a much lamented loss of power. There is a great feeling of hurt in the Muslim world, especially the Arab part of it. Understandably so, since the scars of the colonial era remain. Travelling through Algeria in the early nineteenth century, Tocqueville arrived at a harsh verdict: 'We have brought Muslim society to a far more miserable, more disordered, more ignorant and more barbaric state than it was in before they came to know us.'[9]

Yet the decline of the Islamic world began before it was subjected to colonial interference and continued after the colonial powers withdrew. There's therefore every reason for greater self-examination, and it should not be evaded by continually posing the question of guilt: 'Who has done this to us?' The answer is: ultimately, no one. Responsibility needs to be acknowledged by the Islamic world itself. Its decline was of its own making, a natural outcome of deliberate isolation from the economic and scientific innovations of Europe. The Renaissance, the Reformation, the technological revolution – they all passed most of the Muslim world by virtually unnoticed. The majority of Muslims persisted in seeing Christian Europeans as barbarians, from whom little or nothing could be learned. This introverted attitude on the part of the Muslim world has proven extremely disadvantageous.

That deliberate and profound isolation from Europe lasted for centuries. In his novel *My Name Is Red*, Turkish author Orhan Pamuk portrays the conflict at the Ottoman court that resulted from the introduction of Venetian painting techniques. The painters of miniatures refused to have anything to do with the technique of perspective: 'If the houses on a street were rendered according to man's false perception that they gradually diminish in size as they recede into the distance, wouldn't man then effectively be usurping Allah's place at the centre of the world?' The new way of looking sparked deep fears. It was surely downright heresy to 'draw, from the perspective of a mangy street dog, a horsefly and a mosque as if they were the same size – with the excuse that the mosque was in the background – thereby mocking the faithful who attend prayers'.[10]

Islam sees itself as the successor to, indeed as the ultimate, perfected version of Judaism and Christianity. This inherent superiority of Islam in the eyes of its mainstream followers goes some way to explain why their interest in the Western world developed only at a late stage. Reformers within Islam have tried to put a different slant on it. Nasr Hamid Abu Zayd, for example, describes Islam as 'a closing message and the last word from heaven to earth', meaning above all a recognition 'that humanity had left behind it the stage of immaturity, which required continual tutelage, and had grown up'.[11] Tunisian liberal Muslim thinker Mohamed Charfi says more or less the same thing: the ending of the time of prophesy actually opens up space for people to 'construct their futures in freedom, with individual responsibility and active solidarity'.[12]

So the belief that Islam marked the final chapter of the prophetic tradition can be explained by these scholars as an invitation to independent thought. Yet that call for intellectual freedom only goes to show that the closed attitude is currently dominant. This is all the more striking when we consider that the period in which the Islamic world flourished in the Middle Ages can be regarded as the only link between ancient scholarship and European modernity. Much of the knowledge from classical antiquity that was of such crucial importance during the Renaissance would have been lost without the great scientific and cultural achievements of the Muslim world, which was governed successively from Medina, Damascus, Baghdad, Cairo and Istanbul. The caliphate was not just a rapidly expanding political force; it represented a developing civilization, even in respect to its dealings with other religions.

The ever-critical Bernard Lewis is outspoken in his appraisal of the historical merits of Islam. He points to the lead taken by the liberal democracies in modern times: 'There is nothing in Islamic history to compare with the emancipation, acceptance, and integration of other-believers and non-believers in the West.' At the same time, however, he writes that 'there is nothing in Islamic history to compare with the Spanish expulsion of Jews and Muslims, the Inquisition, the Auto da fés, the wars of religion, not speak of more recent crimes of commission and acquiescence'.[13] From a contemporary point of view, Christians and Jews were certainly second-class citizens in the Islamic world, and they were required to pay a special tax, but by the standards of the time they did have a fair degree of autonomy. They could organize their lives largely as they chose.

After the long centuries in which the Muslim world occupied a central position politically and culturally, its decline came as a bitter blow. Stagnation now blights the core countries of Islam. The *Arab Human Development Report* of 2002 paints a tragic picture. Compiled by scholars from the countries concerned, the report draws attention to three major shortcomings of the Arab world: the lack of democratic freedoms, the weak position of women, and problems in science and education. It gives concrete examples: the total production of translations in the Arab world from the ninth century onwards is equal to the number of translated works published in Spain every year and, to stay with Spain, the total income of that country is greater than the income of all Arab nations combined.

Yet there's no reason to exclude the possibility of Islamic reform out of hand. Lewis refuses to be convinced that Islam cannot in theory be combined with freedom, science and economic development: 'How is it that Muslim society in the past was a pioneer in all three, and this when Muslims were much closer in time to the sources and inspiration of their faith than they are now?'[14] In saying this he means to make clear that the history of Islam suggests possibilities beyond the current doldrums.

There's a general feeling that stories about a flourishing Islamic culture refer to an increasingly distant past. A civilization that derives its legitimacy from such a far-off history has lost much of its power to convince. A split self-image results. The lofty civilization of memory makes the demonstrable time-lag that now separates it from the West – and to an increasing extent even from other countries in Asia – unbearable. This perspective is generally avoided, but under the skin self-criticism is rife. We might call it the malaise within Islam, a whole raft of cultural and religious doubts that cannot be voiced, which therefore find an outlet in aggression and resentment, or in resignation of a kind that refuses to acknowledge any responsibility.

Reformers like Abu Zayd have not failed to notice that their world is languishing. Dependence on the West is obvious in all fields of modern science and technology. 'The form, the material life, is modern and progressive; the content, the intellectual and spiritual life, is traditional and archaic. These contrasts are a direct menace to all kinds of modern ways of life and they threaten the Islamic consciousness with slow suicide.'[15]

This developmental disjunction in the core Islamic countries is reflected in the composition of their populations. Demographic projections suggest that the Arab world, which is to say a group of countries in the immediate vicinity of the expanded European Union, will see its population grow from 280 million in 2000 to somewhere between 410 and 460 million by 2020. In the short term, the rise will place these societies under even greater strain. A majority of the population are minors, almost 40 per cent under the age of 14, which means tens of millions of young people find themselves in a fairly hopeless situation. It's a known fact that a relatively young population is in itself a source of unrest and carries within it the seeds of violence.

The better news is that the pressure will ease from about 2015–20, since the average number of children born per woman is falling. The population will by then be slightly older than it is now. American demographer Philip Longman even speaks of a 'demographic dividend', since resources will come free for infrastructural development and, so he hopes, 'the appeal of radicalism could also diminish as young adults make up less of the population'.[16]

Even if in the longer term the prospects are somewhat brighter, it's clear that rapid population growth will only add to the pressure to migrate. Already many young people say they want to move to Europe or America. This is of course impossible and the deep frustration that already exists will not be reduced if children now growing to adulthood feel imprisoned in a stagnating society, while on the other side of the Mediterranean the wealth and freedom of Europe beckon.

In a Secular Environment

Today's migration flows reveal the true relationship between Europe and the Arab world. People are voting with their feet. In authoritarian Arab states they have thus far had few other means of expression. Those who don't become resigned to their fate or resort to forms of protest leave their native countries and head for the major cities of the former colonial powers, against which their parents' generation fought so hard to achieve independence. The irony of the situation is inescapable, and migrants might well ask themselves why they've been set adrift. Why have poverty and repression, far from decreasing, often increased since decolonization?

Meanwhile, Europe is home to many Muslim immigrants and the malaise within Islam has migrated into our world along with them. It's estimated that within 20 years around 30 million Muslims, twice the current number, will be living in the European Union. This creates a situation unique in the history of Islam, namely the permanent settlement of a large number of Muslims in a liberal and secular society, that of Western Europe, a region made up of the most irreligious countries in today's world. How are they to live as a minority amid Christians and Jews, apostates and heathens?

Within Muslim communities there have been various responses to this challenge. One possible route is liberal reform, with Islam somehow reconciling itself with the principles of a secular society. Quite a few Muslim thinkers are searching in this direction, although their voices are weaker than we might wish. On the other hand, there are clear instances of fundamentalism within the Muslim communities of Europe. As a third possibility, we might expect to find European secularization rubbing off on Muslim immigrants. There are plenty of signs of reduced religious commitment. These are the three possible directions: orthodox, liberal and secular.

Let's first look more closely at signs of secularization, before moving on to examine evidence of radicalization and liberalization. An article written by journalist Gerard van Westerloo about the Dutch branch of the Turkish Muslim movement Milli Görüs, illustrates the fact that migration to the West deeply affects the self-image of Muslims. The problems of permanent settlement as a Muslim in a secular environment are summed up by one member of Milli Görüs, Selami Yüksel: 'It means letting go of an essential part of yourself.' Van Westerloo asks what part he means and notes his interviewee's response. 'He hesitates for a moment and then comes out with a key statement that explains why integration is so painful. "The idea that you're one hundred per cent a Muslim. The idea that you're perfect."'[17]

In a secular environment, religious purity can be experienced only in isolation. Even then there are limits, since in a constitutional state with no place for Islamic law, a traditional Muslim must always accept some degree of affront. The *sharia* attaches legal sanctions to apostasy that are unacceptable in Western countries, such as the dissolution of marriage and deprivation of parental and inheritance rights. The moral convictions enshrined in Islamic legislation are not the same as those recognized in the West; they contravene the principles of freedom and equality for all. Where freedom of conscience exists, religion as a juridical doctrine has no place.

In the view of social scientists Pippa Norris and Ronald Inglehart, the yawning gap between secular European societies and the overwhelmingly religious Muslim world is all about the security of existence. Their argument has the charm of simplicity. There's a powerful inverse relationship between having religious faith and feeling secure. The more vulnerable people are to unpredictable forces in life, the greater their tendency to have faith in God. Conversely, the more secure people feel, the less likely they are to embrace a religion. 'Societies where people's daily lives are shaped by the threat of poverty, disease, and premature death remain as religious today as centuries earlier.'[18] Richer countries, on the other hand, are engaged in a fairly steady process of secularization. 'The need for religious reassurance becomes less pressing under conditions of greater security.'[19]

Based on the research carried out by Norris and Inglehart – and a degree of caution, given the unequivocal nature of their argument – we can draw certain conclusions about migrants and faith. If it's true that there's a close connection between security and secularization, then it's surely no accident that many migrants who find themselves in a relatively marginalized and insecure position cling to religious faith. It's a phenomenon extensively documented in American migrant history. Immigrants have a strong tendency to group up around shared beliefs. One report on Muslims in the Netherlands concludes: 'A certain degree of religious perpetuation is only to be expected, to the extent that religion is bound up with family life, ethnic identity and social ties in immigrant communities.'[20]

If we assume that religion plays a greater than average role in the lives of the children of Muslim immigrants as well as those of their parents, then it's important to think about the changes that religion will undergo in a secular society. Existence as a minority faith in a relatively non-religious environment is an entirely new experience in the history of Islam, and indeed the history of Europe. Because there are no precedents, the outcome is unpredictable. In modern societies, culture and religion have grown apart. Several obstacles need to be removed if we're to make a more or less natural integration of Islam possible and if Muslim believers are to emancipate themselves from the cultures of their countries of origin.

French researcher Olivier Roy has written about the Islamic diaspora in Western Europe. He looks primarily at the children of migrants and detects an increasing individualization of religious experience, speaking of 'the reinvention of an ideal religious community, founded solely on the practice of the faith and personal adherence to it, to the exclusion of the specific traditions and cultures of any one country or geographical area'.[21] In the second generation at least, a split can be seen between culture and religion: 'The greatest innovation brought about by the transition of Islam to the West is the decoupling of Islam as a religion and as a concrete culture.'[22]

Roy believes this lack of social embedding means the faith is increasingly a matter of individual choice for young Muslims: 'Everything that was simple because silently accepted, embedded in custom and consensus . . . , suddenly has to be explicitly formulated. Islam becomes the object of reflection.'[23] This has its consequences: 'The values of the inner life come to the fore: patience, trial, resistance to temptation, or prohibitions are just as much opportunities for spiritual development.'[24]

Many options are available; the future is truly open. Take the story of Salma Ismaili, a Moroccan woman, which reads like a tale of conversion. After a fairly wild youth she suddenly became extremely pious. She wears a headscarf: 'No one talked me into it. It's not necessary, either. I wear it as a symbol. I'm making clear I'm a Muslim!' A little later: 'They can't stand the fact that, when it comes down to it, you recognize no authority other than God. I set a good example, don't I? Who am I threatening by not believing in evolution? What trouble does that cause anyone?'[25] She wants to return to Morocco eventually. The aggrieved tone is conspicuous, but no one would want to challenge her personal choice, as long as her rejection of evolutionary theory doesn't become the opening shot in a new battle over education.

Her story suggests that the individualization of the experience of faith is by no means always the same as its liberalization. In fact, says Roy, if anything the opposite is the case, at least in the short term: 'The individual appropriation of the sacred is generally speaking profoundly orthodox.'[26] Making religion more explicit is not the same as liberalizing it, in fact their articulation will tend to make beliefs more dogmatic: 'The hardening of the discourse about values . . . is taking place in the context of a crisis of those values.'[27] He's more optimistic about the longer-term prospects; ultimately, the liberalization and secularization of Islam in Europe will continue.

In opposition to this turn towards orthodoxy stands Fadoua Bouali, a Moroccan-Dutch nurse, who writes, for example: 'My Islam would never approve of violence towards women and it would never force me to marry a man and give birth only to sons.' Most striking here is the term 'my Islam'. Bouali is demanding and exercising the right to a personal interpretation of the faith. She writes about 'the entire Muslim community which for centuries has watched passively and cooperated as women are made to suffer in the name of Islam'.[28]

These two contrasting life stories indicate that within the Muslim community many different choices are being made. Yet group pressure should not be underestimated. With his stress on the privatization of faith, Roy pays insufficient attention to social pressure within families and the loyalty children feel to their parents, a loyalty that's often at odds with personal preferences but has an effect nonetheless. He writes: 'Neither law nor social pressure nor simple custom forces anyone who is "Muslim" by origin to practise the faith.'[29] That's too hasty a verdict, since there can be no doubt that many people are indeed placed under pressure. Conformism is reinforced by the fact that in European cities more and more ethnic enclaves have grown up, and within them attempts are being made to preserve religious beliefs.

It also remains true that for a Muslim, openly stating that you no longer believe is social suicide. Apostasy actually carries the death penalty in orthodox Islam, as a much-consulted book by Ahmad ibn Naqib al-Misri confirms: 'When a person who has reached puberty and is sane voluntarily apostatises from Islam, he deserves to be killed.'[30] This will seldom happen in liberal democracies, but an apostate is at real risk of exclusion, of being cast out of his or her community or family. This is another reason why it's premature to see Islam as an individual experience of faith. All the same, there's a considerable likelihood that it will move in that direction, since we can expect the already fragmented Muslim community to be less and less able to keep a firm grip on its religion.

There are a good many obstacles yet to be overcome before Islam can take root in a democratic environment, but Norris and Inglehart point out that the conflict mainly concerns personal morality. 'The central values separating Islam and the West revolve far more centrally around Eros than Demos.'[31] Simply put, the most profound differences between secular and religious societies concern relationships between men and women, issues surrounding homosexuality and abortion, and beliefs about the family. This cultural or moral divide has widened spectacularly in the past few decades, mainly because of rapid liberalization in our part of the world, which has broken free from God.

These cultural differences affect migrants directly. Family life and the position of girls and women within it is a source of particularly fierce conflict. Children growing up in Muslim families worry a great deal about what is or is not permitted. Their dilemmas are usually private but they have obvious public consequences. People are too often distracted by the intriguingly modern appearance of many young Muslims, failing to realize that in many respects they are trapped in a fairly traditional morality. The loss of virginity before marriage is seen as a problem. One option is surgical repair of the hymen. A handbook for social workers suggests that when a girl asks about this possibility, 'it is worth first finding out whether there might be other ways of getting blood onto the sheet, such as a minor cut or a prick to the finger or thigh'.[32] It all seems reminiscent of a bygone era, the days of abortions in grimy back rooms, but many girls and boys struggle with this kind of anxiety every day.

Homosexuality remains hidden too, even though it's not exactly unknown in the Arab world. Aggression towards homosexuals sends an unambiguous message: it's increasingly dangerous to come out. Muslims with the wrong sexual orientation lead a double life and face a constant moral dilemma. Hakan puts it like this: 'It's damned hard to be born a homosexual in an Islamic family. You're pretty much doomed from the start to a miserable existence. Your own parents renounce you as if you're a piece of dirt.'[33]

There's a long way to go yet before the moral stance of the average Muslim coincides with that of mainstream liberal society. Many deeply traditional customs from their countries of origin are justified in the name of Islam. For girls, growing up in Muslim communities in the West can be a confusing and sometimes terrible experience. For many years it was assumed that honour killings and other violent practices never, or hardly ever, took place in migrant communities. We now know better. In countries like Germany and the Netherlands many cases are registered annually, and they're the tip of an iceberg of domestic violence. Some years ago the murder of 23-year-old Hatun Sürücü, a Turkish woman living in Berlin, broke the silence in Germany. Three shots were fired at close range by her younger brother, hitting her in the head and face. The two older brothers, who were almost certainly involved in the murder plot, were acquitted. A photograph of them walking out of court smiling, flashing victory signs, was shown all around the world.

What part do religious convictions play in such cases? There's a combination of culture and religion here that's not easy to disentangle. We shouldn't regard honour killing as specific to Islam, if only because it can also be found in Mediterranean cultures with Christian traditions, but Islamic teachings often bring violence against women within easy reach. Investigating the phenomenon in Turkish communities in the Netherlands and Germany, Erdal Gezik, comments: 'Rules of honour and shame are the result of the natural separation of man and woman, such that honour is represented by the man and shame by the woman. Women are expected to be sexually pure before marriage and spiritually pure after marriage.'[34] This inequality between men and women is an essential article of faith for many mainstream Muslims in migrant communities.

We see the same inequality in the debate about the wearing of the headscarf or hijab. It signifies many different things – it's part of a shame culture as well as a religious obligation and a political statement – and it has become a loaded symbol. As a personal choice made in freedom, everyone should accept it, but clearly children are not fully free to choose to wear the hijab. In some countries, including France and Belgium, there's a widespread belief that a ban in schools might contribute to the protection of children and the preservation of a degree of neutrality in the public domain. In other countries too, many schools have banned it.

Fawzia Zouari, born in Tunisia and now living in France, opposes a ban. She believes critics of the headscarf are ignoring something essential, in that many Muslim women believe it's not a matter of subordination to men but of subordination to God. She claims they see the hijab as symbolizing equality of treatment, since it's a way to avoid being seen as a sex object when out in public, a way of moving around without attracting attention. The paradox here, of course, is that in Western societies a woman actually draws attention to herself by wearing a headscarf. It's a highly visible symbol by which she continually declares her religious convictions to the outside world. It marks her out to such a degree that the astonishment we often hear – 'Why does everyone see me as a Muslim?' – seems rather other-worldly.

Another observation by Zouari is more convincing. She says the aim of many women who choose to wear headscarves truly is their own emancipation: 'Their objective is clear: they want to escape from family bonds by means of Islam, to question their parents and their traditions while making sure that such questions cannot be attributed to Western beliefs.' She quotes a Muslim woman called Nouria, who says: 'Having command of Islam is the best means of defending yourself against obscurantism and of resisting traditions that oppress women.'[35] There's something to be said for this notion and some girls who wear the hijab do indeed seem far from timid. In some cases it can be seen as a step towards the outside world, a way of exploring life without interference from the family.

Yet the hijab is commonly seen not as an expression of independence but, rather, as a sign of conformism. In many neighbourhoods it is increasingly hard to walk down the street with no head covering. Conservative imams claim that women who wear headscarves run less risk of sexual intimidation – which amounts to saying that women who do not do so are making themselves vulnerable. Such statements can be interpreted as a concealed threat. True though all this may be, whether it could justify a general ban, in schools for instance, remains an open question. Whether it's a matter of faith or of lifestyle, there's an inherent contradiction in any attempt at forced emancipation.

The government must tread carefully, certainly where adults are concerned. The wearing of a headscarf is ultimately a personal choice, although it ought to be ruled out for those fulfilling certain public functions on behalf of a neutral government, such as police officers. This basic premise is now being challenged. A few years ago a Dutch court refused to take on a student as assistant clerk after she announced that she wanted to wear her headscarf in the courtroom. Those affected by the ban say the blindfold and the hijab go very well together, not only in the case of an assistant clerk of the court but for a judge. Yet the maintenance of neutrality in the courtroom is a thing of great value and it requires some degree of uniformity.

The same goes for the police. In the Netherlands the integration of religious symbols into the uniform is being seriously considered. The proposal by Dutch chief constables to allow an officer to exchange the uniform cap for a turban or headscarf should he or she wish to do so is a good example of the uncertainty that the presence of an increasing number of migrants brings with it. Such genuflections to religious preference are no doubt well intentioned, but it seems people have not asked themselves whether this infringement of uniform regulations is compatible with the goal of equality for all. In jobs where the wearing of uniforms is not compulsory, uniformity is presumably regarded as less important and the wearing of a headscarf need not be a problem.

It's important to make a clear choice in the public domain. Liberal democracy often presents itself as a neutral arena within which cultures can collide and meld. Tolerance means accepting that others have a right to their religious beliefs, and people who want to do away with the separation of church and state or with equal rights for men and women are entitled to voice their opinions. But that neutrality has to stop somewhere and such beliefs must be contradicted by public authorities, one of whose primary tasks is to defend equality. This will give no satisfaction to orthodox religious groups that insist their own cultures must be recognized as of equal worth.

Conservatism and Radicalization

The clashes surrounding *The Satanic Verses* by Salman Rushdie drew our attention to another tendency within Muslim communities in Europe: radicalization can spill over into violence. Rushdie has been the target of public threats in towns like Bradford, such as this statement by the secretary of the Bradford Council of Mosques, Sayed Abdul Quddus: 'Muslims here would kill him and I would willingly sacrifice my own life and that of my children to carry out the Ayatollah's wishes should the opportunity arise.'[36]

In facing such threats it's essential always to make a distinction between doctrinaire Islam, which has moral objections to liberal lifestyles, and a politically motivated rejection of Western society. Conservative attitudes may go together with political radicalism, but in most cases do not. Many people adopt a defensive attitude to a society that seems strange and hostile. Attempting to survive in an enclave is not the same as trying to dislocate a society by intimidation.

In a liberal environment there's nothing neutral about the prospect of integration. Clearly some have more to lose by it than others. What one person calls integration may mean disintegration to someone else. Interaction with an open society turns the notion of a cohesive Pakistani or Turkish community into a fiction. This is the reason many religious leaders try to maintain as great a distance as possible between their followers and the outside world by continually insisting that the decadent society they live in won't give them a chance.

Some say what we're seeing is little more than an Islamic version of orthodox Christian movements, a variation on all too familiar religious hair-splitting. As far as issues surrounding homosexuality or family life are concerned, there's much to be said for this comparison. In other milieus too, modern society is viewed with suspicion. The similarities between conservative Christianity and orthodox Islam are obvious, but they threaten to obscure a number of differences. Dogmatic believers are to be found in all faiths, but they are a minority in Western Christianity, whereas they constitute a majority in the Muslim communities of Europe and certainly beyond, as confirmed by the authors of a recent study: 'The contemporary interpretation of the religious doctrine of Islam is predominantly conservative in nature.'[37]

Another difference is that in most Western countries Christian orthodoxy is concentrated outside the major cities – many countries have a Bible Belt – whereas the rise of Islamic conservatism is an urban phenomenon. The reasons why major European cities such as Amsterdam, Frankfurt, Lyon, London and Copenhagen attract Muslim migrants are largely economic, but cultural differences are maximized by the urban environment. As we have noted before, this transition from the countryside to the city is difficult enough even in migrants' home countries; Algerians or Pakistanis who move to their own major cities have all kinds of problems adjusting.

For all their hostility to the majority culture, home-grown Christian orthodox believers are not affected by the cultural alienation that accompanies migration, and most Muslims are in a weak social position, partly as a result of their history as guest workers. These are further reasons why traditionalism has an effect on the integration of Muslims into society that is quite different from the effect that attendance at churches preaching hellfire and damnation has on believers in the established community.

Some think the dogmatic interpretation of Islam will soften of its own accord. It's often argued that today's liberal societies had a less than enlightened attitude towards homosexuality, for example, in the recent past, so Muslims shouldn't be blamed too harshly for holding similar views today. There's something odd about this notion, since outright conflict with a conservative religion was required to move society forward. There's nothing automatic about the liberalization of religious practices. Open clashes between people with firmly held opinions are an essential part of the process. Anyone who values the emancipation that has taken place over past decades should attach great importance to initiatives aimed at liberalization of a similar kind within Muslim communities.

A gulf yawns between liberal societies and the culture of traditional Muslims. Dutch author Yasmine Allas, who comes from Somalia, offers us a taste of their world: 'I met people who had lived here for years but who really had no idea what the Netherlands was, people who were surrounded only by their own culture and by fellow believers, children who were born and brought up here in this country yet had never had any contact with Dutch children.' Inevitably, there are consequences: 'To my amazement I met people who had opted for this country but at the same time spoke about it with contempt. I met parents who had passed on to their children the distorted image of our society that they'd created for themselves.'[38]

Allas describes how her once liberal mother gradually fell under the spell of an extremely conservative form of Islam. The true faith was drummed into her via cassette recordings. 'Men's voices cheer at the punishment that awaits apostates in the hereafter.'[39] Mother and daughter grew apart: 'I'll never forget her funeral. It was unreal, since the religious extremists who prayed for her said that I, as a woman, was forbidden to attend. "This is men's work," they announced. From far away, between two trees, I tried desperately to catch a final glimpse of her coffin.'[40]

The reinforcement of strict religious convictions can hardly be seen as progress – had they not freed themselves from believers who adhered to an oppressive form of faith, Western societies would never have become so open – but it's a far more serious matter when traditional beliefs become distilled into a radical rejection of liberal democracy. From time to time fiercely hostile pronouncements by imams or other religious leaders reach the outside world. After a flurry of consternation, they're usually quickly forgotten.

We'd be wise not to underestimate the radical minority. There are many such movements and they are gradually trying to gain a foothold in Europe. The Salafists are the best known. They see Europe as *dar-al-kufr*, a region of heretics and unbelievers. One Salafist group will conclude that violence is justified under present circumstances, another that it has every reason to close itself off as far as it can from a morally corrupt environment: 'Salafism is not a coherent, uniform movement, rather it consists of a number of currents, ranging from religious puritanism to violent political-religious activism.'[41]

This is illustrated by the situation in the Netherlands, where radicalization among Muslim youth does not differ greatly from similar tendencies in other Western European countries. In one study, a number of young Salafists were interviewed. Mounir, who adheres to a violent interpretation, formulates his harsh beliefs as follows: 'There can be no compromise between Islam and democracy. Democracy has nothing to teach us; everything has already been said by our religion. What has democracy accomplished up to now? What have they achieved here in the West? Travel to the moon? That was a lie. People say they faked the pictures.' He is convinced of one thing: 'An Islamic state must come; the aim and the means are realistic. Look at the WTC, Madrid and London. Our religion, our prophet and his companions are being insulted. Our brothers are being killed. People who kill us, we must kill.'[42]

What all the radical currents have in common is the conviction that Islam's very existence is under threat. The work of Sayyid Qutb, the most important thinker of the fundamentalist Muslim brotherhood in Egypt in the 1950s, demonstrates the kind of arguments used to support political Islam. Qutb condemns the decadence of the West and above all the separation of religious and worldly affairs, saying that every dividing line between the secular and the sacred suggests that in everyday matters there's more than one supreme authority, and that this in turn implies the existence of more than one God. He fears that liberal ideas would slowly spread to the Islamic world and sees radical engagement as the only fitting response to that threat. Qutb suggests quite baldly that fathoming the truth of the Koran requires not just religious devotion but revolutionary action in the name of Islam.[43]

Such a worldview means it's one easy step from rebelling against liberal values to justifying the use of violence. Radicalization is a slow process, however, since it takes time to sever all links with established society. People need powerful reasons for resorting to violence. The alienation that makes young people receptive to radical Islam is, among other things, an indirect consequence of migration. Mustapha says: 'My family is straying. They no longer practise the faith. All my family thinks about is whether you've got your diploma and whether you're earning a good salary. That's the pursuit of your desires. Their Islam is very weak; they know nothing.'[44] The rift between parents and children that characterizes all migratory processes clearly contributes to radicalization.

A disconcerting number of young Muslims born in the West have set off on their own roads to nowhere. What often surprises people is that so many of these radicalized youngsters were born in European countries. Three of the perpetrators of the attacks on the London Underground of 7 July 2005 – Shehzad Tanweer (22), Hasib Hussein (18) and Mohammad Sidique Khan (30) – come from Asian families in towns and cities such as Leeds. These home-grown terrorists were described by their friends as helpful and open. Their conversion to murderous obsession came as a huge surprise to those around them. Perhaps this banality of terror, the thought that today's friendly boy next door could become tomorrow's suicide bomber, is the most disturbing of all. It's precisely the fact that the violence is so close and can't be dismissed out of hand as the product of a disordered personality that is so worrying.

In sum, radicalization does not stem purely from the consequences of migration; its causes are in part international. A sense of identification with Muslims as victims in Palestine, Chechnya, Iraq and Afghanistan is an important motive. Ibrahim, one of the Salafists interviewed, says: 'I worry about the oppression of Muslims. I empathize with my brothers in the faith. Islam is like a body, the pain is felt all over. So I feel the pain of the Muslims.'[45] There's a logic to terrorism that should be acknowledged. The thinking behind it is that violence in the Muslim world, perpetrated anonymously by the West, must be transferred to the streets of Western cities, since that's the only way to bring change. The concept of retaliation makes it possible to justify murder and to cross the boundary into violence.

This explains why the British government and its security services laboured for a long time under the misapprehension that a clear line could be drawn between terrorism within the country's borders and acts of terror outside them. Radical Islamic groups – such as Abu Hamza's Finsbury Park Mosque – were tolerated on the unspoken assumption that their radicalism would not be aimed at targets on British soil. The attacks of July 2005 brought an abrupt end to this way of thinking. *Daily Mail* columnist Melanie Phillips wrote: 'They finally lifted the veil on Britain's dirty secret in the war on terrorism – that for more than a decade, London had been the epicentre of Islamic militancy in Europe.'[46]

There is a clear relationship between events in the world at large and the radicalization of young Muslims in cities like Lyon, Bradford and Amsterdam, one example being the impact of the Israeli-Palestinian conflict on Muslim communities in Europe, which enables the *intifada* to travel there from the Middle East. In the time when Ed van Thijn was mayor of Amsterdam, there was a belief among some Muslims that they needn't obey the laws of a city governed by a Jewish mayor. The letter left on Theo van Gogh's body by his murderer had an anti-Semitic tenor as well: 'It is a fact that Dutch politics is dominated by many Jews who are a product of Talmudic educational institutions.'[47]

We must not be too quick to psychologize acts of terror. First we should take the perpetrators' convictions seriously. Mohammad Sidique Kahn, one of the men who mounted the attacks on the London Underground, left a video message that testifies to an unshakable conviction: 'We are at war and I am a soldier. . . . Your democratically elected governments continuously perpetuate atrocities against my people and your support of them makes you directly responsible, just as I am directly responsible for protecting and avenging my Muslim brothers and sisters. Until we feel security, you will be our target.'[48] His choice of words demonstrates once again the extent to which international conflict is regarded as a justification for violence at home.

The alienation of radical Muslims from their home environments can't be attributed to any single cause. It has to do with both a worldwide conflict and issues inherent to migration, including a serious inter-generational dispute. Some young Muslims distance themselves from their parents, who for numerous reasons are unable to serve as an example to them, and at the same time they reject a society that sees their faith as merely one among many and which they feel is doing its best to belittle Islam. Their quest for a subculture of their own is in itself understandable. The hope remains that peaceful ways will be found of articulating their protest.

The radical Arab European League, which had a following in Flanders and the Netherlands for several years, seemed to offer just such an alternative. The inspiration behind the movement, the articulate Dyab Abu Jahjah, gave a voice to Muslim discontent, reiterating the old theme: the danger that the Muslim community will be destroyed. In his autobiography he couples assimilation with ethnic cleansing and genocide as 'different methods that lead to the same goal'.[49] He sees a sliding scale from cultural adjustment to physical annihilation and believes that in Belgium all politicians are in favour of assimilation, and therefore the obliteration of the Arab community.

What does Jahjah offer by way of a response? 'We want to foster our own identity and culture while being loyal and valuable citizens of the countries in which we live.'[50] Little can be said against this as it stands, but the danger of his line of reasoning lies in the fact that if the debate about integration becomes burdened by the idea that ultimately it's all about survival as a community, the end may come to justify the means. He alludes to this in his ominous conclusion: 'The choice is yours: Sinn Fein or the IRA, Herri Batassuna or ETA, the AEL or God knows what if you destroy us.' This way of presenting politics and terrorism as alternatives seems above all rhetorical, but it's hard to regard it as anything other than a concealed threat, even though Jahjah goes on humbly: 'We hold out our hands for dialogue and forgiveness.'[51]

Movements like Jahjah's must be given a chance to prove themselves, since if democratic mobilization within the Muslim community is seen to be unproductive, the violent option may gain a broader following, just as student movements in Germany and Italy once spilled over from radicalism into terrorism. Indeed, Roy sees a parallel here: 'People are now wondering about the source of the fascination exercised by Bin Laden on young people who have gone astray, but have we forgotten that exercised by Baader (not to mention Mao)?'[52] Less reassuringly, he adds: 'The great difference is that Islamic radicalism seems to have a potential social base the internationalist Marxists lacked: the uprooted Muslim population.'[53] Such a base can be found in the Islamic world from Morocco to Indonesia, but it undoubtedly exists in the suburbs of European cities too. It really ought to surprise no one that some young people are receptive to the temptation of political Islam. After all, it gives a new significance to lives lived in anonymity.

It would be unforgivably naive not to be aware of the threat, but to what degree is Muslim terrorism, as manifested in the attacks in New York, Madrid and London, a strategic challenge? That such violence can create a climate of fear has been proven, that it can divide population groups along ethnic and religious lines has been amply demonstrated, and that it can influence foreign policy is clear from Spain's decision to withdraw its troops from Iraq. So there is every reason to take these acts of violence seriously, even if the perpetrators sometimes give the impression of being merely teenagers who've gone off the rails.

Is there any real danger, however, that coordinated terrorism will disrupt Western society permanently? Some radical groups certainly have this aim in view, but it's fairly unlikely that anyone is yet in a position to accomplish such a thing. That could change if these groups get their hands on weapons of mass destruction, but terrorism has, historically, always been the weapon of the weak. It can trouble a society for many years, divide people and threaten their civic freedoms, but the political and military resources available to Western societies are so overwhelming that no one need worry too much about the outcome of this trial of strength. Just as long as everyone is prepared for the worst.

Acts of terror are targeted at Muslim communities in the West as well. Radical Muslims believe these communities need to be confronted with a choice: either you try to become part of the receiving society, which means corrupting your faith, or you remain doctrinally pure by keeping your distance as far as you can. From this point of view, it's impossible to be both a good Muslim and a good citizen. More moderate voices deny there's a choice to be made and claim that Muslims can be citizens of a liberal society.

The way the battle against terrorism is fought will help to determine whether Muslims can stand up to intimidation by radical fellow believers. Stringent identity checks in London after the attacks, for example, provoked considerable opposition. If Muslims can see the liberal, constitutional state as protecting them, the battle against Muslim terrorism will not be perceived as a confrontation with Islam as such. The remark of one young Moroccan in a Dutch television debate points in this direction: 'I demand of the government that it protect me against violent people within my community.' At least as important is the degree to which Muslims face up to their own responsibilities. British MP Shahid Malik was right to say, after the attacks in London: 'Condemnation is not enough, and British Muslims must confront the voices of evil head on.'[54]

Reformist Voices

It would help if a more liberal Islam had a greater chance of success, but attempts at reform have been limited up to now. Why do those who favour a more open attitude turn out to be so ineffective? For a start this is a problem common to all world religions. Faith and democracy do not sit easily together, as the long struggle to separate church and state in Europe illustrates. Orthodox believers cling to immutable doctrines and consciously set their faces against the modern world. The reformers who try to modernize their faith often end up leading people to a loss of faith and for that reason they're condemned by more pious fellow believers.

Furthermore, Islam has developed historically as a majority religion in a far from democratic environment. It has therefore rarely been challenged, either by other religions or by secular views of the world. Abdou Filali-Ansary, a reform-minded philosopher from Rabat, points out that the modernization of European societies was carried through in the face of opposition from the Christian churches. Those churches refused to take a step back until forced to do so. There are few places where Islam has been forced to re-examine itself in a similar way, so reform has been harder to initiate.

However limited they've been up to now, attempts to interpret Islam in a more up-to-date way have a significance of their own. Why should we disregard these efforts? It's not simply a matter of choosing between apostasy and dogmatism. A third way may ultimately prove an illusion, but even so, if it leads people to strive for a contemporary interpretation of Islam it could be an extremely productive illusion. Reformers like

Hans Küng and Edward Schillebeeckx offered many believers within the Christian churches the opportunity to expand their horizons and put the certainties of their faith into perspective without qualms. Reform-minded thinkers could play a similar role in Islam, perhaps finding a particularly eager audience among Muslim minorities in the Western world.

Despite their many differences, reformers within Islam share some common ground. For a start they all have a sense of urgency. They acknowledge that the Muslim world has fallen into a state of profound stagnation, partly because of its resistance to outside influences. Abdolkarim Soroush, who comes from Iran, criticizes the concept of *gharb zadegi*, which roughly translates as 'intoxicated by the West'. Those who adhere to this notion advocate a return to tradition, to the things that are theirs. 'Such people never realize that the self must be created, that it does not come prefabricated and maintenance-free.'[55] We should not direct our thoughts primarily towards that which is ours as opposed to that which is foreign, Soroush says. Instead we should simply distinguish between good and bad, truth and falsehood. Nothing has an automatic entitlement to our devotion simply because it originated on our own soil: 'Each culture must disavow certain elements of itself.'[56]

Soroush attempts to reconcile Iran's three cultures: a national tradition that stretches back even beyond the introduction of Islam in the eighth century, the Islamic worldview and Western thinking. All three go to make up the heritage of contemporary Iran, he argues. The country has already rejected the idea of a pure culture free of foreign influences, since anyone thinking along those lines would first have to reject Islam, which came from outside Iran. It's precisely the exchange with other cultures that makes true purification possible.

Moroccan feminist Fatima Mernissi likewise takes stagnation in the Muslim world as the starting point for her discussion. 'And how do we react ... By sliding, sorrowfully, wounded, and infantilized, back toward our origins, toward an anesthetizing past where we were protected, where we had dominion over the rising and setting of the sun.'[57] In her own way, incidentally, she too is held hostage by the ancient texts, since all her efforts are focused on a new reading of the original sources in order to be able to interpret them differently. She realizes, however, that 'appealed to from time to time, our ancestors can be a resource for us, but if they take over, they devour the dawn and the sun and turn our dreams into nightmares'.[58]

It would be a mistake to assume that a self-critical attitude will automatically lead to an embrace of the Western world. Mernissi writes about Western culture as a threat to the identity of Muslim societies: 'America does not have to occupy the Muslim countries in order to bring them to their knees.'[59] Egyptian Muslim thinker Nasr Hamid Abu Zayd, who fled his country and taught at Dutch universities until his death in 2010, spoke fairly regularly of 'the enemy'. The Arab world finds itself in a situation in which 'we ourselves have to defend our own continued existence, now that the enemy has almost succeeded in breaking through our ranks to try to rob us of our true consciousness for ever'.[60] As to the identity of 'the enemy', Abu Zayd leaves no room for doubt: 'Western imperialism and Israeli Zionism.'[61]

It's important for these unconventional thinkers to accept that Muslims themselves are responsible for the decline of Islamic countries, to break the habit of blaming the evil outside world for all their problems. This turn towards self-criticism is key. It will release the energy needed for democratization, which is the only possible basis in the longer term for a civilized 'clash' with Western countries. Up to now, those who place all the blame on the Western world have had the upper hand, and they have chosen to face every possibility except that of their own failure.

Another shared element in reformist thinking is its emphasis on the fact that the history of Islam is nothing other than a history of interpretation. Abu Zayd: 'The belief that the Koran has existed for centuries fossilizes the religious texts and pins down their religious meaning. The belief that the Koran is an event and that the revelation is part of history gives vivacity back to the texts.' To him the important thing is 'to approach the heritage and the study of it from the perspective of our contemporary consciousness'. This involves a more open-minded interpretation, one that takes account of the intentions of the ancient texts rather than simply reiterating them time and again.[62]

He says he's not denying the divine origin of the Koran, merely saying that its origin is hidden, so we cannot study it. The text of the Koran as a 'cultural product', on the other hand, can be fathomed using critical methods derived in part from literary studies. 'The Koran that we read and interpret is in no sense identical with the eternal word of God.'[63] To put it another way, the content of the Koran has been shaped by the linguistic and spiritual horizons of those to whom it was addressed. Before Islamic scripture can be put into a different historical context, those past circumstances must be fully absorbed. The Koran is the product of a culture and at the same time it has shaped a culture. Abu Zayd says there is a 'dialectical relationship' between text and reality.

According to reformist Muslim thinkers, therefore, we must return to the tradition of interpreting scripture, referred to as *ijtihad*. The Koran suggests this possibility explicitly when it says that 'some of its verses are decisive' but that 'others are allegorical' (3:7). The ambivalences or allegories in the Koran are all too obvious, in fact it's possible to say that it contradicts itself in truly essential areas, but then the same is true of the founding texts of all religions.

In his much-read introduction to Islamic theology, Ignaz Goldziher raises the issue of free will and predestination as an example of ambiguity in the Koran. Can a person freely accept or reject his faith? Or is everything ultimately decided by a higher power, with everyone's path in life laid down for him? According to one text, God proposes and disposes: 'And it is not for a soul to believe except by Allah's permission; and He casts uncleanness on those who will not understand' (10:100). Another says much the same: 'Therefore (for) whomsoever Allah intends that He would guide him aright, He expands his breast for Islam, and (for) whomsoever He intends that He should cause him to err, He makes his breast straight and narrow as though he were ascending upwards; thus does Allah lay uncleanness on those who do not believe' (6:125). But there are just as many passages that emphasize freedom of the will, even in relation to whether or not to believe. Take for example the passage 'let him who please believe, and let him who please disbelieve' (18:29). Or, later: 'Surely this is a reminder, so whoever pleases takes to his Lord a way' (76:29).

Clearly justification can be found in the Koran either for a belief in an almighty God who intervenes whenever he chooses or for freedom of choice and the moral responsibility of man that flows from that freedom. These diverse readings have given rise to an enduring battle between different schools of Islam. The Koran is so coded that there have been endless attempts to decode it. The difference between the literal reading and the more liberal interpretation is that the reformers recognize the possibility of different interpretations.

Where does the alternative way of dealing with the Koran lead? One of the most important areas of innovation concerns the position of women. Verse 4:7 states: 'Men shall have a portion of what the parents and the near relatives leave, and women shall have a portion of what the parents and the near relatives leave, whether there is little or much of it; a stated portion.' In the pre-Islamic tradition women had never been rightful claimants, so in that sense it is possible to say that Islam improved the position of women considerably. Still, it's hard to speak of equality of the sexes, given the statement in verse 4:34: 'Men are the maintainers of women.' Or a little further on in the same verse: 'And (as to) those on whose part you fear desertion, admonish them, and leave them alone in the sleeping-places and beat them.' Or in another verse, 2:282: 'Call in to witness from among your men two witnesses; but if there are not two men, then one man and two women.' There are countless further examples, making clear that in Koranic texts women are seen as second-class citizens.

Reformers deal with passages like these by concentrating on identifying the beginnings of a struggle for equality in the context of the time, then projecting that reformism onto the present as normative. Mernissi seeks a rehabilitation of women in Islam. 'All the monotheistic religions are shot through by the conflict between the divine and the feminine, but none more so than Islam, which has opted for the occultation of the feminine, at least symbolically, by trying to veil it, to hide it, to mask it.'[64] By unravelling, through textual criticism and a historian's approach, the most quoted verse of the Koran, which describes the origin of the face-covering veil (33:53), she tries to convince us it was about a form of spatial separation 'that can be understood to be a separation of the public from the private, or indeed the profane from the sacred, but which was to turn into a segregation of the sexes'. The latter is surely another thing altogether.[65]

One final important theme common to Islamic reformers is a contemplation of the relationship between Islam and the idea of secularism. Filali-Ansary reconciles Islam and the secular principle in his own way. He opposes the notion that the Koran carries within it a kind of constitution that describes the functioning of an Islamic state. The form the political community took could have been different, as is proven by the divisive conflict that occurred a few decades after Mohammed's death. Moreover, the prophet did not name a successor, and apart from the fact that it caused a great deal of confusion, this indicates that the formation of states was seen as belonging to a different sphere of life.

Filali-Ansary repeats an old question: 'Was the prophet a king?' He says there's an essential difference between the authority of the prophet over those who have converted to Islam and the authority of a worldly ruler. If Islam explicitly intended to unite spiritual and worldly power, why do we learn nothing about the founding of such a state from either the Koran or the Hadiths (the texts about the life and work of Mohammed)? Filali-Ansary's conclusion is that the religious ideal must be separated from the historical forms within which it has organized itself. He says it's time to recognize that the experiences of the first Muslim community in Medina no longer have any significance as a model.

He believes that being a Muslim is a cultural identity, which is to say a connection to spiritual values; it doesn't mean people must allow their lives to be ruled by Islamic precepts. The bringing into being of a Muslim community takes second place to the individual and free character of the faith. Islam is not a social discipline that can be enforced by a public authority, rather it's a personal engagement, an act of faith, an expression of the will to submit to God.

There are other reformers who likewise see Islam as a spiritual message rather than a legislative system. According to Mohamed Charfi, the Koran doesn't speak of *sharia* as a law but as a path. Of the 6,200 verses in the Koran, between 220 and 250, or no more than 3 to 4 per cent of the total, have a legalistic purport and even then it's mostly a matter of moral guidance, which is often closely bound up with specific circumstances. Charfi speaks of the 'perversion of all prophetic messages from the moment they are placed within the history of man with his passions, interests, cultures, mental horizons and sociological constraints of all kinds'.[66] He seeks a modernization of Islam, which will inevitably bring secularization with it.

Questions about how to deal with the separation of church and state are also being asked, naturally enough, within Muslim communities in the West. As we have seen, Muslims who find themselves a minority in a secular democracy are forced to reconsider their stance. Swiss Muslim philosopher Tariq Ramadan, in particular, has tried to describe the position of Muslims in a secular environment. He says that Muslims must break with the idea of themselves as a diaspora, in other words they must cease to see their presence in Western society in the light of their origins or indeed their possible return.

He criticizes the first generation, which lived too defensively in the West, always with a sense of being on foreign soil. This is unnecessary, since there's another way of understanding the distinction between *dar al-Islam* and *dar al-harb* – 'house of Islam' and 'house of war'. According to one of the four Sunni schools of law, the Hanafi School, the difference lies primarily in the degree of security in which Muslims can live. By that criterion, Ramadan says, Western countries are just as much part of the *dar al-Islam*, perhaps even more so than their countries of origin, since 'sometimes Muslims can feel safer in the West when it comes to the free practise of their faith than in some so-called Muslim countries'.[67]

For this reason Muslims must come out of their shells and adopt a more self-conscious attitude in the Western world: 'It's a matter of integrating all dimensions of life that are not opposed to our orientation and considering them to be entirely our own. It's a matter of clearly going beyond a binary vision and ceasing to hold on to the feeling of being eternal outsiders.'[68] Ramadan talks about a principle of integration: as Muslims we can regard as Islamic everything that is not opposed to Islam. This is an ambiguous formulation, since although it means Muslims should throw themselves open to a great many things that originate outside the Islamic tradition, at the same time they can accept those attainments only by absorbing them into Islam. Clearly Ramadan is not distancing himself from the all-embracing ambition of Islam, since he seems to suggest it's impossible for anything of lasting value to exist outside Islam without potentially being part of it.

Compared to the reformers we've already looked at, Ramadan is circumspect, trying to reconcile all the various currents. He makes no real choice between them. He strives to normalize the presence of Muslims in the West without playing it down. Their role must be self-evident yet not necessarily invisible. This seems to be his ultimate motive, to search for a form of words that will give Muslims confidence in themselves. In this respect his work can be seen as an important contribution. But having set himself up as a reconciler within a deeply divided Muslim community, he needs to give all the various tendencies within Islam their due, even if in daily practice they are mutually exclusive. The ambivalences in the work of Ramadan – which are not veiled but visible to all – arise as a consequence of this.

Believers in an Open Society

Having looked at the factional struggles within and between Muslim communities, we must now turn our attention to the inability of receiving societies to find ways of dealing with Islam. A number of clear choices have to be made, but they will be acceptable only if based on the principle of equal treatment. Nothing feeds suspicion so much as a sense that double standards are being applied.

It's strange, to put it mildly, that the debate the Dutch are now having about Islam takes no account of attempts to tackle the same issues at a time when the Netherlands was doing its best to govern a country with the largest Muslim population in the world. Although colonial rule over a Muslim majority presents a very different challenge from the integration of a Muslim minority, there's nevertheless something to be learned from the debates about Islam in that period. As we shall see, some of the same misconceptions have returned in our own day.

This is perfectly illustrated by a critical study of Dutch colonial policies with regard to Islam called *Nederland en de Islam*, published in 1911 by the well-known orientalist Christiaan Snouck Hurgronje. He reacts strongly to the idea that Muslims ought to be converted and is unimpressed by efforts to this end by Catholic missionaries and Protestant evangelicals. Not that he's completely neutral towards Islam: 'Since the Netherlands has woken to an awareness that its task is to make the peoples of the Archipelago, according to their nature, ready to participate in modern culture and interaction, it therefore has its own Islam question, just like every non-Mohammedan state with Muslim subjects.'[69]

He concludes that for years the government has failed to concern itself with the indigenous population, and more specifically their religion. This indifference has suddenly flipped over into a call for restrictions to be placed on the pilgrimage to Mecca: 'The most innocent Mohammedan religious teachers, pupils at *pesantrens* [religious boarding schools], those who lead services of worship, were then after a period of neglect approached with idiotically generalized distrust, often placed under supervision.'[70] This amounted to saying that 'pilgrims to Mecca come back armed, as it were, with dynamite bombs, that every *hadji* is an agitator'. We may live in new times, but the old debates continue.

How should the Dutch colonizers deal with Islam in the East Indies? Snouck Hurgronje's approach is three-pronged and it can serve as a guide in our own time, even though his thinking ultimately remains within the colonial paradigm. He appeals for 'the most strict and sincere maintenance of the freedom of *religion*, if with an important reservation with regard to the *political* side of the Muslim system and with the holding open of all routes that could lead the Mohammedans to *social* evolution, even to rising above their religious system'.[71]

His aim was therefore first of all to separate religion and politics. Nothing must be put in the way of Islam as a religion – 'the most strict and sincere maintenance of the freedom of *religion*' – and all attempts at conversion would fail, of that he was firmly convinced. At the same time all forms of political Islam, including pan-Islamism, must be combated as a dangerous challenge to the authority of the government. In that regard any passivity would be misplaced.

He found it hard to imagine reform of Islamic law, but its rigid character was such that real life would move away from it: 'What for the new age and its interactions are galling bonds, which the Muslim law wraps around the lives of the adherents of Islam, will loosen of their own accord as soon as our cultural life by one means or another pulls them towards it more powerfully.'[72] Opposing overly ambitious plans to that end, he added: 'The pressure must come from the inside outwards and not the other way around.'[73] He was aware that 'everything that is open to attack rises in value to those who possess it'.[74] Again, the old debates are still significant in our day.

What would relations with Islam on the basis of equal treatment look like? The separation of church and state, on which freedom of religion is founded, is the first priority. That 'most strict and sincere maintenance of the freedom of religion' is crucial. Not only must the state be safeguarded against improper pressure from the church; to an equal or even greater extent the church must be protected against meddling by the state. Certainly where Islam is concerned, as a matter of principle nothing must be laid in the way of Muslims who want to practise their faith openly. Mosques belong here, even though many people will be shocked to learn that the Essalaam mosque in Rotterdam, with its 50-metre-high minarets, is expressly intended as a major feature of the city's skyline.

If we are going to emphasize the principle of equal treatment, then we need to ask ourselves whether Europeans are complying with it. Many countries have regulations that are at odds with the separation of church and state, such as the obligation to pay church taxes in Germany and Denmark. But when Aygül Özkan, a minister in the German state of Lower Saxony, criticized the presence of Christian symbols in public institutions, the nation was outraged. The secularization of institutions needs to go further, and those who ask Muslims to respect religious freedom should feel obliged to summon up a comparable willingness themselves. The recent decision by the European Court that the requirement to display crucifixes in Italian state schools is incompatible with the principle of equality is therefore a move in the right direction.

This certainly does not mean religion must be banished from the public sphere. Behind the unwillingness to accept a highly visible Islam lies the notion that religion is purely a private matter, but the separation of church and state is not the same as the separation of church and society. Religions are an essential part of a pluralist society, which is why Muslims, especially given the differences that exist between them, must venture into the public arena of the countries in which they now live. This is a paradoxical invitation, since as someone remarked: 'You only really want to accept a passive Islam.' Indeed, up to now there's been little willingness in the West to see Islam as part of social life.

Jean Baubérot comments that the greatest advocates of a rigorous separation of church and state exhibit a remarkable inconsistency in that they often welcome statements from the churches that relate to public matters, such as world poverty or the arms race, but are hugely resistant to statements about people's private lives, such as matters surrounding the family or sexuality. If they are so keen to restrict the role of religion to the private domain, surely their reaction should be precisely the reverse.[75]

First of all, then, a clear commitment to the equal treatment of religions is needed. Political Islam can be combated effectively only if the principle of freedom of religion is defended unambiguously. A leading question can then be posed: Doesn't the exercise of the right to religious freedom inevitably bring with it a duty to defend that same freedom for other believers and for non-believers? This is of course exactly what political Islam contests, not only in words but with threats and violence. Which brings us to Snouck Hurgronje's second point. What form should that 'important reservation with regard to the *political* side of the Muslim system' take?

The political ambitions of Islam do not exist in a vacuum, rather they are based on a fairly common habit of dividing the world into Muslims and non-Muslims. Far too often, Muslims withdraw into a believing 'us' that strives to keep its distance from an unbelieving 'them'. When freedom of religion is exploited as a means of spreading contempt towards non-Muslims, the right to that freedom is eroded and sooner or later a time will come when Muslims start to undermine their own ability to live in a democracy characterized by religious diversity. The right of one is after all the duty of another. This holds true for everybody, including members of the Muslim community. If a significant majority cannot summon respect for this rule, Muslims will stigmatize themselves.

Interreligious dialogue, which is under way everywhere, requires a number of principles to be held in common. At the very least such a dialogue has to be based on the acceptance of religious freedom. Experience shows that quite a few religious leaders reject this: 'Yes, it is laid down in the law of European countries, but elsewhere it may be different; higher authorities will have to decide.' We can simply take note of such reactions, but that is to follow the path of least resistance. When it comes to equal treatment a more principled stance would be appropriate from those who lay claim to equality as a matter of principle.

The integration of Islam into democracy therefore requires it to make profound adjustments. Some do not believe such reciprocity is possible. Ayaan Hirsi Ali considers what she calls 'pure Islam' to be incompatible with liberal democracy. Sometimes she refers to 'the excrescences of Islam' or to 'some principles within Islam' as being in conflict with democracy, but this is merely a slightly more diplomatic way of saying that Islam and democracy do not go together. She believes there's no such thing as European Islam or, more generally, reform within Islam.

Perhaps we will eventually have to concede that she's right, but what goal would be served by excluding the possibility of reform? The migration of Muslims has created a unique situation and it's therefore premature to say that Islam as it has developed in the West can never be combined with democratic principles. The assumption that Muslims must abandon their faith if they're to live in a secular environment is not only rather unrealistic, it's incompatible with the principle of religious freedom. There are undoubtedly signs of secularization among European Muslims, but there are plenty of examples too of an increased interest in religion. In short, it's vitally important for Muslims to continue exploring ways of developing Islam as a minority religion in a secular environment. It may prove essential to the stability of Western societies.

Finally, the principle of equal treatment has another inevitable consequence. Anyone claiming freedom of religion for a group must be able to summon a willingness to grant the same freedom to members of that group. Alternative movements are now quite often excommunicated, as Tariq Ramadan is forced to acknowledge. He's extremely critical of the absence of a culture of dialogue within the Muslim community, where denunciation is rife.[76] We need only think of how some of the more wayward groups within Islam, such as the Alevis and the

Ahmaddiya movement, have been excluded. Ramadan believes there's a lack of willingness to enter into dialogue with those who hold different beliefs.

The ways in which disputes within Islam are handled are most problematic of all when it comes to the loss of faith. This relates to the final prong of Snouck Hurgronje's approach: 'The holding open of all routes that could lead the Mohammedans to *social* evolution, even to rising above their religious system.' Most Muslims have exceptional difficulty on this point. But again, anyone who demands the right to practise his religion freely has no choice but to grant that same right to other members of the same religious community. Faith must either be practised in freedom or abandoned. This too is a long way from the situation as it stands, since for Muslims to say openly that they no longer believe means social exclusion or worse. Young Salafists leave no room for doubt about this: 'An intruder inside the house is certainly more dangerous than one outside,' said Mohammed Bouyeri.[77]

The Universal Declaration of Human Rights is perfectly clear on the issue of apostasy: 'Everyone has the right to freedom of thought, conscience and religion; this right includes freedom to change his religion or belief' (article 18). Like many other articles of the Declaration, this has remained a dead letter in many countries, where freedom is restricted in the name of a state religion. In the Western world too, the freedom to abandon the Muslim faith is disputed and ex-Muslims have formed groups in order to stand up for their choice publicly in the face of serious threats. Muslims will have to learn to accept the decisions of those who want openly to bid farewell to their faith.

Freedom of religion does not exclude criticism of religion. On the contrary, part of the price of an open society is that religious traditions can be the subject of public debate. Some sensitivity on the part of critics is only right, since speaking freely about things some people regard as holy can be deeply hurtful. Nevertheless, if Muslims intend to live in liberal democracies while retaining the idea that the Koran or the prophet are above all criticism and must never be the object of ridicule, then they condemn themselves to the role of eternal outsiders. Freedom for Muslims can be defended only if Muslims are willing to defend the freedom of their critics.

Confronted with a similar appeal on an American television programme, one Muslim organization responded in a revealing manner, issuing a public statement that read: 'We as an American Muslim community claim the human right to self-definition.'[78] Since when has 'self-definition' been a human right? Since when have believers had exclusive permission to speak about their holy books? These are astonishing demands that have no place in a democracy. Every faith belongs to everyone in the sense that we can all have opinions about it and are free to express those opinions.

Statements made by the British and Dutch governments as they consider making blasphemy punishable under law once again have not always been sensible either. Why should insulting the gods be any worse than insulting people? Anyone who supports the principle of equal treatment is obliged to regard religious and secular worldviews as equal before the law. The Universal Declaration of Human Rights is clear about this: religion is on a par with other convictions. There are certainly limits to freedom of speech, but we can't draw the line at criticizing or ridiculing a faith, otherwise we'd have to start by tossing onto the pyres *The Praise of Folly* by Erasmus, with its passages about 'folly in the Bible'.

Conflict avoidance is the wrong response when freedom of expression is at stake, not only for reasons of principle but because it does nothing to calm the situation when feelings run high. One evasion leads to another. If a decision is made not to publish any more cartoons, then what about the commotion surrounding an opera on the subject of Aisha, one of the prophet's wives? The performance was abandoned in response to threats. If objections are met in the case of opera, what should be the reaction when a newspaper discovers that even an image of the Koran on the front of its monthly magazine section is reason enough for some delivery boys to refuse to distribute it? The ban on images embraced by part of the Muslim world can never be a guideline for journalistic or artistic expression, if only because it's a short step from banning images to banning spoken statements, and from there to banning comments made in writing. By that point openness has been abandoned altogether.

During a British debate about proposed new legislation on incitement to religious hatred, Timothy Garton Ash confronted the government with its self-declared aim of protecting the Muslim community. He commented that it made him think of 'a man trying to stop a leaking wastepipe with a priceless Raphael drawing'. He went on: 'The Government is preparing to do great damage in the cause of averting damage.' It is the task of every government to balance the competing demands of liberty and of public order. In this case, Garton Ash said, 'they are proposing too great a risk to freedom, for too uncertain a gain in security'.[79]

On balance, freedom of speech contributes to the avoidance of social conflict. Precisely because people are able to convert their anger into words or images, the road that leads from resentment to aggression becomes longer. It's no accident that the Danish cartoons affair eventually led to violence in Middle Eastern countries, where freedom of speech is much more limited and people are therefore more likely to resort to violence as the last available means of expressing their discontent. The idea that limitations on freedom of speech could help to calm feelings within the Muslim community is therefore based on a misconception.

The freedom to practise a religion and the freedom to criticize a religion are inseparable. This is hard for practising Muslims to accept. Equality of treatment, however, doesn't mean that everyone must now suddenly embrace liberal ideas. Just like other traditional believers, conservative Muslims are free to reject institutions like homosexual marriage, as long as they accept that as things stand a majority has made a different decision. In an open society there must be room for traditional interpretations of any faith, as long as the freedom of others isn't limited by them. In practice, it seems, it often is.

The impasse over Islam shows there's still no generally accepted basis for a discussion about its place in a liberal democracy. Diplomatic avoidance doesn't help, whereas honesty about the principle of religious freedom does. Most liberal societies do not yet live up to the ideal of equal treatment. There's every reason for a critical reconsideration of the majority culture and at the same time a need for self-examination on the part of the Muslim minority. Muslims could be far more open about what is happening in the mosques and take a more active stance against expressions of intolerance in their own circles.

Shaping public opinion in this way remains difficult for many Muslims. Solidarity with your own community is often understood as a promise to say nothing about the things that give offence within that community. Often people think: we're not going to hang out our dirty washing, we're vulnerable enough as it is. But room for newcomers in a society actually increases when differences of opinion are made more plainly visible. What Islam needs are whistle blowers, people who're willing to let go of their spurious loyalty to 'the community' and break out of that vicious circle to speak freely about wrongdoing within the divided world of Islam – like the parents who revealed financial mismanagement at an Islamic school, for instance, or the writer who brought to light the way mosques were orchestrating claims for welfare payments, or women who draw attention to tyranny and violence behind the closed doors of the home, or leaders of mosques who inform the security services about extremism they come upon there.

Such whistle blowers will ease relations, counteracting the crude caricatures on both sides that result from distrust. Something that is by no means cohesive – whether it be the culture of the majority or of a minority – is too often seen as monolithic.

To put it another way, peaceful co-existence is an extremely limited interpretation of what integration means. Compare the Europe of before and after 1989. Where there was cold peace and distance there is now space for interaction and rapprochement. The same applies to the multicultural society. We are still too much caught up in the era of diplomacy and non-interference, but society demands more than that. The future of Islam affects everyone, not just Muslims. Trust is another word for integration, and it will develop far more readily if pluralism becomes visible on all sides.

A World Without an Emergency Exit

With the immigration of millions of Muslims, the crisis of Islam has become Europe's crisis too. It remains to be seen whether Gilles Kepel, a French expert on the subject, will be proven right in thinking that the struggle to create a European Islam will be of decisive importance to the modernization of Islam worldwide.[80] The divided Muslim community will in any case engage the attention of Western societies for a long time to come, even though many Westerners may have a feeling that the battle being fought in their midst for the future of Islam takes no account of them.

If Islam can find a place for itself in a secular environment, then Western democracies will have confirmed their leading position in the world. The extent to which the societies affected can encourage such an accommodation is limited. After all, never before has a wave of immigration been so interwoven with an international crisis as the arrival of millions of Muslims in the West. In Europe in particular there's an urgent need to avoid a violent clash of civilizations. In contrast to the situation in 1967, the year of the Six Day War, millions of Muslims now live in Western Europe, four to five million in France alone.

The crisis in the Muslim world is spilling over into aggression against the West. There's therefore every reason for a closer examination of the arguments involved. Ian Buruma and Avishai Margalit, in a study into what they have called 'occidentalism', write that the image of the West as a degenerate society in which moral licentiousness reigns supreme has generated some powerful symbolism. They see a deeper reason behind the attack on New York: 'A deliberate act of mass murder played into an ancient myth – the myth about the destruction of the sinful city.'[81] The classic form of this myth is the fall of whorish Babylon, which in its pride vied with the gods. In this way of seeing the world, Buruma and Margalit recognize a means of dehumanizing Western society: 'To diminish an entire society or a civilization to a mass of soulless, decadent, money-grubbing, rootless, faithless, unfeeling parasites is a form of intellectual destruction.'[82]

It's not just a matter of words but of words that lead to violence.

For a start, there's a need to acknowledge that the threat is real. All the ingredients for a spiral of violence are present. Wars in the Middle East or turmoil in Pakistan may lead to a further radicalization of Muslims all over the world and there's certainly reason to see in the 'war on terror' a dilemma that confronts the liberal democracies with fundamental questions.

The problems faced by Muslim immigrants in Europe must be separated as far as possible from the widespread conflict between the West and politicized Islam in the world at large. This will not be easy, but the signs of a change in mentality are visible everywhere. More and more Muslims have settled in Europe for good and no longer see themselves as part of a 'diaspora'. In the midst of the uproar about the Danish cartoons of the prophet, it became clear that two worlds are slowly but steadily growing apart: that of Muslims in the West and that of their fellow believers in the Arab world. It's surely no accident that the issue exploded on the streets of Damascus and Beirut, not in London or Amsterdam.

There's a striking difference between the United States and Europe in their approaches to radical Islam. In America it's seen mainly as a problem of international politics, whereas in Europe, domestic and foreign affairs are inseparable as far as this threat is concerned. The explanation lies in the different backgrounds and circumstances of their Muslim communities. Muslims in the United States could generally be described as middle class, so the social problems that come to the fore in Europe are less in evidence there. Their numbers in relation to the rest of the population are much smaller – estimates give figures of three to four million US Muslims – and therefore they have much less of an impact on the major cities. Moreover, a considerable number of Muslim believers belong to the black community and are therefore unaffected by problems specific to immigration. Finally, Europe's proximity to the Arab world gives greater weight to conflicts that arise as a result of the presence of Muslims.

Several European countries are engaged in public discussions about how Islam can become part of their national identities. This gives an extra charge to the debate. American researcher John Esposito thinks that the big questions about the place of Islam in America still have to be asked: 'The majority of Americans have yet to realize that Muslims are "us", but many Muslims have not solved the problem of the relationship of their faith to national identity either: will they remain Muslims in America or become American Muslims?'[83]

It's too early to say whether Muslim communities in the Western world will become integrated and whether Muslims will succeed in shielding their lives in the West against the worldwide conflict raging in the background, but there can be no doubt that it's extremely important for them to do so. History offers plenty of examples of migrants being crushed by the larger forces of international conflict. At such moments majorities may be inclined to doubt the loyalty of their fellow citizens. This threatens to happen to Muslim communities, but their own public choices are just as important. To the extent that they start to see their own lives as inherent to the countries in which they now live, to the extent that they choose to see the practice of their faith in the context of religious freedom, they can contribute to a lessening of distrust and ensure that their presence is not continually associated with the 'war on terror'.

The confrontation with political Islam can end well only if receiving societies take a stand against the temptation to divide the world into good and evil along religious lines. The cohesion that exists between Western democracies was produced to a large extent by the contrast between them and totalitarian states during the Cold War. There is now a temptation to draw new dividing lines along old religious boundaries. That would mean once again seeing the fault-line between Western Christianity and Islam as fundamental to the way Europe defines itself.

The current significance of such traditions is the focus of Samuel Huntington's book about the 'clash of civilizations'. The main criticism that has been made of his work has to do with his underestimation of nation-states, which form coalitions for reasons of power politics irrespective of the supposed battle lines between civilizations. European history shows that countless ruinous wars are possible between people who believe themselves to belong to the same civilization, and more recently the First Gulf War demonstrated that Islamic solidarity is fairly weak. We need to keep a close eye on regional and national differences within civilizations.

There's another qualification that should perhaps be set beside the notion of a 'clash of civilizations'. Norris and Inglehart have pointed out that societies in which God is in retreat generally produce fewer children, so much so in fact that they often decline in size. Today's religious societies are experiencing a population explosion. 'In virtually every case they encourage people to produce large numbers of children, and discourage anything that threatens the family, such as divorce, homosexuality, or abortion. Rich, secular societies produce fewer people, but with relatively high investment in each individual.'[84]

These contrasting demographic trends have an unexpected outcome: 'Rich societies are becoming more secular but the world as a whole is becoming more religious.'[85] In short, there have never been so many traditional believers in the world as there are now, which means among other things that religion is increasing in importance, in world politics as elsewhere: 'A growing gap has opened up between the value systems of rich and poor countries, making religious differences *increasingly* salient.'[86] In this sense the authors agree with Huntington that a 'clash of civilizations' is under way. Indeed, religion and culture will continue to put their stamp on international relations – certainly when it comes to the encounter between the world of Islam and the West – which is not to say that differences of this kind inevitably lead to violence.

But Huntington is wrong, Norris and Inglehart say, when he claims that the germ of the present confrontation lies in divergent beliefs about political democracy. Their research in a wide range of Muslim countries shows that when it comes to the subject of democracy the difference between public opinion in the West and in the Arab world is negligible. Democratic aspirations are high among Arab populations, although they do give more weight to the public role of religious leaders.

At the moment a considerable and growing proportion of the world's population leads an insecure existence. Religion is still extremely important in societies where this is the case and as a result cultural divides in the world have widened. This is especially true of the divide between Islam and the West. The malaise in the Islamic world, which of all religious communities is by far the worst off in terms of average income and development in general, goes a long way to explain today's fundamentalism. From this perspective, everyone who wants to prevent religious wars has a major interest in helping to ensure the basic needs of people in the Arab world are met, beginning with support for nascent democratization. In that sense the history of the Western world does not offer much reason for hope; all too often Europe and America have supported authoritarian regimes.

There's another sense in which the democracies are in danger of betraying their own norms. Contemporary terrorism confronts liberal societies with a fundamental problem: How can Muslim communities in the West avoid being riven by conflicts of loyalty? This indicates a responsibility shared by all. Which methods can legitimately be deployed against the terrorist threat? As the controversial treatment of prisoners in Guantánamo Bay has shown, there's a real risk of a tit-for-tat battle with terrorism in which liberal democracy betrays itself.

Even if political Islam is indeed a new form of totalitarianism, the question remains: what attitude should Europe and America have towards their Muslim communities? It was the historical parallel with Fascism that inspired a despairing plea from Italian writer Oriana Fallaci. She asked herself how a culture so backward as that of the Muslims could possibly be a threat to the West. Her answer was as follows: 'They stay in our own countries, in our cities, our universities, our business companies. . . . Worse, they live in the heart of a society that hosts them without questioning their differences, without checking their bad intentions, without penalizing their sullen fanaticism. . . . If we continue to stay inert, they will become always more and more. They will demand always more and more, they will vex and boss us always more and more. 'Til the point of subduing us.'[87]

This type of polemic opens the way to policies of the kind that led to the American internment of Japanese residents during the Second World War, a decision now rightly spoken of with shame. This does not alter the fact that Fallaci's tirade is a frightening illustration of the eternal dilemma faced by an open society. To what extent can liberal principles survive events like 9/11? Which means of self-defence are permissible and which are not? Even more importantly, should open societies respond to the challenge of fundamentalism by seeing the world as a 'war between civilizations', or should they do all they can to avoid exactly that temptation?

While Fallaci regards the defence of the liberal worldview as primary, British philosopher John Gray takes the attacks by Al-Qaeda as a starting point for reflection on the relationship between liberalism and Islamism. He believes self-examination should come first: 'Western thinkers rightly note that Islam has never grasped the need for a secular realm. They fail to note that what passes for secular belief in the West is a mutation of religious faith.'[88] He's referring to Enlightenment thinking, which is based on the assumption that reason and morality go hand in hand. With the growth of knowledge, morality too would increase – that was the expectation, and Gray regards it as a secular religion.

These are valid questions, but they do not obviate the need for self-defence. The vulnerability of the open society was made obvious by the attacks in New York and Washington, Madrid and London. The concern here is first of all physical vulnerability. In an economy so interwoven with the outside world, can adequate security be guaranteed in the face of those determined to abuse their freedom of movement in liberal societies? Would tight border controls not lead to huge economic losses, as we saw in the days and weeks after the attack on the Twin Towers? Within 36 hours some car assembly plants reported they would have to shut down temporarily because of log jams at the US border.

American scientist Stephen Flynn, a former senior officer in the American Coast Guard, thinks that with sufficient investment and new technology much can be done without seriously disrupting world trade. The hunt for terrorists and their networks remains of great importance, but 'the more daunting challenge will be to reduce the vulnerability of the systems of transport, energy, information, finance, and labor'.[89] The infrastructural backbone of an open society – such as the extensive network of high-speed trains that is beginning to reduce distances in Europe – is indeed composed of vertebrae that can cause general paralysis if hit.

Along with its physical vulnerability, a major concern is the moral vulnerability of an open society. Gray points to the paradoxical situation that arises when a liberal society is faced with a terrorist threat. Groups such as Al-Qaeda can rely on considerable mutual trust among their supporters: 'Liberal societies cannot replicate this suicidal solidarity. Values of personal choice and self-realisation are too deeply encrypted within them.'[90] Yet open societies do have to defend themselves, which necessitates greater controls on people within their own territories. 'The price of individualism is proving to be the loss of privacy.'[91]

All over the Western world we see this dilemma time and again. To what extent can and should our private lives be restricted for the sake of defending public order and public safety? Should existing laws be recalibrated to protect the liberal constitutional state more determinedly from its enemies? Must the law be adjusted to make recruiting for the *jihad* a punishable offence? A tightening of the rules might help, but each case needs to be considered on its merits to ensure the means does not corrupt the end. It is essential to ask whether the open society is slowly being undermined from within by those who want to defend it by all available means.

American writer Paul Berman observes that it was a symptom of Eurocentrism to think that in 1989 totalitarianism had met its end – as if Islamism was not spreading at that very moment. He also rejects the image of a clash of civilizations, which after all suggests that in the world of Islam the fundamental principles of liberal democracy will never have a realistic chance. Nevertheless, if we're hoping to disseminate democracy, we must be able to rely on citizens of the Western world to defend democratic principles and propagate them passionately, no matter how difficult that may be.

Self-examination and self-defence do not sit easily together, especially now that the liberal democracies are confronted with a real threat. Yet the Cold War was won by remaining true to the ideal of an open society. Some are now announcing, as they did then, the end of the European democracies. Alarming books with titles like *The Last Days of Europe* and *While Europe Slept* are selling well.[92] In Cold War days it was argued that democracy was doomed by an inner weakness, namely its perpetual self-doubt and open debate. Now too the fervent defenders of the open society, facing a new threat, seem unable to believe in its continuing viability. There are calls for draconian measures. Instead, a combination of openness and resilience is required. The strength of Western societies lies in their ability to combine liberal principles with an effective response to any security challenge that arises.

All of us, in unguarded moments, must have tried to imagine those final minutes in the World Trade Center. The endlessly replayed footage vividly evoked the claustrophobia, the panic of so many people with no way out. Those pictures capture our times. The world has become smaller over the past few years and it will be increasingly difficult in future to escape global disorder. A plane crashes into a New York skyscraper and the whole world, from Vancouver to Islamabad, is dislocated. Immigration, including that of countless Muslims, has strengthened intercontinental ties even further. The call for self-defence must therefore be accompanied by an awareness of increasing interdependence. The perpetual need to find a balance between security and openness demands a great deal from both citizens and governments, but the alternative is a spiral of violence. We live in a world without an emergency exit.

9

Land of Arrival

Rituals of Citizenship

Post-war immigrants were not only numerous, they came from an exceptionally wide range of backgrounds. Migrants from what used to be called the third world are changing Europe and America. Urban populations increasingly reflect every continent in the world and it's no longer unusual for more than 100 different nationalities to live next to and with one another. In all senses this is a unique experience, which by its very nature often causes conflict. Western societies are now so diverse that they are left wondering what holds them together.

Migrants have unintentionally exposed a more general difficulty. The requirement placed upon them to integrate has developed into a quest for contemporary citizenship. Here is the reciprocity we've been seeking throughout this book: integration means all sides must engage in self-examination. For a long time, making demands of newcomers was equated with standing in their way, so little was required of them, but when a person takes on a new nationality it ought to mean not just acquiring rights but consciously accepting duties. In a time of immigration, we need to start out by reconsidering what citizenship means.

Author Fouad Laroui has written, in ironic tones, of his disappointment on gaining Dutch nationality: 'My Dutch wasn't bad. To increase my chances I learned the genealogy of the House of Orange, the height of the mountains(!) and the breadth of the rivers by heart. I read the biography of the great Thorbecke, who gave this country its first democratic constitution. I wandered the corridors of the Amsterdam Historical Museum. In the public library I called up the complete works of the Great Three: Reve, Hermans, Mulisch.'[1] (He is referring to the three major post-war Dutch novelists.) He needn't have bothered. The procedure took less than five minutes and there were no questions, not even any expression of interest; it was purely a formality.

Afshin Ellian, a lawyer who moved to the Netherlands from Iran, has described a similar disillusionment. 'I received the most important decision about my life by post: my Dutch citizenship. It was nothing more than an administrative letter, signed by Nawijn, then director of the Immigration and Naturalization Service. A deep sense of embarrassment and disappointment tempered my joy. The moment of naturalization should be ritualized, out of respect both for the new citizen and for the constitution.'[2] But in the Netherlands, country of avoidance, there was little respect for rituals. People preferred to keep things low-key; a passport through the post or across a counter would do fine.

These voices have now been heeded. In 2006 the Netherlands introduced a naturalization ceremony based on those held by classic countries of immigration like Canada. In Amsterdam the awkwardness was immediately apparent. At the first ceremony on 24 August 2006, the mayor reminded those present that the Netherlands is a country with traditions very much its own: 'Certain things are forbidden by law, but sometimes we feel they should be permitted nonetheless. *Gedogen*, we call it, a word that's difficult to translate. Why? Because other countries are not familiar with the phenomenon in this form.'[3] There are those who might regard lax law-enforcement as a reason for soul-searching, or at any rate not as a tradition to point out to newcomers with pride on the day they receive their new citizenship.

The same awkwardness showed through in the gift new compatriots were given. It was a thoroughly Dutch Delft pottery potato. Designed by a Chinese immigrant to the Netherlands, Ni Haifeng, it seemed intended as an ironic comment on the ceremony. The reality was even worse; this platitude had a serious purpose, as the accompanying text made clear: 'Now you've become what you've already been for a long time. A Netherlander in Amsterdam, an Amsterdammer in the Netherlands. A potato in the mash, a plank in the ship, a stone in the statue.'[4] Anyone looking at the solemn yet emotional faces of all those for whom a Dutch passport marked the end of a long, often difficult story of migration would know that it wasn't an occasion to talk about permissiveness and hand out potatoes.

Nevertheless, the ceremony does mark a break with a time when little or nothing was demanded of people, when the failure to ask questions of applicants made it clear no one was expecting an answer from them. The implicit message was: you'll never be part of this society and we certainly don't expect you ever to have any influence on goings on around here, so stay where you are and by all means preserve your own identity. There was no mention of responsibilities, since the government knew perfectly well that as soon as you make demands of newcomers, you place commitments upon the receiving society.

A gradual change is in sight, marked by new rituals. Other European countries too are introducing naturalization ceremonies and citizenship exams. Britain is one of the places where a new outlook is emerging. A government commission wrote: 'The rights and, in particular, the responsibilities of citizenship need to be more clearly established. ... This should then be formalised into a form of statement of allegiance.'[5] Not long ago just such a ceremony took place. Some 50 immigrants in Birmingham stood in a circle, simultaneously swearing an oath of allegiance, prompted sentence by sentence by a civil servant: 'I will give my loyalty / to the United Kingdom / I will respect its rights and freedoms / I will uphold its democratic values / I will observe its laws faithfully / and fulfil my duties and obligations / as a British citizen.' An Indian man commented on being given his new passport: 'I think it is quite a serious day. It makes you feel welcome, it is an important landmark in my life.' Finally, rather stumblingly, all those present sang the National Anthem.

In France and Germany too, more is now being asked of immigrants who apply for naturalization. Nor is the new focus on citizenship confined to Europe. Australia, a classic country of immigration, is moving away from official multiculturalism. The period of residence after which migrants can become citizens has been extended from two to four years and a citizenship test is in place.

In America the idea of citizenship is far more ritualized. During a speech to a mass demonstration by illegal immigrants in Chicago in May 2006, Senator Barack Obama, as he then was, reminded the demonstrators in no uncertain terms of the rights and duties of American citizens. A few days later he summarized what he had said: 'When I spoke to folks at this rally I insisted that for those undocumented workers who hope some way to have a pathway to citizenship, they have to understand that citizenship involves a common language, a common faith in the country, common commitments and a common sense of purpose.'

As if that were not enough, he added firmly 'and fealty to a common flag', a reference to a controversy that had arisen over the fact that many of the demonstrators had been waving the flags of their own nations, in most cases Mexico. 'I think there are times in these marches where you have seen Mexican flags. I think that is not helpful because it indicates that somehow the traditional pattern of immigrants assimilating to a broader American culture is not what these marchers are seeking. I think they have to seek that because that is the essence of this country – that in diversity we come together as one.'

Europe has a different tradition and differences between nations remain, but in this sense too we can see lessons being learned from countries with longer histories of immigration. All this represents an important change in attitude: the emphasis used to lie on cultural differences, whereas now the main focus of concern is a person's ability to participate as a citizen. Freedom of choice is crucial. A sense of loyalty can never be imposed from above. In the end, migrants have to decide for themselves how to relate to the countries where in all likelihood they'll spend the rest of their lives. The established population must open its doors to their potential contribution, inviting and challenging newcomers to shoulder a shared responsibility.

Although steps are now being taken to make the meaning of citizenship more explicit, it's not yet possible to say that we're being presented with any particularly clear ideas on the subject. Is the new 'us' any broader than the old 'us'? Are we managing to create societies that reach across their current ethnic and religious divides, that strive towards a shared future rather than continually emphasizing differences in origin? Communities are changing and the ways they imagine themselves must change too – a challenging thought in a time when familiar faces and surnames are fast disappearing.

In many countries this has led to debates about what holds society together, such as discussions about French 'national identity', or about 'Britishness'. Contributions to the British debate make the discomfiture instantly visible, such as this from journalist Jeremy Paxman: 'I am fed up to the back teeth with middle-class, soi disant cultural commentators saying there is something contemptible about the idea of Britishness, or suggesting it is exclusively the preserve of thugs.'[6] Commentator Will Hutton has remarked with some scepticism: 'What will happen, I suspect, is that the British will carry on with their understated Britishness.'[7] Philosopher Roger Scruton, meanwhile, is less phlegmatic: 'If people don't have a social and individual identity, they have no way of identifying with their neighbours or anyone else. That way lies social chaos, which is a potentially violent place to be.'[8]

Attempts by the British and French governments to stimulate such debates have produced few results; in fact, they have done more to arouse suspicion than to inspire trust. The internal discord that characterizes an open society makes it undesirable to settle upon a clearly defined notion of national identity. A new idea of what it means to be French or British emerges when more and more people with a background in immigration make their voices heard in the media, sport, politics and literature. Their visibility has, above all, a symbolic significance. Issues that touch upon identity should be spoken of with some restraint in the political sphere, but, as we have seen, it is possible to conceive of citizenship rituals, and in schools more attention could be paid to history and law. The maintenance and handing down of the cultural heritage could be taken in hand with more vigour. At their best, such efforts are an invitation to citizens to develop outlooks that are both concerned and critical.

Debates about national identity have revealed uncertainty about how a society of immigrants might see itself. A commission led by political philosopher Bhikhu Parekh has suggested that Britain should be thought of as a 'community of communities', which, as he puts it, means attempting 'to combine the values of equality and diversity, liberty and solidarity'.[9] But the classical ideals of freedom and equality that constitute the core of an open society already involve a recognition of the diversity of beliefs and lifestyles. Furthermore, it is not accurate to describe society as a community of communities, and such an approach fosters the conservatism of group cultures, no matter how much Parekh wishes to avoid exactly that.

It's not easy to find your place in a society that's at odds with itself. Migrants are being asked to free themselves from group ties and concentrate on their independence as individuals, while at the same time the limits to individualism are under fresh scrutiny and there's a widespread feeling that after a one-sided defence of individual rights the emphasis should now lie on responsibilities towards society as a whole. In short, new currents are moving in different directions, muddying the waters.

The confusion takes many forms. Isn't an emphasis on integration ultimately a betrayal of liberal principles? If girls go out on the street and say, 'In a country of religious freedom we have the right to wear headscarves or veils whenever we like', then on what grounds could anyone contradict them? Yet people who live in an open society and opt for a closed community, using their freedom to embrace a lack of freedom, cross a line as soon as they interfere with the freedom of others. In practice, they soon will, and repeatedly. Is the preaching of tolerance for intolerance not a departure from the principle of equality?

Meanwhile, migrants are caught up in ambiguities of their own. They need to ask themselves why they left hearth and home. Why is it that the countries where they grew up are in such a bad way? Why has independence from colonial powers in so many cases led to more poverty and repression rather than less? And why have they decided to come to countries they used to condemn with such passion and in many cases still look upon with a combination of timorousness and distaste? Could there be something inviting about liberal cultures after all, something hugely attractive that no society in the world can ignore?

Migrants are too strongly influenced by their own hesitancy, even aversion. Of course many are completely taken up with the daily struggle, puzzling out how to survive in a strange country. Still, they could do more, not to speak of their children, who grew up with more opportunities than their parents. Moroccan-Dutch author Abdelkader Benali believes his compatriots need to look more closely at what 'being Dutch' means: 'It seems as if many non-natives here are silently waiting for that, so that at last they can feel properly and fully absorbed into Dutch society.'[10] But there's little point waiting quietly for a place to be allocated; migrants and their offspring must raise their voices. No one can do the talking for them.

Multiculturalism offered an answer that entailed no obligation, by saying that it had become meaningless to talk about 'us', since society was a collection of subcultures. Where this leaves citizenship is unclear. Without 'us', there can be no critical engagement, and society will disintegrate. That 'us' need not necessarily point to shared pride, but can equally well express vicarious shame. Surely it was a sign of progress when Haci Karacaer, spokesman for the North Holland branch of the Turkish Muslim organization Milli Görüs, said: 'We failed in Srebrenica.' By 'we' he meant the Dutch.

In these years of conflict in particular, it's important for migrants to make their voices heard. Dyab Abu Jahjah contradicts himself when he explicitly opts for a 'model of equality' and then abruptly goes on to say: 'There's virtually nothing we can do, since the immigrant population is oppressed by racism and discrimination.'[11] Within a single line of reasoning his perspective shifts from citizenship to victimhood. This won't do. Reciprocity presumes a shared desire to shape society, a shared willingness to be critical of the community to which you belong. In short, everyone's dirty washing must be hung out in public. There's no other way. Holding on to a sense of victimhood amounts to a rejection of freedom and responsibility.

A new 'us' is required. Urban residents old and new don't yet seem to have recognized this clearly enough, or at any rate they don't behave as if they have. We need to be more aware of our mutual dependence. This is more than a matter of pleasantries. The climate in many cities depends to a large extent on the way migrants and their children seize opportunities for the future. Their ambition is essential, but everyone must be receptive to the talents on offer. Institutions can and should be more open than they've been up to now. There's room for a great deal of change in schools, in media organizations, in the police service, everywhere – and still too few signs of it happening.

To what extent are members of the new middle class of migrants willing to engage with problems in their own communities? It's wholly understandable that a Moroccan or Pakistani doctor simply wants to be a good doctor, nothing more. Others in migrant communities regard attitudes among their own emerging middle class as a threat, criticizing what they see as too great a willingness to adjust to the 'white' majority. But even those who set themselves up as spokespeople for the communities to which they're presumed to belong and exercise some form of responsibility don't have an easy time of it. People all too readily reproach them for trading their integrity for political office.

Those able to articulate effectively the interests of their supporters while at the same time criticizing their own communities are of great value to society, as a city councillor in The Hague, Rabin Baldewsingh, made clear in a speech several years ago: 'The immigrant segment of the population of The Hague is not a homogenous community. What you see is that people can be forced to live next to each other but not to live with each other. There's no communality, no common history that binds them. People pitch their tents next to each other in the hope of eventually being able to settle somewhere else. There's no affinity with others in the same street.' For him this is reason enough to appeal for greater involvement in public affairs.[12]

British writer, former broadcaster and one-time mayoral candidate Trevor Phillips, who spent part of his childhood in Guyana, expressed similar concerns about growing segregation in Britain: 'In recent years we've focused far too much on the "multi" and not enough on the common culture. We've emphasized what divides us over what unites us. We have allowed tolerance of diversity to harden into the effective isolation of communities, in which some people think special separate values ought to apply.'[13] The receiving society is continually asked to measure itself against the norm of equality of treatment and therefore to oppose all forms of discrimination, but newcomers have a responsibility of their own: 'We are looking for migrants who have the ability to participate in our national life, and the willingness to interact with the rest of us.'

First there's a need to rescue the word 'us'. Many have rejected black-and-white thinking in terms of 'us' and 'them' and concluded that if we reject the idea of 'them' we must also dispense with 'us'. That seems logical perhaps, but in a democracy there's no other option. Without 'us', without an imagined community, there will be no shared responsibility for society's changing fortunes. That 'us' will have to expand to include today's newcomers, turning them into the established residents of tomorrow.

Everything of Value Must Defend Itself

Integration is often mentioned, but what it means remains rather vague. Let's try to describe it more precisely. When migrants and their children can say 'this country is mine too', everyone will have come a long way. Integration means acquiring a number of skills, but above all it's about a willingness to be part of society, and that inevitably means reassessing traditions brought from elsewhere. At the same time integration requires an environment in which migrants and their children feel invited to take part in social life. An open society must measure itself critically against its own standards of equal treatment. Integration forces both natives and newcomers to take a hard look at themselves.

We can discuss concepts like participation, emancipation and integration endlessly, but it would be better to reformulate the question that needs addressing. Where do people naturally come into contact with the society around them? By concentrating on socialization we can turn a discussion about immigration into a general social issue. Simply put, newcomers are initiated into society within the family, at school and in the workplace. There's another dimension that we won't include here: the neighbourhood. We've discussed that already at length and when it comes to integration it's not really the place to start.

We've looked in detail at what makes the experience of migration so extraordinary and how it brings to light more general problems. In many migrant communities access to society via the family, school and work has been blocked. Communication within families has broken down to such an extent as a result of migration that parents often have little notion of the world in which their children live. Despite all kinds of extra investment in education, many children of migrants drop out of school. Finally, high rates of unemployment among both parents and young people means the workplace cannot do enough to help them identify with their newly adopted countries.

All these broken connections create a gap between migrants and society, but behind specific problems in immigrant communities lie general social shortcomings. The only way forward is by consistently transforming the issue of integration into a question of citizenship that addresses everyone, regardless of background. True equality will lead to social renewal of a kind that goes further than debates about the position of migrants and their families.

To understand the meaning of citizenship we must look at the democratic advances of the past few decades. Citizens have become more articulate and independent and less trusting of traditional authority. This new assertiveness is valuable, but alongside its salutary effects it contains a potential for aggression: reliance on self-control is not always realistic. There has been an increase in violence in the public sphere, specifically against teachers, doctors, police officers, indeed all those directly involved in making it possible for everyone to live together. People still want to believe that freedoms will become more deeply rooted, but it seems freedom itself is being brought into disrepute amid calls for greater public safety. A famous line by Dutch poet Lucebert goes: 'Everything of value is defenceless.' Turning this on its head, we might say: 'Everything of value must defend itself.'

We're now in a position to make a broader assessment of the cultural transformation of the 1960s. The challenge to parental authority, criticisms of schools as institutions and the loosening of the work ethic have on the whole been beneficial, but everywhere people are seeking a new balance. It's clear that the significance of a more or less stable upbringing has been underestimated, that in schools the skills needed for citizenship have been neglected and that too many are without work and dependent on state support. As a result, the places where responsibility is learned – the family, the school and the workplace – are failing to fulfil that task.

Even 40 years ago there were those who believed that the liberation of the 1960s amounted to boundless individualism, and some claimed that the stress on personal development had degenerated into narcissism. In 1979, American sociologist Christopher Lash wrote in his well-known polemic about the self-serving society: 'The new narcissist is haunted not by guilt but by anxiety. He seeks not to inflict his own certainties on others but to find a meaning in life.'[14] A craving for personal fulfilment creates permanent restlessness: 'The poor have always had to live for the present, but now a desperate concern for personal survival, sometimes disguised as hedonism, engulfs the middle class as well.'[15]

The disintegration of hierarchies made room for personal authenticity and experimentation, previously the preserve of an artistic elite. Civic emancipation made democracy richer, but the drawback is that people increasingly make demands of their own while ignoring the needs of others. A society in which everyone tries to monopolize the conversation and fewer and fewer are willing to listen – why would anyone else know better? – hardens attitudes towards others that ultimately restricts the freedom of all.

Liberalism has great difficulty establishing where its boundaries lie. The sexual revolution brought not only freedom but also new forms of dependence. French author Michel Houllebecq has described in his novels the defenceless individualism that accompanies the untamed satisfaction of desires. In telling the story of one of his antiheroes he comments: 'As the lovely word "household" suggests, the couple and the family would be the last bastion of primitive communism in liberal society. The sexual revolution was to destroy these intermediary communities, the last to separate the individual from the market.'[16]

Even without succumbing to cultural pessimism, it's easy to discern the shadow side of a society increasingly dominated by market norms. The potential for constructive criticism inherent in many of the changes of the 1960s has been swallowed up by ever-expanding consumerism. To put it another way, individualization creates choice without necessarily giving people more control over their lives. Their relationship to public affairs has changed; the consumer can drive out the citizen in us.

We're now witnessing both responsible and irresponsible manifestations of individualism. French philosopher Gilles Lipovetsky draws attention to some of them: more effort to care for our bodies along with higher rates of drug addiction; a greater aversion to violence along with a trivialization of crime; more tax evasion along with increases in charitable donations; escalating debt and higher savings. He writes that while individualism is winning out everywhere, the cultural changes that have brought welcome emancipation have some clearly problematic aspects.[17]

There's no way back to the law-abiding society of the 1950s and before, nor should anyone wish there was, but it must be possible to talk in contemporary terms about duties. They don't detract from freedoms; they're part of what freedom is founded upon. We've noted that the right to freedom of speech, for instance, goes hand in hand with the duty to defend that freedom for others, but in the absence of an awareness of history this sense of reciprocity will be lost. Society can be defined as a 'contract between the generations'. Whether born in Europe, America or elsewhere, we all encounter a society created by the efforts of those who went before; each new generation succeeds to an inheritance and must continually re-evaluate that inheritance.

The search for a new balance between rights and responsibilities has inevitably been intensified by the scale of immigration over recent decades. Past migration flows, the results of early industrialization, inspired a civilizing offensive in Europe and America that placed the private lives of families under scrutiny. 'Antisocial families' were supervised by state employees. In the Netherlands these forerunners of today's social workers were initially called 'home inspectors', but whatever they were called, the paternalism was unmistakable, as was the aspiration to edify. In looking at the movement for the Americanization of immigrants we've seen how in the United States the desire to emancipate and the desire to discipline overlapped.

It should come as no surprise that in a time of renewed immigration the call for interference in problem families is being heard once more. Cultural sociologist Gabriël van den Brink appeals for a new 'civilizing offensive', not just to tackle the nuisance caused by troubled families but to hold out clear norms to all citizens. He stresses that after years of 'norm liberalization' in society, there's now a demand for 'norm restoration'.[18] Others speak of an 'educational offensive', but their intentions are much the same, amounting to a contemporary form of paternalism in the name of emancipation. By the nature of things, this is an enterprise riddled with contradictions.

A change of this kind to European and American societies is risky. Paul Frissen, an expert on public administration, writes that any attempt to achieve social coherence through government interference is not only outdated but will erode freedom. 'Moralizing is dangerous as a policy strategy by the state, which can deploy its monopolies.'[19] The state has means of coercion at its disposal, so restraint is required when it comes to moral and cultural preferences. He is worried. 'We know we've lost control and therefore we intensify the rituals that reinforce the myth of social engineering.'[20] Frissen favours an extension of the relatively relaxed attitude that was dominant in the 1960s. That feeling of invulnerability defined the social climate for decades, but nonchalance has come to grief. New forms of responsibility are needed, although they must not stifle the sense of personal autonomy. This is the context in which the debate about the integration of migrants is taking place.

British psychiatrist Theodore Dalrymple draws upon some of the more dramatic examples from his practice to show just how much the underclass has suffered as a result of the liberalization of norms: 'Day after day I hear of the same violence, the same neglect and abuse of children, the same broken relationships, the same victimization by crime, the same nihilism, the same dumb despair.'[21] Here again we see that the impact is widely felt, and not just by migrant families. Dalrymple concludes soberly 'that the majority of the British underclass is white, and that it demonstrates all the same social pathology as the black underclass in America'.[22]

Many migrants live in the same neighbourhoods as the underclass and experience the invitation to integrate as a call to adjust downwards. Sensibly enough, they try to keep their distance. As Dalrymple comments: 'I can quite understand that what they see only reinforces their determination to live according to their own beliefs, and that they do not want their children to become like that underclass.'[23] This survival strategy offers a temporary solution in a difficult environment, but in the long run it's not the answer for children who have to make their way in society.

Ultimately this is not just a matter of an underclass; the middle classes too are uncertain about what prospects to hold out to their children. It's all too easy to blame liberal approaches to childrearing over the past few decades. The decline in parental authority has undoubtedly revealed a great deal of hidden misery in families – think of child abuse – but it's equally clear that the increasing number of one-parent families has produced many children with serious problems. A cautious re-evaluation of the family is now under way and it's here that efforts to achieve social integration must begin. Later we'll look at the importance of education and work to successful socialization.

A Triptych of Integration

Starting a family is above all a decision for the parents-to-be, but at the same time their choice has an impact on society. Demographer Franz-Xaver Kaufmann has written a convincing plea for the raising of children within families to be seen as an investment in human capacity. He is writing about the German situation, which in many ways is ahead of developments in other European countries, since the birth rate is falling dramatically, a fact still obscured to some extent by immigration and a decline in mortality. The average age of Germans has steadily increased.

The problem is not that there are too many older people, but that too few children are being born. This might be described as a breach of the contract between generations, since who will support and care for the elderly? According to Kaufmann, the sharply declining number of children means too little is being invested in human capital. This affects more than just the balance of the workforce, so he prefers to speak of 'human capacity'. Future generations are not merely an economic asset; they are the citizens and parents of the coming decades.[24]

In the richer nations of the world, having children is not, as it once was, a direct investment in your own future, rather it's an indirect investment in the future of all. Children no longer contribute to their parents' livelihood, partly because child labour has been abolished. In an economic sense it's not even particularly rational to have children these days. There is collective provision for those who no longer work, whereas the costs for those not yet in work are covered largely by private citizens. The parents pay. The childless profit from other people's childrearing efforts without contributing a great deal themselves. In a time when so few children are being born and the population is likely to shrink, the family should be valued more.

There are different ways of bringing up children, but the costs of failed or problematic socialization are all too clear. A change in family culture is taking place. Typical of the modern family is a high degree of independence among children, equality between men and women, and minimal interference from relatives in the choice of a partner. De Swaan has described this as a transition from a 'household by writ' to a 'household by negotiation'.[25] It's clear that most migrants from countries like Turkey or Pakistan still rely on an authoritarian style of childrearing. There's therefore a considerable gap between the more traditional family relationships of many migrant families and the modern lifestyles that prevail in most indigenous families. These cultural contrasts affect upbringing, as we have seen. Norms at home, on the street and in school may differ hugely, and in many migrant families this creates a generation gap that's hard to bridge.

The problems involved in raising children in a foreign country mean that immigration offers only a partial answer to the dilemmas raised by the increasing proportion of elderly people. A shrinking population must revise its ideas about the family. The question of how to encourage people to have children, the offspring of migrants included, is fairly urgent. For a long time a decline in the number of children has been seen as a natural phenomenon. Population politics was brought into disrepute in the twentieth century. And not without good reason, of course. Attitudes are slowly changing as the awareness grows that a population that cannot replace itself is less able to renew itself. There's a legitimate concern that the ageing of the population will produce a more inward-looking and fearful society. Surely the central concern should be social quality, not demographic quantity. Kaufmann calls for measures such as a change to the tax system so that resources are redistributed from childless adults to parents: 'Those who don't bring up children don't invest in human capacity for the future and therefore their own care in old age.'[26]

So the debate about immigration and integration throws a new light on the family. The same goes for another institution: school. Past emancipation movements were always concerned about material and intellectual progress. Education was central to such efforts, and understandably so, since in an open society the government is better placed to shape education than anything else. The state can have a more powerful influence there than in either the family, which after all largely belongs to the private sphere, or the workplace, which is affected mainly by the workings of the market.

As well as passing on knowledge and skills relevant to later working practices, education aspires to promote citizenship. The social questions surrounding migrants and their children have given new weight to this aspect of emancipation. That became clear at the point when newcomers ceased to be seen, and to see themselves, as a transient presence. Citizenship is about feeling responsible for the wider social environment, about taking account of people outside your immediate family, and this kind of fellow feeling is of great significance for all children as they grow up.

It's important to ensure that such initiatives fall under the heading of 'freedom of thought' rather than, as the report *The Future of Multi-Ethnic Britain* recommends, 'multicultural and antiracist education'. Schooling should be a matter of opening horizons, not imposing a worldview. So talk about 'skills of deliberation', or knowledge of 'human rights principles' and 'equality legislation' can be defended, but if the moulding of citizens boils down to 'opposition to racist beliefs', as advocated in the report, then it quickly crosses a line, especially in combination with a plea for a multicultural view of society.[27] The boundary between stimulating critical citizenship and intellectual paternalism is all too easily crossed.

A number of countries are considering introducing community internships as part of a child's education. Now that conscription has been abolished more or less everywhere – the army too contributed to social integration – some form of community service might not be a bad idea. In the Netherlands new legislation obliges schoolchildren to work for a number of weeks in public organizations, in hospitals, for example, or nursing homes for the elderly. In view of the aging of the population and the resulting shortages of manpower in many parts of the service sector, extra hands might help. It's also worth considering how schoolchildren could become involved in efforts to help migrants integrate. The children would learn more about a fast-changing urban society and immigrants would come into contact with their new environment more quickly.

A sense of responsibility is not at all the same as an uncritical acceptance of things as they are. In fact an open society depends on the ability of citizens to think independently and judge for themselves. Nevertheless, meaningful differences of opinion rely upon mutual engagement, which in turn requires that more attention be paid to culture and history in education. Citizenship is all about a consciousness that something came before us and something will come after us. A society that regards itself as no longer capable of engaging with earlier generations is in a state of decline.

The creation of a canon is one way to present history in schools. As philosopher Maarten Doorman writes: 'Not the principle of the canon but its content should be the focus of debate. The fact that along with its content cultural values are up for discussion is all to the good, since this underlines the fact that a canon provides the context for an unavoidable debate about identity and diversity.'[28] Such calls have been heeded, leading to the formulation of 50 key events in Dutch history that all school-aged children should know about. We see similar initiatives all over Europe. Denmark, for example, now has a literary canon.

After a fierce debate, the Netherlands has decided to create its own National Historical Museum. There was no shortage of objections, based mainly on a fear that any such institution would become a temple to national pride. That certainly need not be the case. It's a matter of delving into the past as a means of self-examination, not self-glorification. Slavery is part of the Dutch canon. It's important to resist the temptation to sweep away the less appealing aspects of the past, as was in danger of happening in France in 2005 when the Assemblée nationale attempted to pass a law stating that the 'positive work' accomplished in the colonial period must be emphasized in schools. After countless protests the act was withdrawn. In their report, Bhikhu Parekh and his colleagues show a greater sense of reality in their take on the British Empire: 'There has been no collective working through of this imperial experience.'[29]

Citizens should know about the high and low points of national history and all the mediocrity in between. It makes no sense to present the past as a story of gradual progress towards freedom for all – it's of course far more complicated than that. History offers no simple truths and few certainties, but this is no reason to regard the past as a closed chapter and focus purely on the future. The Dutch have done exactly that with gay abandon over past decades, but now they're beginning to realize that culture depends not just on creativity but on continuity as well.

In France too, opinions differ starkly on this point, as demonstrated for example by a debate between philosophers Alain Finkielkraut and Alain Badiou. Finkielkraut is concerned about the handing down of culture: 'As for our heritage, over the past forty years schools have worked with a passion to erode it. More and more French people, the elite included, are now strangers to their language, their literature, their history, their landscape.' Badiou, by contrast, sees an increasing emphasis on heritage and identity as a significant threat to an open society: 'The public debate is currently taking place in between two disastrous positions: on one side the free market consensus and universal commercialism, and on the other frenetic attempts to hold on to an identity, which constitutes a reactionary barrage against globalization and in the end is totally ineffective.'[30]

It is possible to reach beyond this antithesis, since there are plenty of ways of combining heritage and openness without denying the tension between them. No matter how troubling, it ought to go without saying that the history of the arrival and settlement of migrants should feature in any national museum. There are plenty of examples that can serve as inspiration. Take the national museum in Canberra, which didn't shy away from the difficult subject of the original inhabitants of Australia, the Aboriginals, and their tragic history. A museum that recently opened in France, with the inviting slogan 'Their history is our history', is devoted entirely to the history of migrants. Everyone immediately notices the ambiguity of that publicity slogan, which could be understood as a kind of expropriation, and it will prompt a great deal of debate yet, as was clearly the intention. Knowledge of the past is a precondition of a lively culture of citizenship.

Finally, along with the family and school, work is an important domain through which people become involved in society; in fact it may be the quickest route to social integration. Low levels of participation in work among migrants are forcing a reconsideration of state involvement in support for the unemployed, but this should not affect immigrants alone. There's a far wider problem here: the welfare state has trapped many people in positions of dependency and become an obstacle to their social advancement.

Over past decades there has been much cultural criticism of the welfare state, the main target being freedom without responsibility. Dalrymple paints a grim picture of the British social security system as seen through the eyes of a group of visiting Filipino doctors. At first they are full of praise, but gradually the picture starts to shift: 'They see it now as creating a miasma of subsidized apathy that blights the lives of its supposed beneficiaries. They come to realize that a system of welfare that makes no moral judgements in allocating economic rewards promotes antisocial egotism.'[31]

We see the same problem on a larger scale in the migrant communities of continental Europe. Economist Arie van der Zwan has pointed out that jobs in industry offered a 'schooling in modernity'.[32] Tragically, a generation of guest workers was cut off from work by the economic crisis of the early 1970s. In receipt of generous unemployment benefits, migrants were placed on the sidelines and ended up in permanent isolation. The effects can be seen in subsequent generations: 'For two thirds of these population groups the chances of integration are poor. They cannot keep up at school and they occupy the lowest positions in the jobs market.'[33] As far as the chances for migrants in the labour market goes, it's clear that something is wrong with Europe's welfare states. There's little solidarity between natives and newcomers. Researchers have reached the same conclusion: 'The bridging of differences along ethnic lines is undoubtedly the main task.'[34]

Reforms are needed that do not involve unequal treatment, unlike proposals to disqualify immigrants from receiving social welfare payments. In America in the mid-1990s limits were placed on access by newcomers to state support of all kinds. Social provision in the United States is far from bountiful compared to Western Europe, but it seems it was still felt to be too generous towards new arrivals. There are sporadic appeals for similar measures to be introduced in Europe, but it would be far better to implement initiatives across the board aimed at reducing dependence on state aid. The social benefits system needs to be remodelled so that it no longer stands in the way of participation in the workplace. It's beyond dispute that the protection of those in need, a norm of a decent society, has slowly but steadily pushed people into subsidized isolation. Ayaan Hirsi Ali has remarked that for migrants 'to survive it is not absolutely necessary for them to adapt to [the receiving] society. The process of modernization can thus grind to a halt in a welfare situation, where people on the margins of society go on clinging to values that stand in the way of their own emancipation.'[35]

That insight has gained ground. Over the past few years we've seen a slow reversal of the tendency to hand out welfare payments too readily, along with a move towards a greater emphasis on participation in paid work. The specific problem of high unemployment among young people from migrant families should be cause for broader self-examination. We may well wonder why someone who has never worked should have an automatic right to welfare. In this respect there's no difference between migrants and school leavers. Both are newcomers in the market for jobs. The call for immigrants to be made ineligible for unemployment benefits during the first five years of their stay in their new countries must be countered with proposals for a universal requirement to build up rights through work before qualifying for financial support. Young people in the Netherlands can in theory no longer resort to welfare until they reach the age of 27. They have a choice between work and education or training.

One study has identified four functions of the welfare state, concluding: 'It's time for a shift in attention from the functions of insuring and caring to the functions of uplifting and connecting.'[36] This opens up a route towards reconciling economic competitiveness and social justice, since all studies show that countries with strong welfare states do well in today's competitive world economy. External economic pressure is not the most important reason to reform the welfare state; a normative concept of citizenship represents a more pressing motive for trying to introduce change.

A working life is a route to social acceptance. In the specific case of migrants, their visible contribution to the economic well-being of society as a whole helps enormously in justifying their presence. Without it not only do ethnic conflicts threaten, the opportunities for migrants and their children to climb the social ladder are blocked. A decades-old shortcoming of the welfare state has been brought to light in a new way.

Dilemmas of Equal Treatment

It's clear that general social issues lie behind the problems that result from migration. The only way to achieve a good outcome is by remaining true to the principle of all integration: reciprocity on the basis of equal treatment. The American Declaration of Independence begins: 'All men are created equal.' The Dutch constitution says the same thing in a slightly different way: 'All those who find themselves in the Netherlands will in equal cases be treated equally.' Article one of the French constitution begins: 'France shall be an indivisible, secular, democratic and social Republic. It shall ensure the equality of all citizens before the law, without distinction of origin, race or religion.'

In all democratic countries the constitutional principle of equality is carved in stone. Yet just look at the effort needed to live up to it. We've come upon all too many cases of discrimination based on race and religion. Equality turns out to be far from simple to enforce. There's a need to contemplate this constitutional principle afresh and to ask whether as an ideal it requires a government that forgoes moral judgement. Then we'll touch on the issue of positive discrimination and finally devote some thought to the language used to describe immigrant populations, terms originally introduced with preferential treatment for migrants and their children in mind.

Let's first examine the question of whether the principle of equality presupposes moral neutrality. Equality can be understood in two different ways, and neither is necessarily an extension of the other. First there's the legal interpretation. Within the bounds of the law everyone is free to live according to his or her own beliefs and chosen lifestyle. Restraint of conscience has no place in a liberal society, so citizens are at liberty, for example, to adhere to conservative ideas about women, seeing them as subordinates, or to condemn homosexuality as a perversion. People must be given the opportunity to shape their own private lives as they see fit, even if in doing so they depart from what the majority regards as desirable, just as long as they don't restrict the freedom of others.

Then there's the normative interpretation. In the public arena the authorities must propagate a standard of equality that goes further than strict implementation of the law. We can therefore defend government efforts to encourage girls to continue to study after they pass the school leaving age and to live independent lives, even if this conflicts with a traditional interpretation of their role. Governments must also try to foster understanding for homosexuality as a choice in love, even though it's offensive to many traditional believers. This is a question of emancipation, something that must never be imposed as an obligation but can certainly be promoted by governments.

A strictly legalistic interpretation of the principle of equality for all may well clash with a more normative one. In a constitutional state people can't be prevented from withdrawing into authoritarian communities, whether grounded in a secular or a religious worldview. In a general sense there should be no attempt to ban manifestations of religious fervour such as the veil or indeed any other expression of dogmatic beliefs, as long as they don't violate the principles of the constitutional state. Thinking is free, and in principle we should all be free to say what we think.

Freedom of expression is essential, and it's odd to see how often its defenders are tempted to deny that same freedom to religious movements of an orthodox kind. Adherents of fundamentalist faiths, whether Christian, Jewish or Islamic, have a right to hold their own opinions and to propagate them in an open society, within certain legal limits. Appeals for an expurgated version of the Koran are as nonsensical as appeals to give the Koran more protection against its critics by means of blasphemy laws. Freedom of religion and criticism of religion are two sides of the same coin.

This does not mean that governments must leave all options open. A society is held together by more than its legislative principles alone. Social intercourse relies on reciprocity, which cannot be forced. Governments must therefore disseminate it as a norm. The emancipation of women is a recent achievement in many societies and some people wrongly conclude that they are therefore in no position to hold out these norms as an example to others. This reasoning must be turned on its head. Precisely because equality was so difficult to achieve, it remains a fragile norm that needs to be defended, and the rights of women in migrant families are no exception.

Necla Kelek describes the vexed relationship between men and women by telling the story of her own family, which emigrated to Germany from Turkey. Her mother barely had any independent existence at all; from morning to night everything was decided by her mother-in-law and no one ever asked her what she might be planning to do with her life. That attitude was passed on by the mother to the daughters, who were expected above all to be compliant: 'Not that the daughter learns something but that she makes a good impression on the other women. What matters to them is that she shows herself to be docile, dexterous and polite.'[37] On what grounds would anyone criticize such an attitude based on the concept 'each to his own'? Should a government, in the name of neutrality, refuse to pass judgement on a family culture of this kind, when growing girls are manifestly suffering as a result?

Take the case of parents who don't want their children to participate in mixed swimming lessons. Many schools try to keep the peace by giving in to the wishes of the parents. Yet there's a great deal to be said for taking a stand, certainly in state schools, which really ought to hold on to some basic rules of equality of treatment and not bow to attempts to separate boys and girls, even though that was relatively common half a century ago. The new norms are indeed rather different from the generally accepted ideas of earlier times, but no good arguments have been presented in favour of what's generally felt to be a policy of surrendering equality for the sake of apparent neutrality. If parents opt for faith schools in order to make their preferences a reality, we will simply have to accept their choice. This, incidentally, is one more reason to query the notion of access to publicly funded faith schools as a constitutional right.

The more normative concept of equality has a broader reach than its legal formulation, and in any case legislation is often the product of implicit beliefs. When the Moroccan government urged the Dutch government to lower the age at which people could marry to 15, it suddenly became clear that a whole world of ideas lies behind the age limit of 18 that now applies in the Netherlands – specifically the belief that children must acquire a certain maturity, and therefore resilience, before they're able to make an independent choice of marriage partner. We could say the same about the school leaving age of 16. It's a manifestation of ideas about the importance of education for boys and for girls. These are beliefs that other cultures aren't necessarily obliged to share.

Equality of treatment is controversial in another sense too. Everyone agrees that holding on to equality as a norm is the most effective defence against prejudice, but opinions about the ways in which discrimination can best be combated are extremely diverse. Dilemmas have emerged in the battle surrounding positive discrimination. Seeking sanctuary in forms of what the Americans call affirmative action has a serious downside in that it's a departure from the principle of equality. Special preference is given to groups, whereas equality relates to individuals. When students from the black community with lower grades than rival applicants are admitted to good universities, their origins become the deciding factor. Although there is something to be said for affirmative action in the case of America's black population, which endured slavery for many years followed by forced segregation, it's not easy to justify the extension of the idea to migrant groups that do not need to be compensated for any kind of historical injustice.

This is not to say that job-seekers with the same training and capacities always receive equal treatment. Studies of job applications have shown that replacing an Arabic name with a European one makes a difference to the way a letter is handled. Even in economic boom times it's possible to point to forms of exclusion from the world of work. Saïda Sakali, a civil servant at a Flemish ministry, writes: 'We, the second and third generation, were for many years promised a different future. As long as we studied hard, we would get there. Participation in the jobs market would be a logical consequence. We were fed a fairy tale. The future we've ended up in looks very different. In one out of every three vacancies an applicant from a migrant community is treated differently. Subjective and irrational mechanisms are at work here, forms of discrimination large and small.'[38]

For as long as this reproach is justified, it will be hard to speak of full citizenship. Put like this, however, is it really an accurate observation? Some people avoid others in their daily lives based on well-founded generalizations that can nevertheless be unfair to individual members of a group. If criminality in the black community is high, then the reluctance of taxi drivers to pick up black compatriots may be justified, certainly in neighbourhoods with bad reputations, even though such attitudes may be exceptionally hurtful to respectable citizens. Why should a shopkeeper or business manager take on a young person from a migrant community with a poor reputation, thereby deliberately running a greater than average risk that the placement will not work out?

Yet even with this reservation in mind, there are plenty of examples of discrimination in the jobs market that are indeed 'irrational'. The costs of discrimination, both where it exists and where it's presumed to exist, can be high. The sense of alienation in society increases and rare talent is lost. Quite apart from the fact that there are compelling moral reasons to combat discrimination, enlightened self-interest comes into play. As ever it's better if people embrace such insights voluntarily, since there will then be no need to use official quotas to try to force people to change their behaviour or their opinions.

It was the free-market liberal Dutch politician Frits Bolkestein, of all people – ahead of his time in the 1990s in speaking openly about problems of integration – who pointed out to the business community that it had certain responsibilities in this field: 'Perhaps they would like to remember how this problem arose in the first place. Exactly. Employers imported labour in the 1960s (and were helped in doing so by an unbelievably short-sighted government).'[39] The history of guest workers at the very least obliges employers to treat job applicants from migrant communities fairly, he told them.

An emphasis on equality brings something else to the fore, namely a reconsideration of categories such as established and outsider, native and foreign. People continually stumble over the problem of which words to use. Majority and minority, natives and newcomers, the multicultural or multiethnic society – the variety of words used to describe the experience of migration illustrates the uncertainty that arises from the profound social changes it brings. Anthropologist Margaret Mead once suggested that in talking about ethnic or religious groups it's best to do so in adjectives rather than nouns. Indeed, it makes a difference whether you speak about a Pakistani or a Pakistani schoolboy, and calling someone a Jew is not the same as calling him a Jewish shopkeeper.

This goes only a little way towards solving the problem of language, however. The words used by governments are important, since vested interests are attached to the categories selected. Many new words have been introduced into European languages, with the best of intentions. In the 1980s the Dutch settled upon the neologisms 'autochthon' (*autochtoon*) and 'allochthon' (*allochtoon*) as a means of avoiding the term 'foreigner' when referring to first- or second-generation migrants. These relatively neutral monikers are still in everyday use, but they're no longer uncontroversial, mainly because the reality behind them has become a matter of dispute. The division of a population into two parts, such that the descendants of migrants are described as *allochtonen*, is problematic. Generations of people are placed in a category that becomes less specific by the day. Splitting society in two makes communication between different groups all the more awkward. Words introduced to ease discomfort have themselves become a source of discomfort.

Sevtap Baycili, a Dutch writer of Turkish origin, points out that words create their own reality: 'Young Moroccans and Turks who speak the language perfectly, even those who have Dutch nationality, are regarded not as Dutch but as *allochtonen*. It'll be another generation and more before people learn to see beyond that.'[40] We don't have that much time. More impatience is needed. There's no avoiding it: the words must be reassessed. It's sad to hear some migrants say that they don't want their children to grow up in the Netherlands because they'll be trapped in an existence as *allochtonen*. In other words they'll always be outsiders.

The Netherlands is not the only country where great uncertainty exists about the terms that can best be used to refer to migrants and their children. Take the British obsession with colour or race. Countless recent studies speak of the rise of 'multiracial' Britain, but surely the use of that term is a late echo of a time people want to leave behind them, namely a time when Caribbean or Asian immigrants were consistently referred to as 'coloured migrants'? The British seem trapped in an imperial era when racial differences were at the centre of an entire worldview.

In Australia the long-winded 'non-English-speaking background' (NESB) was in use for some years, despite criticism that it placed undue emphasis on language. Now the no less artificial term 'culturally and linguistically diverse' (CALD) has been introduced. Canadians talk of 'visible minorities', again with the best of intentions, but the term seems to denote a remarkable emphasis on colour, or racial difference. In America 'foreign-born' is a common description and France still uses the word '*étranger*', meaning foreigner or, indeed, stranger. In fact, wherever immigration is controversial, the words too are controversial, as they reveal differences while at the same time obscuring similarities. There's really no way to avoid this, since every bureaucratic classification bends the truth to fit.

But why do these classifications exist at all? The paradox is that the fiercest critics of the terms used still want to hold on to the material advantages that bureaucratic categorization brings with it. Does this mean the distinctions aren't valid but the 'positive' discrimination based on them is? Dinesh D'Souza points to the perverse results seen in America. In the heyday of racism the so-called 'one drop rule' applied. Anyone with a single black ancestor was categorized as part of the Negro population; a drop of 'black' blood was enough to get you registered as a black person. Now it's the black organizations themselves who want to hold on to this rule, since the more blacks there are in the ten-yearly census, the greater the flow of subsidy money.[41]

Our words of discomfort are themselves a problem. Their imprecise designations have an impact on society. In this book I've mainly stuck to the term 'migrants and their children'. That seems a good description of the individuals concerned. Alternatives like 'ethnic minority' appear occasionally, but I use them with some reluctance. All too often we talk about a majority and a minority. Shared citizenship ought to be an ideal that everyone can measure himself or herself against. It's better to use words that point forwards, that contain expectations, rather than words that make ballast out of the past. This will help us to break away from prejudices that support and reinforce one another.

Accommodation will not be easy, since letting go of established certainties causes pain all round. It's easier not to ask questions and simply to leave one another alone. The conservative idea of 'each to his own' has failed us. Its main effect now is to reinforce social inequality, whereas what everyone is after is equal treatment. Progress in that direction will shake society up, because taking equality seriously as a principle means asking a great deal of everyone, certainly in a time of mass immigration. Here too, reciprocity is key. Anyone wanting to challenge discrimination against migrants and their children must be prepared to oppose other forms of discrimination too – against unbelievers or homosexuals, for example. We can't demand equal treatment for some but not for all. With this attitude in mind we begin to see the outlines of a society in which people with diverse religious and ethnic backgrounds realize that for all their independence they nevertheless rely on one another.

Tomorrow's Immigrants

Any attempt to integrate newcomers depends on making clear choices when it comes to immigration. Equality inside a country's borders is in many ways predicated upon inequality *at* its borders. Some people find this contradiction unacceptable and resolve it by appealing for immigration controls to be dropped. What they're really saying is that parts of the third world are settling into the first world, which is good for the third world. Anyone championing such a view is in effect claiming that the poverty, illiteracy and traditionalism that accompany mass migration from the poorer regions of the world will inevitably raise their heads more and more frequently in Western societies. Those who oppose a complete opening up of borders do so because they want to go on defending a specific ideal of civilization, which has equality at its heart. Not everyone who wants to can come in.

However understandable the motives of those trying to escape misery in their own countries may be, in the end the needs of the countries they arrive in are decisive as far as labour migration is concerned. Allowing some migrants access because their skills are needed while denying entry to others may be seen as discriminatory. Applicants for refugee status need to fit into certain categories as well. This is inevitable. Any asylum policy would be meaningless otherwise. One story of exile is acknowledged as valid whereas another falls outside the rules. A woman who has suffered for many years as a victim of sexual violence is not allowed into the country, since asylum legislation doesn't cover a case like hers, whereas an accomplice of the old communist regime in Afghanistan is accepted as a political refugee.

Another dividing line exists between people with official permission to stay and illegal residents. There have been suggestions that the distinction between legals and illegals should be abolished as far as possible, but this would mean failing to respect the law as it stands. If someone has been denied a residence permit, then all reasonable measures should be deployed to get him or her to leave. This isn't the same as proposing to bar the children of illegals from education or to exclude illegal residents from medical care, since that would conflict with humanitarian principles. Being illegal is certainly not the same as having no rights. Many countries turn a blind eye to illegal immigrants, not for reasons of principle but simply to oblige the business community. Backstreet clothing factories are one example, as are the labourers we commonly see in market gardening. Businesses that are not economically viable are kept going by people who have no rights. There's nothing charitable about this.

Migrants who hold the nationality of the country in which they now live have a different status from those who have merely been given residence permits. Over recent decades we've seen moves almost everywhere designed to make the difference as small as possible. In some countries, like Sweden and the Netherlands, those legally resident for five years are allowed to vote in local council elections. More recently, there have been moves in the opposite direction, with a renewed emphasis on the significance of state citizenship as a route to full participation, involving rights and duties that have grown up over the centuries. Naturalization is a major step, now rightly marked by some form of ceremony.

This does not exclude the possibility of dual nationality, since different nationalities can be combined in a single human life, the most obvious example being mixed marriage. There are plenty of immigrants who have more than one nationality and who dedicate themselves to public service, or even demonstrate that they identify with their new country by serving in its armed forces. Their legal position may be complicated, but their commitment is none the less for that. The conflation by some of nationality and loyalty, in other words the suspicion that people with dual nationality cannot ever be loyal to their new country, leads nowhere except to resentment.

Clear choices need to be made about which immigrants to allow in; selectivity is essential to successful integration. This idea was resisted for many years, with integration and immigration treated as separate issues. In our examination of American and European immigration history we've seen that policy in the more distant past made a connection between the two. It's often said, without any egregious intent, that national governments have no real control over worldwide migration flows. We've explored at length the inaccuracy of this assertion in a descriptive sense. Governments certainly do have an influence. In a normative sense the argument that migration is beyond governmental control has had a whole range of unintended consequences. Anyone wanting to foster openness needs to think in terms of balanced immigration.

There is no escaping the question of what kind of immigration is actually needed. Based on research, arguments have been advanced for the selection of better educated or skilled immigrants: 'In any case it is clear that if labour migration were to consist primarily of immigration by the uneducated or poorly educated, then the position of uneducated and low-skilled people who are already here would worsen.'[42] Advocates of unrestricted migration are ignoring the relatively high unemployment rate among migrants and their children, and the potential reserves of low-skilled workers in the new countries of the European Union, such as Poland and in the longer term perhaps Turkey. Here is another clear indication that issues surrounding immigration and integration confront society with more general shortcomings.

Treating labour migration as the only way to counteract population shrinkage or to get around a lack of participation in the workplace by the low skilled is unwise. It would be better to resolve the shortages in the labour market as far as possible before opting for the line of least resistance, which anyhow in the long run turns out to be the line that arouses the greatest resistance of all. Nevertheless, labour migration may well be part of the solution. Estimates suggest that if the developed world receives a net average of 2.3 million immigrants a year, then the predicted decline in the working population will be roughly halved, meaning it will fall by around 10 per cent by 2050.[43]

At the moment the classic countries of immigration are absorbing the majority of their new migrants from Asia, while in Europe many newcomers arrive from Africa and the Middle East. European countries have a number of valid reasons to promote immigration from Asian countries, given that they accept the need for immigrants. Rapid economic development in South and East Asia makes the arrival of students and other bearers of cultural capital all the more desirable, since they will strengthen economic ties between Europe and countries such as China and India. In the information technology sector, global networks like the Indus Entrepreneur are emerging, and they may be of huge significance in the future. In the competition to attract highly educated migrants, Europe needs to make up lost ground, since it's currently lagging behind the rest of the developed world.

The sheer diversity of the migrant groups that have settled in America over past centuries is instructive. As we have seen, first to arrive were the Irish and Germans, followed by the Italians and Poles, and in our own time the larger immigrant groups have included Koreans and Mexicans. Some commentators conclude that this fluctuation has aided the gradual development of a 'nation of immigrants'. Extensive and continual immigration from a single country or region has a strong impact on the relationship between generations. As Douglas Massey puts it: 'The character of ethnicity will be determined relatively more by immigrants and relatively less by later generations, shifting the balance of ethnic identity toward the language, culture, and ways of life in the sending society.'[44] It's felt to be better if a single migrant group does not remain dominant for too long, which is another reason why European countries should draw lessons from positive developments in America and try to encourage migration from the countries of the Far East that are in the ascendant.

These choices are based on a rejection of the idea that receiving societies have a humanitarian duty to permit labour migration from the developing world. It's not sensible to be guided by both workforce requirements and developmental issues at the same time. Yet we see this happening time and again. Practical arguments merge with deeply held convictions in a way that's often impossible to fathom. Philippe Legrain's book ends with a cry from the heart of 'Let Them In'. He's hoping for a marriage of convenience between adherents of the free market and advocates of developmental cooperation. In itself this is less strange than it might seem, since globalization is making traditional political dividing lines increasingly irrelevant, in the debate on migration at least. Yet the need for compliant low-skilled workers does not sit easily with humanitarian arguments for a more open attitude on the part of the North towards the South.

Despite the problematic history of guest workers, there are now renewed appeals for the hiring of low-skilled workers from outside the European Union. The language has changed – its advocates now talk about seasonal or cyclical migration – but the intentions are the same as they were almost half a century ago. Whether such schemes are more realistic now than when the first guest workers arrived is doubtful. True, more stringent measures could be put in place to ensure they go back – such as a rule that a proportion of their salaries can be paid only after they return home – but an interest in staying will often weigh more heavily. The degree to which migrants put down roots in a society and start their own family histories within it, making their return an illusion, is still underestimated.

The reduction of the migrant to his labour – which may result in a decision to allow temporary migration but not permanent settlement – demonstrates the one-sided nature of the economic approach. Those who take the risk of leaving their countries will often want to settle in their new homelands and it's better to take this into account from the start. Labour migrants are more than simply workers, they're also fathers, husbands and, the hope is, citizens. The many questions raised by the need to integrate them into society make the appeal for open borders far more than a calculation of economic profit and loss.

Timothy Hatton and Jeffrey Williamson are sceptical about arguments for seasonal migration: 'Temporary immigration programs may be the worst of both worlds: they discourage the immigrant's acquisition of human capital during the period when his or her immigrant status is temporary (or at least uncertain), and they end up as gateways to permanent migration for those who might not have been admitted had their permanent status been anticipated from the start.'[45] So instead of opting for a new influx of guest workers, developed nations should admit well-educated migrants. Economists like Hatton and Williamson ultimately conclude that countries allowing in low-skilled migrants 'get immigrants who assimilate more slowly, crowd out more unskilled natives, placing a greater burden on the welfare state'.[46]

Despite these reservations, we can conclude that migration is here to stay. Demographic projections for European countries such as France and Germany show that by mid-century up to perhaps a third of their populations may consist of migrants and their descendants. This is a dramatic change, which in itself makes a transparent immigration policy essential. It would be worthwhile to hold annual parliamentary debates about the situation surrounding immigration and population developments as a whole, since citizens must be in a position to understand decisions about the nature and extent of immigration. This would help to justify future immigration and therefore contribute to public acceptance of the profound demographic changes that result.

Accepting What We Have Become

The arrival of so many migrants presents a huge opportunity for social renewal. An opportunity, no more and no less. There is nothing automatic about it, but societies that absorb migrants successfully are in a position to open up new routes to the rest of the world from which everyone can benefit. America has proven that a society with many newcomers can create and sustain a vigorous economy and culture. The price of that dynamism has meanwhile become clear to all: great social inequality and deep cultural divides.

There is plenty that makes the American experience unique, yet it turns out to have more in common with that of post-war Europe than Europeans are inclined to think. So often as I read and travel I have thought: see, all this was happening over there already. America teaches us that immigration doesn't necessarily lead to a loss of power in the world. Quite the opposite, in fact. It's no exaggeration to say that the United States is the Rome of our day, with all the symptoms of hubris such a status entails. The dynamism of that country is closely connected to its ability to integrate people of extremely diverse backgrounds. It demonstrates the power of a shared idea about what it means to be an American.

This process was and is accompanied by deep crises. The Civil Rights Movement reminded American society so starkly of its own principles that it remains a source of inspiration to this day. Author James Baldwin wrote with conviction: 'We, the black and the white, deeply need each other here if we are really to become a nation – if we are really, that is, to achieve our identity, our maturity, as men and woman. To create one nation has proved to be a hideously difficult task; there is certainly no need now to create two, one black and one white.'[47] Nevertheless, he believed the maturing of America required a leap of imagination by the whites: 'What it comes to is that if we, who can scarcely be considered a white nation, persist in thinking of ourselves as one, we condemn ourselves ... to sterility and decay, whereas if we could accept ourselves *as we are*, we might bring new life to Western achievements, and transform them.'[48]

The self-description 'a nation of immigrants' conceals a complex reality in which borders have been sometimes open and sometimes closed to newcomers. Recent immigration from developing countries is causing concerns in America comparable to those of Europe. New controversies are arising not just as a result of the increasing drain on welfare resources but because of the declining educational level and low social mobility of some migrant communities. Illegal immigration is causing tension across the United States. The divisive polemic about multiculturalism and political correctness illustrates the prevailing uncertainty about what integration means. The debate is far from over, to judge from a book by Nathan Glazer, whose title belies his scepticism: *We Are All Multiculturalists Now*.

Yet over the past century America has come closer than Europe to the 'unity in diversity' to which it aspires. Its migrants and especially their children identify more quickly with their new country than is usual in Europe, and this should give us pause. Their identification is easier because America has in many ways come to represent globalization writ small. America as a world power is more attractive than the European nations, which with the exception of Britain do not automatically offer access to a world that operates in English.

The New World that America has always aspired to be was founded on a contrast with the Old World, a continent paralysed by competition and conflict between nations. The triumph over old rivalries – inspired in part by the fear that nationalism would cross the ocean along with the migrants – was at the heart of the American creed, in which unity weighs as heavily as diversity. This called for a conscious effort, since there were considerable obstacles on both sides. Again we are reminded of the words of Oscar Handlin: 'The history of immigration is a history of alienation and its consequences.'[49]

European societies are to this day less than wholly successful at integrating newcomers. This is not necessarily a fatal flaw, but it does show that the effects of irreversible demographic change have been seriously underestimated. The avoidance of the question 'Who are we now?' has opened the way for blunt answers. The shock of immigration has been downplayed and, as a result, many opportunities for social renewal have been missed. If pluralism becomes an invitation to productive differences of opinion rather than degenerating into permanent misunderstanding, much will have been gained. Elspeth Huxley was aware of this in the mid-1960s when she remarked: 'Immigrants have created few new problems, they have merely underscored those which already perplex our society. In this case it is a lack of national purpose, of self-confidence.'[50]

This explains why the debate about migration is so enlightening. A society must win the acceptance of newcomers by seeing their arrival as a reason to measure itself against its own ideals. I would like to see migrants and their children becoming more involved in this process.

My wish is that in the not too distant future the contribution made by migrants will become much more obvious. The languages now spoken by many of them are an asset, opening up new avenues to the outside world. I hope we'll succeed in making migration a powerful element of the social dynamism we need in Europe, without necessarily following America in every respect.

After all, the societies of the Old World have a different tradition of social integration. Countries like the Netherlands, Sweden and Germany are harder to penetrate than America because they have drawn the net of solidarity far tighter. Whereas in the streets of New York or Chicago shadow societies of indigents and paupers have grown up, cities like Amsterdam, Berlin and Stockholm are doing all they can to prevent the formation of ghettos or of an underclass. Tolerance of extreme differences is more limited in the Old World, but one advantage of this is that the hope of involving all citizens in society has not been abandoned. The bar is higher, so migrants have to make a greater leap to be included.

There are those who believe globalization means we'll have to abandon the modernist belief in our ability to shape society. Dutch philosopher René Boomkens writes that because economies and cultures across the world are now interwoven, 'notions such as emancipation, civilization and enlightenment' are rapidly losing their significance.[51] To say this is to shake the foundations of Western societies, which see themselves as bearers of the promise of emancipation. Yet he is also aware of the threats posed by globalization: 'Set against the opportunities that uprooting brings are the greater risks that go with it.'[52] He therefore advocates a re-evaluation of the promise of continuity, which he describes as 'an intergenerational responsibility or engagement'.[53] Responsibility for what? Engagement with what exactly? Who will pay attention to the contract between generations in the midst of all this welcome change?

Apparent liberation from a belief in social engineering turns out on further reflection to be a desire for the crossing of boundaries, a desire that up to now has been firmly grounded in a relatively ordered world. Should that cohesion unexpectedly dissolve, should important institutions such as schools or the courts fall prey to a 'new world disorder', then the celebration of globalization will not have a happy sequel. What Stefan Zweig called 'that terrible state of homelessness'[54] becomes obvious only when the certainties of a secure home are thrown into doubt. Under pressure from an expanding world market, the other side of human nature comes into view, namely a longing for security. How do we maintain the correct balance between local public safety and global openness? How do we prevent the native and the foreign from standing in opposition to each other? This is the fundamental question of our times. There are plenty of signs of polarization in Europe, and indeed in

America. A world without borders can easily produce the kind of demagogues who mobilize majorities with slogans like 'our own people first'.

Globalization is not a departure from modernity as a challenge but, rather, an intensification of it. Under these new conditions, the story of emancipation, far from belonging to the past, remains incomplete. In fact, globalization can bring societies closer to their declared norms, although this will require some effort. As we have seen, the arrival of migrants from all parts of the world presents indigenous populations with opportunities to see through their own prejudices. Natives as well as newcomers need to think of themselves as part of a greater whole. Will they regard the migrants of today as fellow citizens? Will they expect their new countrymen to become part of their collective memories and to influence their view of the past?

Behind that quest for a shared outlook on the past lies a fundamental choice. Should we try to create new symbols and rituals by introducing more opportunities to celebrate the Sugar Festival together, by building slavery memorials and by acknowledging migrants to be an essential part of Europe's post-war history? Or should we say: to each his own calendar, his own shops, his own schools and sports clubs, his own festivals, his own memories? The answer ought to be clear. We need to look for new forms of cohesion and for ways to broaden our 'imagined community'.

There's nothing nostalgic about that search for symbols and stories to bring us together. A community requires a shared history and the investigation of the past prompts never-ending debates that, far from being divisive, can create common references. It's possible to overcome a great deal of distrust by sharing responsibility, which makes it vitally important that institutions are open to newcomers. Nevertheless, the historical dimension, a product of interaction between individuals and groups, is crucial as well. Misunderstandings and conflicts are due in part to a difference in length of settlement. Residents of long standing have generations behind them; newcomers need time to secure a position for themselves.

In that sense those who say integration is a matter of time and patience are right, but they would not be right to wait resignedly. Emancipation will not be achieved without pioneers. In the pressure cooker of the past few years there has been an unmistakable quickening of developments. We must acknowledge that the present conflict signifies a departure from the evasions that preceded it and opens the way for accommodation. Conflict avoidance is by no means always a good thing, since it only brings yet more years of walking past each other with barely a sideways glance. Conflict is ultimately a sign of integration, so we should make a clear-eyed assessment of the anger and frustration of many migrants' children. Far more often than we may realize, behind what they say lies a burning ambition to be part of society.

In 1918 sociologist Georg Simmel wrote about the significance of conflict. His verdict on indifference is wholly negative, whereas he believes conflict has something positive at its core: 'Our opposition makes us feel that we are not completely victims of circumstances. It allows us to prove our strength consciously and only thus gives vitality and reciprocity to conditions from which, without such corrective, we would withdraw at any cost.'[55] The dramas of the past few years are part of that conflict, including the riots in the French *banlieues* and the cartoons crisis in Denmark. We must do all in our power to make a virtue of necessity. Communities are built on shared experiences. All the loaded conversations we engage in now can help to create a new 'us', one that includes all those who, regardless of origin, can feel part of the countries in which they now live.

Trust takes time to build, but its value is inestimable. Where routine falls away, and predictability along with it, transaction costs rise. Distrust makes all kinds of explicit rules necessary where previously we acted informally. This applies to the economy and it also holds true for social interaction in a general sense. Only if we succeed in transforming the breach of trust that concerns us here into new ideas about citizenship will we succeed in making immigration beneficial to all.

There are some signs of change. The idea that trust can be strengthened in this way is now more broadly shared. George Alagiah looks ahead: 'Instead of trying to work out where people belong, we should ask what they are doing now that they are here. This is a question about citizenship rather than ethnicity.'[56] The many migrants who work hard to stay afloat and to give their children a better life surely have at least as much right to citizenship as those who have acquired it by birth and consistently fail to live up to the responsibilities that go with it. Alagiah concludes: 'The test of contribution is colour-blind.'[57]

We must aspire to rise above ourselves. In the competition between the Old, the New and the Newest World, Europe could easily fall behind America and Asia. This is not inevitable. The foundations have been laid for a vast single market. By allowing the internal borders on the continent to fall away we have created the potential for great mobility, not only of money and goods but of people and ideas. If Europe succeeds in uniting itself in a peaceful manner, not just by overcoming the old antipathies but by offering migrants the opportunity to make a place for themselves, then there's no reason why the Old World should not discover itself afresh.

Europe's conservatism is understandable. It has much that should be cherished rather than brutally modernized. All the same, the shock of migration must be understood as an invitation to re-examine the principles of an open society. If we can remain true to the ideal of religious freedom and succeed in integrating millions of Muslim migrants into our societies, then we will have stolen a march on the rest of the world. Those who keep insisting there's 'nothing new under the sun' are missing out on an important experience now being gained in the major cities of Europe. Above all, they lack the words needed to turn migration into something everyone values. The arrival of migrants is not just irreversible, it forces us all to rise above our prejudices. That is to ask a great deal, but anyone who doesn't ask a great deal in these times falls a long way short of the mark.

Europe has reached out to touch the world and is increasingly touched by the world in return. Not only have we caused this reciprocity, in many ways we wanted it. The confrontation with militant Islam is obscuring a welcome change. Competition with the Far East can release energies that will help Europe to move beyond its current heaviness of heart. That pressure from outside is sorely needed. The same goes for the arrival of migrants; their presence is an enduring invitation to self-examination. If we acknowledge that it takes effort to perpetuate an open society, then we'll be able to say with conviction to those who come from far and wide: welcome.

Epilogue: After the Multicultural Drama

As ever, it was ultimately personal meetings that shaped my thinking at important moments. During my public wanderings at home and abroad there were many people who influenced me and many of them are named in these pages. Others are present in a more indirect sense. I'm no less indebted to them for that. Opinion-forming is incompatible with aloofness, since there's always a need to hear a response, to test recently acquired ideas against the judgement and experience of others.

Equally, engagement with society requires a degree of detachment. The central character of V. S. Naipaul's *A Bend in the River* says: 'So from an early age I developed the habit of looking, detaching myself from a familiar scene and trying to consider it as from a distance. It was from this habit of looking that the idea came to me that as a community we had fallen behind. And that was the beginning of my insecurity.'[1] Everything I've written has emerged from a comparable sense of uncertainty.

This book is the product not just of academic research but of a public debate that arose after I published an article entitled 'The Multicultural Drama'.[2] Its conclusion was: 'We need a parliamentary inquiry into immigration and integration policy, because entire generations are now being written off in the name of tolerance. The current policy of liberal admission and limited integration worsens inequality and contributes to a sense of alienation. Tolerance is groaning under the burden of overdue maintenance.' With some trepidation I added a final sentence: 'The multicultural drama now unfolding is therefore the greatest threat to social peace.'

That article, published in January 2000, marked the beginning of a major debate in the Netherlands and a turbulent period in Dutch politics. People abroad watched in amazement as this apparently tolerant and laid-back country suddenly turned tense and resentful. Many saw in that agitation a warning to their own societies. If even the easy-going Dutch had trouble getting along with their migrants, what did that say about the rest of Europe? I was caught in the throes of that tumultuous time, and since this book is informed to a great degree by those experiences, I want to take a moment to look at my own involvement.

I had plenty of reasons for writing an article about the multicultural drama: the growing chasm between so-called black and white schools in my home city of Amsterdam, the unbridled aggression of many young Moroccans, the moral issues thrown up by both the admittance and the expulsion of asylum seekers, and the degree to which migrants' children were lagging behind in education. All this generated a creeping unease: I certainly didn't feel society was any the better for it.

An article by Anil Ramdas in which he reproached Dutch writers for excluding immigration from their literary imaginations was the most direct reason for me to begin raising questions. Ramdas wrote: 'Isn't it a tremendous failure on the part of Dutch storytellers not to see that the colour and nature of their society have changed drastically over the past twenty years? While a million citizens swallow their daily doses of humiliation, Dutch writers look the other way. Surely we must eventually start to attribute this to malice and bad faith.'[3] There was no arguing with his assessment of contemporary Dutch literature, but 'bad faith' was overstating the case. What could be read from our literature was above all that the arrival of migrants was entirely absent from the lived or imagined reality of most authors. In that sense, I concluded, writers do not differ greatly from the average citizen.

I took a look at myself, noted that my own tolerance was under strain and decided to say something in response. The strong emphasis on social cohesion in my article about the multicultural drama arose from the knowledge that the open society is fragile. The more aware we become of the conflict, I thought, the better able we'll be to deal with it. The long tradition of conflict avoidance, which had been so fruitful for Dutch society, was clearly not a productive response to migration. I was particularly concerned about social order, believing that immigration would be a severe test of democratic processes.

Then came 9/11 and immediately afterwards the Dutch experienced the rise of Pim Fortuyn and what I've described as a citizens' revolt. Some commentators and politicians explained the success of Fortuyn's populism shortly after the turn of the century as a result of boredom, saying his supporters were simply spoilt, with nothing better to do than to support a political adventure. Riches had led to this embarrassment, the reasoning went. That condescending tone is no longer heard. A visit to one of the many places of commemoration after the murder of Fortuyn was enough to make me realize that a deep insecurity had been exposed.

After his death in May 2002 I tried to take stock: 'Fortuyn has shaken things up and now it's everyone's responsibility to settle them down again. It would have been this way whatever the circumstances. Fortuyn was better at pulling things apart than at putting them back together. The dissatisfaction he tapped into has been seeking an outlet for years. The one person with the civic courage to challenge the establishment with contrary opinions has been stopped short by a violent act. Freedom of expression has suffered a devastating blow. A great many people have been silenced. All that remains to them is to vote for a party without a politician, whereas they were intending to vote for a politician without a party. That makes these elections a soulless exercise.'

In that same article, written a few days before the election that won Fortuyn's party a large number of seats in parliament, I wrote: 'Our image of ourselves as a satisfied and tolerant nation has started to slip. We need to think again about what binds us together as a society and there are no easy answers, but avoiding the question has brought us to the point where an answer that is harsher than desirable lurks in wait.'[4]

To this day, that has been my primary motivation in writing about these issues. It is precisely the failure to ask questions about the problems all migratory movements of any size bring with them that has given populism such power. I would have loved to see the established parties make these issues their own, rather than looking the other way until a significant number of voters pulled the emergency brake. My articles on the multicultural drama were an attempt to stay ahead of such a development by drawing attention to the problems, but some believe I've merely helped to make opposition to immigration socially acceptable.

Then, in November 2004, came another murder, the shooting and stabbing of filmmaker Theo van Gogh not far from where I live. That evening I read out my response on television: 'After Fortuyn another politically motivated murder. It's difficult to get one's thoughts in order, to let it all sink in. This murder too is a traumatic experience, one that will reinforce the widely held belief that there's something seriously wrong with our country. This new murder throws everything out of balance, erodes our self-confidence, leaves less and less intact of the image we once had of ourselves as an open, relaxed and tolerant society. A politically motivated murder: a victim and a perpetrator. Then nothing for a long time. A victim and a perpetrator. There's no such thing as the collective guilt of Muslims; it would be unforgivable if our rage were to be taken out on believers who live peacefully in this country. While there's no collective guilt, there is a special responsibility. There's been too much evasion, too much silence in the Muslim community – too many people who say to me: it's good that you're critical of Islam, it's so hard for us to bring ourselves to be. That has to end. The ship of silence has foundered.'

So with varying degrees of success I've contributed to the formation of public opinion on one of the most important issues of our day. Many of my experiences are reflected in this book, making it the product of both dialogue and research, of innumerable debates as well as solitary hours surrounded by books. One minute there has been the risk of taking a stand in public, the next the relative safety of the study. Since I published my article about the multicultural drama, not a day has gone by without someone speaking to me about it. I'm not keen to avail myself of the often misplaced word 'enrichment', but I have learned a great deal, including many things about myself. As somebody said to me, 'If it isn't hurting, it isn't working.'

One day someone came to my door, unannounced, with a complete meal cooked in his own restaurant. He told me my 'multicultural drama' was something he'd waited years to read. Not that he agreed with everything I'd written, but finally someone had opened his mouth. He added that I wouldn't get very rich from my writing, but he believed that somehow or other it would enrich me. 'After reading your article many people will want to tell you their life stories. And I'm the first. Can we make an appointment?'

Not long after that he told me the story of his migration from India, from the Punjab. How he'd moved to London in the 1960s and how he and his friends had survived there. It wasn't an easy time, to put it mildly. They rented rooms, but Indians weren't allowed to use the front door. Every weekend they stood at the airport until they spotted people from their own district. They picked them up and gave them a rent-free place to stay for a while. Once they were settled they had to start earning money and as soon as they'd saved enough they would buy a house of their own; step by step they took over whole streets and later whole districts that way. His wanderings had brought him to Amsterdam. The restaurant was going reasonably well, but it was a continual struggle to keep his head above water. He told of small instances of discrimination, how he went to a trade fair and was repeatedly redirected towards the second-hand equipment. He thought of a solution: the next time he took with him a thick wad of cash with a couple of business cards inside. When he was redirected for the umpteenth time he ostentatiously pulled out all the money – enough for half a display's worth of coffee machines – and fished from it a card, which he handed over saying, 'Maybe I'll call you some time.' Then he walked off.

It was a long afternoon. One story led to another. He certainly had no desire to take Dutch nationality – he'd had too many bad experiences for that – but he also talked about the obsession with skin-colour in his country of origin, how the bride price would be higher the more light-skinned the bride. A modest man, who'd once wanted to become a chemist, but eventually, like so many migrants, had ended up working below his level of competence. A history of perseverance, of large sacrifices and small steps. Later, in the years of economic decline after the turn of the century, his restaurant went under. A life story to make you stop and think, and in many ways typical of the experiences of countless invisible migrants who have settled in Western countries over recent decades.

Mr Khanna, for that was his name, was certainly proven right. In the past few years I've heard countless stories and witnessed a great many events. Year in, year out, I've taken up almost every invitation to a public debate. Along the way I've justified what I wrote innumerable times. I needed to. Every conversation is a lesson, and in any case I see dialogue as an essential aspect of an open society. Anyone who has direct access to a newspaper, to radio or television must always remember that there are many who don't. The privilege of being able to express an opinion before a large audience brings with it a duty to expose yourself to criticism from all those who don't have a voice in the media. As far as I'm concerned, anyone who limits himself to throwing a stone into the pond violates a basic principle of democracy: the obligation to listen to the other side of the argument.

One day I'm strolling through the Aya Sofia mosque on the Baarsjesweg in Amsterdam. Scores of predominantly older men sit together in the hall watching Turkish television. Tea is served and one conversation flows into another. Along the passageway that runs through this former garage are small shops selling vegetables and rice, as well as sombre Islamic reading materials. The atmosphere is downcast. A longing for past times hangs in the air.

I speak hesitantly with several imams; the translation between Dutch and Turkish makes the conversation all the more halting. 'We've done what was expected of us, haven't we? What do you mean, drama?' A handful of girls in brightly coloured headscarves nod in agreement. But the reform-minded director of the Turkish Muslim organization Milli Görüs says: 'My problem is that my people think they've fallen behind because they're not Muslim enough.' I say that we must get away from thinking in terms of majority and minority. He replies, 'Yes, the time will come when in Amsterdam the majority becomes a minority. I dread the prospect.'

Another day I'm sitting beneath the chandeliers in a convention centre near Rotterdam Central Station, at the enthusiastic launch of Alumnia, a network of highly educated Moroccans. Men in sober suits and dazzling women; not a single headscarf to be seen. The ambitions are sky-high. Here the willingness to look ahead is more than evident.

The anger is unmistakable too, come to that, but I think: without ambition there's no frustration. Even so, I hear far too much bitterness around the table. 'Everything that comes from far away interests you, except the people.' At such moments I always feel constrained by the sense of being seen as an ambassador for the white majority. I keep having to answer the question 'What do you people want from us? Go on, out with it!' Suddenly someone at the other end of the table says, 'In the Netherlands they're doing with us now what they ought to have done with the Jews: hiding us away.'

One day I'm a guest in the Amsterdam suburb of Bijlmer, in a room filled with Surinamers who differ vehemently but cheerfully about the problem of divided loyalty. Can you be Surinamese and Dutch at the same time and what does that mean in practice? Only later does it become clear that Surinamers who live in the Netherlands are not treated very hospitably in Surinam. They've become too Dutch. They grumble that people ought to be punctual; they're no longer used to petty corruption – problems like that. The people in the hall think Surinam should be less indifferent towards its emigrants, but also that Surinamers in the Netherlands ought to do more for their country of origin. With some envy they talk about the generosity of the Turkish community after a recent earthquake in Turkey.

I note down disparate comments during the debate: 'Bijlmer is the first town that Surinamers have taken from the Dutch.' 'I'm sick of the Netherlands with its millions of petty rules.' Reactions to my speech range from someone who remarks testily, 'You're trying to keep us down' to another who is convinced: 'You want to cut a deal with us.' Later someone sneers, 'Look, we're not a hobby or something.' I think to myself: maybe not, but I don't want to make a career out of you either.

Another day and I'm in a suburb of Lelystad attending an Islamic mourning ritual. I sit on a sofa in the living-room, while on the carpet in front of me several men pray fervently in the direction of Mecca. Their foreheads almost touch my stockinged feet. I nod encouragingly to the Lebanese imam as he reads the 56th verse of the Koran, which tells of the last judgement and how infidels will drink hellfire. For someone who's not a believer this is a slightly uncomfortable moment, but it pales into insignificance beside the warm welcome.

Afterwards we speak about the tense situation in the Netherlands, and someone says: 'Muslims are the greatest threat to Islam.' The words of another imam float up from my memory. During a debate he put a question to one of the believers who had just sharply attacked him, a tone of despair in his voice. 'I say to my brother: Allah is watching us. Are we good Muslims as we are now? If we feel we're in a strong position then we stand up for each other, so shouldn't we be a model of harmony?'

One day during my endless tour of the Netherlands I'm in a hall in Zwolle addressing young people from the Turkish community and I can feel how difficult it is to overcome their distrust. What are the real intentions of this speaker who emphasizes all the problems? Why does he keep going on about language deficits? Does he secretly mean to insult us with this concern of his? 'You've supplied the grain the populists grind into flour, that's your tragedy.' Another says: 'There's a big difference between being held accountable and feeling responsible.'

It makes me think of a question put to me by a young Turkish man who was working as a journalist: 'What does this country actually have to offer me?' As he said it I felt a surge of exasperation. Why do I so rarely hear people say they feel grateful for the chance to live here, for being able – like me, I should add – to pluck the fruits of centuries of peaceful and prosperous coexistence? Only at the end of a long afternoon does the air clear and a few days later the organizer writes, in a thank-you note, 'A Turkish saying goes: a true friend may speak bitter words.'

Another day on my wanderings I speak to a branch meeting of a political party in the Slotervaart district of Amsterdam. The hall is deeply divided between longstanding party members and people from migrant communities. A woman whose son is being terrorized by boys from the neighbourhood says: 'The Dutch boys have lost control of the streets to the Moroccans; the payback will come later when they want a job.' It's not long after the murder of Theo van Gogh and someone else remarks simply: 'They've gone too far.'

The Moroccans present refuse to take that lying down. 'When will you start seeing me as a Dutchman. I've done everything I can not to stand out, haven't I?' Indeed, the invitation to migrants to take an active part in society seems ambiguous, since for many of them silence is a means of survival, a strategy of circumspect assimilation. 'We've had bad experiences with visibility.' But we are prisoners of ambivalence on both sides. Remember that contradictory request made by migrants and their children: 'Don't judge me by my background but never forget where I come from.'

Yet another day and I visit a member of parliament and later a professor, both of whom have received threats as a result of things they've said about Islam. Face to face with a group of security men, feeling my chest tighten, I ask myself what kind of country I've landed up in. The blithe assumption that freedom of speech is valued everywhere suddenly belongs to a distant and improbable past. How could we have felt so invulnerable? How could two migrants, one from Somalia, the other from Iran, have managed to confront the country with its own shortcomings like this?

The member of parliament – Ayaan Hirsi Ali – suddenly takes aim at me during our conversation: 'I don't mean it personally, but you always opt for safety, for distance. Writing articles, giving lectures and always griping about how parliament, our most vital institution, has fallen into decline. But actually doing something yourself? No, you stand shouting from the sidelines. Taking a risk. That's something you people aren't much good at.' I explode. 'What do you mean "you people"? Can't we keep this personal? And who decides what the centre is and where the sidelines are? There are so many ways of taking responsibility. Perhaps writing is the prime example, because you're always the weakest link, you can never hide behind anyone else.'

So it went, again and again: the past few years have been a rough, heart-wrenching voyage of discovery in my own country – call it the ideal citizenship test if you like. The countless conversations, letters, debates and critical comments that my 'multicultural drama' produced in the Netherlands, and later in other countries, make clear how concerned and involved many people feel. The reactions, no matter how rude they may sometimes have been, ultimately inspire hope. In recent years it's often been said that immigration shouldn't become a matter for public debate. The wrong note would quickly creep in and unpleasant clichés raise their ugly heads. That's exactly what happened and it did indeed prove difficult to talk in a reasonably frank way about the ambiguities of a country in which many newcomers live.

A motley array of critics has mistaken my plea to include people for a desire to exclude them. The appeal for more attention to be paid to the countless problems of adjustment the arrival of immigrants brings with it isn't at all the same as a call to close the borders. They will stay open, one way or another. Yesterday's guest workers have stayed, they have families now, and new immigrants keep arriving. It's not proximity and contact that are undesirable but distance and avoidance. While some people are wary of too much interference in society by migrants and their children, my fear has always been that the divide will remain too great, that newcomers will keep their distance for too long.

Among minorities there's often a prickly reaction to the debate about multiculturalism, revealing an insecurity about their status in the countries where they now live. Many have only just created a place for themselves in a new land and for perfectly understandable reasons they don't want to be equated with disadvantage. At the same time they come up against researchers and people in authority who in their subtle approaches fail to appreciate the seriousness of the problems. All this skirting of issues has created a culture of avoidance. But we can't keep dodging around each other and so we must speak in public about the integration of all who live and work in our countries. It's not a matter of defending the interests of the 'indigenous' as opposed to 'non-natives' but of ways in which we can get closer to the ideal of an open society. The question that has preoccupied me all these years is how we can guard against new forms of inequality and segregation, so that Western nations remain open in their dealings with migrants.

I live in a country of immigration, a place where many people have arrived from far and wide and where others have lived for generations. The change this produces is a sensitive matter and the debate is often fierce, because a great deal is at stake. In a reaction to my article about the multicultural drama, Kader Abdolah, an author who came to the Netherlands from Iran as a refugee, wrote: 'Paul Scheffer, stand aside. This country is ours too.'[5] I answered him by saying there was room for both of us but that I liked the fact he had said 'This country is ours too.' Later it occurred to me that we'd be a step further along the road if he'd written, 'This country is mine too.'

But perhaps we are forced to conclude that this country now belongs to fewer and fewer people, that it threatens to slip beyond everyone's grasp. Of all those who live here, how many see themselves as part of society as a matter of course and can claim without hesitation, 'This country is mine'? There's a sense of loss on both sides, so we can easily be played off against one another. In that sense the changes brought about by immigration in a globalizing world need to be addressed by everyone.

My search began with the thought 'this far and no further', which inevitably became 'this far and now further'. A typing error helped me along. Somewhere in an article I remarked that migrants who will stay in the Netherlands for the rest of their lives might make more of an effort to master the language. Rereading the draft version I saw I'd written not 'the rest of their lives' but 'the rest of my life'. I changed it, but now I think I ought to have written 'for the rest of their lives and mine'. Only when we take both points of view seriously can we finally say: the rest of our lives.

Acknowledgements

The detachment Naipaul speaks about seems to me a precondition for being able to fathom the land you're born into. Time spent in other countries has changed my view of my own. Surprise at the contrast makes us take a fresh look at what was once so familiar. Meetings with other people, especially those who didn't grow up in the same environment, can have a similar effect. They make the things you take for granted suddenly seem special.

Many people have helped me with their stories, comments and criticism. In thanking some by name, I'm no doubt short-changing most. For all my meetings and conversations with them I would like to thank Samira Abbos, Ahmed Aboutaleb, Yasmine Allas, Khadija Arib, Zeki Arslan, Sevtap Baycili, Mohamed Benzakour, Jos de Beus, Frits Bolkestein, Gabriël van den Brink, Peter de Bruin, Peggy Burke, Ian Buruma, Paul Cliteur, René Cuperus, Jeroen Dijsselbloem, Jan Willem Duyvendak, Fatima Elatik, Han Entzinger, Sylvain Ephimenco, Paul Frissen, Ruben Gowricharn, Sadik Harchaoui, Ayaan Hirsi Ali, Marcel ten Hooven, John Albert Jansen, Hans Jansen, Sjoerd de Jong, Alma Mahawat Kahn, Hikmat Mahawat Kahn, Paul Kalma, Haci Karacaer, Arthur Kibbelaar, Margalith Kleijwegt, Len de Klerk, Ruud Koopmans, Mark Kranenburg, the Lamraoui family, Fouad Laroui, Marc Leijendekker, Geert Mak, Jan Mansvelt-Beck, Ahmed Marcouch, Claartje Mulder, Sako Musterd, Gert Oostindie, Wim Ostendorf, Marco Pastors, Dick Pels, Rinus Penninx, Herman Philipse, Baukje Prins, Omar Ramadan, Anil Ramdas, Rene Roelofs, Chris Rutenfrans, the Sadouq family, Stephan Sanders, Marien van Schaik, Sanne Scheffer, Hendrik Jan Schoo, Jan Stassen, Georg Seferens, Eddy Terstall, Rita Verdonk, Jaffe Vink, Hans Wansink, Leon de Winter, Syp Wynia, Michaël Zeeman and Anton Zijderveld. Without their wisdom and dissent this book would never have become what it is.

I would also like to express my profound thanks to the translator of this book, Liz Waters, for her endless patience and her commitment. I'm also greatly indebted to Suzanne Holtzer at my Dutch publishing house De Bezige Bij. Finally, my thanks to John Thompson, Sarah Lambert and Clare Ansell of Polity for their confidence, critical comments and flexibility.

Notes

Chapter 1 A Suitcase in the Hall

1 Erika Kuijpers, *Migrantenstad*, ch. 2.
2 Oscar Handlin, *The Uprooted*, Introduction, p. 4.
3 Oscar Handlin, *The Uprooted*, Introduction, p. 5.
4 Oscar Handlin, *The Uprooted*, p. 116.
5 Oscar Handlin, *The Uprooted*, p. 141.
6 Oscar Handlin, *The Uprooted*, p. 285.
7 Oscar Handlin, *The Uprooted*, p. 189.
8 Oscar Handlin, *Boston's Immigrants*, p. 206.
9 Oscar Handlin, *Boston's Immigrants*, p. 184.
10 Robert E. Park, *Race and Culture*, p. 150. See also Ulf Hannerz, *Exploring the City*, p. 44.
11 Svetlana Boym, *Future of Nostalgia*, Introduction p. xiv.
12 Svetlana Boym, *Future of Nostalgia*, Introduction p. xv.
13 Anil Ramdas, *De papagaai, de stier en de klimmende bougainvillea*, p. 12.
14 Anil Ramdas, *De papagaai, de stier en de klimmende bougainvillea*, p. 95.
15 Norman Podhoretz, *Making It*, pp. 3–27.
16 Achmed, as quoted in Anil Ramdas, *Het geheugen van de stad*, p. 128.
17 Koemar, as quoted in Anil Ramdas, *Het geheugen van de stad*, p. 15.
18 Robert E. Park, in Louis Wirth, *The Ghetto*, Foreword, p. ix.
19 Robert E. Park, *Race and Culture*, p. 350.
20 Robert E. Park, *Race and Culture*, p. 354.
21 Gérard Noiriel, *Le Creuset français*, p. 163.
22 Farah Karimi, in *De Gelderlander*, 25 February 2000.
23 Kader Abdolah, *De reis van de lege flessen*, p. 18.
24 Kader Abdolah, *De reis van de lege flessen*, p. 77.
25 Hafid Bouazza, *Paravion*, p. 168.

26 Robert E. Park and Herbert A. Miller, *Old World Traits*, p. 56.
27 Necla Kelek, *Die verlorenen Söhne*, p. 138.
28 Necla Kelek, *Die fremde Braut*, p. 260.
29 Atabey, as quoted in Anil Ramdas, *Het geheugen van de stad*, p. 31.
30 Gérard Noiriel, *Le Creuset français*, p. 193.
31 Kristian Hvidt, *Flight to America*, p. 118.
32 John Bodnar, *The Transplanted*.
33 John Bodnar, *The Transplanted*, p. 209.
34 Fouad Laroui, *Judith en Jamal*, p. 91.
35 Fouad Laroui, *Judith en Jamal*, p. 125.
36 Saïd, as quoted in Ali Eddaoudi, *Hollandse nieuwe*, p. 26.
37 Margalith Kleijwegt, *Onzichtbare Ouders*, p. 21.
38 Margalith Kleijwegt, *Onzichtbare Ouders*, p. 54.
39 Monica Ali, *Brick Lane*, p. 17.
40 Monica Ali, *Brick Lane*, p. 82.
41 Fatiha, as quoted in Ali Eddaoudi, *Hollandse nieuwe*, p. 85.
42 Oscar Handlin, *The Uprooted*, p. 255.
43 Fatiha, as quoted in Ali Eddaoudi, *Hollandse nieuwe*, pp. 92–3.
44 WRR, *Nederland als immigratiesamenleving*, p. 120.
45 George Alagiah, *A Home from Home*, p. 48.
46 Interview with Dyab Abu Jahjah, 'Held en demon', *de Volkskrant*, 7 December 2002.
47 Interview with Zohra Acherrat-Stitou, 'Je bent een leenkind', *de Volkskrant* 5 March 1997.
48 Robert E. Park & Herbert A. Miller, *Old World Traits*, p. 67.
49 Güner Yasemin Balci, *Arabboy*.
50 Lucienne Bui Trong, *Violences urbaines*, p. 33.
51 Fouad Laroui, *Judith en Jamal*, p. 77.
52 Aisha, as quoted in Ali Eddaoudi, *Hollandse nieuwe*, p. 57.
53 *All White in Barking*, directed by Marc Isaacs.
54 Ruth Glass, *London's Newcomers*, p. 212.
55 Ruth Glass, *London's Newcomers*, p. 217.
56 Barack Obama, 'A More Perfect Union', speech in Philadelphia, 18 March 2008.
57 Maria Kefalas, *Working-Class Heroes*, p. 4.
58 Maria Kefalas, *Working-Class Heroes*, p. 5.
59 Maria Kefalas, *Working-Class Heroes*, p. 57.
60 John Hartigan, *Racial Situations*, p. 46.
61 John Hartigan, *Racial Situations*, p. 32.
62 Maria Kefalas, *Working-Class Heroes*, p. 100.
63 Maria Kefalas, *Working-Class Heroes*, p. 121.
64 Maria Kefalas, *Working-Class Heroes*, p. 129.
65 Timothy Hatton & Jeffrey Williamson, *International Migration in the Long-Run*, p. 25.
66 Jutta Chorus, *Afri*, pp. 57–8.
67 Pim Fortuyn, *De islamisering van onze cultuur*, p. 77.

68 Rowan Atkinson, 'The Opposition's Case', in Lisa Appignanesi (ed.), *Free Expression Is No Offence*, p. 600.
69 Gérard Noiriel, *Le Creuset français*, p. 274.
70 Ziauddin Sardar, *Balti Britain. A Journey through the British Asian Experience*, p. 88.
71 Hans Magnus Enzensberger, *Die grosse Wanderung*, p. 59.
72 Samuel Huntington, *Who Are We?*, p. 315.
73 David van Reybrouck, *Pleidooi voor populisme.* p. 42.
74 Henry Pratt Fairchild, *Immigration*, p. 426.
75 Henry Pratt Fairchild, *Immigration*, p. 425.
76 Christopher Caldwell, *Reflections on the Revolution in Europe*, p. 17.
77 Christopher Caldwell, *Reflections on the Revolution in Europe*, p. 11.
78 Denis Lacorne, *La Crise de l'identité américaine*, p. 12.
79 German Marshall Fund of the United States, *Transatlantic Trends 2009*, p. 6.
80 German Marshall Fund of the United States, *Transatlantic Trends 2009*, pp. 10 & 12.
81 German Marshall Fund of the United States, *Transatlantic Trends 2009*, p. 15.
82 International Organization for Migration, *World Migration 2008*, p. 455ff; German Marshall Fund of the United States, *Transatlantic Trends 2009*.
83 Sako Musterd, 'Social and Ethnic Segregation in Europe', p. 338.
84 Geert Mak, *Nagekomen flessenpost*, p. 62.
85 Stephen Castles & Mark J. Miller, *The Age of Migration*, p. 239.
86 Klaus Bade, *Europa in Bewegung*, p. 452.
87 Gordon W. Allport, *The Nature of Prejudice*.
88 Dorien Pessers, *Liefde, solidariteit en recht*, p. 46.
89 Leo Lucassen, *The Immigrant Threat*, p. 212.
90 Irshad Manji, *The Trouble with Islam*, p. 152.
91 John Mollenkopf, 'Assimilating Immigrants', p. 208.
92 WRR, *Nederland als immigratiesamenleving*, pp. 162–3.

Chapter 2 The World in the City

1 Panikos Panayi, *The Impact of Immigration*, p. 68, document 2.5.
2 Lewis Mumford, *The Culture of Cities*, pp. 145–6.
3 Peter Hall & Ulrich Pfeiffer, *Urban Future 21*, p. 4.
4 Lewis Mumford, *The Culture of Cities*, p. 171.
5 Upton Sinclair, *The Jungle*, p. 258.
6 Lewis Mumford, *The Culture of Cities*, p. 191.
7 Lewis Mumford, *The Culture of Cities*, p. 161.
8 Louis Wirth, 'Urbanism as a Way of Life', in Richard T. LeGates & Frederic Stout (eds.), *The City Reader*, p. 98.
9 Louis Wirth, 'Urbanism as a Way of Life', in Richard T. LeGates & Frederic Stout (eds.), *The City Reader*, p. 99.
10 Lyn Lofland, *A World of Strangers*, pp. 177–8.
11 Lyn Lofland, *A World of Strangers*, p. 45.

12 Lyn Lofland, *A World of Strangers*, p. 82.
13 Paul Knox & Steven Pinch, *Urban Social Geography*, p. 168.
14 Paul Knox & Steven Pinch, *Urban Social Geography*, p. 175.
15 George Washington, as quoted in Arthur M. Schlesinger, *The Disuniting of America*, p. 24.
16 Figures on segregation from Paul L. Knox & Linda McCarthy, *Urbanization*, pp. 310–11; Douglas Massey & Nancy Denton, *American Apartheid*, chs. 2 and 3.
17 Sako Musterd, *Social and Ethnic Segregation in Europe*.
18 *Bruggen Bouwen* (Report by the Temporary Committee of Investigation into Integration Policy), p. 409.
19 Peter Hall, *Cities of Tomorrow*, pp. 425–6.
20 Douglas Massey & Nancy Denton, *American Apartheid*, p. 181.
21 Douglas Massey & Nancy Denton, *American Apartheid*, p. 164.
22 Eric Maurin, *Le Ghetto français*, p. 13.
23 Jan Rath, *Het mooist van Mokum*, p. 15.
24 Alejandro Portes & Robert D. Manning, 'The Immigrant Enclave', p. 160.
25 Philip Kasinitz, et al., *Inheriting the City*, p. 343.
26 Philip Kasinitz, et al., *Inheriting the City*, p. 344.
27 Yann Moulier-Boutang, *La Revolte*, p. 99.
28 Theodore Dalrymple, *Our Culture, What's Left of It*, p. 306.
29 Israel Cohen, *Jewish Life in Modern Times*, pp. 37–8, as quoted in Louis Wirth, *The Ghetto*, p. 125.
30 Louis Wirth, *The Ghetto*, p. 26.
31 Louis Wirth, *The Ghetto*, p. 222.
32 Louis Wirth, *The Ghetto*, p. 291.
33 Louis Wirth, *The Ghetto*, p. 216.
34 Jaco Dagevos, *Minderheden in Amsterdam*, p. 18.
35 Jaco Dagevos, *Minderheden in Amsterdam*, p. 29.
36 Hind Fraihi, *Undercover in klein-Marokko*, p. 38.
37 Hind Fraihi, *Undercover in klein-Marokko*, p. 38.
38 Hind Fraihi, *Undercover in klein-Marokko*, p. 136.
39 Bassam Tibi, *Islamische Zuwanderung*, p. 91.
40 Philip Roth, *The Human Stain*, p. 108.
41 Philip Roth, *The Human Stain*, p. 109.
42 Karen Montet-Toutain, *Et pourtant, je les aime*, p. 54.
43 Karen Montet-Toutain, *Et pourtant, je les aime*, p. 106.
44 Karen Montet-Toutain, *Et pourtant, je les aime*, pp. 24–5.
45 Eric Maurin, *Le Ghetto français*, p. 58.
46 Eric Maurin, *Le Ghetto français*, p. 26.
47 Wetenschappelijke Raad voor het Regeringsbeleid, *De verzorgingsstaat herwogen*, p. 241.
48 Amartya Sen, *Identity and Violence*, p. 119.
49 SCO-Kohnstamm Instituut, *Onderwijssegregatie in Amsterdam*, p. 43.
50 Jaco Dagevos, *Minderheden in Amsterdam*, p. 35.
51 Eric Maurin, *Le Ghetto français*, p. 55.

52 WRR, *De verzorgingsstaat herwogen*, p. 237.
53 Jaco Dagevos, *Minderheden in Amsterdam*, p. 31.
54 Ryszard Kapuscinski, *Lapidarium*, p. 130.
55 Dick de Ruijter, *Een culturele blik op de Afrikaanderwijk en de Bloemhof* p. 88.
56 Gemeente Rotterdam, *Rotterdam zet door. Op weg naar een stad in balans*, p. 7.
57 Peter Hall, *Cities of Tomorrow*, p. 459.
58 Herbert Gans, *People and Plans*, p. 175.
59 Jan Willem Duyvendak & Lex Veldboer, *Meetingpoint Nederland*, p. 194.
60 Setha Low, *Behind the Gates*, p. 11.
61 Setha Low, *Behind the Gates*, p. 230.
62 *Geschiedenis van Amsterdam*, part IV, p. 15.
63 Ebenezer Howard, as cited in Peter Hall, *Cities of Tomorrow*, p. 161.
64 Manuel Castells, 'European Cities', in Richard T. LeGates & Frederic Stout (eds.), *The City Reader*, p. 483.
65 Manuel Castells, 'European Cities', in Richard T. LeGates & Frederic Stout (eds.), *The City Reader*, p. 484.
66 Leonardo Benevolo, *The European City*, p. 15.
67 Ali Madanipour, 'Social Exclusion and Space', in Richard T. LeGates & Frederic Stout (eds.), *The City Reader*, p. 185.
68 Robert Putnam, *E pluribus unum*, pp. 148–9.
69 Robert Putnam, *E pluribus unum*, p. 164.
70 Peter Sloterdijk, *Sphären II, Globen*, p. 311.
71 Peter Sloterdijk, 'Globalisierungsdrama', in *Im Weltinnenraum des Kapitals*, p. 15.

Chapter 3 The Great Migration

1 F. van Heek, 'Chineesche Immigranten in Nederland', in Frank Bovenkerk & Lodewijk Brunt (eds.), *De rafelrand van Amsterdam*, p. 112.
2 Stephen Castles & Mark J. Miller, *The Age of Migration*, p. 2.
3 International Organization for Migration (IOM), *World Migration 2008*, pp. 403–91.
4 IOM, *World Migration 2008*, p. 36.
5 See for example Philip Legrain, *Immigrants: Your Country Needs Them*, pp. 53–8.
6 IOM, *World Migration 2008*, p. 288.
7 Piet Emmer & Hans Wansink, *Wegsturen of binnenlaten?*, p. 104.
8 Piet Emmer & Hans Wansink, *Wegsturen of binnenlaten?*, p. 108.
9 Myron Weiner, *The Global Migration Crisis*, p. 25.
10 See GMFUS, *Transatlantic Trends 2009*.
11 WRR, *Nederland als immigratiesamenleving*, p. 100.
12 Berlin Institut für Bevölkerung und Entwicklung, 'Ungenutzte Potenziale', January 2009, p. 81.

13 WRR, *Nederland als immigratiesamenleving*, p. 19.
14 Hans Roodenburg, et al., *Immigration and the Dutch Economy*, p. 14.
15 'Arbeidsmigratie in de twintigste eeuw: noodzaak of last?', pp. 85–6.
16 Christopher Caldwell, *Reflections on the Revolution in Europe*, p. 32.
17 John Higham, *Strangers in the Land*, p. 317.
18 Gérard Noiriel, *Le Creuset français*, p. 314.
19 Daniel Cohn-Bendit & Thomas Schmid, *Heimat Babylon*, p. 166.
20 George Borjas, *Heaven's Door*, p. 13.
21 Han Entzinger & Jelle van der Meer (eds.), *Grenzeloze Solidariteit*, p. 116.
22 Michael S. Teitelbaum & Jay Winter, *A Question of Numbers*, p. 45.
23 Franz-Xaver Kaufmann, *Schrumpfende Gesellschaft*, p. 49.
24 UNPD, *Replacement Migration*.
25 Michael S. Teitelbaum & Jay Winter, *A Question of Numbers*, p. 241.
26 Eurostat, *Statistics in Focus*, 81/2008.
27 Franz-Xaver Kaufmann, *Schrumpfende Gesellschaft*, Ch. 4, 'Soziale Folgen des Bevölkerungsrückgangs.'
28 Piet Emmer & Hans Wansink, *Wegsturen of binnenlaten?*, p. 69.
29 Piet Emmer & Hans Wansink, *Wegsturen of binnenlaten?*, p. 61.
30 Thomas Sowell, *Race and Culture*, p. 44.
31 'Bos: soepel zijn met immigratie', in *NRC Handelsblad*, 8 December 2003.
32 James Jupp, *From White Australia*, p. 8.
33 Peter Li, *Destination Canada*, p. 19.
34 Peter Li, *Destination Canada*, p. 23.
35 David Reimers, *Unwelcome Strangers*, p. 22.
36 IOM, *World Migration 2008*. Figures for Australia, Canada and America at pp. 481, 425 & 424 respectively.
37 Will Kymlicka, *Finding our Way*, p. 5.
38 James Jupp, *From White Australia*, p. 67.
39 Geoffrey Blainey, *All for Australia*, p. 58.
40 James Jupp, *From White Australia*, p. 145.
41 Peter Li, *Destination Canada*, p. 86.
42 George Borjas, *Heaven's Door*, p. 12.
43 Theo Veenkamp, et al., *People Flow*, p. 23.
44 Theo Veenkamp, et al., *People Flow*, p. 67.
45 Philip Legrain, *Immigrants: Your Country Needs Them*, p. 330.
46 Philip Legrain, *Immigrants: Your Country Needs Them*, p. 186.
47 Stephen Castles & Mark J. Miller, *The Age of Migration*, p. 133.
48 IOM, *World Migration 2005*, pp. 269 & 273.
49 Eurostat, *Newsrelease* 20/2010, 11 February 2010.
50 Philip Legrain, *Immigrants: Your Country Needs Them*, pp. 166–7; Nigel Harris, *Thinking the Unthinkable*, p. 86.
51 Nigel Harris, *Thinking the Unthinkable*, p. 89.
52 Nigel Harris, *Thinking the Unthinkable*, p. 91.
53 Peter Singer, *Een wereld*, pp. 79–81.
54 Michael Dummett, *On Immigration and Refugees*, p. 69.
55 Paul Kennedy, *Preparing for the Twenty-First Century*, p. 42.

56 Paul Kennedy, *Preparing for the Twenty-First Century*, p. 94.
57 Paul Kennedy, *Preparing for the Twenty-First Century*, p. 44.
58 Jacques Attali, *Millennium: Naar een nieuwe wereldorde*, p. 78.
59 Michael Dummett, *On Immigration and Refugees*, p. 73.
60 This is the line of reasoning found in Jacqueline Stevens, *States without Nations*.
61 Michael Walzer, *Spheres of Justice*, p. 39.
62 Michael Walzer, *Spheres of Justice*, p. 39 (the term is derived from Henry Sidgwick's *The Elements of Politics*).
63 Myron Weiner, *The Global Migration Crisis*, p. x.
64 Myron Weiner, *The Global Migration Crisis*, p. 217.
65 Myron Weiner, *The Global Migration Crisis*, p. 156.
66 Michael Dummett, *On Immigration and Refugees*, p. 35.
67 The story of Hazrat in Katrien de Klein, et al. (eds.), *26.000 gezichten*.
68 The story of Quiru Liao in Annerieke Goudappel & Zhimin Tang, 'Gestrand in Dalfsen.'
69 Patrick Weil, *La France et ses étrangers*, p. 319.
70 Pippa Norris, *Radical Right*, part III, 'Electoral Demand', pp. 129–87.
71 Jean-Marie Guéhenno, *Het einde van de democratie*, p. 8.
72 Jean-Marie Guéhenno, *Het einde van de democratie*, p. 27.
73 Filip Dewinter, *Baas in eigen land*, p. 8.
74 Filip Dewinter, *Baas in eigen land*, pp. 32–3.
75 Filip Dewinter, *Baas in eigen land*, p. 51.
76 Filip Dewinter, *Baas in eigen land*, p. 61.
77 Filip Dewinter, *Baas in eigen land*, p. 10.
78 Filip Dewinter, *Baas in eigen land*, pp. 198–9.
79 Manu Claeys, *Het Vlaams Blok in elk van ons*, p. 75.
80 Manu Claeys, *Het Vlaams Blok in elk van ons*, p. 83.
81 Geoffrey Blainey, *All for Australia*, p. 50.
82 Geoffrey Blainey, *All for Australia*, p. 154.

Chapter 4 The Netherlands: A Culture of Avoidance

1 Ernest Kossmann, 'Een land leeft zolang er debat is', *NRC Handelsblad*, 7 March 1995.
2 James Kennedy, in Pieter van Os (ed.), *Nederland op scherp*, p. 216.
3 Christian Chartier, *Het verdriet van Nederland*, p. 30.
4 Edmondo de Amicis, in Rene van Stipriaan, *Een land om bij te huilen*, p. 62.
5 Christian Chartier, *Het verdiet van Nederland*, p. 43.
6 Anil Ramdas, in Rene van Stipriaan, *Een land om bij te huilen*, p. 168.
7 Simon Schama, *The Embarrassment of Riches*, p. 378.
8 Rentes de Carvalho, *Waar die andere God woont*, p. 168.
9 Geert van Istendael, *Het Belgisch labyrint*, p. 15.
10 Erik de Kuyper, *Een vis verdrinken*, p. 69.
11 'Hatred engulfs a liberal land', in *The Times*, 13 November 2004; 'Haines raciales en terre de tolérances', in *Libération*, 12 November 2004.

12 Magdi Allam, in Pieter van Os (ed.), *Nederland op scherp*, p. 115.
13 Jonathan Israel, in Pieter van Os (ed.) *Nederland op scherp*, p. 108.
14 Mario Vargas Llosa, 'Hirsi Ali is voor de leeuwen gegooid', in *NRC Handelsblad*, 6 June 2006.
15 Ernest Kossmann, 'Een land leeft zolang er debat is', *NRC Handelsblad*, 7 March 1995.
16 Peter van der Veer, 'Nederland bestaat niet meer', *De gids*, 745.
17 Johan Huizinga, *Verzamelde Werken* VII, p. 291.
18 Sylvain Ephimenco, 'Niemandsland.'
19 Ernest Gellner, *Conditions of Liberty*, p. 107.
20 Hans Knippenberg & Ben de Pater, *De eenwording van Nederland*, p. 41.
21 Jan & Annie Romein, *Erflaters van onze beschaving*, p. 772.
22 G. A. Bredero *The Spanish Brabanter*, p. 85 (lines 1168–1171).
23 Enno van Gelder, *Getemperde vrijheid*, p. 19.
24 Piet de Rooy, *Geschiedenis van Amsterdam*, part IV, p. 579.
25 A. Th. van Deursen, 'De Republiek der Zeven Verenigde Nederlanden', p. 177.
26 Remieg Aerts, 'Living apart together?', p. 73.
27 Johan Huizinga, *Nederland's Geestesmerk* (1935), in *Verzamelde Werken* VII, p. 291.
28 El-Moumni, as quoted in 'Homo-beweging woedend op imam', in *NRC Handelsblad*, 4 May 2001.
29 Wim Eijk, as quoted in 'Bisschop: homo's kunnen niet liefhebben', in *NRC Handelsblad*, 18 August 1999.
30 Figures for employment participation by Moroccan and Turkish migrants from Sociaal en Cultureel Planbureau, *Jaarrapport integratie 2005*, p. 83.
31 Hafid Bouazza, 'Nederland is blind voor moslimextremisme', in *NRC Handelsblad*, 20 February 2002.
32 Ali Eddaoudi, *Hollandse nieuwe*, p. 139.
33 Anton Zijderveld, 'Minderheden in Nederland meest gebaat bij verzuiling', in *NRC Handelsblad*, 23 December 1991.
34 Arend Lijphart, *Verzuiling, pacificatie en kentering in de Nederlandse politiek*, p. 94.
35 Anton Zijderveld, 'Minderheden in Nederland meest gebaat bij verzuiling', in *NRC Handelsblad*, 23 December 1991.
36 Jan Peter Balkenende, in *Trouw*, 3 November 2003.
37 August Hans den Boef, *Nederland seculier!*, p. 169.
38 Hafid Bouazza, 'Nederland is blind voor moslimextremisme', in *NRC Handelsblad*, 20 February 2002.
39 SCP, *Moslim in Nederland. Religieuze dimensies, etnische relaties en burgerschap: Turken en Marokkanen in Rotterdam*, pp. 61–89.
40 Geert Mak, *Gedoemd tot kwetsbaarheid*, p. 61.
41 Ahmed Aboutaleb, as quoted in 'Wethouder: geef verdachten aan', in *NRC Handelsblad*, 4 November 2004.
42 Sylvain Ephimenco, 'Open brief aan de moslims van Nederland', in *Trouw*, 5 October 2001.

43 Johan Rudolf Thorbecke, *Een woord in het belang van Europa*, pp. 6–7.
44 Henk Wesseling, *Europa's koloniale eeuw*, p. 368.
45 Herman Langeveld, *Dit leven van krachtig handelen*, p. 59.
46 Gert Oostindie, *Postkoloniaal Nederland*, p. 56.
47 Tjalie Robinson, as quoted in Wim Willems, *De uittocht uit Indië*, p. 244.
48 Rob Nieuwenhuys, *Vergeelde Portretten uit een Indisch familiealbum*, p. 180.
49 J. A. A. van Doorn, *Indische lessen*, p. 154.
50 J. A. A. van Doorn, *Indische lessen*, p. 126.
51 Edgar du Perron, *Country of Origin*, p. 259.
52 Gert Oostindie (ed.), *Het verleden onder ogen*, p. 9.
53 Hendrik Constantijn Cras, as quoted in Angelie Sens, 'Mensaap, heiden, slaaf', p. 115.
54 Johan Huizinga, *Nederland's Geestesmerk* (1935), in *Verzamelde Werken* VII, p. 290.
55 *NRC Handelsblad*, 4 November 2006.
56 N. C. F. van Sas, *De metamorfose van Nederland*, p. 65.
57 *Bruggen Bouwen*. (Report by the Temporary Committee of Investigation into Integration Policy), p. 537.
58 Ian Buruma, 'Letter from Amsterdam', in *The New Yorker*, 3 January 2005.
59 *Het nieuwe Rijksmuseum*, p. 24 (Shervin Nukuee) & p. 15 (Fieke Konijn).
60 *Het nieuwe Rijksmuseum*, p. 39 (Arie van der Zwan) & p. 37 (Rutger Wolfson).
61 'De moraal van het verleden', in *de Volkskrant*, 30 October 2004.
62 Interview with American historian Hayden White, in *De Groene Amsterdammer*, 28 October 2005, pp. 22–5.
63 Willem F. Hermans, *Tranen der Acacia's*, p. 575 in *Volledige Werken* I, p. 270.
64 Jan & Annie Romein, *Erflaters van onze beschaving*, p. 772.

Chapter 5 European Contrasts

1 Gérard Noiriel, *Le Creuset français*, p. 20.
2 Jan Lucassen & Rinus Penninx, *Nieuwkomers, Nakomelingen, Nederlanders*, p. 19.
3 Lord Curzon, as quoted in Klaus Bade, *Europa in Bewegung*, p. 276.
4 José Ortega y Gasset, *The Revolt of the Masses* p. 7.
5 Saskia Sassen, *Guests and Aliens*, p. 102.
6 Saskia Sassen, *Guests and Aliens*, pp. 135–6.
7 Saskia Sassen, *Guests and Aliens*, p. 155.
8 Saskia Sassen, *Guests and Aliens*, p. 140.
9 Klaus Bade, *Europa in Bewegung*, pp. 86, 91 & 67.
10 Klaus Bade, *Europa in Bewegung*, pp. 86 & 91.
11 Klaus Bade, *Europa in Bewegung*, p. 67.
12 Leo Lucassen, *The Immigrant Threat*, p. 28.
13 Alex Will, 'Les Étrangers dans le Pays Noir', in *Le Réveil du Nord*, 6, 8 & 12,

March 1914. This document is reproduced in Janine Ponty, *L'Immigration dans les textes*. pp. 92–3.

14 'The Irish in Nineteenth-century Britain: Problems of Integration', in Roger Swift & Sheridan Gilley (eds.), *The Irish in the Victorian City*, p. 29.

15 In Roger Swift (ed.), *Irish Migrants in Britain, 1815–1914*, p. 38.

16 Christoph Klessmann, 'Einwanderungsprobleme im Auswanderungsland: das Beispiel der "Ruhrpolen"', in Klaus J. Bade, *Deutsche im Ausland, Fremde in Deutschland*, pp. 305–6.

17 Christoph Klessmann, 'Einwanderungsprobleme', p. 208.

18 Emile Temime (ed.), *Migrance* (part II), ch. 3: 'Concurrence et affrontements: les Vêpres Marseillaises.'

19 Gérard Noiriel, *Le Creuset français*, p. 334.

20 Klaus Bade, *Europa in Bewegung*, pp. 270–3.

21 Georges Mauco, as quoted in Patrick Weil, *La France et ses étrangers*, p. 71.

22 Jean-Marie Le Pen, second sitting of the Assemblée nationale on 29 January 1958, as cited in *Journal officiel, Débats parlementaires, Assemblée nationale* (1958), pp. 310–11.

23 Dominique Schnapper, *La France de l'intégration*, p. 79.

24 Dominique Schnapper, *La France de l'intégration*, p. 167.

25 Jean-François Mattéi, 'Le bûcher des illusions', in Raphaël Draï & Jean-François Mattéi (eds), *La République brûle-t-elle?*, p. 195.

26 Marcel Gauchet, *La Religion dans la démocratie*, pp. 41–82.

27 Senator Eugène Lintilhac as quoted in Jean Baubérot, *Laïcité 1905–2005*, p. 90.

28 Jeanne-Hélène Kaltenbach & Michèle Tribalet, *La République et l'islam*, p. 122.

29 Jeanne-Hélène Kaltenbach & Michèle Tribalet, *La République et l'islam*, p. 328.

30 Christian Joppke, *Immigration and the Nation-State*, p. 91.

31 Ralph Giordano, *Wird Deutschland wieder gefährlich?*, p. 51.

32 Ralph Giordano, *Wird Deutschland wieder gefährlich?*, p. 269.

33 Bodo Morshäuser, *Warten auf den Führer*, p. 100.

34 Christian Joppke, *Immigration and the Nation-State*, p. 69.

35 Daniel Cohn-Bendit & Thomas Schmid, *Heimat Babylon*, p. 265.

36 Daniel Cohn-Bendit & Thomas Schmid, *Heimat Babylon*, p. 248.

37 Necla Kelek, *Die fremde Braut*, p. 12.

38 Guido Knopp, *Die grosse Flucht*, pp. 356–411.

39 Wilhelm Heitmeyer, et al., *Verlockender Fundamentalismus*, p. 177.

40 Daniel Cohn-Bendit & Thomas Schmid, *Heimat Babylon*, p. 55.

41 Isensee, as quoted in Christian Joppke, *Immigration and the Nation-State*, p. 198.

42 Bassam Tibi, *Islamische Zuwanderung*, p. 179.

43 Necla Kelek, *Die verlorenen Söhne*, p. 203.

44 Necla Kelek, *Die fremde Braut*, p. 211.

45 Wilhelm Heitmeyer, et al., *Verlockender Fundamentalismus*, p. 192.

46 Hans Magnus Enzensberger, *Die grosse Wanderung*, p. 31.

47 Peter Glotz, *Die deutsche Rechte*, p. 148.
48 Elspeth Huxley, *Back Street New Worlds*, p. 169.
49 Sam King, as quoted in Mike & Trevor Phillips, *Windrush*, p. 17.
50 V. S. Naipaul, *The Enigma of Arrival*, p. 130.
51 V. S. Naipaul, *Letters Between a Father and Son*, p. 44.
52 Cited in Mike & Trevor Phillips, *Windrush*, p. 59.
53 Mike & Trevor Phillips, *Windrush*, p. 97.
54 Mike & Trevor Phillips, *Windrush*, p. 156.
55 Michael Banton, *The Coloured Quarter*, p. 150.
56 Cited in Ruth Glass, *London's Newcomers*, p. 100.
57 Cited in Ruth Glass, *London's Newcomers*, pp. 156–7.
58 Ian Spencer, *British Immigration Policy*, pp. 101–2.
59 Ian Spencer, *British Immigration Policy*, p. 118.
60 Clifford Hill, *Immigration and Integration*, p. 30.
61 Memorandum quoted in Panikos Panayi, *The Impact of Immigration*, p. 46.
62 Ian Spencer, *British Immigration Policy*, p. 4.
63 Hugh Gaitskell, as quoted in Clifford Hill, *Immigration and Integration*, p. 34.
64 Union report, as quoted in Panikos Panayi, *The Impact of Immigration*, p. 179.
65 Ian Spencer, *British Immigration Policy*, pp. 130–4.
66 Enoch Powell, as quoted in Panikos Panayi, *The Impact of Immigration*, p. 142.
67 Mike & Trevor Phillips, *Windrush*, p. 295.
68 Ziauddin Sardar, *Balti Britain*, pp. 377–8.
69 Michael Banton, *The Coloured Quarter*, p. 214.
70 Ziauddin Sardar, *Balti Britain*, p. 128.
71 Elspeth Huxley, *Back Street New Worlds*, p. 166.
72 George Alagiah, *A Home from Home*, p. 183.
73 Adrian Favell, *Philosophies of Integration*, p. 231.
74 Christian Joppke & Ewa Morawska (eds.), *Toward Assimilation and Citizenship*, p. 1.
75 *Community Cohesion*, 2001 (known as the 'Cantle Report'), p. 5.
76 Abram de Swaan, 'Identificatie in uitdijende kring', in *Bakens in Niemandsland*, pp. 24–44.
77 Saskia Sassen, *Guests and Aliens*, p. 155.
78 Jan Peter Balkenende, 'Om Europese identiteit behoort geen hek', in *de Volkskrant*, 7 December 2004.
79 'Wir Kulturvölker, wir wissen jetzt, dass wir sterblich sind.' 'Nous autres, civilisations, nous savons maintenant que nous sommes mortelles.' Paul Valéry, *Oeuvres*, vol. I, p. 988.

Chapter 6 The Cosmopolitan Code

1 Arnold Toynbee, *Civilization on Trial*, pp. 83–4 & 89.
2 David Livingstone, as quoted in Niall Ferguson, *Empire*, p. 155.

3 David Livingstone, as quoted in Niall Ferguson, *Empire*, p. 129.
4 David Abernethy, *The Dynamics of Global Dominance*, p. 183.
5 David Landes, *The Wealth and Poverty of Nations*, p. 177.
6 David Landes, *The Wealth and Poverty of Nations*, p. 179.
7 David Landes, *The Wealth and Poverty of Nations*, p. 250.
8 David Landes, *The Wealth and Poverty of Nations*, pp. 401–2.
9 David Abernethy, *The Dynamics of Global Dominance*, p. 34.
10 David Abernethy, *The Dynamics of Global Dominance*, p. 190.
11 David Abernethy, *The Dynamics of Global Dominance*, p. 12.
12 Henk Wesseling, *Europa's koloniale eeuw*, pp. 367–8.
13 David Hume, *On National Characters*, p. 208.
14 Article 110 of the *Fundamental Constitutions of Carolina* (1669), the text of which is largely attributed to John Locke.
15 Camper, as quoted in Angelie Sens, 'Mensaap, heiden, slaaf', p. 53.
16 Charles Darwin, *The Descent of Man*, pp. 130–41.
17 Charles Darwin, *The Descent of Man*, Vol. 2, p. 403.
18 Charles Darwin, *The Descent of Man*, p. 131.
19 Charles Darwin, *The Descent of Man*, p. 135.
20 Charles Darwin, as quoted in Dinesh D'Souza, *The End of Racism*, p. 130, from *The Voyage of the Beagle*, pp. 205–6.
21 Lord Salisbury, as quoted in Henk Wesseling, *Europa's koloniale eeuw*, p. 177.
22 Madison Grant, as quoted in Oscar Handlin, *Race and Nationality in American Life*, p. 97.
23 Aldous Huxley, *The Hidden Huxley*, p. 154.
24 Franz Boas, *The Mind of Primitive Man*, p. 31.
25 Franz Boas, *The Mind of Primitive Man*, p. 29.
26 Franz Boas, *The Mind of Primitive Man*, p. 179.
27 Franz Boas, *The Mind of Primitive Man*, pp. 180–1.
28 Melville Herskovits, *Man and His Works*, p. 76.
29 Franz Boas, *The Mind of Primitive Man*, p. 203.
30 Melville Herskovits, *Man and His Works*, pp. 77, 78.
31 Michel de Montaigne, *Essays*, Book 1, Ch. 31.
32 Ton Lemaire, *Over de waarde van kulturen*, p. 166.
33 Ton Lemaire, *Over de waarde van kulturen*, p. 159.
34 Tzvetan Todorov, *Nous et les autres*, pp. 58–62.
35 Ayaan Hirsi Ali, *De zoontjesfabriek*, p. 69.
36 Claude Lévi-Strauss, *Race et histoire*, p. 52.
37 Ruth Benedict, *Patterns of Culture*, p. 17.
38 Norman Podhoretz, *Making It*, pp. 3–27.
39 Horace M. Kallen, *Culture and Democracy*, p. 108.
40 Will Kymlicka, *Finding Our Way*, p. 16.
41 Tariq Modood, *Multiculturalism*, p. 98.
42 Tariq Modood, *Multiculturalism*, p. 42.
43 Tariq Modood, *Multiculturalism*, p. 55.
44 Tariq Modood, *Multiculturalism*, p. 61.

45 Peter Li, *Destination Canada*, pp. 50–7.
46 Will Kymlicka, *Finding Our Way*, p. 29.
47 Will Kymlicka, *Finding Our Way*, p. 29.
48 Hans Vermeulen, 'Cultuur en ongelijkheid', p. 39.
49 Necla Kelek, in *Spiegel Online*, 22 March 2007.
50 N. F. van Manen & A. J. Hoekema, *Gemeenschappen komen tot hun recht*, p. 253.
51 George Alagiah, *A Home from Home*, p. 207.
52 William Graham Sumner, *Folkways*, p. 13.
53 William Graham Sumner, *Folkways*, p. 58.
54 William Graham Sumner, *Folkways*, p. 45.
55 Claude Lévi-Strauss, as quoted in Taguieff, *La Force du préjugé*, p. 246.
56 Norbert Elias, *The Established and the Outsiders*, p. xxiii.
57 Norbert Elias, *The Established and the Outsiders*, pp. xxxxiii & xix.
58 Norbert Elias, *The Established and the Outsiders*, p. xvi.
59 Norbert Elias, *The Established and the Outsiders*, p. xxviii.
60 Hans Magnus Enzensberger, *Die grosse Wanderung*, pp. 11–13.
61 Norbert Elias, *The Established and the Outsiders*, p. xxx.
62 Gordon Allport, *The Nature of Prejudice*, p. 195.
63 Gordon Allport, *The Nature of Prejudice*, p. 365.
64 Gordon Allport, *The Nature of Prejudice*, p. 451.
65 Gordon Allport, *The Nature of Prejudice*, p. 454.
66 Gordon Allport, *The Nature of Prejudice*, p. 149.
67 Eva Hoffman, *De ziel van de dialoog*, p. 32.
68 Eva Hoffman, *De ziel van de dialoog*, p. 33.
69 Jean-Jacques Rousseau, *Emile* I, p. 249.
70 Stefan Zweig, *Die Welt von Gestern*, pp 462–463.
71 Stefan Zweig, *Die Welt von Gestern*, p. 442.
72 Alain Finkielkraut, *Comment peut-on être croate?*, p. 58.
73 Cited by Kwame Anthony Appiah in his introduction to Chinua Achebe, *Things Fall Apart*, p. xii.
74 Alain Finkielkraut, *L'Ingratitude*, p. 43.
75 Alain Finkielkraut, *L'Ingratitude*, p. 116–117.
76 Kwame Anthony Appiah, *The Ethics of Identity*, p. 213.
77 Kishore Mahbubani, *The New Asian Hemisphere*, p. 102.
78 Timothy Garton Ash, *Free World*, p. 192.
79 Michael Ignatieff, *Whose Universal Values?*, p. 13.

Chapter 7 The Rediscovery of America

1 Samuel Huntington, *Who Are We?*, p. 39.
2 Samuel Huntington, *Who Are We?*, p. 39.
3 Stephan Thernstrom (ed.), *Harvard Encyclopedia of American Ethnic Groups*, p. 284.
4 Aristide Zolberg, *A Nation by Design*, p. 464.
5 Samuel Huntington, *Who Are We?*, p. 40.

6 John de Crèvecoeur, *Letters from an American Farmer*, p. 44.
7 James Russel Lowell, as quoted in Merle Curti, *The Roots of American Loyalty*, p. 120.
8 Frederic Turner, as quoted in John Higham, *Strangers in the Land*, p. 22.
9 Merle Curti, *The Roots of American Loyalty*, p. 6.
10 Oliver Wendell Holmes, as quoted in John Higham, *Strangers in the Land*, p. 21.
11 Aravind Adiga, *The White Tiger*, p. 305.
12 Kishore Mahbubani, *The New Asian Hemisphere*, p. 126.
13 Ralph Waldo Emerson, as quoted in Merle Curti, *The Roots of American Loyalty*, p. 202.
14 John Higham, *Strangers in the Land*, p. 118.
15 From the 1912 election programme of Theodore Roosevelt's Progressive Party, as quoted in John Higham, *Strangers in the Land*, 238.
16 Francis Kellor, *Immigration and the Future*, p. 39.
17 Francis Kellor, *Immigration and the Future*, p. 68.
18 Chairman of the League, as quoted in Edward George Hartmann, *The Movement to Americanize the Immigrant*, p. 94.
19 Francis Kellor, *Immigration and the Future*, p. 25.
20 John Higham, *Strangers in the Land*, p. 262.
21 Dennis Lacorne, *La Crise de l'identité américaine*, p. 234.
22 Francis Kellor, *Immigration and the Future*, p. 264.
23 Nathan Glazer & Daniel Patrick Moynihan, *Beyond the Melting Pot*, p. 17.
24 Nathan Glazer & Daniel Patrick Moynihan, *Beyond the Melting Pot*, p. 313.
25 Leonard Dinnerstein & David Reimers, *Ethnic Americans*, pp. 198–9.
26 Samuel Huntington, *Who Are We?*, p. 38.
27 Leonard Dinnerstein & David Reimers, *Ethnic Americans*, p. 54.
28 Benjamin Franklin, *Observations Concerning the Increase of Mankind*, section 23.
29 Aristide R. Zolberg, *A Nation by Design*, p. 7.
30 Aristide R. Zolberg, *A Nation by Design*, p. 16.
31 Aristide R. Zolberg, *A Nation by Design*, p. 127.
32 *The Philadelphia Sun*, as quoted in Tyler Anbinder, *Nativism & Slavery*, p. 75.
33 Abraham Lincoln in a letter to Joshua Speed (1855), as quoted in Tyler Anbinder, *Nativism and Slavery*, p. 266.
34 Tyler Anbinder, *Nativism and Slavery*, p. 125–6.
35 Oscar Handlin, *Boston's Immigrants*, p. 55.
36 John Hawgood, *The Tragedy of German-America*, p. xv.
37 John Hawgood, *The Tragedy of German-America*, p. 37.
38 John Hawgood, *The Tragedy of German-America*, p. xviii.
39 John Hawgood, *The Tragedy of German-America*, p. 52.
40 John Higham, *Strangers in the Land*, p. 61.
41 Henry Pratt Fairchild, *Immigration*, p. 412.
42 Henry Pratt Fairchild, *Immigration*, p. 431.
43 John Higham, *Strangers in the Land*, p. 97.

44 Leonard Dinnerstein & David Reimers, *Ethnic Americans*, p. 99.
45 Philip Gleason, 'American Identity and Americanization', p. 46.
46 Aristide R. Zolberg, *A Nation by Design*, p. 464.
47 David M. Reimers, *Unwelcome Strangers*, p. 70.
48 David M. Reimers, *Unwelcome Strangers*, p. 133.
49 David M. Reimers, *Unwelcome Strangers*, p. 29.
50 Ira Berlin, *Generations of Captivity*, p. 13.
51 Alexis de Tocqueville, *De la Démocratie en Amérique*, p. 369.
52 John Hope Franklin, *From Slavery to Freedom*, p. 144.
53 Ira Berlin, *Generations of Captivity*, p. 6.
54 Edward P. Jones, *The Known World*, p. 109.
55 Merle Curti, *The Roots of American Loyalty*, p. 160.
56 Abraham Lincoln, as quoted in John Hope Franklin, *From Slavery to Freedom*, p. 281.
57 John Hope Franklin, *From Slavery to Freedom*, p. 571.
58 Booker T. Washington, *Up From Slavery*, p. 234.
59 W. E. B. Du Bois, *Writings*, p. 363.
60 W. E. B. Du Bois, *Writings*, p. 489.
61 W. E. B. Du Bois, *Writings*, p. 365.
62 W. E. B. Du Bois, *Writings*, p. 484.
63 W. E. B. Du Bois, *Writings*, p. 1243.
64 Lyndon B. Johnson, as quoted in John Hope Franklin, *From Slavery to Freedom*, p. 639.
65 Gunnar Myrdal, *An American Dilemma*, p. 1004.
66 Philip Gleason, *American Identity and Americanization*, p. 52.
67 Remarks on Afrocentrism as quoted in Arthur Schlesinger Jr, *The Disuniting of America*, pp. 62–8.
68 Frederick Douglass, as quoted in Arthur M. Schlesinger Jr, *The Disuniting of America*, p. 82.
69 James Baldwin, *Collected Essays*, p. 333.
70 Arthur M. Schlesinger Jr, *The Disuniting of America*, p. 15.
71 Lyndon B. Johnson, as quoted in Dinesh D'Souza, *The End of Racism*, p. 217.
72 Thomas F. Pettigrew, 'New Patterns of Prejudice: The Different Worlds of 1984 and 1964', p. 53.
73 Peter D. Salins, *Assimilation, American Style*.
74 Alejandro Portes & Rubén G. Rumbaut, *Legacies*, pp. 278–80.
75 Alan Wolfe, 'Native Son', p. 123.
76 Barack Obama, *Dreams from My Father*, p. 81.
77 Aristide R. Zolberg, *A Nation by Design*, p. 459.

Chapter 8 The Divided House of Islam

1 John Berger, *Stemverheffing*, p. 67.
2 Carl Brown, *Religion and State*, p. 22.
3 Franco Cardini, *Europa und der Islam*, p. 13.

4   C. Busken Huet, *Het land van Rembrand*, p. 31.
5   V. S. Naipaul, *Beyond Belief*, p. 31.
6   V. S. Naipaul, *Beyond Belief*, p. 72.
7   Fatima Mernissi, *The Veil and the Male Elite* p. 153.
8   Amin Maalouf, *The Crusades*, p. 264.
9   Alexis de Tocqueville, *Rapports sur l'Algérie* (*Oeuvres* III), p. 813.
10 Orhan Pamuk, *My Name is Red*, p. 158.
11 Nasr Hamid Abu Zayd, *Vernieuwing in het islamitisch denken*, p. 90.
12 Mohamed Charfi, as quoted in Rachid Benzine, *Les Nouveaux Penseurs de l'islam*, p. 240.
13 Bernard Lewis, *What Went Wrong?*, p. 114.
14 Bernard Lewis, *What Went Wrong?*, p. 156.
15 Nasr Hamid Abu Zayd, *Vernieuwing in het islamitisch denken*, p. 44.
16 Philip Longman, 'The Global Baby Bust', p. 68.
17 Selami Yüksel, as quoted in Gerard Van Westerloo, 'Revolutie bij de zwarte-kousenmoslims', p. 19.
18 Pippa Norris & Ronald Inglehart, *Sacred and Secular*, p. 216.
19 Pippa Norris & Ronald Inglehart, *Sacred and Secular*, p. 18.
20 SCP, *Moslims in Nederland*, p. 87.
21 Olivier Roy, *L'Islam mondialisé*, p. 9.
22 Olivier Roy, *L'Islam mondialisé*, p. 17.
23 Olivier Roy, *L'Islam mondialisé*, p. 81.
24 Olivier Roy, *L'Islam mondialisé*, p. 104.
25 Salma Ismali, 'Ik deed alles wat Allah verbood.'
26 Olivier Roy, *L'Islam mondialisé*, p. 92.
27 Olivier Roy, *L'Islam mondialisé*, p. 70.
28 Fadoua Bouali, 'Film Ayaan ontroert door puurheid', in *de Volkskrant*, 1 September 2004.
29 Olivier Roy, *L'Islam mondialisé*, p. 106.
30 Ahmad ibn Naqib Al-Misri, *Reliance of the Traveller*, p. 595.
31 Pippa Norris & Ronald Inglehart, *Sacred and Secular*, p. 134.
32 Rekha Ramsaran & Bregje Spaans, *Wankele waarden*, p. 134.
33 Hakan, as quoted in Imad el Kaka & Hatice Kursun, *Mijn geloof en mijn geluk*, p. 122.
34 E. Gezik, *Eer, identiteit en moord*, p. 15.
35 Fawzia Zouari, *Ce voile qui déchire la France*, pp. 42 & 60.
36 Melanie Phillips, *Londonistan*, p. 46.
37 Frank J. Buijs, et al., *Strijders van eigen bodem*, p. 141.
38 Yasmine Allas, *Ontheemd en toch thuis*, pp. 40–5.
39 Yasmine Allas, *Ontheemd en toch thuis*, p. 38.
40 Yasmine Allas, *Ontheemd en toch thuis*, pp. 39–40.
41 Frank J. Buijs, et al., *Strijders van eigen bodem*, p. 129.
42 Mounir, as quoted in Frank J. Buijs, et al., *Strijders van eigen bodem*, p. 82.
43 For a summary of Qutb's thinking, see Paul Berman, *Terror and Liberalism*, pp. 52–76.
44 Mustapha, as quoted in Frank J. Buijs, et al., *Strijders van eigen bodem*, p. 62.

45 Ibrahim, as quoted in Frank J. Buijs, et al., *Strijders van eigen bodem*, p. 65.
46 Melanie Phillips, *Londonistan*, p. 11.
47 Letter written by Mohammed Bouyeri, 'Je zal jezelf stuk slaan op de islam', in *NRC Handelsblad*, 5 November 2004.
48 Quoted in Melanie Phillips, *Londonistan*, pp. 132–3.
49 Dyab Abu Jahjah, *Tussen twee werelden*, p. 163.
50 Dyab Abu Jahjah, *Tussen twee werelden*, p. 207.
51 Dyab Abu Jahjah, *Tussen twee werelden*, p. 331.
52 Olivier Roy, *L'Islam mondialisé*, p. 25.
53 Olivier Roy, *L'Islam mondialisé*, p. 186.
54 Shahid Malik, as quoted in Andrew Rawnsley, 'Nothing can ever be the same', in *The Observer*, 17 July 2005.
55 Abdolkarim Soroush, *Reason, Freedom, and Democracy in Islam*, p. 165.
56 Abdolkarim Soroush, *Reason, Freedom, and Democracy in Islam*, p. 167.
57 Fatima Mernissi, *The Veil and the Male Elite*, p. 19.
58 Fatima Mernissi, *The Veil and the Male Elite*, p. 19.
59 Fatima Mernissi, *The Veil and the Male Elite*, p. 18.
60 Nasr Hamid Abu Zayd, *Vernieuwing in het islamitisch denken*, p. 59.
61 Nasr Hamid Abu Zayd, *Vernieuwing in het islamitisch denken*, p. 103.
62 Nasr Hamid Abu Zayd, *Vernieuwing in het islamitisch denken*, p. 68.
63 Nasr Hamid Abu Zayd, as quoted in Benzine, *Les Nouveaux Penseurs de l'islam*, p. 205.
64 Fatima Mernissi, *The Veil and the Male Elite*, p. 81.
65 Fatima Mernissi, *The Veil and the Male Elite*, p 101.
66 Mohamed Charfi, as quoted in Rachid Benzine, *Les Nouveaux Penseurs de l'islam*, p. 231.
67 Tariq Ramadan, *Les Musulmanes d'occident*, p. 118.
68 Tariq Ramadan, *Les Musulmanes d'occident*, p. 101.
69 Christiaan Snouck Hurgronje, *Nederland en de islam*, p. 53.
70 Christiaan Snouck Hurgronje, *Nederland en de islam*, p. 73.
71 Christiaan Snouck Hurgronje, *Nederland en de islam*, p. 77.
72 Christiaan Snouck Hurgronje, *Nederland en de islam*, p. 67.
73 Christiaan Snouck Hurgronje, *Nederland en de islam*, p. 67.
74 Christiaan Snouck Hurgronje, *Nederland en de islam*, p. 55.
75 Jean Baubérot, *Laïcité 1905–2005*, p. 225.
76 Tariq Ramadan, *Les Musulmanes d'occident*, p. 350.
77 Mohammed Bouyeri, as quoted in Frank J. Buijs, et al., *Strijders van eigen bodem*, p. 45.
78 Press statement by the Muslim Public Affairs Council, 15 March 2005.
79 Timothy Garton Ash, 'Save our Raphael', in Lisa Appignanesi (ed.), *Free Expression is No Offence*, p. 68 & 71.
80 Gilles Kepel, *Fitna*, pp. 286–334.
81 Ian Buruma & Avishai Margalit, *Occidentalism*, p. 14.
82 Ian Buruma & Avishai Margalit, *Occidentalism*, p. 10.
83 Yvonne Haddad & John Esposito, *Muslims on the Americanization Path?*, p. 3.

84 Pippa Norris & Ronald Inglehart, *Sacred and Secular*, p. 233.
85 Pippa Norris & Ronald Inglehart, *Sacred and Secular*, p. 217.
86 Pippa Norris & Ronald Inglehart, *Sacred and Secular*, p. 217.
87 Oriana Fallaci, *The Rage and the Pride*, p. 97.
88 John Gray, *Al-Qaeda and What it Means to be Modern*, p. 116.
89 Stephen Flynn, 'America the Vulnerable', in *The War on Terror*, p. 148.
90 John Gray, *Al-Qaeda and What it Means to be Modern*, p. 83.
91 John Gray, *Al-Qaeda and What it Means to be Modern*, p. 83.
92 Bruce Bawer, *While Europe Slept: How Radical Islam Is Destroying the West From Within*; Walter Laqueur, *The Last Days of Europe: Epitaph for an Old Continent*.

Chapter 9 Land of Arrival

1   Fouad Laroui, 'Hoe ik Europeaan werd.'
2   Afshin Ellian, 'Leve de monoculturele rechtsstaat.'
3   Job Cohen, speech delivered on 24 August 2006.
4   Ni Haifeng, *Kunst als gift.*
5   Ted Cantle, *Community Cohesion*, p. 20.
6   *Observer*, 31 July 2005, p. 18.
7   *Observer*, 31 July 2005, p. 18.
8   *Observer*, 13 June 2004, p. 16.
9   Parekh Report, *The Future of Multi-Ethnic Britain*, p. 105.
10 Abdelkader Benali, 'Waarom zwijgen de Nederlandse schrijvers?'
11 Interview with Dyab Abu Jahjah, in *Bijeen*, May 2003, p. 39.
12 Rabin Baldewsingh, 'Ken je buren: samenleven is samenwerken', speech delivered on 12 February 2000 in The Hague.
13 Trevor Phillips, 'After 7/7: Sleepwalking to segregation', speech to the Manchester Council for Community Relations, 22 September 2005.
14 Christopher Lash, *The Culture of Narcissism*, p. 23.
15 Christopher Lash, *The Culture of Narcissism*, p. 129.
16 Michel Houellebecq, *The Elementary Particles*, p. 94.
17 Gilles Lipovetsky, *Le Crépuscule du devoir*, p. 17.
18 Gabriël van den Brink, *Schets van een beschavingsoffensief*, pp. 139–50.
19 Paul Frissen, *De staat van verschil*, p. 28.
20 Paul Frissen, *De staat van verschil*, p. 54.
21 Theodore Dalrymple, *Life at the Bottom*, p. ix.
22 Theodore Dalrymple, *Life at the Bottom*, p. ix.
23 Theodore Dalrymple, 'Reader, She Married Him – Alas', *City Journal*, Spring 1995.
24 Franz-Xaver Kaufmann, *Schrumpfende Gesellschaft*, p. 224.
25 Abram de Swaan, *De mens is de mens een zorg. Opstellen 1971–1981*, pp. 81–115.
26 Franz-Xaver Kaufmann, *Schrumpfende Gesellschaft*, p. 224.
27 Parekh Report, *The Future of Multi-Ethnic Britain*, p. 149.
28 Maarten Doorman, *Kiekertak en Klotterbooke*, p. 15.

29 Parekh Report, *The Future of Multi-Ethnic Britain*, p. 25.
30 *Nouvel Observateur*, 17 December 2009.
31 Theodore Dalrymple, 'What is Poverty?', *City Journal*, Spring 1999.
32 Arie van der Zwan, *De uitdaging van het populisme*, p. 108.
33 Arie van der Zwan, *De uitdaging van het populisme*, p. 97.
34 WRR, *De verzorgingsstaat herwogen*, p. 15.
35 Ayaan Hirsi Ali, *The Caged Virgin*, p. 60.
36 WRR, *De verzorgingsstaat herwogen*, p. 16.
37 Necla Kelek, *Die verlorenen Söhne*, p. 127.
38 Saïda Sakali, 'Ze zijn niet zo lief meer, meneer', in *De Morgen*, 6 December 2002.
39 Frits Bolkestein, *Woorden hebben hun betekenis*, p. 203.
40 Sevtap Baycili, 'Ik wil in Nederland blijven', p. 105.
41 Dinesh D'Souza, *The End of Racism*, p. 554.
42 WRR, *De verzorgingsstaat herwogen*, p. 60.
43 IOM, *World Migration 2008*, p. 36.
44 Douglas Massey, as quoted in Samuel Huntington, *Who Are We?*, p. 196.
45 Timothy J. Hatton & Jeffrey G. Williamson, *Global Migration and the World Economy*, p. 386.
46 Timothy J. Hatton & Jeffrey G. Williamson, *Global Migration and the World Economy*, p. 25.
47 James Baldwin, *Collected Essays*, p. 342.
48 James Baldwin, *Collected Essays*, p. 340.
49 Oscar Handlin, *The Uprooted*, p. 4.
50 Elspeth Huxley, *Back Street New Worlds*, p. 179.
51 René Boomkens, *De nieuwe wanorde*, p. 32.
52 René Boomkens, *De nieuwe wanorde*, p. 247.
53 René Boomkens, *De nieuwe wanorde*, p. 201.
54 Stefan Zweig, *Die Welt von Gestern*, p. 442.
55 Georg Simmel, *On Individuality and Social Forms*, p. 75.
56 George Alagiah, *A Home from Home*, p. 264.
57 George Alagiah, *A Home from Home*, p. 265.

Epilogue: After the Multicultural Drama

1 V. S. Naipaul, *A Bend in the River*, p. 22.
2 Paul Scheffer, 'Het multiculturele drama', in *NRC Handelsblad*, 29 January 2000.
3 Anil Ramdas, 'Moedwil en kwade trouw bij blanke schrijvers', in *NRC Handelsblad*, 14 March 1997.
4 Paul Scheffer, 'De ontkende opstand', in *NRC Handelsblad*, 11 May 2002.
5 Kader Abdolah, *Een tuin in de zee*, p. 125.

References

Abdolah, Kader. *De reis van de lege flessen*. Breda, De Geus, 1997.
Abdolah, Kader. *Een tuin in de zee*. Breda, De Geus, 2001.
Abernethy, David B. *The Dynamics of Global Dominance. European Overseas Empires 1415–1980*. New Haven, Yale University Press, 2000.
Abu Jahjah, Dyab. *Tussen twee werelden. De roots van een vrijheidsstrijd*. Amsterdam, Meulenhoff, 2003.
Abu Zayd, Nasr Hamid. *Vernieuwing in het islamitisch denken. Een wetenschappelijke benadering*. Amsterdam, Bulaaq, 1996.
Achebe, Chinua. *Things Fall Apart* (1958). New York, Knopf, 1992.
Acherrat-Stitou, Zohra. 'Je bent een leenkind.' Interview in *de Volkskrant*, 5 March 1997.
Adiga, Aravind. *The White Tiger*. London, Atlantic Books, 2008.
Adorno, Theodor W., et al. *Der autoritäre Charakter. Studien über Autorität und Vorurteil*. Vols. 1 & 2. Amsterdam, Verlag de Munter, 1968.
Aerts, Remieg. 'Living apart together? Verdraagzaamheid in Nederland sinds de zeventiende eeuw.' In Marcel ten Hooven (ed.), *De lege tolerantie. Over vrijheid en vrijblijvendheid in Nederland*. Amsterdam, Boom, 2001.
Alagiah, George. *A Home from Home. From Immigrant Boy to English Man*. London, Little Brown, 2006.
Al-Azm, Sadik. *Kritiek op godsdienst en wetenschap. Vijf essays over islamitische cultuur*. Amsterdam, El Hizjra, 1996.
Ali, Monica. *Brick Lane*. London, Doubleday, 2003.
Ali, Tariq. *The Clash of Fundamentalisms. Crusades, Jihads and Modernity*. London, Verso, 2002.
Allam, Magdi. 'Politieke zelfmoord.' In Pieter van Os (ed.), *Nederland op scherp. Buitenlandse beschouwingen over een stuurloos land*. Amsterdam, Bert Bakker, 2005.
Allas, Yasmine. *Ontheemd en toch thuis*. Amsterdam, De Bezige Bij, 2006.
Allport, Gordon W. *The Nature of Prejudice*. Boston, The Beacon Press, 1954.

Anbinder, Tyler. *Nativism and Slavery. The Northern Know Nothings and the Politics of the 1850s.* New York, Oxford University Press, 1992.

Anderson, Benedict. *Imagined Communities. Reflections on the Origin and Spread of Nationalism.* London, Verso, 1983.

Appadurai, Arjun. *Modernity at Large. Cultural Dimensions of Globalization.* Minneapolis, University of Minnesota Press, 1996.

Appiah, Kwame Anthony. *The Ethics of Identity.* Princeton, Princeton University Press, 2005.

Appignanesi, Lisa (ed.). *Free Expression Is No Offence.* London, Penguin, 2005.

Attali, Jacques. *Millennium. Naar een nieuwe wereldorde.* Utrecht, Kosmos, 1992.

Bade, Klaus J. *Deutsche im Ausland, Fremde in Deutschland. Migration in Geschichte und Gegenwart.* München, Beck, 1992.

Bade, Klaus J. *Europa in Bewegung. Migration vom späten 18. Jahrhundert bis zur Gegenwart.* München, Beck, 2000.

Balci, Güner Yasemin. *Arabboy. Eine Jugend in Deutschland oder Das kurze Leben des Rashid A.* Frankfurt, Fischer, 2008.

Baldwin, James. *Collected Essays.* New York, The Library of America, 1998.

Banton, Michael. *The Coloured Quarter. Negro Immigrants in an English City.* London, Jonathan Cape, 1955.

Barker, Pat. *The Regeneration Trilogy.* London, Viking, 1995.

Baubérot, Jean. *Laïcité 1905–2005, entre passion et raison.* Paris, Editions du Seuil, 2005.

Bawer, Bruce. *While Europe Slept: How Radical Islam Is Destroying the West From Within.* New York, Doubleday, 2006

Baycili, Sevtap. 'Ik wil in Nederland blijven. Ik hou van dit land.' In Steve Austen, *Kaaskoppen. 20 jonge landgenoten over de toekomst van Nederland.* Amsterdam, Cossee, 2005.

Baycili, Sevtap. *Donderpreken. Aforismen over Nederland.* Amsterdam, Prometheus, 2006.

Beck, Ulrich. *Was ist Globalisierung? Irrtümer des Globalismus – Antworten auf Globalisierung.* Frankfurt, Suhrkamp, 1997.

Beck, Ulrich. *Weltrisikogesellschaft. Auf der Suche nach der verlorenen Sicherheit.* Frankfurt, Suhrkamp, 2007.

Becker, Frans, et al. (eds.). *Transnationaal Nederland.* Amsterdam, Wiardi Beckman Stichting, 2002.

Benali, Abdelkader. 'Waarom zwijgen de Nederlandse schrijvers?' In *Vrij Nederland,* 14 September 2002.

Benedict, Ruth. *Patterns of Culture.* Boston, Houghton Mifflin, 1934.

Benevolo, Leonardo. *The European City.* Oxford, Basil Blackwell, 1993.

Benzine, Rachid. *Les Nouveaux Penseurs de l'islam.* Casablanca, Tarik Editions, 2004.

Berger, John. *Stemverheffing. Een visie op de afgelopen drie jaar.* Amsterdam, De Bezige Bij, 1992.

Berger, Peter L. & Huntington, Samuel P. (eds.). *Many Globalizations. Cultural Diversity in the Contemporary World.* Oxford, Oxford University Press, 2002.

Berlin, Ira. *Generations of Captivity. A History of African-American Slaves.* Cambridge, MA, Harvard University Press, 2003.

Berman, Paul. *Terror and Liberalism.* New York, W. W. Norton, 2003.

Berns, Walter. *Making Patriots.* Chicago, University of Chicago Press, 2001.

Bessems, Kustaw. *En dat in Nederland! De roerige jaren sinds 11 september.* Amsterdam, L. J. Veen, 2006.

Beus, Jos de. *Een cultus van vermijding.* Utrecht, Forum, 1998.

Blainey, Geoffrey. *All for Australia.* Sydney, Methuen Haynes, 1984.

Blokland-Potters, Talja. *Wat stadsbewoners bindt. Sociale relaties in een achterstandswijk.* Kampen, Kok Agora, 1998.

Blumrosen, Alfred W. & Ruth G. *Slave Nation. How Slavery United the Colonies and Sparked the American Revolution.* Naperville, IL, Sourcebooks Inc., 2005.

Boas, Franz. *The Mind of Primitive Man* (rev. edn 1938). Westport, Greenwood Press, 1983.

Bodnar, John. *The Transplanted. A History of Immigrants in Urban America.* Bloomington, Indiana University Press, 1985.

Boef, August Hans den. *Nederland seculier! Tegen religieuze privileges in wetten, regels, praktijken, gewoonten en attitudes.* Amsterdam, Van Gennep, 2003.

Bok, Edward W. *The Americanization of Edward Bok. The Autobiography of a Dutch Boy Fifty Years Later.* New York, Charles Scribner's Sons, 1922.

Bolkestein, Frits. *Woorden hebben hun betekenis.* Amsterdam, Prometheus, 1992.

Boll, Alfred M. *Multiple Nationality and International Law.* Leiden, Martinus Nijhoff, 2007.

Boomkens, René. *De nieuwe wanorde. Globalisering en het einde van de maakbare samenleving.* Amsterdam, Van Gennep, 2006.

Borjas, George J. *Heaven's Door. Immigration Policy and the American Economy.* Princeton, Princeton University Press, 1999.

Botje, Harm. *Een eiland in het westen.* Amsterdam, Nieuwezijds, 2001.

Bouali, Fadoua. *Bevrijd door Allah. Waarom een moslimvrouw haar mannen niet hoeft te gehoorzamen.* Amsterdam, Van Gennep, 2006.

Bouazza, Hafid. 'Nederland is blind voor moslimextremisme.' In *NRC Handelsblad*, 20 February 2002.

Bouazza, Hafid. *Paravion.* Amsterdam, Prometheus, 2003.

Bovenkerk, Frank & Brunt, Lodewijk (eds.). *De rafelrand van Amsterdam. Jordaners, pinda-chinezen, ateliermeisjes en venters in de jaren dertig.* Meppel, Boom, 1977.

Boym, Svetlana. *The Future of Nostalgia.* New York, Basic Books, 2001.

Bredero, G. A. *The Spanish Brabanter. A Seventeenth-Century Dutch Social Satire in Five Acts.* Trans. H. David Brumble III. Binghamton, NY, 1982.

Brenner, Neil & Keil, Roger (eds.). *The Global Cities Reader.* London, Routledge, 2006.

Brink, Gabriël van den. *Schets van een beschavingsoffensief. Over normen, normaliteit en normalisatie in Nederland.* Amsterdam, Amsterdam University Press, 2004.

Brink, Gabriël van den. *Culturele contrasten. Het verhaal van de migranten in Rotterdam.* Amsterdam, Bert Bakker, 2006.

Broeck, Bob van den & Foblets, Marie-Claire (ed.). *Het failliet van de integratie? Het multiculturalismedebat in Vlaanderen.* Leuven, Acco, 2002.

Brown, Carl L. *Religion and State. The Muslim Approach to Politics.* New York, Columbia University Press, 2000.

Bruggen, Carry van. *Vaderlandsliefde, menschenliefde en opvoeding.* Baarn, Hollandia-Drukkerij, 1916.

Bruggen Bouwen. Eindrapport van de Tijdelijke Commissie Onderzoek Integratiebeleid. Den Haag, Sdu Uitgevers, 2004.

Brugman, J. *Het raadsel van de multicultuur. Essays over islam en integratie.* Amsterdam, Meulenhoff, 1998.

Bui Trong, Lucienne. *Violences urbaines. Des vérités qui dérangent.* Paris, Bayard, 2000.

Buijs, Frank J., et al. *Strijders van eigen bodem. Radicale en democratische moslims in Nederland.* Amsterdam, Amsterdam University Press, 2006.

Bulliet, Richard W. *The Case for Islamo-Christian Civilization.* New York, Columbia University Press, 2004.

Buruma, Ian. 'Brief uit Amsterdam.' In Pieter van Os (ed.), *Nederland op scherp. Buitenlandse beschouwingen over een stuurloos land.* Amsterdam, Bert Bakker, 2005.

Buruma, Ian & Margalit, Avishai. *Occidentalism: The West in the Eyes of Its Enemies.* New York, Penguin, 2004.

Buruma, Ian. *Dood van een gezonde roker.* Amsterdam, Atlas, 2006.

Busken Huet, C. *Het land van Rembrand. Studiën over de Noordnederlandsche beschaving in de zeventiende eeuw* (1882). Haarlem, Tjeenk Willink & Zoon, 1946.

Caldwell, Christopher. *Reflections on the Revolution in Europe. Immigration, Islam and the West,* London, Allen Lane, 2009.

Cardini, Franco. *Europa und der Islam. Geschichte eines Misverständnisses.* München, Beck, 2000.

Carr, E. H. *The Twenty Years' Crisis 1919–1939.* New York, Harper Torchbooks, 1939.

Castells, Manuel. 'European Cities, the Information Society and the Global Economy' (1993). In Richard T. Le Gates & Frederic Stout (eds.), *The City Reader.* London, Routledge, 2003.

Castles, Stephen & Miller, Mark J. *The Age of Migration. International Population Movements in the Modern World.* New York, The Guilford Press, 2003.

Césaire, Aimé. *Discours sur le colonialisme.* Paris, Editions Réclame, 1950.

Chapoulie, Jean-Michel. *La Tradition sociologique de Chicago 1892–1961.* Paris, Seuil, 2001.

Chartier, Christian. *Het verdriet van Nederland. Een Fransman stoeit met de Hollandse ziel.* Amsterdam, Prometheus, 1992.

Chorus, Jutta. *Afri. Leven in een migrantenwijk.* Amsterdam, Contact, 2009.

Claeys, Manu. *Het Vlaams Blok in elk van ons.* Leuven, Van Halewyck, 2001.

Cliteur, Paul. *Moderne Papoea's. Dilemma's van een multiculturele samenleving.* Amsterdam, De Arbeiderspers, 2002.

Cohn-Bendit, Daniel & Schmid, Thomas. *Heimat Babylon. Das Wagnis der multikulturellen Demokratie.* Hamburg, Hoffman und Campe, 1992.

Collins, Sydney. *Coloured Minorities in Britain. Studies in British Race Relations Based on African, West-Indian and Asiatic Immigrants.* London, Butterworth Press, 1957.

Community Cohesion. A Report of the Independent Review Team Chaired by Ted Cantle. London, Home Office, 2001.

Couwenberg, S. W. (ed.). *Nationale identiteit. Van Nederlands probleem tot Nederlandse uitdaging.* Budel, Damon, 2001.

Crèvecoeur, J. Hector St. John de. *Letters from an American Farmer* (1782). Pennsylvania, The Franklin Library, 1982.

Curti, Merle. *The Roots of American Loyalty.* New York, Columbia University Press, 1946.

Dagevos, Jaco. *Minderheden in Amsterdam, contacten, concentratie en integratie* (WRA essays 2, 2003).

Dalrymple, Theodore. *Life at the Bottom: The Worldview That Makes the Underclass.* Chicago, Ivan R. Dee, 2001.

Dalrymple, Theodore. *Our Culture: What's Left of It.* Chicago, Ivan R. Dee, 2005.

Darwin, Charles. *The Descent of Man and Selection in Relation to Sex.* Chicago, Rand, McNally & Company, 1874.

Davis, Mike. *Magical Urbanism. Latinos Reinvent the US City.* London, Verso, 2001.

Davis, Mike. *Dead Cities and Other Tales.* New York, The New Press, 2002.

Desai, Kiran. *The Inheritance of Loss.* London, Hamish Hamilton, 2006.

Deursen, A. Th. van. 'De Republiek der Zeven Verenigde Nederlanden (1588–1780).' In J. C. H. Blom & E. Lamberts (eds.), *Geschiedenis van de Nederlanden.* Amsterdam, Agon, 1994.

Dewinter, Filip. *Baas in eigen land.* Brussel, Egmont, 2000.

Dinnerstein, Leonard & Reimers, David M. *Ethnic Americans. A History of Immigration.* New York, Columbia University Press, 1999.

Djaït, Hichem. *La Grande Discorde. Religion et politique dans l'Islam des origines.* Paris, Gallimard, 1989.

Djavann, Chahdortt. *Bas les voiles!* Paris, Gallimard, 2003.

Donzelot, Jacques. *L'Invention du social. Essai sur le déclin des passions politiques.* Paris, Fayard, 1984.

Donzelot, Jacques. *Quand la ville se défait. Quelle politique face à la crise des banlieues?* Paris, Editions du Seuil, 2006.

Doorman, Maarten. *Kiekertak en Klotterbooke. Gedachten over de canon.* Amsterdam, Amsterdam University Press, 2004.

Doorn, J. A. A. van. *Indische lessen. Nederland en de koloniale ervaring.* Amsterdam, Bert Bakker, 1995.

Douglass, Frederick. *Autobiographies.* New York, The Library of America, 1994.

Draï, Raphaël & Mattéi, Jean-François (eds.). *La République brûle-t-elle? Essai sur les violences urbaines françaises.* Paris, Editions Michalon, 2006.

D'Souza, Dinesh. *The End of Racism. Principles for a Multiracial Society.* New York, The Free Press, 1995.

Du Bois, W. E. B. *Writings.* New York, The Library of America, 1986.

Dummett, Michael. *On Immigration and Refugees.* London, Routledge, 2001.

Duyvendak, Jan Willem & Veldboer, Lex (eds.). *Meeting Point Nederland. Over samenlevingsopbouw, multiculturaliteit en sociale cohesie.* Amsterdam, Boom, 2001.

Eddaoudi, Ali. *Hollandse nieuwe. Drie generaties Marokkanen aan het woord.* Rotterdam, Ad. Donker, 2000.

Elias, Norbert. *The Established and the Outsiders. A Sociological Enquiry into Community Problems* (1965). London, Frank Cass & Co, 1994

Ellian, Afshin. 'Leve de monoculturele rechtsstaat.' In *NRC Handelsblad*, 30 November 2002.

Ellison, Ralph. *Invisible Man* (1952). New York, Random House, 2002.

Emerson, Ralph Waldo. *Essays and Lectures.* New York, The Library of America, 1983.

Emmer, Piet. *De Nederlandse slavenhandel 1500–1850.* Amsterdam, De Arbeiderspers, 2000.

Emmer, Piet & Wansink, Hans. *Wegsturen of binnenlaten? Tien vragen en antwoorden over migratie.* Amsterdam, De Arbeiderspers, 2005.

Entzinger, Han. 'Arbeidsmigratie in de twintigste eeuw: noodzaak of last?' In Frans Becker, et al. (eds.), *Transnationaal Nederland. Immigratie en integratie.* Amsterdam, De Arbeiderspers, 2002.

Entzinger, Han & Van der Meer, Jelle (eds.). *Grenzeloze Solidariteit. Naar een migratiebestendige verzorgingsstaat.* Amsterdam, De Balie, 2004.

Enzensberger, H. M. *Die grosse Wanderung. 33 Markierungen.* Frankfurt, Suhrkamp, 1992.

Enzensberger, H. M. *Aussichten auf den Bürgerkrieg.* Frankfurt, Suhrkamp, 1993.

Ephimenco, Sylvain. 'Niemandsland.' In *De Groene Amsterdammer*, 1 March 2000.

Ephimenco, Sylvain. 'Open brief aan de moslims van Nederland.' In *Trouw*, 5 October 2001.

Ephimenco, Sylvain. *Gedwongen tot weerbaarheid. Islamkronieken.* Antwerpen, Houtekiet, 2005.

Eryilmaz, Aytaç, et al. (eds.). *Projekt Migration.* Köln, DuMont Literatur und Kunst Verlag, 2005.

Esposito, John L. & Voll, John O. *Makers of Contemporary Islam.* Oxford, Oxford University Press, 2001.

Eurostat. *Statistics in Focus.* 81/2008.

Fairchild, Henry Pratt. *Immigration. A World Movement and its American Significance* (rev. edn). New York, Macmillan, 1925.

Fallaci, Oriana. *The Rage and the Pride.* New York, Rizzoli, 2002.

Favell, Adrian. *Philosophies of Integration. Immigration and the Idea of Citizenship in France and Britain.* New York, Palgrave, 2001 (2).

Ferguson, Niall. *Empire. How Britain Made the Modern World.* London, Allen Lane, 2003.

Ferro, Marc (ed.). *Le Livre noir du colonialisme. xvie–xxie siècle: de l'extermination à la répentance.* Paris, Robert Laffont, 2003.

Filali-Ansary, Abdou. *L'Islam est-il hostile a la laïcité?* Arles, Actes Sud, 2002.

Finkielkraut, Alain. *De ondergang van het denken.* Amsterdam, Contact, 1988.

Finkielkraut, Alain. *Le Mécontemporain. Péguy, lecteur du monde moderne.* Paris, Gallimard, 1991.

Finkielkraut, Alain. *Comment peut-on être croate?* Paris, Gallimard, 1992.

Finkielkraut, Alain. *L'Ingratitude. Conversation sur notre temps.* Paris, Gallimard, 1999

Florida, Richard. 'Cities and the Creative Class.' In Jan Lin & Christopher Mele (eds.), *The Urban Sociology Reader.* London, Routledge, 2005.

Flynn, Stephen E. 'America the Vulnerable.' In *The War on Terror.* New York, W. W. Norton, 2002.

Fontana, Josep. *The Distorted Past. A Reinterpretation of Europe.* Oxford, Blackwell, 1995.

Fortuyn, Pim. *De islamisering van onze cultuur. Nederlandse identiteit als fundament.* Rotterdam, Karakter, 2001 (2).

Fraihi, Hind. *Undercover in klein-Marokko. Achter de gesloten deuren van de radicale islam.* Leuven, Van Halewyck, 2006.

Francis, Diane. *Immigration. The Economic Case.* Toronto, Key Porter Books, 2002.

Franklin, Benjamin. *Observations Concerning the Increase of Mankind.* 1751.

Franklin, John Hope. *From Slavery to Freedom. A History of Negro Americans* (1947). New York, Knopf, 1966 (3).

Freeman, Gary P. & Jupp, James (eds.). *Nations of Immigrants. Australia, the United States, and International Migration.* Melbourne, Oxford University Press Australia, 1992.

Frissen, Paul. *De Staat.* Amsterdam, De Balie, 2002.

Frissen, Paul. *De staat van verschil.* Amsterdam, Van Gennep, 2007.

Fukuyama, Francis. *Trust. The Social Virtues and the Creation of Prosperity.* New York, The Free Press, 1995.

Fukuyama, Francis. 'Identiteit, immigratie en de toekomst.' In *Nexus* 44, 2006.

Gans, Herbert. *People and Plans. Essays on Urban Problems and Solutions.* New York, Basic Books, 1968.

Garton Ash, Timothy. *Free World. Why a Crisis of the West Reveals the Opportunity of Our Time.* London, Allen Lane, 2004.

Gauchet, Marcel. *La Religion dans la démocratie.* Paris, Gallimard, 1998.

Geertz, Clifford. *The Interpretation of Cultures. Selected Essays.* New York, Basic Books, 1973.

Geertz, Clifford. *Available Light. Antropological Reflections on Philosophical Topics.* Princeton, Princeton University Press, 2000.

Gelder, H. A. Enno van. *Getemperde vrijheid. Een verhandeling over de verhouding van Kerk en Staat in de Republiek der Verenigde Nederlanden.* Groningen, Wolters-Noordhoff, 1972.

Gellner, Ernest. *Conditions of Liberty. Civil Society and Its Rivals*. London, Hamish Hamilton, 1994.

German Marshall Fund of the United States. *Transatlantic Trends 2009*.

Gezik, E. *Eer, identiteit en moord. Een vergelijkende studie tussen Nederland, Duitsland en Turkije*. Utrecht, Nederlands Centrum Buitenlanders, 2003.

Ginkel, Rob van. *Op zoek naar eigenheid. Denkbeelden en discussies over cultuur en identiteit in Nederland*. Den Haag, Sdu Uitgevers, 1999.

Giordano, Ralph. *Wird Deutschland wieder gefährlich? Mein Brief an Kanzler Kohl – Ursachen und Folgen*. Köln, Kiepenheuer & Witsch, 1993.

Glass, Ruth. *London's Newcomers. The West Indian Migrants*. Cambridge, MA, Harvard University Press, 1961.

Glazer, Nathan. *We Are All Multiculturalists Now*. Cambridge, MA, Harvard University Press, 1997.

Glazer, Nathan & Moynihan, Daniel Patrick. *Beyond the Melting Pot. The Negroes, Puerto Ricans, Jews, Italians, and Irish of New York City*. Cambridge, MA, MIT Press and Harvard University Press, 1963.

Gleason, Philip. 'American Identity and Americanization.' In Stephan Thernstrom (ed.), *Harvard Encyclopedia of American Ethnic Groups*. Cambridge, MA, Harvard University Press, 1980.

Global Commission on International Migration. *Migration in an Interconnected World: New directions for action*. 2005.

Glotz, Peter. *Die deutsche Rechte. Eine Streitschrift*. Stuttgart, Deutsche Verlags-Anstalt, 1989.

Goldziher, Ignaz. *Introduction to Islamic Theology and Law* (1910). Princeton, Princeton University Press, 1981.

Göle, Nilufer. *The Forbidden Modern. Civilization and Veiling*. Ann Arbor, University of Michigan Press, 1998.

Goodhart, David. *Progressive Nationalism. Citizenship and the Left*. London, Demos, 2006.

Goudappel, Annerieke & Tang, Zhimin. 'Gestrand in Dalfsen. Chinese vluchtelingen wachten op het paradijs.' In *NRC Handelsblad*, 11 November 2000.

Gowricharn, Ruben. *Andere gedachten. Over de multiculturele samenleving*. Utrecht, Forum, 2000.

Grant, Madison. *The Passing of the Great Race Or the Racial Basis of European History*. New York, Charles Scribner's Sons, 1918.

Gray, John. *Al-Qaeda and What it Means to be Modern*. London, Faber & Faber, 2003.

Grodzins, Morton. *The Loyal and the Disloyal. Social Boundaries of Patriotism and Treason*. Chicago, University of Chicago Press, 1956.

Groen, Janny & Kranenberg, Annieke. *Strijdsters van Allah. Radicale moslima's en het Hofstadnetwerk*. Amsterdam, Meulenhoff, 2006.

Guéhenno, Jean-Marie. *Het einde van de democratie*. Tielt, Lannoo, 1994.

Guénif Souilamas, Nacira. *Des beurettes*. Paris, Editions Grasset & Fasquelle, 2000.

Gutmann, Amy. *Identity in Democracy*. Princeton, Princeton University Press, 2003.

Haddad, Yvonne & Esposito, John L. (eds.). *Muslims on the Americanization Path?* Oxford, Oxford University Press, 2000.

Hall, Peter. *Cities of Tomorrow.* Oxford, Blackwell, 2002.

Hall, Peter & Pfeiffer, Ulrich. *Urban Future 21. A Global Agenda for Twenty-First Century Cities.* London, Spon Press, 2002.

Handlin, Oscar. *The Uprooted. The Epic Story of the Great Migrations that Made the American People.* Boston, Little, Brown and Company, 1952.

Handlin, Oscar. *Race and Nationality in American Life.* Boston, Little, Brown and Company, 1957.

Handlin, Oscar. *Boston's Immigrants. A Study in Acculturation* (1941). Cambridge, MA, Harvard University Press, 1959 (2).

Handlin, Oscar (ed.). *Children of the Uprooted.* New York, George Braziller, 1966.

Hannerz, Ulf. *Exploring the City. Inquiries Toward an Urban Anthropology.* New York, Columbia University Press, 1980.

Hansen, Marcus L. *The Atlantic Migration 1607–1860. A History of the Continuing Settlement of the United States* (1940). Safety Harbor, Simon Publications, 2001.

Hansen, Marcus Lee. *The Immigrant in American History.* Cambridge, MA, Harvard University Press, 1940.

Harris, Nigel. *Thinking the Unthinkable. The Immigration Myth Exposed.* London, Tauris, 2002.

Harrison, Lawrence E. & Huntington, Samuel P. (eds.). *Culture Matters. How Values Shape Human Progress.* New York, Basic Books, 2000.

Hartigan, John. *Racial Situations: Class Predicaments of Whiteness in Detroit,* Princeton, Princeton University Press, 1999.

Hartmann, Edward George. *The Movement to Americanize the Immigrant.* New York, Columbia University Press, 1948.

Harvey, David. *Spaces of Hope.* Edinburgh, Edinburgh University Press, 2000.

Haseth de, Carel. *Slaaf en meester.* Schoorl, Conserve, 2002.

Hatton, Timothy & Williamson, Jeffrey. *International Migration in the Long-Run: Positive Selection, Negative Selection and Policy.* Discussion Paper, Institute for the Study of Labour, Bonn, 2004.

Hatton, Timothy J. & Williamson, Jeffrey G. *Global Migration and the World Economy. Two Centuries of Policy and Performance.* Cambridge, MA, MIT Press, 2005.

Havenaar, Ronald. *Muizenhol. Nederland volgens Willem Frederik Hermans.* Amsterdam, Van Oorschot, 2003.

Hawgood, John A. *The Tragedy of German-America. The Germans in the United States During the Nineteenth Century – and After.* New York, Putnam's Sons, 1940.

Heitmeyer, Wilhelm, et al. *Verlockender Fundamentalismus. Türkische Jugendliche in Deutschland.* Frankfurt, Suhrkamp Verlag, 1997.

Held, David. *Democracy and the Global Order. From the Modern State to Cosmopolitan Governance.* Cambridge, Polity Press, 1995.

Hermans, Willem Frederik. *Volledige Werken* I. Amsterdam, De Bezige Bij, 12th printing, 1971.

Herskovits, Melville J. *Man and His Works. The Science of Cultural Anthropology.* New York, Knopf, 1948.

Higham, John. *Strangers in the Land. Patterns of American Nativism 1860–1925.* New Brunswick, Rutgers University Press, 1955.

Hill, Clifford. *Immigration and Integration. A Study of the Settlement of Coloured Minorities in Britain.* Oxford, Pergamon Press, 1970.

Hirsi Ali, Ayaan. *De zoontjesfabriek. Over vrouwen, islam en integratie.* Amsterdam, Augustus, 2002.

Hirsi Ali, Ayaan. *De maagdenkooi.* Amsterdam, Augustus, 2004.

Hirsi Ali, Ayaan. *The Caged Virgin. An Emancipation Proclamation for Women and Islam.* New York, Free Press, 2006.

Hobsbawm, E. J. *Nations and Nationalism Since 1780. Programme, Myth, Reality.* Cambridge, Cambridge University Press, 1990.

Hoffman, Eva. *De ziel van de dialoog.* In *Nexus* 26, 2000.

Houellebecq, Michel. *The Elementary Particles.* New York, Vintage Books, 2001.

Hughes, Robert. *Culture of Complaint. The Fraying of America.* New York, Oxford University Press, 1993.

Huizinga, Johan. *Verzamelde Werken II. Nederland.* Haarlem, Tjeenk Willink & Zoon, 1948.

Huizinga, Johan. *Verzamelde Werken VII. Geschiedwetenschap. Hedendaagse Cultuur.* Haarlem, Tjeenk Willink & Zoon, 1950.

Hume, David. *Essays. Moral, Political and Literary* (1741). Indianapolis, Liberty Fund, 1987.

Huntington, Samuel P. *The Clash of Civilizations and the Remaking of World Order.* New York, Simon & Schuster, 1996.

Huntington, Samuel P. *Who Are We? The Challenges to America's National Identity.* New York, Simon & Schuster, 2004.

Huxley, Aldous. 'What is Happening to Our Population?' (1934). In David Bradshaw (ed.), *The Hidden Huxley. Contempt and Compassion for the Masses.* London, Faber & Faber, 1994.

Huxley, Elspeth. *Back Street New Worlds. A Look at Immigrants in Britain.* New York, William Morrow and Company, 1965.

Hvidt, Kristian. *Flight to America. The Social Background of 300,000 Danish Emigrants.* New York, Academic Press, 1975.

Ignatieff, Michael. *Whose Universal Values? The Crisis in Human Rights.* Amsterdam, Praemium Erasmianum Essay, 1999.

International Organization for Migration (IOM). *World Migration 2005. Costs and Benefits of International Migration.* Geneva, 2005.

International Organization for Migration (IOM). *World Migration 2008. Managing Labour Mobility in the Evolving Global Economy.* Geneva, 2008

Ismaili, Salma. 'Ik deed alles wat Allah verbood.' Interview in *NRC Handelsblad*, 21 August 2004.

Israel, Jonathan. 'Culturele zelfmoord.' In Pieter van Os (ed.), *Nederland op scherp. Buitenlandse beschouwingen over een stuurloos land.* Amsterdam, Bert Bakker, 2005.

Istendael, Geert van. *Het Belgisch labyrint. Wakker worden in een ander land.* Amsterdam, De Arbeiderspers, 1989.

Jefferson, Thomas. *Writings.* New York, The Library of America, 1984.

Jenks, Jeremiah W. & Lauck, W. Jett. *The Immigration Problem. A Study of American Immigration Conditions and Needs.* New York, Funk & Wagnalls Company, 1922.

Jones, Edward P. *The Known World.* New York, HarperCollins, 2003.

Joppke, Christian. *Immigration and the Nation-State. The United States, Germany and Great Britain.* Oxford, Oxford University Press, 1999.

Joppke, Christian & Morawska, Ewa (eds.). *Toward Assimilation and Citizenship. Immigrants in Liberal Nation-States.* New York, Palgrave, 2003.

Joustra, Arendo (ed.). *Vreemde ogen. Buitenlanders over de Nederlandse identiteit.* Amsterdam, Prometheus, 1993.

Jupp, James. *From White Australia to Woomera. The Story of Australian Immigration.* Cambridge, Cambridge University Press, 2002.

Kaka, Imad el & Kursun, Hatice. *Mijn geloof en mijn geluk. Islamitische meiden en jongens over hun homoseksuele gevoelens.* Amsterdam, Schorerboeken, 2002.

Kallen, Horace M. *Culture and Democracy in the United States* (1924). New Brunswick, Transaction, 1998.

Kaltenbach, Jeanne-Hélène & Tribalet, Michèle. *La République et l'islam. Entre crainte et aveuglement.* Paris, Gallimard, 2002.

Kant, Immanuel. *Zum ewigen Frieden: Ein philosophischer Entwurf.* Königsberg, bey Friedrich Nicolovius (1795).

Kapuscinski, Ryszard. *Lapidarium. Observaties van een wereldreiziger 1980–2000.* Amsterdam, De Arbeiderspers, 2003.

Kasinitz, Philip, et al. *Inheriting the City. The Children of Immigrants Come of Age.* Cambridge, MA, Harvard University Press, 2008.

Kaufmann, Franz-Xaver. *Schrumpfende Gesellschaft: Vom Bevölkerungsrückgang und seinen Folgen.* Frankfurt, Suhrkamp, 2005.

Kefalas, Maria. *Working-Class Heroes. Protecting Home, Community, and Nation in a Chicago Neighborhood.* Berkeley, University of California Press, 2003

Kelek, Necla. *Die fremde Braut. Ein Bericht aus dem Inneren des türkischen Lebens in Deutschland.* Köln, Kiepenheuer & Witsch, 2005.

Kelek, Necla. *Die verlorenen Söhne. Plädoyer für die Befreiung des türkisch-muslimischen Mannes.* Köln, Kiepenheuer & Witsch, 2006.

Kelley, Ninette & Trebilcock, Michael. *The Making of the Mosaic. A History of Canadian Immigration Policy.* Toronto, University of Toronto Press, 1998.

Kellor, Frances. *Immigration and the Future.* New York, George H. Doran Company, 1920.

Kennedy, James. 'Radicale bekering.' In Pieter van Os (ed.), *Nederland op scherp. Buitenlandse beschouwingen over een stuurloos land.* Amsterdam, Bert Bakker, 2005.

Kennedy, James. 'Oude en nieuwe vormen van tolerantie in Nederland en Amerika: Tolerantie als ideologie maakt verdraagzaamheid kwetsbaar.' In Marcel ten Hooven (ed.), *De lege tolerantie. Over vrijheid en vrijblijvendheid in Nederland.* Amsterdam, Boom, 2001.

Kennedy, Paul. *Preparing for the Twenty-First Century.* New York, Random House, 1993.

Kepel, Gilles. *Fitna. Guerre au coeur de l'islam.* Paris, Gallimard, 2004.

Klausen, Jytte. *The Islamic Challenge. Politics and Religion in Western Europe.* Oxford, Oxford University Press, 2005.

Kleijwegt, Margalith. *Onzichtbare ouders. De buurt van Mohammed B.* Zutphen, Plataan, 2005.

Klein, Katrien de, et al. (eds.). *26.000 gezichten. Dertig fotografen, eenentwintig schrijvers en zesentwintigduizend gezichten.* Amsterdam, Stichting 26.000 gezichten, 2006.

Knippenberg, Hans & Pater, Ben de. *De eenwording van Nederland. Schaalvergroting en integratie sinds 1800.* Nijmegen, SUN, 1988.

Knopp, Guido. *Die grosse Flucht. Das Schicksal der Vertriebenen.* München, Econ, 2001.

Knox, Paul L. & McCarthy, Linda. *Urbanization. An Introduction to Urban Social Geography.* Upper Saddle River, Pearson, 2005 (2).

Knox, Paul & Pinch, Steven. *Urban Social Geography. An Introduction.* Harlow, Pearson, 2006.

Koch, Koen & Scheffer, Paul (eds.). *Het nut van Nederland. Opstellen over soevereiniteit en identiteit.* Amsterdam, Bert Bakker, 1996.

Koran, in the translation by Muhammad Shakir, *Holy Qur'an,* New York, Tahrike Tarsile Qur'an Inc., 1987.

Kossmann, Ernest H. *Een tuchteloos probleem. De natie in de Nederlanden.* Leuven, Davidsfonds, 1994.

Kossmann, Ernest H. *Vergankelijkheid en continuïteit. Opstellen over geschiedenis.* Amsterdam, Bert Bakker, 1995.

Kristeva, Julia. *De vreemdeling in onszelf.* Amsterdam, Contact, 1991.

Kuijpers, Erika. *Migrantenstad. Immigratie en sociale verhoudingen in 17e-eeuws Amsterdam.* Hilversum, Verloren, 2005.

Kundera, Milan. *Le Rideau. Essai en sept parties.* Paris, Gallimard, 2005.

Kuyper, Eric de. *Een vis verdrinken. Een niet-Nederlander tussen de Nederlanders.* Nijmegen, SUN, 2001.

Kymlicka, Will. *Multicultural Citizenship: A Liberal Theory of Minority Rights.* New York, Oxford University Press, 1995.

Kymlicka, Will. *Finding Our Way. Rethinking Etnocultural Relations in Canada.* New York, Oxford University Press, 1998.

Lacorne, Denis. *La Crise de l'identité américaine. Du melting-pot au multiculturalisme.* Paris, Gallimard, 2003.

Landes, David S. *The Wealth and Poverty of Nations. Why Some Are So Rich and Some So Poor.* New York, W. W. Norton, 1998.

Lang, Jack & Le Bras, Hervé. *Immigration positive.* Paris, Odile Jacob, 2006.

Langeveld, Herman. *Dit leven van krachtig handelen. Hendrikus Colijn 1869–1944.* Amsterdam, Balans, 1998.

Laqueur, Walter. *The Last Days of Europe: Epitaph for an Old Continent.* New York, St Martin's Press, 2007.

Laroui, Fouad. *Judith en Jamal.* Amsterdam, Van Oorschot, 2001.

Laroui, Fouad. 'Hoe ik Europeaan werd.' In *Contrast,* no. 4, 31 January 2002.

Lash, Christopher. *The Culture of Narcissism. American Life in An Age of Diminishing Expectations.* New York, Warner Books, 1979.

Lawrence, Bruce (ed.). *Messages to the World. The Statements of Osama Bin Laden.* London, Verso, 2005.

Lee, Chang-Rae. *Native Speaker.* New York, Riverhead Books, 1995.

LeGates, Richard T. & Stout, Frederic (eds.). *The City Reader.* London, Routledge, 2003.

Legrain, Philippe. *Immigrants. Your Country Needs Them.* London, Little Brown, 2006.

Lemaire, Ton. *Over de waarde van kulturen. Tussen europacentrisme en relativisme. Een inleiding in de kultuurfilosofie.* Baarn, Ambo, 1976.

Lemaire, Ton. *Twijfel aan Europa. Zijn de intellectuelen de vijanden van de Europese cultuur?* Baarn, Ambo, 1990.

Levering Lewis, David & Du Bois, W. E. B. *Biography of a Race, 1868–1919.* New York, Henry Holt, 1993.

Levering Lewis, David & Du Bois, W. E. B. *The Fight for Equality and The American Century, 1919–1963.* New York, Henry Holt, 2000.

Lévi-Strauss, Claude. *Race et histoire* (1952). Paris, Denoël, 1987.

Lewis, Bernard. *Race and Slavery in the Middle East. An Historical Enquiry.* Oxford, Oxford University Press, 1990.

Lewis, Bernard. *Islam and the West.* Oxford, Oxford University Press, 1993.

Lewis, Bernard. *What Went Wrong? The Clash Between Islam and Modernity in the Middle East.* London, Weidenfeld & Nicolson, 2002.

Lewis, Bernard. *The Crisis of Islam. Holy War and Unholy Terror.* New York, Modern Library, 2003.

Lewis, Philip. *Islamic Britain. Religion, Politics and Identity Among British Muslims.* London, Tauris, 2002.

Li, Peter S. *Destination Canada. Immigration Debates and Issues.* Don Mills, Oxford University Press, 2003.

Lijphart, Arend. *Verzuiling, pacificatie en kentering in de Nederlandse politiek.* Amsterdam, J. H. de Bussy, 1976 (2).

Lin, Jan & Mele, Christopher. *The Urban Sociology Reader.* London, Routledge, 2005.

Lincoln, Abraham. *Speeches and Writings 1859–1865.* New York, The Library of America, 1989.

Lipovetsky, Gilles. *Le Crépuscule du devoir. L'éthique indolore des nouveaux temps démocratiques.* Paris, Gallimard, 1992.

Lofland, Lyn H. *A World of Strangers. Order and Action in Urban Public Space.* New York, Basic Books, 1973.

Longman, Phillip. 'The Global Baby Bust.' In *Foreign Affairs*, May/June 2004, pp. 64–79.

Low, Setha. *Behind the Gates. Life, Security, and the Pursuit of Happiness in Fortress America*. New York, Routledge, 2004.

Lucassen, Jan & Penninx, Rinus. *Nieuwkomers, Nakomelingen, Nederlanders. Immigranten in Nederland 1550–1993*. Amsterdam, Het Spinhuis, 1994.

Lucassen, Leo. *The Immigrant Threat. The Integration of Old and New Migrants in Western Europe Since 1850*. Chicago, University of Illinois Press, 2005.

Lucassen, Leo, et al. (eds.). *Paths of Integration. Migrants in Western Europe (1880–2004)*. Amsterdam, Amsterdam University Press, 2006.

Maalouf, Amin. *The Crusades Through Arab Eyes* (1983). London, Saqi, 2004.

Maalouf, Amin. *Les Identités meurtrières*. Paris, Grasset, 1998.

Mahbubani, Kishore. *The New Asian Hemisphere. The Irresistible Shift of Global Power to the East*. New York, Public Affairs, 2008.

Mak, Geert. *De engel van Amsterdam*. Amsterdam, Atlas, 2002 (rev. edn).

Mak, Geert. *Gedoemd tot kwetsbaarheid*. Amsterdam, Atlas, 2005.

Mak, Geert. *Nagekomen flessenpost*. Amsterdam, Atlas, 2005.

Mandanipour, Ali. 'Social Exclusion and Space' (1998). In Richard T. LeGates, & Frederic Stout (eds.), *The City Reader*. London, Routledge, 2003.

Manen, van N. F. & Hoekema, A. J. 'Gemeenschappen komen tot hun recht. Zeven kernproblemen bij onderzoek naar recht, multiculturaliteit en sociale cohesie.' In P. B. Cliteur, & V. van den Eeckhout (eds.), *Multiculturalisme, cultuurrelativisme en sociale cohesie*. Den Haag, Boom Juridische Uitgevers, 2001.

Manji, Irshad. *The Trouble with Islam. A Wake-up Call for Honesty and Change*. Toronto, Random House Canada, 2003.

Massey, Douglas & Denton, Nancy. *American Apartheid. Segregation and the Making of the Underclass*. Cambridge, MA, Harvard University Press, 1993.

Maurin, Eric. *Le Ghetto français. Enquête sur le séparatisme social*. Paris, Editions du Seuil, 2004.

Mayo Smith, Richmond. *Emigration and Immigration. A Study in Social Science*. New York, Charles Scribner's Sons, 1890.

McLeod, Cynthia. *Slavernij en de Memorie*. Schoorl, Conserve, 2002.

Memmi, Albert. *Portrait du colonisé. Portrait du colonisateur* (1957). Paris, Gallimard, 1985.

Memmi, Albert. *Portrait du decolonisé arabo-musulman et de quelques autres*. Paris, Gallimard, 2004.

Mernissi, Fatima. *The Veil and the Male Elite: A Feminist Interpretation of Women's Rights in Islam*. New York, Addison-Wesley, 1991.

Modood, Tariq. *Multiculturalism. A Civic Idea*. Cambridge, Polity, 2007.

Mollenkopf, John. 'Assimilating Immigrants in Amsterdam.' In Leon Deben, et al. (eds.), *Understanding Amsterdam. Essays on Economic Vitality, City Life and Urban Form*. Amsterdam, Het Spinhuis, 2000.

Montaigne, Michel de. *Essays*, Book I, Ch. 31. 'On Cannibals.' London, Penguin, 1958.

Montet-Toutain, Karen. *Et pourtant, je les aime . . . .* Neuilly-sur-Seine, Editions Michel Lafon, 2006.

Morshäuser, Bodo. *Warten auf den Führer*. Frankfurt, Suhrkamp, 1993.

Moulier-Boutang, Yann. *La Révolte des banlieues ou les habits nus de la république*. Paris, Editions Amsterdam, 2005.

Mumford, Lewis. *The Culture of Cities* (1938). New York, Harcourt Brace & Company, 1970.

Mumford, Lewis. *The City in History. Its Origins, Its Transformations and Its Prospects*. New York, Harcourt, Brace & World, 1961.

Musterd, Sako. 'Social and Ethnic Segregation in Europe: Levels, Causes and Effects.' In *Journal of Urban Affairs*. Vol. 27, no. 3, 2005.

Musterd, Sako. *Social and Ethnic Segregation in Europe. Levels, Causes and Effects*. Paper for the Urban Affairs Association Conference held in Washington 2004.

Musterd, Sako. 'Segregation and Integration: A Contested Relationship.' In *Journal of Ethnic and Migration Studies*. Vol. 29, no. 4, July 2003, pp. 623–41.

Myrdal, Gunnar. *An American Dilemma. The Negro Problem and Modern Democracy*. New York, Harper & Brothers, 1944.

Naipaul, V. S. *A Bend in the River*. London, Andre Deutsch, 1979.

Naipaul, V. S. *The Enigma of Arrival*, New York, Knopf, 1987.

Naipaul, V. S. *Beyond Belief. Islamic Excursions among the Converted Peoples*. London, Little, Brown and Company, 1998.

Naipaul, V. S. *Letters Between a Father and a Son*. London, Little, Brown and Company, 1999.

Naqib al-Misri, Ahmad ibn. *Reliance of the Traveller. A Classic Manuel of Islamic Sacred Law*. Beltsville, Amana, 1994.

Nieuwenhuys, Rob. *Vergeelde portretten uit een Indisch familiealbum*. Amsterdam, Querido, 1954.

Nimwegen, Nico van & Beets, Gijs (eds.). *Bevolkingsvraagstukken in Nederland anno 2000*. Den Haag, NiDi, 2000.

Nimwegen, Nico van & Esveldt, Ingrid (eds.). *Bevolkingsvraagstukken in Nederland anno 2006. Grote steden in demografisch perspectief*. Den Haag, NiDi, 2006.

Noiriel, Gérard. *Le Creuset français. Histoire de l'immigration xixe–xxe siècle*. Paris, Editions du Seuil, 1988.

Norris, Pippa. *Radical Right. Voters and Parties in the Electoral Market*. Cambridge, Cambridge University Press, 2005.

Norris, Pippa & Inglehart, Ronald. *Sacred and Secular. Religion and Politics Worldwide*. Cambridge, Cambridge University Press, 2004.

Obama, Barack. 'A More Perfect Union.' Speech in Philadelphia, 18 March 2008.

Obama, Barack. *Dreams from My Father. A Story of Race and Inheritance*. New York, Three Rivers Press, 2004 (2).

Obdeijn, Herman & Mas, Paolo de. *De Marokkaanse uitdaging. De tweede generatie in een veranderend Nederland*. Utrecht, Forum, 2001.

Ogata, Sadako. *The Turbulent Decade. Confronting the Refugee Crises of the 1990s*. New York, W. W. Norton , 2005.

Oostindie, Gert (ed.). *Het verleden onder ogen. Herdenking van de slavernij*. Amsterdam, Arena, 2002.

Oostindie, Gert. *Postkoloniaal Nederland. Vijfenzestig jaar vergeten, herdenken, verdringen.* Amsterdam, Bert Bakker, 2010.

Oostrom, Frits van (ed.). *Entoen.nu. De canon van Nederland.* Rapport van de commissie ontwikkeling Nederlandse canon. Den Haag, Ministerie van OCW, 2006.

Ortega y Gasset, José. *The Revolt of the Masses* (1930). New York, Mentor Books, 1950.

Os, Pieter van (ed.). *Nederland op scherp. Buitenlandse beschouwingen over een stuurloos land.* Amsterdam, Bert Bakker, 2005.

Pamuk, Orhan. *My Name Is Red.* London, Faber & Faber, 2001.

Panayi, Panikos. *The Impact of Immigraton. A Documentary History of the Effects and Experiences of Immigrants in Britain Since 1945.* Manchester, Manchester University Press, 1999.

Parekh Report. *The Future of Multi-Ethnic Britain.* London, Profile Books, 2000.

Park, Robert E. *Race and Culture. The Collected Papers Vol. I.* Glencoe, The Free Press, 1950.

Park, Robert E. & Burgess, Ernest W. *The City. Suggestions for Investigation of Human Behavior in the Urban Environment* (1925). Chicago, University of Chicago Press, 1984.

Park, Robert E. & Burgess, Ernest W. *An Introduction to the Science of Sociology.* Chicago, University of Chicago Press, 1924 (2nd rev. edn).

Park, Robert E. & Miller, Herbert A. *Old World Traits Transplanted.* New York, Harper & Brothers, 1921.

Perron, E. du. *Het land van herkomst* (1935). Amsterdam, Contact, 1948.

Perron, Edgar du. *Country of Origin* (1935). Cambridge, MA, University of Massachusetts Press, 1984.

Pessers, Dorien. *Liefde, solidariteit en recht. Een interdisciplinair onderzoek naar het wederkerigheidsbeginsel.* Amsterdam, dissertation, 1999.

Pettigrew, Thomas F. 'New Patterns of Prejudice: The Different Worlds of 1984 and 1964.' In Fred L. Pincus & Howard J. Ehrlich (eds.), *Race and Ethnic Conflict. Contending Views on Prejudice, Discrimination, and Ethnoviolence.* Boulder, Westview Press, 1994.

Phillips, Mike & Phillips, Trevor. *Windrush. The Irresistable Rise of Multiracial Britain.* London, Harper Collins, 1998.

Phillips, Caryl. *Het Atlantisch lied.* Amsterdam, De Bezige Bij, 2000.

Phillips, Melanie. *Londonistan. How Britain is Creating a Terror State Within.* London, Gibson Square, 2006.

Podhoretz, Norman. *Making It.* New York, Random House, 1967.

Ponty, Janine. *L'Immigration dans les textes. France, 1789–2002.* Paris, Editions Berlin, 2003.

Popper, Karl. *The Poverty of Historicism.* London, Routledge & Keegan Paul, 1961

Portes, Alejandro & Manning, Robert D. 'The Immigrant Enclave: Theory and Empirical Examples.' In Jan Lin & Cristopher Mele (eds.), *The Urban Sociology Reader.* London, Routledge, 2005.

Portes, Alejandro & Rumbaut, Rubén G. *Legacies. The Story of the Immigrant Second Generation.* Berkeley, University of California Press, 2001.

Prins, Baukje. *Voorbij de onschuld. Het debat over integratie in Nederland.* Amsterdam, Van Gennep, 2004 (2).

Pronk, Jan. *De kritische grens. Beschouwingen over tweespalt en orde.* Amsterdam, Prometheus, 1994.

Putnam, Robert D. 'E Pluribus Unum. Diversity and Community in the Twenty-First Century.' In *Scandinavian Political Studies.* Vol. 30, no. 2, 2007.

Qutb, Sayyid. *In the Shade of the Qur'an.* Vol. 30. New Delhi, Islamic Book Service, 2001.

Qutb, Sayyid. *Milestones.* Damascus, Dar al-Ilm, 1964.

Ramadan, Tariq. *Les Musulmans d'occident et l'avenir de l'islam.* Paris, Actes Sud, 2003.

Ramadan, Tariq. *The Messenger. The Meanings of the Life of Muhammad.* London, Allen Lane, 2007.

Ramdas, Anil. *De papegaai, de stier en de klimmende bougainvillea.* Amsterdam, De Bezige Bij, 1992.

Ramdas, Anil. 'Moedwil en kwade trouw bij blanke schrijvers; niemand heeft oog voor het vreemde.' In *NRC Handelsblad,* 14 March 1997.

Ramdas, Anil. *Het geheugen van de stad.* Amsterdam, Balans, 2000.

Ramsaran, Rekha & Spaans, Bregje. *Wankele waarden. Levenskwesties van moslims belicht voor professionals.* Utrecht, Forum, 2003.

Rath, Jan. *Het mooist van Mokum.* Amsterdam, Vossiuspers, 2007.

Reeber, Michel. *Petite sociologie de l'islam.* Toulouse, Editions Milan, 2005.

Reimers, David M. *Unwelcome Strangers. American Identity and the Turn Against Immigrants.* New York, Columbia University Press, 1998.

Reiss, Albert J. (ed.). *Louis Wirth on Cities and Social Life. Selected Papers.* Chicago, University of Chicago Press, 1964.

Rentes de Carvalho, J. *Waar die andere God woont.* Amsterdam, De Arbeiderspers, 1982.

Reybrouck, David van. *Pleidooi voor populisme.* Amsterdam, Querido, 2008.

Riis, Jacob A. *How The Other Half Lives. Studies Among The Tenements Of New York* (1890). New York, Dover, 1971.

Romein, Jan. *Het vergruisde beeld. Over het onderzoek naar de oorzaken van onze opstand.* Haarlem, Tjeenk Willink & Zoon, 1939.

Romein, Jan & Annie. *Erflaters van onze beschaving. Nederlandse gestalten uit zes eeuwen.* Amsterdam, Querido, 1956.

Roodenburg, Hans, et al. *Immigration and the Dutch Economy.* Den Haag, Centraal Planbureau, 2003.

Roosevelt, Theodore. *Letters and Speeches.* New York, The Library of America, 2004.

Rooy, Piet de (ed.). *Geschiedenis van Amsterdam. Deel IV: Tweestrijd om de hoofdstad 1900–2000.* Amsterdam, SUN, 2007.

Roth, Philip. *The Human Stain.* London, Jonathan Cape, 2000.

Roy, Olivier, *L'Islam mondialisé*, Paris, Seuil, 2002.

Ruijter, Dick de. *Een culturele blik op de Afrikaanderwijk en de Bloemhof.* Gemeente Rotterdam, 2008.

Rutgers, Rob & Molier, Gelijn (eds.). *Het multiculturele debat. Integratie of assimilatie?* Den Haag, Boom Juridische Uitgevers, 2004.

Sackmann, Rosemarie. *Zuwanderung und Integration. Theorien und empirische Befunde aus Frankreich, den Niederlanden und Deutschland.* Wiesbaden, Verlag für Sozialwissenschaften, 2004.

Safranski, Rüdiger. *Wieviel Globalisierung verträgt der Mensch?* München, Carl Hanser Verlag, 2003.

Said, Edward. *Out of Place. A Memoir.* New York, Knopf, 1999.

Said, Edward. *Reflections on Exile and Other Essays.* Cambridge, MA, Harvard University Press, 2000.

Sakali, Saïda. 'Ze zijn niet zo lief meer, meneer.' In *De Morgen*, 6 December 2002.

Salins, Peter D. *Assimilation, American Style.* New York, Basic Books, 1997.

Sanders, Stephan. *Gemengde ervaring, gemengde gevoelens.* De Rushdie-affaire; een besluit tot inmenging. Amsterdam, De Balie, 1989.

Sardar, Ziauddin. *Balti Britain. A Journey Through the British Asian Experience.* London, Granta, 2008.

Sas, N. C. F. van. 'Nederland. Een historisch fenomeen.' In *De metamorfose van Nederland. Van oude orde naar moderniteit 1750–1900.* Amsterdam, Amsterdam University Press, 2004.

Sassen, Saskia. *Guests and Aliens.* New York, New Press, 1999.

Sassen, Saskia. *The Global City. New York, London, Tokyo.* Princeton, Princeton University Press, 2001.

Sayad, Abdelmalek. *La Double Absence. Des illusions de l'émigré aux souffrances de l'immigré.* Paris, Editions du Seuil, 1999.

Schama, Simon. *The Embarrassment of Riches. An Interpretation of Dutch Culture in the Golden Age,* London, Collins, 1987.

Scheffer, Paul. 'Het multiculturele drama.' In *NRC Handelsblad,* 29 January 2000.

Scheffer, Paul. 'De ontkende opstand.' In *NRC Handelsblad,* 11 May 2002.

Schlesinger Jr, Arthur M. *The Disuniting of America. Reflections on a Multicultural Society.* New York, Norton, 1992.

Schnabel, Paul. *De multiculturele illusie.* Utrecht, Forum, 2000.

Schnapper, Dominique. *La France de l'intégration. Sociologie de la nation en 1990.* Paris, Gallimard, 1991.

Schnapper, Dominique. *La Relation à l'autre. Au coeur de la pensée sociologique.* Paris, Gallimard, 1998.

Schoo, H. J. *De verwarde natie. Dwarse notities over immigratie.* Amsterdam, Prometheus, 2000.

Sen, Amartya. *Identity and Violence. The Illusion of Destiny.* New York, W. W. Norton, 2006.

Sens, Angelie. *'Mensaap, heiden, slaaf.' Nederlandse visies op de wereld rond 1800.* Den Haag, Sdu Uitgevers, 2001.

Sidgwick, Henry. *The Elements of Politics*. London, Macmillan, 1897.

Simmel, Georg. *On Individuality and Social Forms*. Chicago, University of Chicago Press, 1971.

Sinclair, Upton. *The Jungle* (1906). New York, Penguin, 2006.

Singer, Peter. *Een wereld. Ethiek in een tijd van globalisering*. Rotterdam, Lemniscaat, 2003.

Sloterdijk, Peter. *Sphären II. Globen. Makrosphärologie*. Frankfurt, Suhrkamp, 1999.

Sloterdijk, Peter. *Sphären III. Schäume. Plurale Sphärologie*. Frankfurt, Suhrkamp, 2004.

Sloterdijk, Peter. *Im Weltinnenraum des Kapitals. Für eine philosophische Theorie der Globalisierung*. Frankfurt, Suhrkamp, 2005.

Snouck Hurgronje, C. *Nederland en de islam. Vier voordrachten gehouden in de Nederlandse bestuursacademie*. Leiden, E. J. Brill, 1911.

Sociaal en Cultureel Planbureau (SCP), *Rapportage minderheden 2003. Onderwijs, arbeid en sociaal-culturele integratie*. Den Haag, 2003.

Sociaal en Cultureel Planbureau (SCP). *Moslim in Nederland. Religieuze dimensies, etnische relaties en burgerschap: Turken en Marokkanen in Rotterdam*. Den Haag, 2004.

Sociaal en Cultureel Planbureau (SCP) et al. *Jaarrapport Integratie 2005*. Den Haag, 2005.

Soroush, Abdolkarim. *Reason, Freedom, and Democracy in Islam. Essential Writings*. Oxford, Oxford University Press, 2000.

Sowell, Thomas. *Race and Culture. A World View*. New York, Basic Books, 1994.

Sowell, Thomas. *Migrations and Cultures. A World View*. New York, Basic Books, 1996.

Sowell, Thomas. *Affirmative Action Around the World. An Empirical Study*. New Haven, Yale University Press, 2004.

Spencer, Ian R. G. *British Immigration Policy since 1939. The Making of Multiracial Britain*. London, Routledge, 1997.

Spengler, Oswald. *Der Untergang des Abendlandes. Umrisse einer Morphologie der Weltgeschichte* (1917). München, Beck, 1990.

Stalker, Peter. *De feiten over internationale migratie*. Rotterdam, Lemniscaat, 2003.

Sterckx, Leen & Bouw, Carolien. *Liefde op maat. Partnerkeuze van Turkse en Marokkaanse jongeren*. Amsterdam, Het Spinhuis, 2005.

Stevens, Jacqueline. *States without Nations. Citizenship for Mortals*. New York, Columbia University Press, 2010.

Stipriaan. René van. *Een land om bij te huilen. Buitenlandse schrijvers over Nederland*. Amsterdam, Athenaeum–Polak & Van Gennep, 2001.

Stokkom, Bas van. *Emotionele democratie. Over morele vooruitgang*. Amsterdam, Van Gennep, 1997.

Stonequist, Everett V. *The Marginal Man. A Study in Personality and Culture Conflict*. New York, Scribner's Sons, 1937.

Sumner, William Graham. *Folkways. A Study of the Sociological Importance of*

Usages, Manners, Customs, Mores and Morals. Boston, Ginn and Company, 1906.

Swaan, Abram de. *Perron Nederland*. Amsterdam, Meulenhoff, 1991.

Swaan, Abram de. 'Uitgaansbeperking en uitgaansangst; over de verschuiving van bevelshuishouding naar onderhandelingshuishouding.' In *De mens is de mens een zorg. Opstellen 1971–1981*. Amsterdam, Meulenhoff 1981.

Swaan, Abram de. *Bakens in Niemandsland. Opstellen over massaal geweld*. Amsterdam, Bert Bakker, 2007.

Swift, Roger (ed.). *Irish Migrants in Britain, 1815–1914. A Documentary History*. Cork, Cork University Press, 2002.

Swift, Roger & Gilley, Sheridan (eds.), *The Irish in the Victorian City*. Beckenham, Croom Helm, 1985.

Taguieff, P. A. *La Force du préjugé. Essai sur le racisme et ses doubles*. Paris, Gallimard, 1987.

Taylor, Charles, et al. *Multiculturalism. Examining the Politics of Recognition*. Princeton, Princeton University Press, 1994.

Taylor, Charles. *A Secular Age*. Cambridge, MA, Harvard University Press, 2007.

Teitelbaum, Michael S. & Winter, Jay. *A Question of Numbers. High Migration, Low Fertility and the Politics of National Identity*. New York, Hill & Wang, 1998.

Temine, Émile (ed.). *Migrance. Histoire des migrations à Marseille*. i. La préhistoire de la migration (1482–1830). ii. L'expansion marseillaise et 'l'invasion italienne' (1830–1918). iii. Le cosmopolitisme de l'entre-deux-guerres (1919–1945). iv. Le choc de la décolonisation et les données nouvelles de la migration (1945–1990). Aix-en- Provence, Edisud, 1989.

Thernstrom, Stephan (ed.). *Harvard Encyclopedia of American Ethnic Groups*. Cambridge, MA, Harvard University Press, 1980.

Thomas, William I. & Znaniecki, Florian. *The Polish Peasant in Europe and America* (1918). Edited and abridged by Eli Zaretsky. Urbana, University of Illinois Press, 1984.

Thorbecke, J. R. *Een woord in het belang van Europa bij het voorstel der scheiding tusschen België en Holland*. Leiden, S. & J. Luchtmans, 1830.

Tibi, Bassam. *Der Islam in Deutschland. Muslime in Deutschland*. Stuttgart, Deutsche Verlags-Anstalt, 2000.

Tibi, Bassam. *Islamische Zuwanderung. Die gescheiterte Integration*. Stuttgart, Deutsche Verlags-Anstalt, 2002.

Tocqueville, Alexis de. *Oeuvres II: De la Démocratie en Amérique*. Paris, Gallimard, 1992.

Tocqueville, Alexis de. *Oeuvres III: Rapports sur l'Algérie*. Paris, Gallimard, 1991.

Todd, Emmanuel. *Le Destin des immigrés. Assimilation et ségrégation dans les démocraties occidentales*. Paris, Editions du Seuil, 1994.

Todorov, Tzvetan. *Nous et les autres. La réflexion française sur la diversité humaine*. Paris, Editions du Seuil, 1989.

Toynbee, Arnold J. *Civilization on Trial*. London, Oxford University Press, 1948.

United Nations Development Programme (UNDP). *Arab Human Development Report. Creating Opportunities for Future Generations.* New York, UNDP, 2002.

United Nations Population Division (UNPD). *Replacement Migration: Is It a Solution to Declining and Ageing Populations?* New York, United Nations Publications, 2001.

United Nations Population Division (UNPD). *World Population to 2300.* New York, United Nations Publications, 2004.

United Nations Development Programme (UNPD). *Human Development Report 2004. Cultural Liberty in Today's Diverse World.* New York, UNDP, 2004.

Valéry, Paul. *Oeuvres. Tome I: Poésies – Mélange – Variété.* Paris, Gallimard, 1957.

Vargas Llosa, Mario. 'Hirsi Ali is voor de leeuwen gegooid'. In *NRC Handelsblad,* 6 June 2006.

Veenkamp, Theo, et al. *People Flow. Managing Migration in a New European Commonwealth.* London, Demos, 2003.

Veenman, Justus. *Molukse jongeren in Nederland. Integratie met de rem erop.* Assen, Van Gorcum, 2001.

Veer, Peter van der. 'Nederland bestaat niet meer.' In *De Gids,* September 2000.

Vermeulen, Hans & Penninx, Rinus (eds.). *Immigrant Integration. The Dutch Case.* Amsterdam, Het Spinhuis, 2000.

Vermeulen, Hans. 'Cultuur en ongelijkheid.' In Jan Lucassen & Arie de Ruijter (eds.), *Nederland multicultureel en pluriform? Een aantal conceptuele studies.* Amsterdam, Aksant, 2002.

Visker, Rudi. *Vreemd gaan en vreemd blijven. Filosofie van de multiculturaliteit.* Amsterdam, SUN, 2005.

Vuijsje, Herman. *Vermoorde onschuld. Etnisch verschil als Hollands taboe.* Amsterdam, Bert Bakker, 1986.

Vuijsje, Herman. *Lof der dwang.* Baarn, Anthos, 1989.

Wacquant, Loïc. *Parias Urbaines. Ghetto – Banlieues – Etat.* Paris, Editions la Découverte, 2006.

Walzer, Michael. *Spheres of Justice. A Defense of Pluralism and Equality.* New York, Basic Books, 1983.

Walzer, Michael. *On Toleration.* New Haven, Yale University Press, 1997.

Washington, Booker T. *Up From Slavery. An Autobiography.* New York, Doubleday, Page & Co., 1901.

Weber, Max. *Die Protestantische Ethik I. Eine Aufsatzsammlung.* Hamburg, Siebenstern Taschenbuch Verlag, 1975.

Weil, Patrick. *La France et ses étrangers. L'aventure d'une politique de l'immigration de 1938 à nos jours.* Paris, Gallimard, 2004 (2).

Weiner, Myron. *The Global Migration Crisis. Challenge to States and to Human Rights.* New York, Harper Collins, 1995.

Weiner, Myron & Teitelbaum, Michael S. *Political Demography, Democratic Engineering.* New York, Berghahn Books, 2001.

Werdmölder, Hans. *Marokkaanse lieverdjes. Crimineel en hinderlijk gedrag onder Marokkaanse jongeren.* Amsterdam, Balans, 2005.

Wesseling, H. L. *Europa's koloniale eeuw.* Amsterdam, Bert Bakker, 2003.

Westerloo, Gerard van. 'Revolutie bij de zwartekousenmoslims.' In *NRC Handelsblad, M Magazine,* 7 February 2004.

Wetenschappelijke Raad voor het Regeringsbeleid (WRR). *Nederland als immigratiesamenleving.* Den Haag, Sdu Uitgevers, 2001.

Wetenschappelijke Raad voor het Regeringsbeleid (WRR). *De verzorgingsstaat herwogen. Over verzorgen, verzekeren, verheffen en verbinden.* Amsterdam, Amsterdam University Press, 2006.

Willems, Wim. *De uittocht uit Indië 1945–1995.* Amsterdam, Bert Bakker, 2001.

Willems, Wim. *De kunst van het overleven. Levensverhalen uit de twintigste eeuw.* Den Haag, Sdu Uitgevers, 2004.

Wirth, Louis. *The Ghetto.* Chicago, University of Chicago Press, 1928.

Wolfe, Alan, 'Native Son. Samuel Huntington Defends the Homeland.' In *Foreign Affairs.* Vol. 83, no. 3, May/June 2004.

Wood, Peter. *Diversity: The Invention of a Concept.* San Francisco, Encounter Books, 2003.

Yerli, Nilgun. *De garnalenpelster.* Amsterdam, De Arbeiderspers, 2001.

Zahn, Ernest. *Regenten, rebellen en reformatoren. Een visie op Nederland en de Nederlanders.* Amsterdam, Contact, 1989.

Zangwill, Israel. *The Melting-Pot. Drama in Four Acts.* New York, The Macmillan Company, 1909.

Zijderveld, Anton. 'Minderheden in Nederland meest gebaat bij verzuiling.' In *NRC Handelsblad,* 23 December 1991.

Zizek, Slavoj. *Pleidooi voor intolerantie.* Amsterdam, Boom, 1998.

Zolberg, Aristide R. *A Nation by Design. Immigration Policy in the Fashioning of America.* Cambridge, MA, Harvard University Press, 2006.

Zonneveld, Peter van. 'Indische literatuur van de twintigste eeuw.' In Theo D'Haen (ed.), *Europa buitengaats. Koloniale en postkoloniale literaturen in Europese talen* (2 vols.). Amsterdam, Bert Bakker, 2002.

Zouari, Fawzia. *Ce Voile qui déchire la France.* Paris, Ramsay, 2004.

Zwan, Arie van der. *De uitdaging van het populisme.* Amsterdam, Meulenhoff, 2003.

Zweig, Stefan. *Die Welt von Gestern. Erinnerungen eines Europäers.* Stockholm, Bermann-Fischer Verlag, 1947.

Name Index

Abdolah, Kader 10–11, 333
Abernethy, David 185, 187
Abizaid, General John 220–1
Aboutaleb, Ahmed 117, 129
Abu Zayd, Nasr Hamid 256, 258, 273–4
Acherrat-Stitou, Zohra 18
Adiga, Aravind 221
Adorno, Theodor 207, 208
Aerts, Remieg 120
Aksu, Sezen 29
Alagiah, George 17, 177, 204, 323
Ali, Monica 15–16
Allam, Magdi 112
Allas, Yasmine 267
Allport, Gordon 37, 207–9
Amin, Idi 75
Anbinder, Tyler 229
Anderson, Benedict 116–17
Anderson, Tryphena 170
Appiah, Kwame Anthony 212
Asante, Molefi Kete 245
Atkinson, Rowan 25
Attali, Jacques 95

Bade, Klaus 37, 143, 146, 180
Badiou, Alain 306
Baldewsingh, Rabin 298
Baldwin, James 246, 319
Balkenende, Jan Peter 180
Banton, Michael 170–1, 175
Barker, Pat 181
Baubérot, Jean 158, 159, 280
Bayle, Pierre 109
Baycili, Sevtap 313

Benali, Abdelkader 297
Benedict, Ruth 197
Benevolo, Leonardo 69
Berlin, Ira 238, 240
Berman, Paul 290
Bin Laden, Osama 271
Bismarck, Otto von 150, 185
Blainey, Geoffrey 89, 107
Blocher, Christoph 104
Blumrosen, Alfred and Ruth 240
Boas, Franz 193–4, 195
Bodnar, John 13
Boef, August van den 127
Bolkestein, Frits 312
Boomkens, René 321
Borjas, George 82, 90
Bouali, Fadoua 261
Bouazza, Hafid 11, 122, 128
Boutang, Yann Moulier 53
Bouyeri, Mohammed 130, 282
Boym, Svetlana 6
Bredero, Gerbrand 119
Brink, Gabriël van den 301
Brown, Carl 252
Bruggen, Carry van 114–15
Bui Trong, Lucienne 19, 53
Burns, Anthony 229
Buruma, Ian 137, 285
Bush, George W. 249
Busken Huet, Conrad 253–4

Caldwell, Christopher 34
Camper, Petrus 190
Cardini, Franco 253
Carnot, Sadi 145

Castells, Manuel 68
Castles, Stephen 36, 73, 92–3
Charfi, Mohamed 256, 276–7
Chartier, Christian 111
Claeys, Manu 106
Cohen, Israel 54
Cohn-Bendit, Daniel 162, 164
Coleman, David 81
Colijn, Hendrikus 131
Columbus Christoffel 182, 202, 246
Coolidge, Calvin 88
Cras, Hendrik Constantijn 134
Curti, Merle 219, 241

Dagevos, Jaco 55, 61
Dalrymple, Theodore 54, 302, 307
Darwin, Charles 190–1
De Crèvecoeur, John 218
De Gaulle, Charles 153
Denton, Nancy 50
Deursen, Arie van 120, 138
Dewinter, Filip 105–6
Dinnerstein, Leonard 226, 235
Donzelot, Jacques 53
Doorman, Maarten 305
Doorn, Jacques van 133
Douglass, Frederick 245
D'Souza, Dinesh 314
Du Bois, W. E. B. 242–3
Duinmeijer, Kerwin 129
Dummett, Michael 94, 98
Duyvendak, Jan Willem 65

Elias, Norbert 205, 206–7
Eliot, T. S. 211
Ellian, Afshin 293
El-Moumni, Khalil 121
Emerson, Ralph Waldo 222
Emmer, Piet 74
Engels, Friedrich 150
Entzinger, Han 80, 82
Enzensberger, Hans Magnus 28, 167–8, 206
Ephimenco, Sylvain 116, 130
Erasmus, Desiderius 283
Esposito, John 286

Fairchild, Henry Pratt 32–3, 233–4
Fallaci, Oriana 288–9
Favell, Adrian 177
Ferenczi, Sandor 145
Ferguson, Niall 184
Ferry, Jules 156

Filali-Ansary, Abdou 272, 276
Finkielkraut, Alain 211, 212, 306
Flynn, Stephen 289
Ford, Henry 223
Fortuyn, Pim 25, 104, 326–7
Fraihi, Hind 55–6
Franklin, Benjamin 227
Franklin, John Hope 238, 239–40, 241
Frisch, Max 165
Frissen, Paul 302

Gaitskill, Hugh 173
Gallagher, Charles 29
Gandhi, Mahatma 199
Gans, Herbert 65
Garton Ash, Timothy 213, 283
Gauchet, Marcel 158
Gelder, Enno van 119
Gellner, Ernest 116
Gezik, Erdal 263
Giordano, Ralph 161
Glass, Ruth 21
Glazer, Nathan 226, 320
Gleason, Philip 235, 245
Glotz, Peter 168
Gogh, Theo van 26, 113, 122, 129, 130, 137, 269–70, 327
Goldziher, Ignaz 275
Gompers, Sam 225
Grant, Madison 192
Gray, John 289
Grotius (Hugo de Groot) 119
Guéhenno, Jean-Marie 104

Haider, Jörg 104
Haifeng, Ni 293
Hall, Peter 50, 64
Handlin, Oscar 4, 5, 13, 16, 20, 230, 320
Harris, Nigel 93
Hartigan, John 22
Hatch, Orin 236
Hatton, Timothy 23, 90, 318
Hawgood, John 231, 232
Heitmeyer, Wilhelm 167
Hermans, Willem Frederik 110, 139
Herskovits, Melville 194
Higham, John 81, 223, 224–5, 233, 234
Hill, Clifford 172
Hirsi Ali, Ayaan 113, 196, 281, 307, 331–2
Hoffman, Eva 210
Holmes, Oliver Wendell 220, 221

Houellebecq, Michel 300
Howard, Ebenezer 68
Huizinga, Johan 115, 121, 136
Hume, David 190
Huntington, Samuel 105, 214, 217,
   248–9, 287, 288
Hussein, Hasib 269
Hutton, Will 295
Huxley, Aldous 192
Huxley, Elspeth 169, 176, 320
Hvidt, Kristian 13

Ignatieff, Michael 215
Inglehart, Ronald 260, 262, 287
Isensee, Josef 165
Ismaili, Salma 261
Israel, Jonathan 112–13
Istendael, Geert van 112

Jahjah, Dyab Abu 270–1, 297
Jefferson, Thomas 218, 238, 239, 240
Johnson, Lyndon 243, 246–7
Jones, Edward P. 240–1
Joppke, Christian 76, 107, 161, 162,
   177
Jupp, James 87, 89, 90

Kallen, Horace 198, 246
Kaltenbach, Jeanne-Hélène 159
Kant, Immanuel 181, 190
Kapuscinski, Ryszard 61
Karacaer, Haci 297
Karimi, Farah 10
Kaufmann, Franz-Xaver 84, 303, 304
Kefalas, Maria 22, 23
Kelek, Necla 12, 162, 165, 166, 202,
   310
Kellor, Frances 223, 224, 225
Kennedy, James 110
Kennedy, John F. 231
Kennedy, Paul 95
Kennedy, Ted 236
Kepel, Gilles 285
King, Mackenzie 87
King, Martin Luther 243
King, Sam 169
Kleijwegt, Margalith 15
Klessmann, Christoph 151
Knippenberg, Hans 117
Knopp, Guido 163
Knox, Paul 47–8
Kossmann, Ernest 110, 114
Kuijpers, Erika 2–3
Küng, Hans 273

Kuyper, Eric de 112
Kymlicka, Will 89, 198, 200

Lacorne, Denis 35, 225
Landes, David 185–6
Laqueur, Walter 34
Laroui, Fouad 14, 19–20, 292–3
Lash, Christopher 300
Le Pen, Jean-Marie 104, 154
Legrain, Philippe 79, 92, 317
Lemaire, Ton 195
Lévi-Strauss, Claude 196, 205
Lewis, Bernard 257
Li, Peter 90, 200
Liao, Quiru 102
Lijphart, Arend 125
Lincoln, Abraham 229, 241
Lindsay, Martin 171–2
Lipovetsky, Gilles 301
Livingstone, David 184
Locke, John 190
Lofland, Lyn 46–7
Longman, Phillip 258
Low, Setha 66
Lowell, James Russell 219
Lucassen, Jan 141, 142
Lucassen, Leo 38, 147, 148–9, 151
Lucebert 300

Maalouf, Amin 255
Madanipour, Ali 69
Magellan, Ferdinand 182
Mahbubani, Kishore 213, 221
Mak, Geert 36, 129
Malcolm X, 243
Malik, Shahid 272
Mandela, Nelson 92
Manji, Irshad 39
Manning, Robert 51
Mansfield, Lord 240
Margalit, Avishai 285
Massey, Douglas 50, 317
Mattéi, François 157
Mauco, Georges 153
Maurin, Eric 51, 58, 60
Mead, Margaret 312
Meer, Jelle van der 82
Memmi, Albert 188–9
Meredith, James 244
Mernissi, Fatima 254, 273, 276
Miller, Mark 36, 73, 92–3
Mitterrand, Francois 53
Modood, Tariq 198–9
Mollenkopf, John 40

Montet-Toutain, Karen 57–8
Morawska, Ewa 177
Morse, Samuel 228
Morshäuser, Bodo 161
Moynihan, Patrick 226
Muck, Karl 232
Mulisch, Harry 292
Mumford, Lewis 44, 45
Musterd, Sako 35, 49
Myrdal, Gunnar 244

Naipaul, V. S. 170, 254, 325
Naqib al-Misri, Ahmad ibn 262
Nawijn, Hilbrand 293
Nieuwenhuys, Rob 132–3
Noiriel, Gérard 10, 13, 27, 81, 141,
  152
Norris, Pippa 103, 104, 260, 262

Obama, Barack 21, 22, 250, 251,
  294
Ogata, Sadako 100
Oostindie, Gert 132, 134
Ortega y Gasset, José 144

Pamuk, Orhan 256
Parekh, Bhikhu 198, 296, 306
Park, Robert E. 6, 9, 18
Pater, Ben de 117
Paxman, Jeremy 295
Penninx, Rinus 142
Perron, Edgar du 133
Pessers, Dorien 38
Pettigrew, Thomas 247
Phillips, Melanie 269
Phillips, Mike 175
Phillips, Trevor 175, 298
Portes, Alejandro 51, 249
Powell, Enoch 174, 175
Putman, Robert 70

Quddus, Saed Abdul 265
Qutb, Sayyid 268

Ramadan, Tariq 277–8, 281–2
Ramdas, Anil 8, 111, 326
Rath, Jan 51
Reimers, David 226, 235, 236
Rentes de Carvalho, J. 112
Reve, Gerard 292
Reybrouck, David van 30
Riis, Jacob 191
Robinson, Tjalie 132
Romein, Annie 117, 140

Romein, Jan 117, 125, 140
Roosevelt, Franklin 243
Roosevelt, Theodore 222, 223
Rooy, Piet de 67, 120
Roth, Philip 56–7
Rousseau, Jean-Jacques 210
Roy, Olivier 260–1, 262, 271
Roth, Philip 56
Rumbaut, Rubèn 249
Rushdie, Salman 265

Sakali, Saïda 311
Salisbury, Lord 192
Sardar, Ziauddin 28, 175, 176
Sarkozy, Nicolas 53
Sas, Niek van 136
Sassen, Saskia 142, 146, 147
Schama, Simon 111
Scheffer, Paul 333
Schillebeeckx, Edward 273
Schlesinger, Arthur 202, 246
Schmid, Thomas 162, 164
Schnapper, Dominique 156, 157
Schopenhauer, Arthur 213
Schubert, Franz 213
Scruton, Roger 295
Sen, Amartya 59, 199
Sidique Khan, Mohammad 269,
  270
Simmel, Georg 323
Sinclair, Upton 45
Singer, Peter 94
Sloterdijk, Peter 71
Snouck Hugronje, Christiaan 278–9,
  280, 282
Socrates, 213
Somerset, James 240
Soroush, Abdolkarim 273
Sowell, Thomas 85, 247
Spencer, Ian 172, 173
Spengler, Oswald 183
Stravinsky, Igor 213
Studt, Heinrich Konrad von 150–1
Stuyvesant, Peter 218
Sumner, William Graham 204, 205
Sürücü, Hatun 263
Swaan, Abram de 179, 303

Tanweer, Shehzad 269
Teitelbaum, Michael 83
Thijn, Ed van 269
Thorbecke, Johan Rudolf 130
Tibi, Bassam 56, 165–6
Tocqueville, Alexis de 239, 255

Todorov, Tzvetan 195
Toynbee, Arnold 183
Tribalat, Michèle 159
Tuathaigh, Gearoid O 150
Turner, Frederic Jackson 219

Valéry, Paul 181
Vargas Llosa, Mario 113
Veer, Peter van der 115
Vermeulen, Hans 201
Voltaire 190
Vondel, Joost van den 139

Wallace, George 244
Walzer, Michael 98–9
Wansink, Hans 74
Washington, Booker T. 241–2
Washington, George 48, 238
Weber, Max 186
Weil, Patrick 103, 153, 154

Weiner, Myron 75, 99
Wesseling, Henk 131, 187–8
Westerloo, Gerard van 259
Wibaut, Floor 68
Wieren, Hans van 139–40
Wilde, Oscar 32
Williamson, Jeffrey 23, 90, 318
Wilson, Woodrow 232, 234
Winter, Jay 83
Wirth, Louis 45–6, 54

Yüksel, Selami 259

Zangwell, Israel 222
Zheng-He, Admiral 185
Zijderveld, Anton 124, 126
Zolberg, Aristide 227–8, 249, 251
Zouari, Fawzia 264
Zwan, Arie van der 86, 307
Zweig, Stefan 210–11, 321

Subject Index

affirmative action 245–8, 311 *see also*
   positive discrimination
Africa
   slavery 238
   urbanization 44
   voyages of discovery 182
   colonialism 188–9
Afrocentrism 245–6
ageing population 83–4, 303–4
Ahmaddiya movement 282
Al-Qaeda 289, 290
Alevis movement 281–2
Algerian migrants 144, 153–5
alienation 4, 5, 13, 20, 32, 53, 107,
   157, 164, 197, 268, 270, 312,
   320
Aliens Act (1905) (Britain) 145
All White in Barking (film) 20–1
allochtonen 313
Alumnia 329
American Civil War 219, 232–3, 240,
   241
American Federation of Labour
   234
American Protective Association
   234
Americanization of immigrants 222–5,
   301
Amsterdam 2, 14, 26, 37, 40, 59, 64,
   68, 110, 119, 129, 269, 293,
   328–31
Angolan immigrants 144

anti-Semitism 26, 129, 130, 207,
   269
antisocial families 301
Antwerp 21, 31–2
apostasy 3, 282
Arab European League 270
Arab Human Development Report
   (2002) 257
Arab world 39, 185, 257–9, 288
arranged marriages 15–16, 166
Asian migration 88, 107, 247, 317
assimilation (of immigrants) 6, 32,
   106, 133, 177, 189, 270
   in United States 222–3, 224, 225–6,
   232, 233, 246, 248–9, 251
asylum-seekers 74–5, 99–101, 108,
   162, 315, 326
   attacks on in Germany 161–2
   see also refugees
Australia 75, 86, 88–9, 91, 107, 177,
   313
   Asian migration to 88, 107
   and citizenship 294
   'dictation test' 87
   economy and immigration 89–90
   immigration history 87, 88–9
   refugee policy 100
   terms used for migrants 313
   welfare and immigration 82
avoidance, conflict and accommodation
   cycle 6, 22, 23, 26, 36–7, 48, 110,
   199, 251, 283–4, 322

banks 77
banlieues (France) 19, 57–8, 157
    riots in 53–4, 157, 159–60, 178
Belgium 30, 106, 125
Berlin 21, 61
Berlin Wall, fall of (1989) 147
bias 195, 205, 207, 208–9
birth rates 84, 152–3, 155, 167–8, 258,
    303–4
black community (US) 220, 237–44,
    245–8, 251
black ghettos (US) 49, 50–1, 244
blasphemy 3, 25, 122, 283, 310
border controls 72, 76, 92, 97–8, 108,
    179–80, 250, 289, 314–6
brain drain 92–3
Bradford 35, 49, 176, 265
Britain 21, 35, 145, 168–77, 313
    anti-discrimination legislation 174
    and decolonization 168–9
    debate about Britishness 295
    fertility rates 83
    growth in number of migrants 173
    mixed marriages 170–1
    and multiculturalism 176, 298
    naturalization ceremony 294
    opposition to early immigrants
        149–50, 170–1
    Pakistanis in 144, 176, 178
    Polish migrants 85
    and Powell's 'rivers of blood' speech
        (1968) 174
    race riots 171, 172, 174–5, 176
    refugee policy 100
    restrictions on immigration 171–2,
        173–4
    segregation in 49, 176–77, 178, 298
    social security system 307
    terms used for migrants 313
    West Indian immigrants 169–70
British Empire 182, 184, 185
British Nationality Act (1981) 174
Brussels 55–6
Bush, George W. 221

Canada 75, 86, 88–9, 91, 125, 293
    Asian migration 88
    educational level of migrants 91
    immigration and economy 90
    immigration history 87, 88–9
    population growth and immigration
        84
    refugee policy 100
    and *sharia* law 202

Canberra
    National Museum of Australia 306
canon 305
Cantle Report 178
capitalism
    and colonization 186
Catholic Church (France) 158–9
Catholic migrants
    early opposition to 147, 149–50,
        206, 233
    in Netherlands 118, 120, 124, 128
    in United States 206, 226, 228–9,
        230–1, 233
Chicago 9, 18, 22, 23, 45, 49, 249
child mortality 44–5
childrearing 303
China 102, 185, 187
Chinese Exclusion Act (1882) (US) 87,
    235
Chinese illegals, death of (2000) 72
Christianity 154–5, 187, 189
    clash with Islam 252–3, 256
church
    relationship with state 39, 119–20,
        158–9, 218, 254–5, 279–80
cities 42–71
citizens' revolt 103–8
citizenship 31, 33, 139, 299–300, 304,
    305, 315–16, 323
    European 178
    rituals of 282–8
    shared 29–30, 32, 177, 197, 244,
        249, 314
    world 209–15
Civil Rights Act (1964) (US) 243
civil rights movement 220, 243, 247,
    319
'clash of civilizations' 214, 287–8, 290
Cold War 290
colonialism/colonization 144, 189, 214
    economic consequences of 188
    European 182–8
    Islamic 254
    and universalism 214–15
Commission for Equality and Human
    Rights 174
Commonwealth 168–9
Commonwealth Immigrants Act (1962)
    (Britain) 173, 174
community internships 305
compartmentalization (in Netherlands)
    118, 124–5, 127–8, 135
conflict avoidance (in Netherlands)
    109–10, 114, 117–18, 130, 326

conservatism
  and Islam 127, 260–4, 265–7
  and migrants 7–14
consumerism 300–1
cosmopolitanism 168, 209–13
countries of origin 2, 8, 14, 15, 28, 29,
    37, 39, 40, 105
  and remittances 93
credit crisis 77
crime 18–19, 43, 57–8, 61–2, 66, 123,
    139–40, 149, 299–300
crusades 253–4, 255
cultural pluralism 133, 199
cultural relativism 188, 193–7, 204,
    213, 214, 215
Czech Republic 180
Czechoslovakia
  expulsion of Sudeten Germans
    142

Danish cartoons affair 25–6, 283,
    286
Darwinian evolution 190–1
Declaration of Independence, US
    (1776) 238, 239, 240, 308
decolonization 48, 131, 168, 183, 198,
    212
democracy 30, 32, 55, 77, 103, 104–5,
    128, 139, 172, 186, 213–15
  and Islam 268, 272, 282, 284, 288,
    290
demographic trends 73–4, 76, 83–5,
    95, 107, 152–3, 167–8, 303–4
  see also population
Detroit 22
development
  and migration 91–7
development aid 94
discrimination 17, 21, 30, 31–2, 172,
    174, 175, 192, 208, 247, 298,
    309, 311–12, 314, 328
  positive 158, 160, 245, 247, 248,
    309, 311–12
dispersal of migrants 62–7
displacement 10, 44, 142, 217
diversity 29, 51, 52, 63–4, 70, 178,
    198, 222, 294, 296, 298
dual nationality 40, 316
Dutch National History Museum
    31
Dutch Revolt 125

East India Company 184
economic crisis (1973) 146

economic issues
  and immigration 23, 47–52, 76–7,
    79–83, 86, 89–91, 92–4, 102–3,
    149, 153–4, 164–5, 223–4, 306–8,
    316, 318–9
education 200, 299, 304–6
  and community service 305
  faith schools 311
  rise of religious schools 59
  segregation in schools 57–62
  and socialization 302
educational level
  and immigrants 90
Egypt
  labour emigration 92–3
el-Moumni affair 121
elderly 83
Empire Windrush, SS 169–70
Enlightenment 190
equality 32, 37–8, 77, 82, 93, 94, 97,
    123, 132, 152, 153, 155, 157–8,
    198, 201, 219, 239, 240, 246,
    254, 280, 284, 296, 298, 299,
    314–5, 325
  dilemmas of 308–14
  legal interpretation of 309, 310, 311
  normative interpretation of 309, 311
  of men and women 263–4, 275,
    303
  segregation and 47–52
established-outsider relationships
    204–7
ethnic enclaves 51–2, 165, 262
Ethnic Heritage Studies Program Act
    (1974) 245
ethnicity 29, 47, 56, 159, 187, 199,
    226, 317
ethnocentrism 204–5, 208, 209, 213
eugenics 192
Eurocentrism 290
Europe 141–81, 216, 249–50, 320
  categories of immigrants 144–5
  colonial conquest by 182–6
  comparison with United States 34–6,
    216
  early opposition to immigration
    147–52
  history of immigration 143–6
  and increased freedom of movement
    108
  and Islam 286
  migration from 87, 142–3, 144
  and Muslim immigration 259
  number of illegal immigrants 101

population growth 143–4
promotion of immigration from
    Asian countries 317
refugee movements 142–3
state intervention and immigration
    145–6
see also Britain; France; Germany;
    Netherlands
European citizenship 178
European Court 280
European Union 85, 95
    expansion of 85
    immigration statistics 35
    population growth and immigration
        84
exclusion 17, 53, 69, 115, 137, 146,
    174, 243–4, 247–8
expulsions 75–6
extended family 200

faith schools 311
families, migrant see migrant families
family reunification 76, 146, 155, 165,
    166, 173
fertility rates 83
Finsbury Park Mosque 269
First World War 77, 143, 145, 181,
    183, 224, 232, 234
fortress Europe 37, 76
France 35, 145, 152–60, 305–6
    Algerian migrants and return of to
        Algeria 154–5
    asylum legislation 75
    Catholic Church 158–9
    constitution 309
    demographic decline 152, 153
    early opposition to migrants
        149
    education 155–6
    fertility rates 83
    headscarf issue 159
    heritage issue 306
    and illegal immigrants 103
    immigration history 141, 152–60
    impact of colonialism on
        immigration 153–4
    and integration of migrants 155,
        157, 178
    and Islam 158, 159
    Italian migrants 147–8, 149, 151,
        156
    naturalization 156–7, 158
    political principles 152
    principle of ius soli 156–7

republican ideal of equality 156–8,
    159
riots in the banlieues 53–4, 157,
    159–60, 178
segregation in 51
selection of migrants 153
state and church relations
    158–9
freedom of expression 3, 25, 30, 33,
    38, 122, 128, 310, 327
freedom of movement 79, 85, 95, 97,
    108, 154, 169, 172, 179–80,
    235–6, 314–6
freedom of religion see religious
    freedom
freedom of speech 24, 122, 283–4,
    301, 331
French Revolution 152
Front National 104, 106, 154
Frontex 108
Future of Multi-Ethnic Britain report
    304

Gambia 92
garden city movement 68
gated communities 66, 99
gedogen 123
German-American Alliance 232
German immigrants
    in Netherlands 141–2
    in United States 40, 220, 227,
        231–2, 248
Germany 35, 56, 145, 160–8, 178
    ageing and declining of population
        167–8, 303
    asylum legislation 75, 162
    attempts to reduce immigrant
        numbers 164–5
    early opposition to Polish migrants
        150–1
    fertility rates 83
    history of immigration 163–5
    Inländervorrang practice 145
    nationality laws 163–4
    non-naturalized migrants and right
        to vote issue 165
    pensions at risk in 83
    recruitment of guest workers 164
    refugees 145
    return of ethnic Germans 163
    Turkish community in 12, 82, 164,
        165–7
Ghana 92
gharb zadegi concept 273

ghettos
  black 49, 50–1, 244
  culture of 53–7
  Jewish 54–5
globalization 6, 26, 27, 51, 72–3, 74,
    78, 79, 97, 105, 136, 317, 321–2
Going to Britain? (BBC series) 171
governments
  impact of on attracting immigrants
    75–6
Greece 142, 180
Guantánamo Bay 288
guest workers 2, 7, 75, 80, 82–3, 85,
    124, 146, 307, 318
Gulf states, migration regulation 75

Haiti 76
Hanafi School 277
headscarves *see* hijab
Herero 188
heritage 306
hierarchy of races and cultures 188,
    189, 190, 193, 194, 213
hijab (headscarf) 263–4
'hillbillies' 22–3
history 38, 305–6
Hollandgänger 141–2
home ownership 64
homelessness 210, 321
homosexuality 24, 121, 263, 267,
    309
honour killings 199, 263
horticulture 81, 94
Huguenots 142
human rights 212, 213, 214–15
humanitarian intervention 215
humanitarian issues 91–2
Hungary 180

illegal immigration/immigrants 35, 72,
    101–3, 108, 315
  amnesties for 102
  number of 101
  in United States 101, 102, 236, 250,
    320
illiteracy, early 186
imagined community 26, 116–17
Immigrant Reform and Control Act
    (1986) 250
immigration
  benefits of 107
  classic countries of 86–91
  costs of 107
  opposition to 24, 69, 147–52

Immigration Act (US)
  (1924) 88
  (1965) 89
immigration control 74–7
Immigration Restriction Act (Australia)
    87
Immigration Restriction League (US)
    234
imperialism
  and Islam 252–8
India 93, 185, 188
individualism 46, 166, 196, 218, 290,
    296, 300–1
Indonesia 131, 188, 254
Indus Entrepreneur 317
industrialization 44, 81, 143, 191
insecurity
  feeling of by native populations 5,
    10, 22, 24, 107, 208
institutional racism 247
integration (of migrants) 26, 27–33,
    36, 37, 41, 177, 266, 296, 298–9,
    302–3, 322
  and education 304–6
  and family 303–4
  in France 155, 157, 178
  selectivity as essential to successful
    316
  in United States 219–22, 232, 235,
    246, 248–9, 251
  and work domain 306–8
intergenerational conflict 11, 14, 16,
    270, 299
Irish migrants 141, 147, 148, 149
  early opposition to in Britain 149–50
  in United States 40, 230–1, 250
Irish Nationalist Party 150
Islam 24–6, 39, 128, 252–91, 324
  attempts at reform 272–8
  clash with Christianity 252–3, 256
  confrontation with political 285–7
  conservatism and radicalization
    265–72, 286
  decline 255–6, 257
  and democracy 268, 272, 281, 282,
    284, 288, 290
  differences between US and
    European responses to radical 286
  expansion of 254, 255
  and France 158, 159
  headscarves issue 263–5
  and homosexuality 263
  and imperialism 252–8
  isolation from Europe 256

and Koran 274–5, 276–7, 310
and liberalism 289
in Netherlands 117, 124–30, 260,
    265, 278–9
political ambitions of 280–1
relations with based on equal
    treatment 278–85
relationship between society and
    state 255
and secular society 258–65, 276–7,
    281
values separating West from 262–3
visibility of in public places as bone
    of contention 25
and women 262–3, 275–6
Islamic fundamentalism 36, 259
Islamophobia 26, 129
Israeli-Palestinian conflict 269
Istanbul 9
Italian migrants
    in France 147–8, 149, 151, 156
    in United States 144
Italy 83–4, 180
ius soli principle 156–7

Japan 83, 186
Japanese immigrants
    in United States 220, 235
Jeunesse Ouvrière Chrètienne (JOC)
    158–9
Jewish ghettos 54–5
Jews 2, 119, 120, 129, 130, 157, 186,
    202, 218, 257, 270, 330
    see also anti-Semitism
judiciary 76
July bombings (London) (2005) 269,
    270

Karlowitz, Treaty of (1699) 253
Know Nothing movement 228–30, 232
Koran 274–5, 276–7, 310
Kosedag family 137
Kosovo refugees 100
Ku Klux Klan 234–5
Kurds 137

labour migration/migrants 74, 77,
    78–86, 89, 92–3, 126, 143, 149,
    154, 164, 315, 316–19
    see also guest workers
language 11–12, 17, 30, 50–1, 54, 61,
    166, 178, 223, 321
    downplaying of importance of in
        Netherlands 114–16, 125

Latin America 88
Lebanon 76, 93
legal residence status 35, 82, 101, 102,
    236
liberalism 300
life expectancy
    in developing countries 94
literacy 30, 186
London 20–1, 43, 68, 173, 176, 183,
    328
    bombings (2005) 269, 270, 272
    Notting Hill 42, 171
    population 44
low-skilled migrants see labour
    migration/migrants

Madrid bombings (2004) 253
Malmö 63, 99
marriage
    arranged 15–16, 166
    mixed 170–1, 204
    in Netherlands 311
Marseille, riots (1881) 151
'Martyrs of Córdoba' 253
'melting pot' doctrine 198, 221–7,
    233
Mexican immigrants
    in United States 88, 91, 248–9, 250
Mexico
    payments sent home by migrants 93
middle class of migrants 17–18, 47,
    69, 297
migrant families
    culture of 303–4
    intergenerational tensions within 11,
        14–15, 16, 299
    strain caused by loss of father's
        status 11
    see also family reunification
migrants/migration
    costs and benefits of 3, 23, 39–40,
        76–7, 79–83, 89–91, 92–3, 102–3,
        122, 153, 164–5, 306–8, 316–9
    numbers of and distribution across
        continents 73–4
    reasons for 4, 7
    words used to describe 312–14
Milli Görüs 259, 297, 329
mixed communities, attempts to create
    63–5
mixed marriages 170–1, 204
mobility, morality of 97–103
Moluccans 132
Morocco/Moroccans 1, 18, 40–1

multiculturalism 37, 92, 176, 197–203,
    245, 297, 298, 320, 332
  objections to 199–203
Murat D 139–40
museums 31, 306
Muslims 24–6, 31–2, 38, 39, 55–6,
    121, 124–130, 154, 159, 165–6,
    186–7, 202, 252–291, 327, 330
  see also Islam
'myth of return' 3–4, 12, 13

nation-states 99, 104–5, 110, 116, 287
National Association for the
    Advancement of Colored People
    (NAACP) 243
national identity 114, 179, 285–6
native populations, unease felt by 20–7
natural selection 191
naturalization/naturalization ceremony
    293–4, 315–16
Netherlands 25, 30, 35, 60–1, 103,
    109–40, 206, 325–6
  and asylum-seekers 75, 101, 108
  children and community internships
    305
  citizens' revolt 104
  and compartmentalization 118,
    124–5, 127–8, 135
  conflict avoidance 109–10, 114,
    117–18, 130, 326
  constitution 125–6, 308–9
  creation of National Historical
    Museum 305
  downplaying importance of language
    114–16, 125
  East Indies émigrés 132–3
  el-Moumni affair 121
  ethnic divisions 126
  fertility rates 83
  gaining citizenship in 292–3
  guest workers in 80, 124, 126
  identity and openness 135–40
  impact of colonial history on
    treatment of ethnic minorities
    130–5
  Islam and Muslim communities in
    117, 124–30, 260, 265, 278–9
  law-enforcement culture 123
  marriage laws 311
  migration and nation-building 113–18
  Moluccan terrorism in 132
  and murder of Theo van Gogh 113,
    122, 129, 130, 137, 269–70, 327
  naturalization ceremony 293

refugees 108, 145
Rijksmuseum renovation debate
    137–8
secularization of society 128, 130
separation of church and state
    119–20
  and slavery 134–5, 305
  terms used to refer to migrants 313
  and tolerance 110–13, 118–24
New York 40, 44–5, 49, 52, 226, 231,
    239, 241
9/11 (2001) 36, 39, 129, 220, 221,
    285, 289, 290–1, 326
'noble savage' 194
norms, liberalization of 301–2
North American Civic League for
    Immigrants 223–4, 225
North/South divide 94, 96, 103

occidentalism 285
one-parent families 247, 302
open borders, appeal for 98–9, 318

Pakistan 76
Palestinian refugees 76
Parekh Report 198, 296, 306
paternalism 133, 244, 301, 305
pensions 83
People Flow (pamphlet) 92
Philippines
  payments sent home by migrants 93
Poland 142, 180
Polish migrants 85, 147, 148, 149,
    150–1, 230, 316
political parties 103–4
polygenesis 190
population 304
  decline 83–4
  growth of in Arab world 258
  growth of in developing countries 95
  growth of in Europe 143–4
  immigration and growth of 84–5
  total world 95
population transfers 142
positive discrimination 158, 160, 245,
    247, 248, 309, 311–12
prejudice 21, 32, 36–7, 128, 194–5,
    203–9, 225, 311, 314, 322, 324
printing 186–7
Protestantism 186, 218, 228–9, 230

Race Relations Act (Britain) 174
race relations cycle 6
racial inequality 189–90

8097

Racial and Religious Hatred Bill 25
racism 21, 26, 188–92, 195, 204, 247
  institutional 247
  scientific 189–90, 192, 193
  and social Darwinism 190–2
reciprocity 31, 32, 37–8, 225, 281,
  292, 297, 301, 308, 314, 323
Reformation 186
Refugee Convention (1951) 99–100
refugees 7, 37, 74, 99–101, 142–3,
  144–5, 315
religion 4–5, 38–9, 208, 287–8
religious freedom 25–6, 31, 39, 119,
  218, 280, 281, 282, 284, 287, 324
religious schools 59
remittances 93
replacement fertility 83
Replacement Migration 84–5
resources, competition for 23
rights 3, 31, 38, 63, 76, 98–9, 107,
  132, 154, 157, 162, 165–6,
  212–15, 310
  see also human rights
Rijksmuseum (Netherlands) 137–8
Rotterdam 24, 62–3, 99, 117, 121,
  279, 329
Russian Revolution 142
Rwanda 212

St Louis
  Pruitt-Igoe project 64
Salafists 267–8, 282
schools 31, 39, 50, 125, 139, 155,
  228–9, 280, 295, 304–6
  and segregation 57–62, 67, 127,
  159, 199, 244, 264
scientific racism 189–90, 192, 193
seasonal migration 85, 318
  see also guest workers
Second World War 142
second-generation migrants 14–20, 41,
  52, 86, 127, 174, 226, 249, 261
secularization
  and Muslim migrants 259–65,
  276–7, 281
  in Netherlands 128, 130
segregation 23, 35, 55, 57, 62, 67
  benefits of ethnic enclaves 51
  and black ghettos in United States
  49, 50–1, 244
  causes of 47–8
  in cities 46–52
  and 'culture of poverty' 50, 52
  and dispersal 62–7

extent of 48–9
  and schools 57–62
  and social inequality 50–2
  segregation index 48–9
selectivity
  and integration 316
sexual revolution 300
shared citizenship 29–30, 32, 177, 197,
  244, 249, 314
sharia 38, 202, 259, 276
slavery 188, 190
  campaign against 184
  and Islam 254
  and Netherlands 134–5, 305
  and United States 237–44, 251
socialization 299, 302
Société Générale d'Immigration 153
South Africa
  emigration of medical personnel 92
South America
  urbanization 44
South Korea 78
Spain 35, 180
  fertility rates 83
  and illegal immigrants 101, 108
Sri Lanka 100
state
  immigration and intervention of 143,
  145
  relationship with the church 39,
  119–20, 158–9, 218, 254–5,
  279–80
status, loss of among immigrants 11
Supreme Order of the Star-Spangled
  Banner 228
Surinamers 26–7, 42–3, 133–4, 144,
  330
Switzerland
  ban on building of minarets 25

terrorism 26, 108, 113, 129, 137, 269,
  271–2, 286, 287, 288
third world 34, 95, 103, 144, 292,
  315
Thirty Years War 120
tolerance
  and Netherlands 110–13, 118–24
trade policy 94, 96
Turkish migrants
  in Germany 12, 82, 164, 165–7

Uganda 75
underclass 50, 62, 64, 66, 79, 175,
  302

unemployment
in migrant communities 39–40, 51,
        299, 308, 316
United Nations 182–3
United States 86, 126, 178, 216–51,
        319, 319–20
    and affirmative action 245–8
    Americanization of migrants 222–5,
        301
    Asian immigrants in 247
    assimilation and integration of
        migrants 219–22, 232, 235, 246,
        248–9, 251
    black community in 220, 237–44,
        245–8, 251
    black ghetto formation 49, 50–1,
        244
    Catholic immigration 226, 228–9,
        230–1, 233
    and citizenship rituals 294
    colonial population 217–18
    comparison with Europe 34–6, 216
    decline in immigration 235
    diversity of migrants in 317
    economic benefits of immigration
        90
    family-based immigration 89
    German immigrants in 40, 220, 227,
        231–2, 248
    and illegal immigration 101, 102,
        236, 250, 320
    immigration history 87–8
    immigration statistics 35
    influence of world wars on migrant
        integration 220, 224–5
    Irish immigrants in 40, 230–1, 250
    Japanese immigrants in 220, 235
    melting pot image 198, 221–7
    Mexican immigrants 88, 91, 248–9,
        250

    Muslims in 286
    nation-building 219
    opposition to immigration 91,
        227–32, 233–5, 236–7, 250
    population growth and immigration
        84
    restrictions on immigration 7, 87–8,
        233–7
    self-image of as 'nation of
        immigrants' 34, 91, 141, 216–17,
        219, 221, 222, 227, 237, 245,
        249, 251, 317, 319–20
    separation of church and state 218
    and slavery 237–44, 251
    welfare and immigrants 82
United States Steel Company 225
Universal Declaration of Human Rights
        98, 212, 282, 283
universalism 209, 211, 214, 214–15
urbanization 44, 45, 143

victimhood 18, 297
Vlaams Belang 21, 104, 105

'war on terror' 286, 287
welfare state 39, 41, 82–3, 307–8
West India Company 218
White Australia Policy 87
white flight 20, 47, 58
women
    and arranged marriages 16, 166
    and Islam 262–3, 275–6
    rights of in migrant families 310
work domain 306–8
world citizen/citizenship 209–15
World Trade Organization 94

xenophobia 5, 21, 203

Yugoslavia 212

DATE DUE

JAN 0 3 2007			